TALLAHASSEE
LIBRARY
COMMUNITY COLLEGE

Edwin O. Reischauer
and the American Discovery of Japan

Edwin O. Reischauer and the American Discovery of Japan

GEORGE R. PACKARD

Columbia University Press *New York*

Columbia University Press
Publishers Since 1893
New York Chichester, West Sussex

Library of Congress Cataloging-in-Publication Data
Packard, George R.
Edwin O. Reischauer and the American discovery of Japan / George R. Packard.
p. cm.
Includes bibliographical references.
ISBN 978-0-231-14354-7 (cloth : alk. paper) — ISBN 978-0-231-51277-0 (ebook)
1. Reischauer, Edwin O. (Edwin Oldfather), 1910–1990.
2. Japanologists—United States—Biography. 3. Scholars—United States—Biography.
4. Ambassadors—United States—Biography. 5. Japan—Relations—United States.
6. United States—Relations—Japan. I. Title.

E840.8. R45P33 2010
327.2092—dc22
[B]

2009038015

Columbia University Press books are printed on permanent
and durable acid-free paper.
This book is printed on paper with recycled content.

Printed in the United States of America
c 10 9 8 7 6 5 4

For Lavinia

Contents

Preface

The idea of writing a biography of Edwin Reischauer occurred to me as early as 1965, after I had served for two years as his special assistant in the U.S. Embassy in Tokyo. I saved notes and documents from the period, but soon found myself caught up in new challenges as diplomatic correspondent for *Newsweek* and managing editor of the *Philadelphia Bulletin*. The next decade was turbulent and all-consuming for a journalist, with coverage of the Vietnam War; the assassinations of Dr. Martin Luther King and Robert F. Kennedy; the antiwar protests; the social, racial, and sexual revolutions of the 1960s and 1970s; the election of Richard Nixon; and the Watergate scandal. Japan seemed far away. I ventured briefly into politics, running for the U.S. Senate in 1976 and losing in the primary.

I returned to the scholarly world as deputy director of the Woodrow Wilson International Center for Scholars from 1976 to 1979 under the charismatic leadership of Dr. James H. Billington. Jim, who would become librarian of Congress, was in charge of the "living memorial" to Woodrow Wilson. He was fascinated by the notion of scholars who can influence policymakers. He had already set up an institute honoring George F. Kennan, and he encouraged me to write the story of a scholar-turned ambassador who single-handedly changed the relationship between Japan and the United States. I worked up an outline and a few chapters for the book, and told Reischauer of my intention. He gave me no encouragement, but did agree to sit for several extended interviews.

Then life took another twist. For my sins, I was appointed dean of the Johns Hopkins School of Advanced International Studies, a position I held from 1979 to 1993 and that allowed little time for personal research and writing. I continued to make plans for the book, but in 1986 a new challenge fell out of the sky: Reischauer published his own autobiography, *My Life Between Japan and America.*[1] After reading it, I decided that he had told his own story sufficiently well and that there was not much left for me to cover.

But, as you can see, I changed my mind. The late 1980s and early 1990s were a time of trauma in U.S.–Japan relations. Reischauer died in September 1990 at the age of seventy-nine, fearing that all his efforts to improve understanding between the two nations might go down the drain in the trade wars and ugly media portrayals of a Japan threatening to destroy Americans' jobs and security. Attacked by leftist scholars and "revisionist" journalists, he went to his grave wondering if his life had been a failure.

Then three things happened. With the bursting of Japan's economic bubble and the rise of a new enemy—Saddam Hussein of Iraq—the squabbles between the United States and Japan were all but forgotten. Japan entered a long period of stagnation and recovery. I also got a chance to see the original manuscript of Reischauer's book, thanks to his assistant at Harvard, Nancy Deptula. Nancy felt that his editors had eviscerated some of the most interesting aspects of his life, as did Marius Jansen, a close friend and, with Reischauer, coauthor of *The Japanese Today*.[2] I agreed.

I knew from personal experience that Reischauer wrote all his books in longhand on yellow lined pads, making many revisions. Once his secretary typed up these pages, he continued to revise and rework the manuscript until he was completely satisfied. The manuscript that Nancy gave me was a finished product—731 double-spaced, typewritten pages—the fourth and final iteration of the book he wanted published. As I read it through, I realized that it had enough new and important material to warrant a more complete story of his life. The words on the cover sheet in his handwriting, "complete unabridged manuscript," told me that it was not some hasty first draft, but rather the version of his life that Reischauer wanted to tell the world. Peter Grilli, one of his former students at Harvard, confirmed this point. At a book-and-author event at the Japan Society in New York, Reischauer said that the published book contained the trunk and main branches of his story, but the twigs had been cut off. His wife, Haru Reischauer, told Marius Jansen that the editors had knocked out big gobs of what Ed had written about his embassy years, and she even considered writing her own version of those years.[3] I have tried to mine some of the nuggets in that longer version and in my own observations.

The most important reason for this book is that we now have a broader perspective of Reischauer's life and his role in helping to shape U.S.–Japan relations. His own book is sophisticated and graceful—the work of an accomplished scholar and writer—and nothing I have written should supplant it. Because he was a meticulous historian, the facts and dates he provides are invaluable. But he could not have known his full impact on Japan and America—he seldom reflected on his own place in history—nor could he foresee that his confidence in Japan would be justified. With the passage of several decades, it is easier to assess his contributions and situate his role in history. Japan's development as a peace-loving democracy and America's acceptance of Japan as a vital partner have more than justified his faith, although he could not live to see it.

Embarking on the book once again in 1994, I was amazed to discover how many lives Reischauer had touched in both America and Japan, and how large was his impact on academic studies of Japan. I was also stunned by the harshness and vitriol of the attacks against him by those with opposing viewpoints. Finally, I was surprised to see how he has been forgotten by some of those who profited most from his life's work.

As I continued to write, I could feel the critical eye of the sensei (teacher) watching me and warning me to get the facts right. Having his autobiography at my side was a blessing and a curse. He was an intensely private person, shrewd but without guile, as one of his former students put it. I have tried to round out the complex human being who often hid behind a scholarly facade.

Some of Reischauer's harshest critics have declared in advance that this book will be mere hagiography, and several have tried to prevent its publication. Their zeal has driven me forward. If Reischauer got Japan right in most essentials, then these critics were mostly wrong. Even revisionists need to be revised, as John Lewis Gaddis has wisely noted.

I am keenly aware of Anthony Grafton's cautionary words, however: "To write the history of the learned, in short, one had to be more learned than they were."[4] I make no claim to such learning. But I have lived in and with Japan as an army officer, Foreign Service officer, journalist, and scholar for many of the past fifty-two years and have had a front-row seat to observe and test Reischauer's judgments about the nation and its people. I am convinced that no one else could have thrown more light on the "dark side of the moon." He seized a unique moment in history—a moment when East Asia began its return to the position of economic center of the world—and helped Americans to understand why this mattered.

A Note on Language

I have followed the Japanese custom of placing Japanese surnames first and have omitted the macron over long vowels on the ground that readers of Japanese will know where they belong and those who don't read Japanese will not care.

Acknowledgments

I am indebted to many people for help in writing this book. Although it is by no means an authorized biography, Edwin Reischauer's three children, Ann, Robert, and Joan, agreed to be interviewed and cheerfully responded to my queries. With the combination of modesty, reserve, irreverence, humor, and self-confidence that I discovered in their father, they seemed mildly amused and slightly surprised that anyone would be writing a biography about him at this late date. I can only hope they will recognize the figure that emerges in these pages.

I am grateful to the late Nancy Monteith Deptula, Reischauer's longtime assistant and friend at Harvard, for sharing with me the unedited manuscript of his autobiography, parts of which have never before been cited, as well as copies of both his letters to his family from 1961 to 1966 while he served as U.S. ambassador to Japan and his letters to others later in his career. I owe thanks also to Jill Conway Villatoro, who served as an assistant to Reischauer at Harvard and then as my assistant and colleague at the John Hopkins School of Advanced International Studies and at the U.S.–Japan Foundation.

I am deeply grateful to John Curtis Perry, a former student of Reischauer and John K. Fairbank and now the Henry Willard Denison Professor of Diplomatic History at the Fletcher School of Law and Diplomacy at Tufts University, for sharing his insights, encouragement, and wise comments on the manuscript. In addition, I am grateful to Gerald L. Curtis, Burgess Professor of Political Science at Columbia University, for reading the entire manuscript and offering thoughtful suggestions.

I owe much to James H. Billington, librarian of Congress, for his strong encouragement to proceed with the project when I served as his deputy at the Woodrow Wilson International Center for Scholars in Washington, D.C., from 1976 to 1979. President Steven Muller and Provost Richard P. Longaker of Johns Hopkins University were inspiring supporters of Japan and China studies. The late James C. Thomson Jr., who had much to do with Reischauer's appointment as ambassador to Japan, shared his recollections of serving in the Kennedy and Johnson administrations.

Two of Reischauer's Harvard colleagues, Albert M. Craig and Howard S. Hibbett, were generous with their time and made thoughtful comments on parts of the manuscript. Other scholars and former students who offered valuable insights were George Akita, Robert N. Bellah, Marshall M. Bouton, Roger W. Bowen, Roger Brown, Kent E. Calder, Richard Dyke, Henry F. Graff, Peter Grilli, Robert M. Immerman, David Janes, Merit E. Janow, Donald Keene, James W. Morley, Fred Notehelfer, Susan J. Pharr, Sumner Redstone, John D. Rockefeller IV, Robert A. Scalapino, Orville Schell, Arthur W. Schlesinger Jr., Benjamin Schwartz, Shinoda Tomohito, Michael J. Smitka, Yoshi Tsurumi, and Ernest Young. None of these individuals should be held responsible for any errors of fact or opinion in the book; I alone am responsible.

A number of journalists helped fill in the picture: Alan Murray and Jacob Schlesinger of the *Wall Street Journal*; Kawachi Takashi, Omori Minoru, and Komori Yoshihisa of *Mainichi Shimbun*; and Sam Jameson of the *Chicago Tribune* and *Los Angeles Times*.

I am grateful to my colleagues at the U.S.-Japan Foundation, especially to our courageous chairman, Tom Johnson, and his board of trustees, and to Teresa Sham, who patiently guided me into the digital world of the twenty-first century, as well as Christine Manapat-Sims, Elizabeth Gordon, and Kanayo Oshima Schlumpf, who lent their moral support.

Among my Columbia graduate students, Joshua Savitch and Kevin Burgwinkle provided outstanding research assistance. I am grateful also to Tina Yin, Noguchi Yasunori, Abe Yasuhito, Akiko Nemoto Pace, Daniel A. De Simone, Yokouchi Yoko, Sukegawa Yasushi, and Koide Ayako for their contributions. Tobias Harris, a doctoral student at MIT, also provided excellent assistance.

I also owe thanks to former government officials Mike Mansfield, Thomas Hughes, William C. Sherman, William L. Givens, John Newhouse, Donald P. Gregg, Robert A. Fearey, Albert Seligmann, Winthrop Knowlton, and Roy Mlynarchik. I also thank Saito Setsuko, Carol Shaw, Shirley Fearey, Lee Sneider, and Selma Janow for their useful insights.

I owe an enormous debt to my mentors who introduced me to Japanese history, politics, and foreign policy: Allan. B. Cole, Marius Jansen, Ishida Takeshi, and Eto Shinkichi of Tokyo University, as well as Matsumoto Shigeharu and Kato Mikio of the International House of Japan, and Professors Homma Nagayo and Inoki Masamichi.

I am grateful to members of the staff of the John F. Kennedy Memorial Library; Linda M. Seelke of the Lyndon B. Johnson Memorial Library; Roland M. Bauman at the Oberlin College Archives; Linda Carlson of the Johns Hopkins School of Advanced International Studies Library; Tim Driscoll and his wonderful staff at the Harvard University Archives; Robert A. Wampler of the National Security Archive at George Washington University; Jonathan Green, research associate at the Ford Foundation; and Kimberly Gould Ashizawa, senior associate at the Japan Center for International Exchange.

I am forever indebted to Kakishima Kazunobu, chief editor of the Translation Book Division at Kodansha, and Moriyama Naomi, translator and researcher for Kodansha, for their patience, good humor, and meticulous fact checking. Similarly, I shall always be grateful to Anne Routon, editor at Columbia University Press, without whose encouragement and faith in the project I could not have pushed forward; to Annie Barva, whose meticulous copyediting vastly improved the final product; and to Anne Holmes, for her superb work on the index.

Finally, I owe more than I can say to my beloved Lavinia, who tolerated my long hours of isolation with admirable good humor, grace, and understanding. To her, I joyfully dedicate this book.

Edwin O. Reischauer
and the American Discovery of Japan

1 Born in Japan

In September 1945, just a month after Japan surrendered to the United States, ending the bloodiest war in history, a shy, thirty-four-year-old, Harvard-trained American scholar sat down with a pencil and pad of yellow lined paper and wrote a short book in two months. He called it Japan: Past and Present.

Remarkably, Edwin O. Reischauer used no history texts, reference works, or notes. The book grew out of a series of four or five hours of lectures on Japanese history that he had given while serving as a lieutenant colonel in the U.S. Army during the war. "I . . . figured that the three years away from history books had allowed inessential details to drop out of my mind, leaving the basic outline of Japanese history all the clearer."[1]

Even more remarkable was the fact that Reischauer had no formal training as a specialist in Japanese history. He could not find a teacher in the 1930s who knew the subject and had decided instead to specialize in ancient Chinese history. His years of Ph.D. research focused on the diary and travels in China of the ninth-century Japanese Buddhist monk Ennin (Jikaku Daishi).

Japan: Past and Present was an overwhelming success. Written for the general reader, free of scholarly jargon, and devoid of the hatred and racism that marked all references to the "Japs" of the Pacific War, the book gave Americans a surprisingly positive look at the nation that had attacked Pearl Harbor in 1941. Sir George Sansom, then dean of Japanese historians, wrote, "I can truthfully say that I do not know of any short book on Japanese history which gives so much useful information in so brief and simple a form."[2]

This little book and its revised editions in l952 and 1964 became the standard account of Japanese history in the United States and elsewhere for the next twenty-five years and would become a major influence on several generations of students, scholars, government officials, and the media. Reischauer wrote and rewrote the book for most of his scholarly career, expanding on his major themes and adding colorful details in *The Japanese* (later titled *The Japanese Today*).[3]

Japan: Past and Present offered Americans an extraordinary new look at Japan. Wartime propaganda in the United States had painted a picture of the Japanese as fanatic subhumans, apes, and vermin who needed to be exterminated. In contrast to the notion of a "good German," there were no "good Japanese."[4] Reischauer saw Japan's descent into militarism and aggression in the 1930s as a tragic aberration rather than as an inevitable continuation of the warlike samurai or feudal tradition. He pointed out the beauty and originality of Japanese culture to a nation that had looked down on the Japanese largely as pathetic imitators of more advanced societies. He portrayed the great leaders of modern Japan as quite different from the kamikaze pilots who blindly sacrificed their lives for their emperor. He placed Japan squarely in the main currents of modern world history and refused to see it as some sort of exotic outlier.

His interpretation of modern Japanese history flew in the face of prevailing theory among left-wing Japanese and Western scholars: he found in Tokugawa Era Japan (1603–1868) the benign origins of modernization where influential Marxist historians saw only the dark shadow of feudalism. He viewed Japan's efforts to avoid being colonized and to catch up with the West in the Meiji Period (1868–1912) as an extraordinary triumph for a non-Western nation. He placed a high value on Japan's early experimentation with parliamentary democracy and believed that Japanese citizens were fully capable of managing democratic government under their new constitution of 1947. In short, Reischauer shook up the received wisdom about Japan on both sides of the Pacific. He cast a spotlight on the dark side of the moon.

By 1960, Reischauer's preeminence at Harvard as America's leading Japan specialist brought him to the attention of President-elect John F. Kennedy, who appointed him ambassador to Japan in April 1961. For the next five and a half years, he became a beloved public figure in Japan. Almost single-handedly, he ended the "occupation mentality" of the U.S. officials who treated the Japanese as defeated inferiors. No American, with the possible exception of George F. Kennan (another of Kennedy's ambassadors), has had greater influence over a relationship with a foreign nation. But the death of President Kennedy in 1963 and the escalating war in Vietnam cast dark clouds over Reischauer's mission. Antiwar critics would accuse him of being an agent of "American imperialism" in Asia.

In 1964, Japan's best American friend was the victim of a bizarre stabbing attack by a deranged Japanese youth at the front door of the U.S. Embassy chancery. Wounded in the leg by a rusty kitchen knife, Reischauer almost bled to death. The blood he received in a nearby Japanese hospital was infected with viral hepatitis C, leaving him with permanent liver damage that led to a painful death in 1990.

Late in his life, he would become the subject of savage attacks by "revisionists" in the 1980s, who would charge that he was an "apologist" for Japan, too soft on the Japanese government, and naive about the prospects for Japanese democracy. Unshaken, he held to his faith in the common sense of ordinary Japanese citizens and in their capacity to grow and change. To a remarkable extent, his faith in Japan has been vindicated. In his final years, he turned to the challenge of educating young Americans for life in the twenty-first century. With prophetic insight, he warned against our provincialism in a dangerous world and anticipated the terrorist threats we face today.

How did Reischauer gain such firm and, for his era, original views? What experiences gave him the confidence to claim that he understood ordinary Japanese citizens? As a scholar whose Japanese acquaintances were mostly other intellectuals, how could he claim to understand the "common man" in Japan? How could he know that democracy would take root in a society saturated with hierarchy, inequality, and emperor worship? What was it about this mild-mannered professor that infuriated other scholars and journalists? That is the story of this book.

From the moment of his birth in a missionary family on the lovely green campus of Meiji Gakuin University, Edwin Reischauer's life would be defined by the missionary spirit. Meiji Gakuin, where his father, Dr. August Karl Reischauer, worked, had been founded in 1863 by two American missionary societies: the Northern Presbyterian Church, to which his parents belonged, and the Calvinist Dutch Reformed Church.

Edwin's great-grandfather, Matthias Reischauer, and his family left their home in upper Austria near Salzburg in 1853 and settled in a farming area near Jonesboro, Illinois, in a community of Austrian and German Protestant immigrants.[5] Edwin's grandfather, Rupert, born in 1841, came along as a young boy. Rupert served in the Northern army in the American Civil War until he was medically discharged with an intestinal disease in 1864. He never fully recovered and died an early death in 1888, when Edwin's father was only nine years old. Edwin never knew him. His grandmother, Maria Gattermeier, however, lived to the age of eighty-four and spoke only German.

Edwin's mother, Helen Sidwell Oldfather, had older roots in America. Her ancestors were Protestant Germans from Berlin who first arrived in Baltimore in 1769 seeking religious freedom and then moved on to Pennsylvania and Ohio. Edwin's maternal grandfather, Jeremiah Oldfather, after fighting through the Civil War for an Ohio regiment, entered the Presbyterian ministry and in 1872 set out to become a missionary in Persia, as Iran was known then. Edwin's maternal grandmother, Felicia Narcissa Rice, came from a family from the Palatinate, or German-speaking Switzerland. Her ancestors first came to Pittsburgh in 1755 and moved on to Kentucky and Indiana, where Felicia was born in 1848.

Felicia lived to the ripe old age of ninety-three and was the only one of his grandparents whom Edwin knew well. He remembers her as "a voracious reader who had decided opinions on most subjects. Despite her own and her husband's Germanic backgrounds, she conveyed the feeling to the whole family that we were of Scottish descent, presumably because of our Presbyterian affiliations."[6] Reischauer would later note that his "father was peeved that I described [our ancestors] as coming from 'sturdy, taciturn, God-fearing peasant stock.'"[7]

Felicia and Jeremiah spent eighteen hazardous years in Azerbaijan, Persia. Edwin's mother, Helen, was born there, but because good schools were lacking, Jeremiah abandoned missionary work and became pastor at Hanover College in southeastern Indiana. Helen in her turn became a teacher of Latin at Hanover and met August Reischauer, Edwin's father, there.

Edwin recalled in his autobiography that his grandmother's family "obviously made the transition back to the United States with success; yet I have always been struck by the paucity of Iranian influences and the lack of feeling for the country that they brought back with them after spending eighteen years in Persia. This stands in sharp contrast with the feel for Japan which my early years in that country gave me."[8]

Edwin's father, August Karl Reischauer, born in 1879, spoke only German at home and attended schools where the language of instruction was German, but later switched to an English-language Presbyterian high school and then to Hanover College. Originally a Lutheran, he joined the Presbyterian Church after college and went on to the McCormick Theological Seminary in Chicago. Graduating in 1905, he prepared to embark on a career as a foreign missionary, with Brazil as his first choice of assignment and Japan as his second. Because there was no opening in Brazil, he accepted a teaching position at Meiji Gakuin in Tokyo.[9]

Japan was a daunting challenge for Christian missionaries. Portuguese Jesuits, led by Francis Xavier, had gained a tiny foothold there in the 1540s and in the next half century won thousands of converts to the Catholic faith. It has been estimated that by 1580 there were 150,000 Christians in Japan and perhaps twice that number in the early seventeenth century. But Hideyoshi, the peasant general who unified the country, feared that the Christians might become a subversive influence and officially banned them in 1587, crucifying nine missionaries and seventeen of their converts in 1597.

Hideyoshi's successor, the shogun Tokugawa Ieyasu, renewed the persecution of Christians in 1612 and after many executions did his best to put an end to Christianity in Japan in 1637–38 at Shimabara, where an uprising of some 20,000 Christian peasants was brutally suppressed. For the next 220 years, Christianity was banned in Japan, and Japanese were forbidden to travel abroad. Foreigners, mainly Chinese and Dutch traders, were limited to Deshima, Tsushima, and Okinawa. Japan entered its long period of semi-isolation.

After Commodore Matthew Perry and his "black ships" forced open Japan in 1853–54, Protestant missionaries from Europe and America ventured back into Japan and in fact were the single largest group of foreigners in the treaty ports in the 1860s. By 1873, the ban on Christianity was lifted entirely, and missionaries rode in on a brief wave of Japanese enthusiasm for westernization in the 1870s and early 1880s. They engaged mainly in language study and translation and in the teaching of their native languages, with attempts to "incorporate a religious message into their teachings."[10]

The period from 1880 to 1893 saw an amazing growth of missionary activity in Japan: mission expenditures more than tripled, amounting at their peak to about four-fifths of those in the longer established China field.[11] A rough estimate in 1883 puts the number of Japanese Protestant converts at 6,598 and the number of Protestant missionaries active at the time at 225.[12] The missionaries focused mainly on improvement of social conditions in urban areas. In 1890, Japan was home to 175 ordained Protestant missionaries, of whom 146 were Americans, 20 were British, and 9 were Canadian. Of the 146 Americans, 21 were Presbyterians.[13] By 1900, five dominant Protestant denominations counted 603 foreign missionaries, 379 organized churches, and more than 40,000 church members. In addition, Protestant missionaries ran 15 boys' boarding schools, 44 girls' boarding schools, and 74 day schools, with a total enrollment of nearly 10,000.[14]

It is important to note, however, that China rather than Japan was the major target of American missionaries at the time A. K. Reischauer undertook his mission in Japan. In 1906, 1,037 American missionaries were in China, compared to 594 in Japan. By 1916, there were 2,862 American missionaries in China and only 858 in Japan.[15] These numbers had consequences. Because of their strong sympathy for and identification with the Chinese people as well as their claims to modest success, the American missionaries in China would influence public opinion at home far more than their counterparts in Japan would. In order to keep the funds flowing from congregations at home, they eagerly and effectively portrayed a China that was ready to embrace Christian and democratic values. As China and Japan headed for war in 1931, American sympathies were clearly on the side of China.

Who were these bold Americans? "The missionary was basically a minister or church-worker who surrendered home, family, friends, and professional advancement for the sake of spending a lifetime preaching to or working with apathetic aliens," explains James A. Field Jr.[16] Generally Caucasian, middle-class Americans born in the United States, they were reasonably well educated by the standards of the times and came mostly from New England, New York, and the rural areas to the west of New York.

Ironically, at the same time that they taught their flocks to believe in a spiritual kingdom where money and worldly possessions were meaningless, they were also fund-raisers, constantly striving to convince their supporters back home that they were having great success in converting the natives in order to assure a continuing flow of financial support. They came to Japan armed with what they believed was their own superior faith while also preaching racial equality. And, of course, the very presence of these peaceful Christians in Japan was made possible by U.S. naval power. The idealistic young missionaries could not have recognized the ironic connection that doomed their enterprise from the outset.

American missionaries brought far more than religious zeal. Of American missionaries in China, Harvard professor John K. Fairbank, who would become a close colleague of and coauthor with Edwin O. Reischauer, wrote:

> They were apostles of liberty under law, of one-class egalitarianism (except for the anomaly of black slavery), and of the self-determination of peoples. When the Second Great Awakening of religious fervor in the early years of the [Nineteenth] Century sent forth missionaries devoted to the spreading of the Protestant gospel of individual salvation through faith in Christ, the foreign missions thus launched many of the features of American life in general: a strong sense of personal responsibility for one's own character and conduct; an optimistic belief in progress toward general betterment, especially through the use of education, invention and technology; a conviction of moral and cultural worth, at times even superiority, justified both by religious teachings of the Holy Bible and by the political principles of the Founding Fathers.[17]

It is not surprising that many of the leaders of Meiji Japan (1868–1912) looked askance at these brash young Americans who were critical of their established political and social order. At a time when these leaders were building up state Shinto and emperor worship as a means to enhance the state's power, the Christians must have seemed dangerously subversive. Buddhist and Shinto leaders joined the Meiji oligarchs to oppose this foreign "contagion." The pendulum that had swung the doors open in the 1870s began to swing back against Western influence and religion in the late 1880s.

August Karl Reischauer, freshly ordained, arrived in Tokyo with his young bride in 1905. One must marvel today at the mixture of self-confidence, generosity of spirit, optimism, hubris, and deep faith that inspired him to leave home in rural southern Illinois to bring the word of God to Japan in this period. He had to believe that he possessed universal answers to ultimate questions for all humanity, that the Japanese people were thirsting for those precious answers, and that they would gladly forsake their native Shinto beliefs, not to mention centuries-old Buddhism and Confucianism, for these new truths.

But he could not have chosen a worse year to spread his faith. Growing Japanese nationalism, fed by military victories over China (1895) and Russia (1905), led to a sharp turn against America. There was vast public indignation against the Portsmouth Treaty of 1905 brokered by President Theodore Roosevelt, a settlement that seemed to cheat Japan out of its rightful gains in the war against Russia. Protest riots broke out in Hibiya Park and elsewhere. A. K. Reischauer noticed that Japanese troops were stationed on the campus of Meiji Gakuin to protect Americans from angry mobs.[18]

In 1910, the year of Edwin Reischauer's birth, Japan annexed Korea and began its long march toward conquest in Manchuria on a path that would eventually lead it to war with the United States. The U.S. Empire, stretching in 1899 to Hawaii and the Philippines, lay dangerously close to Japan's colony of Taiwan. Tension mounted, and war scares would arise periodically from 1906 until the outbreak of war in 1941.

In California, anti-Japanese feelings were festering. An influx of immigrants from Japan led to calls for ending Asian immigration. In 1905, the San Francisco public schools closed their doors to children of Japanese immigrants. (Not by chance, this was the same year in which an Asian power, Japan, defeated a Caucasian power, Russia, for the first time in modern history.) Racism exploded. The *San Francisco Chronicle* warned darkly that "if Japanese immigration is unchecked it is only a question of time when our rural population will be Japanese, our rural civilization Japanese, and the white population hard pressed in our cities and towns."[19] The crisis was temporarily resolved by the negotiation in 1908 of the "Gentlemen's Agreement," whereby Japan undertook to curb the outward flow of its citizens.

It was at this juncture that we can see the beginnings of American schizophrenia regarding Japan and China. Up to 1905, the Japanese were perceived as friendly and docile younger brothers, a new nation willing and eager to learn from Americans' "superior" civilization. American religious, business, and military leaders championed Japan's rise in national power. In 1905, U.S. Navy lieutenant Henry E. Rhoads wrote, "[The Japanese] . . . are kindly, generous, large-hearted, good mannered, and as loyal and honest a people as one could hope for."[20] By 1914, however, this image had all but disappeared. Those who wished to end Japanese immigration into California painted a starkly different portrait: "The Japanese are non-assimilable and undesirable," wrote Sidney L. Gulick, a professor and missionary at Doshisha University who was sympathetic to Japan, in an attempt to describe the general view then held; "they are immoral, untrustworthy, tricky, clannish; they are, therefore, intrinsically unpleasant, untrustworthy, unacceptable. It is impossible to like them and dangerous to welcome them into our political and social system and especially into our family life."[21]

China, by contrast, had been seen as made up of a backward, stagnant people ruled by corrupt officials and a feeble central government. All this changed dramatically after Japan appeared to threaten U.S. interests in East Asia. Sun Yatsen's revolution of 1911 scratched a new image of China in the American mind.[22] For the next three decades, American missionaries, businessmen, soldiers of fortune, and journalists combined to paint a picture of a China that was a budding democracy, a lucrative market, a pro-Western, potentially Christian nation, and an innocent victim of the predatory Japanese. American missionaries in China sent wildly optimistic reports to their home congregations. Ignoring the appalling urban poverty, official corruption, prostitution, and crime there, one such report commented on "the unprecedented ripeness of the field for Christian harvest."[23] American audiences loved this portrait. The romance with China would last until Mao Zedong and the Chinese Communists took over the mainland in 1949. By then, Japan would once again be the new docile younger brother.

If the threat of Japanese expansion alarmed Americans, the reverse was also true. President Theodore Roosevelt announced that "America must dominate the Pacific."[24] Seen from Tokyo, American ambitions seemed threatening. As Gulick observed in 1914,

> [The United States] proposed to neutralize the Manchurian Railways by four European powers without consulting the wishes of Japan and Russia; Americans supported a railway scheme in Manchuria which would

greatly reduce the value of the Russo-Japanese line; newspapers agitated against the alleged Japanese rebate in Manchuria; American financiers played a prominent part in the proposed "four-powers loan" to China, which excluded Russia and Japan; America independently recognized the Chinese republic, in spite of an agreement among leading powers to act together in this matter; California, after repeated mutterings, passed an antialien [*sic*] land law which seriously hampers the prospects of Japanese residing in America and the government at Washington upholds the law. And finally, many newspapers and politicians have for years indulged in the most extraordinary misrepresentations of Japan and in reckless assertions in regard to her doings and purposes calculated to evoke wide-spread suspicion of Japan and readiness to believe any evil report. All these things have been done in spite of Japan's desire for friendship with America. Is it strange that Japan is hurt and estranged?[25]

In 1909, Homer Lea, an American "soldier of fortune," published a sensational book called *The Valor of Ignorance*,[26] in which he warned of an approaching war between Japan and the United States for supremacy of the Pacific. Citing the "Yellow Peril" that threatened America from Asia, he argued that Japan had the naval and military power to seize the Philippines, Alaska, and Hawaii from the United States and then invade the West Coast, easily occupying Washington, Oregon, and California. The book produced hysteria among Caucasian settlers in California, leading the state legislature to bar Japanese immigrants from owning property. As fears and rumors of a Japanese invasion mounted, Senator Hiram W. Johnson of California was able to persuade the U.S. Congress to pass the infamous Exclusion Act of 1924, which singled out Asians as unfit for immigration into the United States and was clearly aimed at Japan. Edwin Reischauer remembered that at the age of thirteen he was indignant at the passage of this act.

In short, had Reischauer's father known of the rising tensions that would lie in the path of his Christian mission to Japan, he might have turned back and chosen a different field of work. But August Karl Reischauer proved to be different from most missionaries. While holding fast to his conviction that Christianity was superior to any of Japan's traditional religions, he nevertheless brought humility and intellectual curiosity to the study of the strange new culture in which he found himself. Instead of becoming discouraged, he quickly plunged into the study of Japanese history and religion with immense energy and enthusiasm.

"My father," recalled Edwin many years later, "despite his farm background in a Protestant, German-speaking, Austrian community in Southern Illinois, was by nature an intellectual and scholarly man. He was deeply religious, having been affected by his father's early death, and his first book was a small essay entitled *Personal Immortality*."[27] He was clearly a serious man of high purpose.

Arriving in Tokyo at the age of twenty-six, August could not have known much if anything about Japanese culture, history, religion, or politics. He spoke not a word of Japanese. If he had read about Japan at all, he may have absorbed the rather gauzy portraits of idyllic samurai life painted in the 1890s by the American journalist Lafcadio Hearn. He may also have read the first volume of James Murdoch's voluminous three-volume *A History of Japan*, which began to appear in 1903. Another possible source of information would have been *A Handbook for Travellers in Japan*, published in 1891 by Basil Hall Chamberlain and W. B. Mason, Britain's leading Japanologists of the day.[28] But none of these works could have anticipated the changes in Japan that accompanied its rapid industrialization and bold quest to become a self-sufficient great power in Asia.

August's intellectual growth and energy over the next eight years was nothing short of extraordinary. He plunged immediately into study of the Japanese language, spending most of his first two years doing his best to learn it without textbooks or trained teachers. In addition to adapting to life in a strange new land, August and Helen became the parents of Robert Karl (1907), Edwin Oldfather (1910), and Felicia (1914).

By 1912, just seven years after arriving in Tokyo, August published a translation of *Shinshu Hyakuwa* under the title "A Catechism of the Shin Sect" in the *Transactions of the Asiatic Society*.[29] In the following year, he gave a series of lectures at New York University that marked his arrival as one of the leading scholars of Buddhism in the Western world.[30] While teaching ethics and philosophy at Meiji Gakuin and caring for his growing family, he had mastered current and classical Japanese and Chinese texts, worked in Sanskrit as well, and wrote in depth of the history of the various sects of Buddhism in Japan. His selected bibliography lists the following types of works in Japanese: six dictionaries, eight texts and commentaries, five histories, five biographies, ten essays, and three lectures and commentaries. His text was sprinkled with erudite references to leading thinkers of his day, both Japanese and Western. This was a prodigious feat of scholarship, especially considering that there were no schools or texts for educating foreigners in those days, and he was almost entirely self-taught. From this time on, lecturing on non-Christian religions and their relationship to Christianity became his major interest.

"The missionary impact on the American mind may have been more profound than its impact on the non-Western mind," wrote Arthur M. Schlesinger Jr. years later.[31] This was certainly true in the case of A. K. Reischauer. The young Christian who had arrived in Tokyo burning to save heathen souls became intrigued with Shinto, Buddhism, and Confucianism. At first, he sought in these established religions clues for how he might introduce Christianity to their believers. Then later, while insisting on his faith in Jesus Christ, he evolved from a zealous propagator of Christian theology into a serious intellectual who dedicated himself to educating the American people about Japanese culture and religion. "I felt quite certain that if Christian workers knew more about Japan's own spiritual heritage as represented by the non-Christian religions, they would have a better understanding of what are really the great essentials of Christianity itself."[32]

He recognized early on the critical role that Buddhism played in bringing knowledge to Japan, "for just as truly as Christian missionaries from Europe and America have been the apostles of a superior civilization to the backward nations of the world, so have the Buddhists often been to Japan the messengers of progress and light."[33] The idea of progress toward a higher form of civilization was deeply rooted among American intellectuals of his day and would later be apparent in the thought of his son Edwin, as would his fascination with the process whereby Japan absorbed foreign influences without losing its own identity.

By 1913, A. K. Reischauer admitted to himself that converting Japan to Christianity would not be easy: "Whatever one may think of the place which the old religions of Japan, and Buddhism in particular, will occupy in the future of this people's life, they are forces with which one must reckon."[34] He became convinced that Buddhism was the enemy of Christianity in Japan and that there could be no compromise between the two ancient faiths. "Toward the end of the eighties [1880s] and early in the nineties [1890s] came the reaction against everything Western, and the conservative Buddhists sought to profit by this. They were loudest among those who pointed out the self-sufficiency of everything Japanese." But he remained optimistic about the prospects for Christianity. He argued that the Japanese students who had studied abroad in the 1880s and 1890s were imbued with the "scientific spirit and devoted to the historico-critical method" and that this fact would "give a tremendous shock to the ordinary claims of Japanese Buddhists." He also noted that Christianity was successful in the Korea of his day because it was "the vehicle of western civilization and not simply because it is a superior religion."[35]

By the age of thirty-four, August had come around to the view that "the human race is one in its needs and in its attempts to meet those needs. . . . It is impossible to have a keen appreciation and full understanding of Christianity unless one sees it in the light of the world's other great religions. It is high time that Western scholars take a wider outlook upon the world, and through a knowledge of Oriental thought help lay the foundations for that sympathy for Asia's millions which alone can make the inevitable meeting of East and West a blessing rather than a curse."[36] This belief would guide his son Edwin's entire career.

A. K. Reischauer ventured beyond religion to observe, "It must be remembered that a Japanese, true to the fundamental principle of his native Shinto, is first a patriot and then a man of religion. When the two conflict, religion is apt to be the loser. To this day this seems to be a characteristic of the average Japanese. Religion is presented by its advocates as something good for the welfare of the state. The greatest obstacle which Christianity has met in Japan is the claim on the part of its enemies that it undermines the state."[37]

His early observations of Japanese history are full of insights that would inform the works of his sons: the Japanese of the sixth century, "though very simple in their manner of life, were intellectually well gifted and later proved to be endowed with extraordinary aesthetic ability." He remarked on the ancient Japanese "tendency to overcome alien beliefs by compromise and absorption." And writing of the learned Japanese priests of the ninth century A.D. who brought Buddhism to Japan, he noted "that deep-rooted Japanese characteristic which is quick to adopt anything new but always only after some slight modifications and a mingling with something from other sources." And this: "It is more natural for the Japanese mind to look upon life and the things of life as good, for Japan is above all else 'the land of the gods' and Japanese are the offspring of 'the sons of heaven.' "[38]

Noting the inflow into Japan of four great Buddhist sects between 1175 and 1253, he observed: "The student who reads with an unbiased mind this movement and the lives of the great men who led the way, cannot fail to be impressed with the positive contribution made by Japan to at least one of the world's great religions. To know this period of Japanese history will cure any man of the superficial thought so often expressed by Westerners that the Japanese have borrowed everything they possess and that they are only imitators."[39] In this one passage, we can see two of the convictions that Edwin O. Reischauer would later adopt: first, that the Japanese are far more than mere imitators and, second, that great individuals rather than impersonal forces create history.

Another of his father's opinions would apparently influence Edwin's understanding of Tokugawa history: August portrayed in glowing terms the "great Tokugawa Shogunate, which ruled the land with such skill and firmness for about two centuries and a half that there was hardly so much as a dogfight on this blood-drenched soil." The Tokugawa's "gave peace and order to Japan for more than 250 years." Leftist historians would bitterly attack Edwin Reischauer's similarly positive evaluation of the Tokugawa Era in his later years. Here lay the seeds of the bitter arguments about feudalism and modernization described later in the book. Elsewhere in his work on Japanese Buddhism, though, A. K. Reischauer did observe that official Confucianism "became really corrupt and helped rivet upon Japan that formalism and dead uniformity so characteristic of much of the life during the Tokugawa period."[40]

At the time August was lecturing, it was widely believed in America that Perry's arrival had caused the overthrow of the Shogunate and had helped bring about the Meiji Restoration of 1868. He disagreed: "The Restoration was, of course, hastened by the appearance of Commodore Perry's ships in 1853, but it was not really caused by this as some Westerners fondly imagine. It was really a very minor factor in a very complex movement the core of which was in the religious and philosophic life of the nation during the two centuries preceding."[41] This view, too, would become an article of faith for Edwin Reischauer.

We can see in the father's works some of the characteristics of the son's later scholarship: a colorful writing style, a tendency to make bold generalizations, a willingness to reject conventional wisdom, an ability to organize myriad details into easily understandable patterns, a reliance on Japanese source materials that had never been used by Western scholars, and an eagerness to educate his countrymen about this vast unknown region. And there was the supreme missionary-like confidence in the validity of his intellectual arguments. This period of A. K. Reischauer's deep immersion in Japanese religion exactly coincides with the boyhood and young adult years of his two sons. "My father provided us with an admirable role model," Edwin later recalled.[42]

The father planted the seeds for Edwin's ambition. He preached that missionaries were not the only foreigners who should study Asian cultures and religions: other representatives from the Western world, such as government officials, businessmen, educators, and the like would also benefit from such study. "Such knowledge would make them far more effective in their respective fields, since it would undoubtedly result in their having greater respect for these people, and this, in turn, would make such representatives from the Western world less arrogant and condescending than has been all too frequently the case."[43] This point would become a second article of faith for the son: the more one knew about Japan, the greater one would respect its culture. Late in his life, however, his critics would challenge this faith, arguing that if one *really* understood the Japanese, one would understand that "they are out to get us."

By the time of Edwin Reischauer's birth in 1910, Japan had gotten rid of the unequal treaties, but still faced discrimination from the Western powers. At the peace negotiations at Versailles in 1919 following World War One, President

Woodrow Wilson of the United States and Prime Minister Lloyd George of Great Britain refused to insert into the charter of the League of Nations a clause supporting racial equality. In the Washington Naval Treaty of 1921–22, Japan was forced to accept a lesser ratio of capital ships (three) than Great Britain (five) or the United States (five). In addition, Japan was pressured into accepting the status quo in China, meaning that whereas European powers had gained special privileges and territory (such as Hong Kong), Japan was to be barred from extending its influence on the China mainland, and it was pressured into abandoning its Treaty of 1902 with Great Britain, leaving it without an ally in the dangerous neighborhood of Northeast Asia.

By 1925, at age forty-six, A. K. Reischauer had become a severe critic of Western imperialism and racism, as well as of some of his fellow missionaries. In a series of lectures at Princeton Theological Seminary, he noted that Western influences had awakened the peoples of East Asia to the idea of progress, but at the same time he cited "the appalling fact that approximately nine-tenths of the world's territory is under the control of the White race. How this control was obtained is a story of many chapters and at least some of these chapters make rather uncomfortable reading for anyone with a Christian conscience."[44]

He was extremely critical of Western economic dominance and lamented that "in many cases our Western civilization, with its emphasis on man's mastery over matter, has broken down Asia's spiritual mood and really impoverished Asia's soul." And in an obvious reference to President Woodrow Wilson's rejection of a racial equality clause in the League of Nations charter of 1919, he declared, "Something must be done to check the overbearing attitude which the White peoples of the West have assumed towards the Brown peoples of the East." Missionaries in this new world needed "to work *with* Japanese as our friends and equals" rather than lording it over them.[45] They should also take it upon themselves to explain and interpret Japan to America. For a Caucasian American to accept the idea of Asians' equality may seem natural enough today, but it was a radical notion for an American from the segregated "Jim Crow" society of the 1920s. Few Americans saw themselves as "imperialists" in that era; rather, they considered it America's "manifest destiny" to move ever westward.

Late in his life, Edwin Reischauer confided to me that he was infuriated by the picture of the missionary movement that John K. Fairbank and other China scholars painted at Harvard—a picture of missionaries backed by gunboat diplomacy and greedy businessmen who made converts in China by giving them food ("rice Christians") and bilked their congregations at home of more funding by claiming that Christianity was capturing Chinese hearts and minds.[46] Reischauer believed that the missionary movement in Japan—of which his parents were a part—was different: "There is, of course, some truth to these characterizations, particularly in China. But basically it gives a very misleading picture of the missionary movement as a whole. Missionaries are usually motivated by the noble desire to share with others what they value most."[47] Their record in Japan, he argued in our conversation, was admirable:

> The native Japanese church took over the leadership very quickly. There were very sincere, strong converts, samurai who were trying to find something to substitute for Confucianism, and it made for a very strong church. The whole thing became associated with liberalism and education and the less militaristic and organized dictatorial aspect of Japan was always associated with Christianity. So Christianity has always been admired in Japan as something good and liberal and progressive, and their work was all in schools. My father's work in starting the women's university, and my mother's work in starting deaf education, and things like that were great accomplishments.

Reischauer offered an even stronger defense of the missionary movement in his 1955 book *Wanted: An Asian Policy*:

> Probably no other single group of outsiders proved more subversive to the traditional regimes and institutions of Asia than American missionaries. They taught an ethical system that was not compatible with native concepts and institutions; they introduced ideas that were not only subversive to the native political regimes but ate away at the roots of the whole society; on top of this they helped supply the technological foundations for the revolution in Asia—English, the language for contact with the outside world, new educational systems, Western medical and scientific knowledge, even such things as improved agricultural techniques. Our missionaries were as much revolutionaries in Asia as any Communist agents, whether they realized it or not.[48]

Despite his heartfelt defense of his parents' work, Edwin could not share their faith. "It never once occurred to me to follow my parents in Christian missionary work," he told me, "and I easily slipped into a very different attitude toward organized religion than they had, but I have always respected their beliefs and have taken pride in their accomplishments. Without doubt, I drew many of my ideals as well as personal traits from my missionary background."[49]

What, in fact, were the forces that shaped this child of a missionary family in Japan? Fred Notehelfer, a distinguished professor of history at the University of California in Los Angeles and himself the son of missionaries in Japan, was one of Edwin Reischauer's students in the 1950s. He notes that the missionary background "makes for strong independent personalities. There is also a good deal of isolation in the missionary child's life. You have to do a lot of relying on yourself. Moreover there is a strong emphasis on inner values. Reischauer was very much his own man."[50]

By his own account, Edwin had a happy childhood, with loving and attentive parents. But it was hardly typical of the boyhood he might have enjoyed in rural Illinois surrounded by family and friends. Conscience, duty, and character were foremost in his family life:

> We did much together as a family, such as reading aloud in the evenings. My mother imbued us with a strong sense of what we would now call women's rights as well as social justice for the less privileged. Both our parents also tried to give my brother and me as normal an American boyhood as possible and succeeded in doing so to a surprising degree. Growing up in Japan, I failed to develop the skills in carpentry, electric wiring, and tinkering with internal combustion engines that my contemporaries in America picked up. . . . But my mother was determined that we should grow up accustomed to manual work and not be like Japanese *o-botchan*, as the pampered sons of the well-to-do were derisively called.[51]

Edwin told of the simple, farming life of his father's family. They were "hardworking, direct people not given to wasting words or devoting attention to social frills and idle pleasures. Life, both of the body and the spirit, was a serious, almost solemn matter to be faced with directness and earnestness." His father, he recalled, "always sought to penetrate to the general truth behind detailed facts, and the ultimate reality behind these general truths. He had a genius for seeing the big picture where others might be lost in petty details. He was, in short, a far-seeing philosopher rather than a subtle psychologist, a strategist rather than a tactician."[52]

Edwin adored his mother, whom he described as perfectly complementing his austere father. Possessed of "a certain boisterous conviviality," she was interested in people as individuals and loved "the little things that made life pleasant and beautiful. Where he [August] might be overly frank in dealing with others, she was always gracious and thoughtful. Where he might have been content with an austere home, lacking in beauty, she always strove to make our home attractive and the life within it comfortable. Typically, it was she that led in organizing intimate parties for students and friends and skillfully laid out the lawns, flower gardens, bushes and trees around out house at the Tokyo *Joshi Daigaku*."[53] It was Helen Reischauer who instilled a love for game playing in her sons: mah-jong or card games such as gin rummy were their favorites. Edwin would pass this love on to his children.

Felicia, youngest of the three Reischauer children, was born in 1914, when Edwin was four. Helen Reischauer had contracted German measles during her pregnancy, and the family soon discovered that Felicia was deaf and mute. These disabilities had a profound impact on their family life. It meant that Helen would undertake a series of long trips to the United States seeking treatment for Felicia, which proved to be a major drain on meager family resources and deprived Edwin of his mother's care and attention when he needed it most. Felicia never learned to lip-read or sign. As it happened, Edwin "developed a special rapport with her and probably greater skills of communication than any of the other members of the family."[54] Despite her obvious intelligence, Felicia would remain locked in her silent prison, isolated from reality, unable to live a normal life, remaining a burden on her family until her death at the age of seventy-nine. "She never fully developed, and then went really peculiar after a breakdown," Reischauer wrote to his daughter Ann in 1964.[55] The job of raising the two boys fell largely on the father and the household maids. In an era when intellectually challenged people were often sent off to special facilities, the Reischauer family was far ahead of its times in treating her with respect and love, and including her in family activities to the extent possible.

Being the son of A. K. Reischauer could not have been much fun. He was a taciturn, humorless man who had no real friends. His granddaughter remembered him as "a nonpeople person . . . very intellectual, pretty gruff. On Sundays he would call us heathens if we didn't go to church."[56] Edwin drew the best possible portrait of his father: "He may have lacked some of my mother's social graces and was known to fall asleep when he found himself stuck with a boring dinner guest, but he was very much of a gentleman in all the best senses of the word. He was always firm in his principles and convictions, and was a good companion to us boys."[57]

"My brother and I used to joke about my father," he recalled in an essay about his father, "saying that, while he was devoted to the cause of higher education for Japanese women, he had never recognized the face nor known the name of a single Japanese college girl. Of course this was not true, but it was the importance of higher education for women as a whole that interested my father, not the individual women who might receive this education."[58]

August, prodded by Helen, found time to teach his boys tennis and baseball. He took them fishing and led them on long, rambling hikes. He became a powerful influence in their lives, and they clearly competed for his approval. But Helen was the dominant influence on the boys, and, from all accounts, she doted on Robert. She had been forced to spend years away from Edwin in her efforts to help Felicia deal with her deafness, and his mother's absence left him feeling lonely and isolated. Deprived of the love and emotional support that he clearly longed for, he developed a defense that would become a lifelong habit: he would bury himself in books and live in a lively intellectual world of his own creation. He learned to shut down or hide his feelings behind an outwardly cool, rational, and intellectual exterior. He was never able to confide in any male friend, and in his life's crises he turned to women, often Japanese women, for moral support.

Later in his life, Edwin would say that Robert was the greatest influence on his career and personality. "His greater self-confidence and more sparkling personality as the oldest child probably helped shape my own combination of shyness, determination, and whatever else makes up my character. In any case, I can remember periods in my early life when I felt quite browbeaten by him."[59]

As he confesses in his autobiography, he had very little chance to associate with "ordinary citizens" of Japan. Raised in a strict missionary household on the sheltered campus of Meiji Gakuin, he admits that "the children of this area were not suitable playmates for me in those class conscious days."[60] He attended English-language schools, played with other missionary children, and spent summer holidays in the mountain village of Karuizawa, Nagano Prefecture, where other Western families gathered to escape the heat of Tokyo. With the exception of his first-grade fall semester, when he attended public school in Champaign, Illinois (1916), and his sophomore year of high school (1924–25), when he attended a public school in Springfield, Ohio, his entire education before college was in Japan.

The American School in Japan was a joyful experience for the boy. It was destroyed by the great earthquake of 1923, when Edwin was thirteen, but it reopened the following year opposite the Red Cross Hospital in Takagi-cho. He would remember playing baseball there in the spring of 1924.

> It included a two-mile hike in spikes on paved roads to the so-called Yoyogi Parade Grounds, later the "Washington Heights" of the Occupation, and the Olympic Village of 1964 where baseball competed with the Imperial Army going through skirmish maneuvers. *Soba* (noodles) became a feature

of school life at this time. All of us on our way home after basketball or baseball had to take in one or two bowls of *soba* to tide us over to a late supper at home. [Robert was the star pitcher on the baseball team] and I at 13 was the peanut left-fielder. The easiest spot to play on the team because of a mountain of charcoal sacks on the field we usually used made it about half the size of the other fields.[61]

No account of Edwin Reischauer's boyhood would be complete without mention of E. Herbert Norman. Born in 1909, a year ahead of Reischauer, in rural Nagano Prefecture, Herbert Norman was the son of Canadian missionary parents. When the boys were between eight and twelve years old, they became friends and played tennis together in Karuizawa. Then their paths diverged. Norman would go on to college in Canada, and Reischauer would study at Oberlin. Their paths crossed again when both studied for doctoral degrees at Harvard in 1938 under Serge Elisseeff. Both reached maturity during the worldwide depression of the 1930s. But then their careers split: Norman pursued his graduate studies in England, joined the Communist Party, and became a leading scholar of the history of modern Japan. He accepted the Marxist interpretation of the Tokugawa period. He joined the Canadian Foreign Service. Reischauer rejected Marxism and, as a Harvard professor, proposed a much different theory of Japan's modernization. The counterpoint of their lives encapsulates the intellectual wars that would rage among scholars of modern Japan, as we shall see.

The Japanese citizens Reischauer did get to know were mainly Christian internationalists and elite associates of his parents, such as Dr. Nitobe Inazo and Dr. Ibuka Kajinosuke, president of Meiji Gakuin University; Maeda Tamon, vice mayor of Tokyo and later Japan's delegate to the International Labor Organization in Geneva; and Tokyo University professor Anesaki Masaharu.

Dr. Nitobe was an extraordinarily interesting contact for the Reischauer family. He had become a Christian early in his life, studied English literature and economics at Tokyo University, pursued doctoral research at Johns Hopkins University from 1884 to 1887 along with Woodrow Wilson, spent three more years getting his Ph.D. from Halle University in Germany, married an American Quaker woman from Philadelphia, and wrote *Bushido: The Soul of Japan* in 1899—the most widely read English-language book about Japan of his time.[62] A distinguished educator at Tokyo University, Dr. Nitobe would go on to attend the Versailles Peace Conference in 1919 and remain in Geneva as the undersecretary-general of the newly formed League of Nations—an organization that his Johns Hopkins classmate Woodrow Wilson had championed but failed to sell to the U.S. Senate.

Dr. Ibuka Kajinosuke, president of Meiji Gakuin University beginning in 1891, was a former samurai who became a Christian pastor and brought the YMCA to Japan.

Another family friend, Maeda Tamon was viewed as one of Japan's leading internationalists. He was deputy mayor of Tokyo, and from 1928 to 1938 he worked as an editorial writer for the *Tokyo Asahi Shimbun*. During the war years, he served as governor of Niigata Prefecture. He is best remembered as the minister of education just after World War Two, when he helped Prime Minister Shidehara Kijuro draft the rescript in which the emperor renounced his divinity. Later he was active in the United Nations Educational, Scientific, and Cultural Organization (UNESCO) and in the movement for "clean elections."

Professor Anesaki Masaharu, an expert on Sanskrit at Tokyo University, became a close friend of A. K. Reischauer. The two were active in the Asiatic Society of Japan, which was headed by the British ambassador to Tokyo. Reischauer was one of three vice presidents of the society. The other two were Anesaki and Sir George Sansom, the British diplomat and founder of Japanese studies in the West. The society met monthly to hear learned papers on Japan. "It is probably no accident that my brother and I became scholars in the Japanese field," Edwin would recall. "After my brother had already won his Ph.D., I happened to give my maiden scholarly presentation before the Society in 1936. On this occasion, Sir George jokingly asked my father whether he was trying to found a dynasty of Japanese scholars."[63]

When the senior Reischauers returned to the United States in March 1941 to get medical treatment, they never suspected that Japan would launch a surprise attack on America before the year was over. For the next two years, A. K. lectured to church audiences about his work in Japan—a task he found difficult after the attack on Pearl Harbor. "While we never condoned the Pearl Harbor attack or the aggression of Japanese militarists, we always stressed the fact that many Japanese never wanted or expected this war with our country. And we also told our audiences that if there were any real Christians in the modern world, some of them were in Japan."[64]

From 1943 to 1952, when he retired, A. K. Reischauer and his wife lived at Union Theological Seminary in New York, where he taught the history of religion. After the war, he raised money and collected clothing for Tokyo Joshi Daigaku and helped plan the launching of the multidenominational International Christian University in Tokyo.

Edwin's isolation from ordinary Japanese citizens and his early association with elite intellectuals raises a fascinating question: How did he come to believe that he understood the needs and desires of ordinary Japanese people? A clue can be found in his autobiography: "I never had to discover Japan, and nothing about it has ever seemed strange or exotic to me." In fact, America was strange and exotic to this boy, and everything in Japan was "natural and normal."[65] Japan was and always would be home.

At the age of five, Edwin would later recall, his first visit to the United States produced memories of a strange and exotic land, where, looking down from the deck of his ship docking in San Francisco, there were white men working as stevedores and black men mixed among them. "At that time almost the only Westerners in Japan were missionaries, teachers, diplomats, businessmen, and occasional tourists. I had never seen a white man doing manual labor."[66] On another trip to the United States at the age of thirteen, he noted with indignation that all the steerage passengers on the ship were lined up on the deck in San Francisco, and those who looked Chinese were unceremoniously yanked out of the line by American immigration officers on the suspicion that they might be ethnic Chinese posing as Filipinos."[67]

The second answer to the question posed earlier was that his loving, dedicated, and intellectually energetic missionary parents were completely egalitarian in their religious beliefs and practical in their daily work. Early on, they drifted away from "saving souls" and instead devoted themselves to addressing the needs of Japan's rapidly changing urban society. Helen was active in the Women's Christian Temperance Union and in settlement work for the poor. After the birth of their deaf third child, Felicia, she established in 1920 the first school in Japan for deaf and mute children, Japan Oral School for the Deaf (Nippon Rowa Gakko), and introduced what was then a new oral method of teaching deaf children. And in 1918, August helped to raise two hundred thousand dollars to buy land and buildings for the founding of the Women's Christian College of Japan, Tokyo Joshi Daigaku (known today as Tokyo Women's Christian University) in Ogikubo, Tokyo—a revolutionary development in the Japan of his day. Dr. Nitobe Inazo was its first president, and August served as executive secretary of its Board of Trustees from 1918 to 1941. The two schools continue to exist to this day.

Beyond social work and religion, the Reischauer family identified with Japan's nationalist aspirations and supported its quest for equality with the Western imperialist powers that had imposed "unequal treaties" on it in 1858. "My sympathy for Japanese nationalism spilled unconsciously over into a general Asian nationalism," Edwin recalled. "The empires of the Western powers seemed to me unjust, and I was incensed by the way Westerners living in other parts of Asia looked down on the 'natives.'"[68]

These views were of course abstract and intellectual perceptions gained from his parents, his education in Japan, at Oberlin, and in graduate school at Harvard. They would dominate his thinking throughout his life. But another more personal force also clearly affected his view of the Japanese people—the influence of the household female servants (*jochusan*) who helped raise the young boys when their parents were away or busy: Haru, Kiku, and Kiyo.

Haru and Kiku "played a large role in my early years and, no doubt, helped shape my personality and sense of values," he wrote. They taught him "kitchen Japanese," a Japanese lullaby ("Nennoko Botchan"), and the story of Momotaro.[69] These women clearly provided the emotional support that may have been lacking in the rather stern, driven lives of his missionary parents. Many years later he remarked: "The strong people of Japan are the women, not the men. But the women do not join 'women's liberation movements.' They are too proud to act that way."[70] In the last year of his life, he went a step farther: "Japanese women have always been felt to be the stronger of the two sexes, having a lot more guts than the men do. The men have their own particular type of Japanese macho that they flaunt, but still the Japanese women are the ones who have the real inner strength."[71]

He recalled, "The maids had a deep influence on me in ways that are hard to define. Perhaps I owe to them my typically Japanese tendency to be more self-conscious about the impression I make on others than judgmental on how they impress me." Haru, from an impoverished samurai family, had retained her "samurai pride, honesty, strength of will and sense of loyalty. . . . As a quasi-mother, paralleling my own mother in inner strength and bravery, she gave me much for which I shall always be grateful."[72] In the unpublished manuscript version of his autobiography, Reischauer was even more effusive: "She was as admirable a person as I have ever known, and I like to think that some of her traditional Japanese virtues rubbed off on me."[73]

Any American who has had the privilege of raising small children in Japan (as I have) with the help of a Japanese housekeeper or nanny will know instantly how the young Edwin felt. Little boys especially are treated as "young masters" who can do no wrong. They are loved, cajoled, indulged, and even spoiled in ways that give them huge self-confidence. There can be no doubt that the maids played a critical role in fostering the warmth that Reischauer would later express toward the Japanese people. In no other writing does he reveal the degree of affection and pure joy that he associated with these women.

In 1926, Reischauer left Japan at the age of sixteen to attend Oberlin College and Harvard and to embark on a career of scholarship and diplomacy. His understanding of Japanese history and current affairs would become broader and deeper and more sophisticated, but his feelings about Japan—his love for its people, his respect for their culture, and his sense of complete equality between Westerners and Japanese were already deeply rooted and would never change. He later wrote a friend, "I remember the first girl I imagined myself in love with was Japanese."[74]

2

Japan, "the Dark Side of the Moon"

The gangly sixteen-year-old who arrived at Oberlin College in the fall of 1927 appeared to be a typical high school student more interested in sports and girls than in academic studies.[1] But his academic record over the next six years—four at Oberlin and two at Harvard—was hardly that of a playboy. Rather, we can see a highly motivated young man aspiring to become a serious scholar and perhaps even a player in the foreign-policy arena. In his autobiography, Reischauer describes his intellectual journey as a series of random occurrences, but a close reading of his account makes it clear that very little was left to chance. He was from the start ambitious, intellectually gifted, competitive, and determined to make a mark in East Asian affairs. Because modesty was a prized virtue in his missionary upbringing, this ambitious side of his character would not reveal itself until much later.

Edwin chose Oberlin College—a small, liberal arts institution in rural northern Ohio—mainly because his older brother, Robert, was already enrolled there. Robert had chosen Oberlin because his best friend, a young man from a Congregational missionary background, had decided to go there. The Reischauer parents' faith clearly played a large role in the choice of Oberlin, with its tradition of training missionaries, and it is ironic that both their sons would rebel against Christian beliefs in their college years. Robert was a senior and a popular man on the campus when Edwin, a shy teenager, entered the college as a freshman at the age of sixteen. For Edwin, Robert was at once a hero and role model, on one hand, and a competitor, on the other.

Edwin spent his first two years at Oberlin acclimating himself to American student life. To make ends meet, he washed pots and pans, and scrubbed floors in his student quarters. In the summer after his freshman year, he worked on his uncle's farm in southern Illinois. He often hitchhiked in the cars of total strangers. After his second and third college years, he worked as a counselor at the University of Michigan Fresh Air Camp, an institution that took in underprivileged children from the big industrial cities. Back at Oberlin, he played on the varsity soccer team, was captain of the tennis team, and sang in the glee club. All of these experiences served to make him comfortable with his fellow Americans and to reinforce his new identity as an American citizen rather than as an exotic outsider. These multiple facets to his identity would help him to deal with American military officers later in his life. Even as a renowned Harvard intellectual, he would retain the ability to relate with a folksy midwestern cheerfulness to Americans of all backgrounds.

The Reischauer boys had lived in reasonable comfort in Tokyo, with several servants, a Western-style home on the campus of Meiji Gakuin, and the chance to escape from Tokyo's hot and humid summers in the cool mountain air of Karuizawa. But they were by no means wealthy. There was little extra cash, and Oberlin's tuition costs (three hundred dollars per year) put a strain on the family resources. Edwin had to struggle to survive by winning scholarships and by doing odd jobs around campus and during the summer vacations. "Anyone raised in the 'poverty' of a missionary family at the time of the depression is likely to be very money-conscious, or 'insecure moneywise,' as you put it," he wrote his daughter, Ann, in 1964.[2] Reischauer's frugality would become legendary among his children and friends. He never ate in a restaurant unless he had no other choice, and he once traveled around the world without a wallet or money by staying with friends.

The college was small, with only about three hundred students in each of four undergraduate classes. Including its famous conservatory of music and its graduate school of theology, the total student body was less than two thousand. "The students were mainly from Northern Ohio and Western Pennsylvania, but quite a few also came from a long strip of territory settled by Congregational New Englanders, stretching westward from Boston all the way to Iowa. There were even some from old Congregational mission fields such as Hawaii and China," Reischauer would later recall.[3]

Reischauer had made only three scattered visits to the United States in his first sixteen years and regarded Japan as home, but he sought to create an image of himself as "an American who happened to be born in Japan rather than [as] a resident of Japan who happened to be an American citizen."[4] Here was a clue to the character of a man who would throughout his life seek to fit into "the system" and work within it for change rather than to overthrow it. This quality would prompt John K. Fairbank, his Harvard colleague and coauthor, to remark years later, not without a touch of condescension, "As ambitious young academics in parallel fields we [Reischauer and I] had a sort of sibling rivalry, but I always felt he was on the inside track in the establishment while I was more on the fringe. Since area specialists, according to one theory, take on the characteristics of the people they study, perhaps this accounts for Ed's establishmentarianism. The Japanese are the most prudently successful people of modern times, while the Chinese are still struggling to put their act together."[5] Reischauer's desire to fit in may also help explain why he was never attracted to the Marxist ideas that proved fascinating to so many young intellectuals of his generation in the wake of the Soviet Revolution of 1917.

Oberlin, with its small community of students and faculty in its rural setting, proved to be the perfect place for Reischauer to discover his American roots and nurture his interest in international affairs. Founded in 1833, the college prided itself on providing an academic environment that welcomed diverse views and encouraged social reform. From its early days, the college was open to women; it claims today to have been the first truly coeducational college in America. (Edwin would eventually marry Adrienne Danton, who graduated from Oberlin a year after he did.) It was also one of the first to accept African Americans, and many of its faculty members favored abolishing slavery well before the American Civil War settled the issue. John Mercer Langston, an Oberlin graduate from Virginia in the mid-nineteenth century, was the first black man to be elected to the U.S. Congress in 1888. The college retained the historically strong Christian influence of its founders and prided itself on having sent about one thousand missionaries to foreign and domestic sites by 1900.

Under President James Harris Fairchild, elected in 1866, students were encouraged to be deeply engaged in moral issues: "The ideal student was both judge and activist, forcefully applying Christian moral principles to all human situations and institutions."[6] Knowledge was valuable when applied to the building of character. Faculty was hired based on depth of loyalty to evangelical religion. Prayer and religious services were required in those early days, and students were expected to adhere to a strict code that forbade alcohol and tobacco, a set curfew, and limited time spent with the opposite sex.

Change came to Oberlin, as it came to many universities in America, beginning in the 1870s. Students came to demand higher academic standards and to worry less about their professors' moral or religious character. Johns Hopkins University, founded in 1876, was the first American university to follow the German model, offering graduate degrees and remaining free of any religious affiliation or influence. Other colleges soon followed.

At Oberlin, Charles Darwin's *Origin of Species*, first published in 1859, became the subject of popular debate among students. At first, some faculty members tried to reconcile the theory of evolution with the traditional Christian explanation that the earth and all living creatures had been created by God some six thousand years earlier. A writer in the *Oberlin Review* asserted in 1874: "Science and religion . . . had separate spheres [and] as along as each confined itself to its proper work—science to explain nature and religion to explain the spiritual and ethical dimensions of existence—there would be no conflict between the two." As one student argued in 1876, the new science could purify faith if "by its doctrine of evolution it can show that man, instead of being cursed with a nature irrevocably vicious, is endowed with a perpetual tendency to improvement."[7] The idea of progress would become central to Edwin's view of history in later years.

Oberlin expanded its course offerings in the 1880s to include evolution, political economy, and international law, and it shifted its focus from Christian emphasis on inward character development to outward social reform and good works. Primary issues of concern were immigration, poverty, temperance, egalitarian reform, and restoration of class harmony. In addition, elective courses in modern language and literature were introduced. Oberlin became a beacon for the idea of progress in human affairs and a leader of liberal internationalism. Such was the atmosphere in which Edwin Reischauer absorbed his early ideas about politics and foreign policy.

By the time Reischauer arrived at Oberlin in 1927, the winds of liberalism—the belief in every individual's innate ability to use the power of reason to arrive at truth—had largely replaced the influence of pure faith in God as a guide to human behavior. Darwin's theory of evolution had led some thinkers to a widely shared belief in the inevitable progress of the human race. Enlightenment thinkers such as Baruch Spinoza, John Locke, and Thomas Jefferson, among others, had taught that human beings, liberated from the shackles of blind religious faith, could arrive at wise choices about their own welfare, government, and politics. Herbert Spencer, the British philosopher, developed the notion of "social Darwinism." Nations, he contended, like living organisms, were subject to evolutionary struggle. Only the fit would survive.

For Edwin Reischauer, the conflict between his parents' religious faith and the new science posed an excruciating dilemma. The Presbyterian Mission Board that paid his father's salary provided a twenty-five-dollar monthly supplement that his parents sent him each month, a princely sum for a student in those days. His parents insisted that they exchange letters once a week, even though the letters took a month to reach their destination. This became a habit that lasted throughout his parents' lives.[8] Reischauer doubtless felt a huge debt of gratitude to the Mission Board and to his parents for sending him to college, and this feeling would make his break from the Christian faith even more painful. Not once was he ever critical of their mission, but at Oberlin he began to doubt the theological underpinnings of their faith. From the time he left his parents in Tokyo, he never again attended church.

We have no precise account of Reischauer's rejection of the Christian faith. Was it a gradual erosion of faith or a sudden conversion? We cannot know, but it is clear that he gravitated toward the secular humanism that prevailed on the Oberlin campus of the 1920s. For a budding historian, this view meant that the study of history was the study of humankind in all its manifestations rather than the study of man as a creature of divine origin. Earlier historians had pursued the study of man as revealing God's purposes. The new breed of secular historians found intrinsic interest in the study of humanity quite apart from the existence of a divine creator.

We know that Reischauer at some point, probably before he was twenty years old, became skeptical of the Christian faith and of all religions. He is uncharacteristically silent on this subject in his autobiography and elsewhere, clearly because he did not wish to hurt his parents or to denigrate their life's work.

His falling away from his Christian roots caused him much pain and embarrassment. Throughout his life, Christian associates and friends of his parents would seek his advice on religious matters, and Reischauer would always politely demur and change the subject when he could. On one occasion, when he was U.S. ambassador to Japan and an interviewer from *Presbyterian Life* magazine asked him why he had not followed his parents into missionary work, he replied with a smile, "Oh, but I am a missionary!"[9] He went on to explain that he was a missionary for democracy.

There are only a few solid clues to his innermost thoughts about religion. In 1981, I pressed him in a recorded interview to explain his thoughts on religion. "I am in no sense a member of an organized church nor a believer in organized religion as such," he said. "I wouldn't deny the fact that there may be a god, but I don't know, and if there is a god, I think he is wise enough to take pity on a person like myself, a god who is not asking anybody to go through a ceremony of some sort." He added, "Organized religions, quite frankly, as such, have probably done more harm in the world than good. In many cases, they are on the wrong side, and you can see that all the time. I mean the kind of thing that's going on in Northern Ireland is absolutely disgraceful. And in Iran as well."[10]

In his later years, Reischauer lived in the beautiful Boston suburb of Belmont, Massachusetts, in a home that had separate living quarters for a young couple. William Shaw, a graduate student at Harvard, and his young wife, Carol, occupied these quarters in the 1970s. Carol, a deeply religious Christian, took it upon herself to try to "win back" Edwin to her faith. She engaged him in discussions about Jesus, salvation, and the afterlife in heaven. She recalled with sadness Reischauer's total rejection of her faith as "superstition" and how he rejected, albeit in a kind but resolute manner, all her efforts to get him to attend church services.[11]

The four years Reischauer spent at Oberlin (1927–31) saw tumultuous changes in Japan and in the world. After the period of "Shidehara diplomacy" of the mid-1920s, in which Japan tried to cooperate with Western powers, army officers plotted with ultranationalists to destroy the fragile "Taisho democracy." In 1927, a bank crisis brought about the fall of the Kenseikai Party cabinet. In 1928, the Kwantung army engineered the murder of the Manchurian warlord Chang Tso-lin. Prime Minister Tanaka Gi'ichi promised the emperor that he would investigate, but failed to do so. Taken to task by the emperor, he resigned and died shortly afterward. In 1930, civilian prime minister Hamaguchi was assassinated, and in 1932 Prime Minister Inukai was also murdered, ending civilian government until 1945. By 1931, the Kwantung army arranged an incident that led to the invasion of Manchuria—the first step toward the Pacific War.

Meanwhile, the New York stock-market crash of 1929 led to a worldwide depression. In Germany, a shattered economy provided the seedbed for the rise to power of Adolf Hitler and the Nazi Party in 1933. In Italy, a new dictator, Benito Mussolini, set up a fascist government and invaded Ethiopia. The Depression led to severe poverty in rural Japan, creating desperation and a vast pool of recruits for the army. The League of Nations, which had been the product of President Woodrow Wilson's idealism, was revealed as powerless. Japan withdrew in 1933; the United States never joined and took refuge in isolationism.

Reischauer, on the Oberlin campus of rural Ohio, was probably only vaguely aware of these developments in Japan. "Japan was in no one's mind. It might as well have been on the dark side of the moon. The college offered no instruction about Japan, and, like most contemporary college students, we never read any newspapers, which had virtually no news about Japan in any case. For four years I did not have a bit of Japanese food or hear a word of Japanese, except for an occasional greeting with one of the two or three Japanese students in the school of theology."[12] He could have been only dimly aware of Japan's slide into militarism and aggression from news in his parents' weekly letters.

Reischauer was bored with the basic courses that were required in his first two years at Oberlin—English composition, French, and zoology—but he enjoyed his history courses and decided again to follow in his brother's footsteps and major in history, with a minor in political science. He became aware of his talent for memorizing names, dates, and figures. In the second half of his junior year, he recalled that "I had a grade record which I was surreptitiously told was the highest on record in Oberlin history for a single semester. This won me a full scholarship for my senior year."[13] He finished fourteenth in his class of 265 students, according to the transcript sent to Harvard by Oberlin on September 21, 1931. He graduated magna cum laude and was elected to Phi Beta Kappa.

An early hint of his interest in current international affairs can be seen in his role as founder of the Oberlin Peace Society in his senior year, 1930–31. He and his fellow members resolved never to participate in war. Another field that interested him was the history of architecture; some of his most eloquent writing as a scholar was on art and architecture. He also took a course in public speaking "since I was terrified of speaking in front of an audience. Unfortunately it did me no good. Even though I received my usual A, I ended up as afraid of public speaking as I had been before."[14] This timid student would in later life become one of Harvard University's most popular lecturers.

Oberlin offered very little on Asia, but Reischauer did write a 213-page paper on Commodore Perry's expedition to Japan titled "American Japanese Relations Before 1860," for which he won a two-hundred-dollar prize. He had no faculty guidance and remembered it as "a very badly written and unimaginative effort. . . . You can see my dedication to Japanese studies was weak, and my interest in sports was certainly greater than any of my intellectual interests at least until my junior year in college. Even in my senior year I turned up for my final honors examination very indifferently prepared and dressed in my tennis clothes, much to the distress of my professors, since I was about to play a varsity tennis match. (I was captain of the team.)" [15] For another course, he wrote a 35-page paper titled "Buddhism in India and Japan."[16]

Reischauer's unusual upbringing in Japan set him apart from other American students of history. Traditional college history texts of his day described the rise of Western civilization, starting with the Sumerians in Mesopotamia and continuing through Egyptian, Greek and Roman, and Judaeo-Christian civilizations to the rise of western Europe, as if the innate superiority of European culture was somehow natural and preordained. China and Japan were introduced, if at all, as part of an historical backwater that was discovered by Western explorers starting in the sixteenth century. Reischauer approached the study of history without that Eurocentric bias and from his earliest days found Chinese and Japanese culture and history as interesting and important as European culture and history. Only a tiny handful of American historians shared this approach in the 1930s.

In the final days of Reischauer's senior year at Oberlin, when a favorite professor had to be away from the college at the end of the semester, he asked Reischauer to correct his examinations and grade his courses—a great honor for a college senior, and Reischauer obviously relished the task.[17]

The Oberlin experience, then, offered hints of a career that would eventually involve the study of East Asia, Buddhism, history, international affairs, and perhaps an academic life of teaching and writing. Ironically, at the moment when the world was heading toward the cataclysm of World War Two, Reischauer and many of his more idealistic fellow college students believed that progress for the human race was inevitable. The progressive, liberal values of Oberlin would shape his politics. It was at Harvard over the next two years that all these strands came to together.

The idealistic twenty-year-old who headed east from Oberlin to Harvard in the summer of 1931 found himself in the middle of the Depression, where jobs were scarce or nonexistent, unemployment was rampant, and America was turning still more away from the world. The Smoot-Hawley Tariff Act of 1930 was intended to protect U.S. industry against foreign imports, but in fact deepened the Depression and damaged U.S. exporters. World trade shrank. The threat of war hung gloomily on the horizon.

Harvard was in fact Reischauer's third choice for further education. His first choice was to win a prestigious three-year Rhodes Scholarship for study at Oxford University in England. Nominated by an Oberlin professor, he was one of two selected from the state of Ohio, but lost in the six-state regional competition that followed. At age twenty, he was considered too young, and, anyway, his goal of studying East Asia could not have been achieved at Oxford because Oxford had only one course on China and none on Japan. He next thought of applying for an internship at the League of Nations in Geneva, Switzerland, but just as he applied, the Depression forced the league to retrench and cancel the internship program.

Graduate study of East Asia was his third option. The three leading universities in this field were Columbia, the University of California at Berkeley, and Harvard, and none of them had more than a few scattered courses on East Asia. He chose Harvard because it had the Harvard-Yenching Institute, which had been established in 1928 and offered some fellowships, and because his brother, Robert, had once again led the way.

Reischauer won a grant of six hundred dollars for each academic year from 1931 to 1933, but still had to pay Harvard four hundred dollars in tuition for each year. This left him with two hundred for living expenses, a tiny sum that his parents supplemented with an interest-free loan. For the next few years, he would have to live a Spartan life, which he described as a "monastic experience of unremitting study."[18] For him, life had become a serious mission involving sustained learning and the striving for intellectual excellence.

He chose to isolate himself from the social life typical of graduate students. He looked down upon the all-male Harvard undergraduate college as "a very aristocratic, parochial New England institution," dominated by prep school graduates and snobbish student clubs that made him feel like a second-class citizen. Nevertheless, it was exhilarating to him to be part of a scholarly community in the graduate school, and he plunged into his studies with single-minded intensity.[19]

Because there was no Department of East Asian Studies, he entered the Department of History in the fall of 1931, once again following in Robert's footsteps, and earned his master of arts degree the following spring. As usual, he excelled with straight A's in most of his courses. He also sought out language courses in Chinese and Japanese. The only course in Japanese was too elementary, so he took an introductory course in Chinese and a half-course of reading in Chinese history.

The Chinese-language course turned out to be a nightmare. The professor, James R. Ware, knew nothing of the tonal system for pronouncing the spoken language. In fact, in most approaches to Chinese in those days, Reischauer later wrote, "the object was to learn to read Chinese, not to speak it, and some of the leading Sinologists of Europe prided themselves on having been in China little if at all. Sinology had grown up in the spirit of Egyptology, treating Chinese as if it were a dead language and not the living tongue of close to a quarter of the human race."[20]

Edwin shared a room in Perkins Hall with Arthur Hogue, a fellow Oberlin graduate. Hogue became a close friend who "even tolerated my maddening habit of studying Chinese every evening from 8:00 PM until midnight with my radio blaring jazz beside me."[21] Each evening, Edwin would walk over to Holden Green, where Robert and his new bride, Jean, would provide dinner—his one good meal of the day. Robert and Edwin would discuss their studies of Chinese language and Japanese history, leaving Jean entirely out of the conversation. Robert in these years was moving steadily toward becoming one of America's most outstanding historians of modern Japan, and Edwin clearly accepted that he was walking in his brother's shadow. In later years, he would write: "Bob, I feel, was a person of great promise. Even though he taught at Princeton only a year or two, he obviously was a great success and people still tell me of what an inspiring teacher he was. He had an outgoing personality, was an interesting talker, and something of a showman. . . . With outstanding talents as a writer, speaker and teacher, [he] would very probably have been the dominant figure in the field of Japanese studies of his generation if he had lived longer."[22]

It is almost impossible to describe the difficulty for a Western beginner of learning even contemporary Chinese characters. The task involves rote memorization of perhaps twenty-five to fifty totally new ideographs each day, with the goal of knowing three thousand just to have the minimal literacy of a high school student in China. It is a lonely pursuit, and there are no shortcuts. A fine memory and an appreciation of the calligraphic beauty of written Chinese helps, but one must be motivated by a single-minded and relentless desire to master the language. The beginning, simpler characters may have three to eight brush strokes, which must be written in a precise order. As one progresses, the characters become more complex, with up to twenty-five or more strokes. After learning the meaning and pronunciation of each character, one sees patterns begin to emerge. Elements of one character appear in another, more complex character, and it becomes possible to make intelligent guesses about the meanings. Progress is uneven, the rewards are in the distant future, and almost every beginner goes through periods of abject discouragement.

If Edwin ever flagged in his pursuit of literacy in Chinese, he does not admit it in his autobiography, but he does point out some of the difficulties he encountered. In his second semester, for example, he was assigned to translate a section on Japan from a third-century Chinese history, the *Weizhi*. Of course, it was written in classical Chinese and not the contemporary *baihua* Chinese that he had studied in the first semester. Classical Chinese has no division of phrases and sentences by punctuation. The only dictionary available, a 1909 revision of an 1874 work by S. Wells Williams, was more confusing than enlightening. "For even the simplest of Chinese characters, it would give a bewildering array of meanings, with no indication as to which were primary meanings and which unusual usages. During the more than three millennia Chinese characters have been in use, the words they represent have naturally evolved and proliferated in meaning and been put to many curious idiomatic uses," explains Reischauer in telling of this episode in his life.[23]

> I was forced to prepare a 3- by 5-inch card for each character in the text, with the Chinese character brushed in my clumsy calligraphy on one side

> and Williams' multiple translations typed on the other. These I arranged in the order of the text with their translation side up, then puzzled over the almost infinite possibilities of translation until I hit upon one that seemed to make some sense in the context. . . . I cannot imagine a way to start classical Chinese that would require so much labor for such small returns, but I did become familiar with a lot of Chinese characters, and this contributed to my learning to read written Japanese. . . . I was able to combine my knowledge of spoken Japanese with the characters I learned through Chinese to develop a reading knowledge of Japanese.[24]

Today, this clumsy, inefficient approach to the study of Chinese and Japanese would be unthinkable. Students are equipped from the start with electronic dictionaries and texts with translations that can be instantly called up on a computer screen. Pronunciation is taught with the aid of audio-visual equipment. The four main tones of Chinese are taught by native Chinese speakers in classroom drills and with voice recorders. Contemporary television programs in Chinese or Japanese are available to students as a means of enhancing their interest and motivation. Many American students can spend a year or two in China devoting themselves to language study through total immersion in the local culture.

That Reischauer had none of these aids available to him is a testimony to his dogged and tireless pursuit of his goal, but also explains why he never became as fluent in Chinese or Japanese as he would like to have been. As a youth in Tokyo, he had learned elementary spoken Japanese and a few Chinese characters (*kanji*) that were used in streetcar destinations and signs over shops. He would later learn classical Chinese and scholarly Japanese for his doctoral research on Ennin (Jikaku Daishi), but the vast area in between these extremes—the normal everyday conversation, slang, jokes, and banter of daily life in Japan and the more formal idiom—were never part of his education and experience. When he became ambassador to Tokyo in 1961, he announced immediately that he would not give speeches or conduct government business in Japanese, even though he could easily read the morning newspapers.

The major turning point in Edwin's graduate education came in the summer of 1932 when he enrolled in a seminar on Chinese studies at Harvard. Funded by the Rockefeller Foundation, the seminar featured Langdon Warner, Harvard's great pioneer in Japanese and Chinese art, and Arthur W. Hummel, a former missionary in China, who would later head the division of Orientalia at the Library of Congress. Hummel taught early Chinese history. His son, Arthur, would rise through the Foreign Service to become U.S. ambassador to China in the 1980s.

In this seminar, Edwin met Hugh Borton and Charles Burton Fahs, two eager young students of Japan who would become his lifelong friends. Borton would go on to a distinguished career as founder of Japanese studies at Columbia, and Fahs, after serving at the Rockefeller Foundation, would become cultural minister to Japan under Ambassador Reischauer in 1962. This seminar would also be the beginning of a long and productive relationship between Edwin and the Rockefeller family. Edwin later recalled that Borton and Fahs, "together with myself and two or three others, were to form the total body of professional Japanese specialists outside of government service until the outbreak of war with Japan in 1941."[25]

The next great stroke of luck came when Edwin encountered the charismatic Serge Elisseeff, whom he described as "probably at that time the leading professional scholar in the Japanese field in the Western world."[26] Elisseeff, a Russian émigré, was born into a family of great wealth based on his grandfather's wine-importing firm and a department store in St. Petersburg. Serge went to Japan in 1908 to and managed to get himself into Tokyo Imperial University, the present Tokyo University. Extraordinarily, he mastered the Japanese language, wrote a thesis in Japanese on Basho, and graduated in 1912 near the top of his class in the field of Japanese literature. Elisseeff liked to joke that the Meiji Emperor, who bestowed the degrees at his graduation, was so shocked to see a Caucasian face among the graduates that he never recovered and died soon afterwards (July 30, 1912).

Not long after Elisseeff's return to Russia, the revolution wiped out his fortune and prospects, and he fled to Finland and then to France, where he obtained a position at the Sorbonne. In 1932, Harvard made him a visiting professor for a year, and his meeting with Edwin Reischauer that year would be a life-changing event for the younger scholar. "Elisseeff was a devoted and inspiring teacher and one of the most charming persons I have ever known," Reischauer would later write. "During a quarter of a century of working closely together, he never once spoke unkindly or in irritation to me. He was a marvelous conversationalist and grand raconteur—sometimes to the point of excess. His most outstanding characteristics, however, were his insistence on high scholarly standards and his devotion to his students. He, if anyone, deserves the title of the father of Japanese studies in the United States."[27]

Elisseeff himself had rebelled against the tradition of treating East Asian languages and cultures as if they belonged to a dead tradition, and he quickly laid out a course of study for the young Reischauer that would take Reischauer to Japan and China and change his life forever. In the spring of 1933, as Reischauer was about to receive his master's in history, Elisseeff proposed that he undertake a five-year program of doctoral study abroad—two in Paris and three in Japan and China, after which he would return to Harvard, and with his Ph.D. in hand, join its Department of Far Eastern Languages. Elisseeff thus pushed his willing young student toward a scholarly career in ancient Chinese and Japanese civilizations.

Reischauer had briefly considered a career in international relations, but when he arrived on the job market after college in 1931, the Great Depression had caused job openings in the field to dry up. "A business career never once entered my mind. It was simply not a family tradition to go into anything but the professions, and I had been raised to think that the purpose of life was to make one's maximum contribution to society, however humble that might be," he later wrote.[28] Government service, involving bureaucratic struggles and boring administrative chores, never appealed to him—at least, not until he became ambassador to Japan. Research and writing came easily to him, and history was his passion, so when Serge Elisseeff cleared a career path for him involving five years of travel, graduate research, and a secure teaching position at Harvard, the choice was easy, and Edwin leaped at the opportunity.

He noted later the irony of his turning his research toward ancient times, when Japan was eagerly importing elements of the T'ang Dynasty's advanced civilization from China, just as Japan's modern army was attempting to conquer China. The war between Japan and China would change his life and inevitably bring him back to contemporary affairs in the 1940s.[29]

Edwin Reischauer would later recall his two years of study in Paris as "a sort of golden age for me."[30] He lived in a pension in the Latin Quarter of Paris, traveled extensively through France, with side trips to Germany, Austria, Italy, Hungary, Spain, England, and Holland. He taught himself enough French to take classes at the Sorbonne, gained a serviceable use of German (the first language of his Austrian grandfather and American father), and took two years of Russian as well. He feasted on museums, cathedrals, and opera. He reveled in the freedom to travel, to learn, and to immerse himself in foreign cultures.

Best of all, he fell in love with Adrienne Danton and pursued her in a summer romance that would lead to their engagement. These days were doubtless the happiest of his life. Released for a moment from his scholar's chains, he allowed himself to savor the joys of Paris with this attractive young woman. Never again would life be so joyful and carefree.

Adrienne was ideally suited to the life of a graduate student in East Asian studies. Her parents had taught at Qinghua University in Beijing from 1917 to

1927, and she had lived in Beijing from age six to sixteen, learning to speak Chinese with a beautiful accent. She was a year behind Edwin at Oberlin, but the two had scarcely known each other there. In 1932, she went on to Radcliffe to take a master's in fine arts, and in Cambridge she and Edwin became friends. In the summer of 1933, she went to Paris for further study, and there they began the serious relationship that would culminate in marriage in 1935.

Edwin would later recall that idyllic summer. Studying French with a family in Etampes, thirty miles south of Paris, "I went . . . to Paris each weekend while she was there, and she introduced me to the museums, art and architecture of the city and its environs. We danced in the streets . . . on Bastille Day, and one day while sitting in the Luxembourg Gardens, realized we were engaged." After Adrienne left for her exchange program in Vienna that fall, the two started a daily correspondence that would continue for the next two years. "Combining love and our studies, I always wrote in French and she in German," he remembered.[31] They would be married two years later in Tokyo.

Ed's friends in later years would note that behind his serious mien as a scholar, there was often a twinkle in his eye and a tendency toward self-deprecating humor that would surprise and delight his students. This lighter side is evident in his account of traveling through Italy:

> Although meaningful contacts with the French people were few, my life in Paris was conducted almost exclusively in the French language, and I did absorb something of the French spirit from the environment. I realized this most clearly at the end of my stay when I was making a trip through Italy on my way from Paris to Tokyo. On an Italian train, I found myself in an altercation with the ticket inspector. French was our only common language, and we entered into a spirited argument in it that quickly attracted an appreciative audience. To make such a public spectacle of myself went entirely against my whole Japanese and American upbringing, but I found that I did not mind it in the slightest. In fact, when in the middle of the dispute I suddenly realized that I was in the wrong, I simply argued all the louder. I had become more French than I had suspected.[32]

Reischauer's time in Paris was not productive from an academic standpoint for a budding young scholar of East Asian history. Courses in this field were few and weak, and its professors were inaccessible. An exception was Professor Maeda Yoichi, who came to Paris to study French literature in 1934. Maeda's father, Maeda Tamon, had been a friend of Edwin's father, and Maeda Yoichi offered to help Edwin translate articles from Japanese scholarly journals into

English. The two became lifelong friends; Maeda would eventually become a distinguished professor at Tokyo University, and his son-in-law, Iriye Akira, would study for his Ph.D. under Reischauer and Fairbank at Harvard and go on to become a leading historian at the University of Chicago and then Harvard. Other than this work with Maeda, however, Edwin never had a real seminar in Paris or received guidance for his Ph.D. thesis. "In this sense I was essentially self-taught—a hazard one must accept when entering a new field."[33]

But Edwin's time in Europe was not wasted. He made a sentimental pilgrimage to his grandfather's home village in Scharten, near Efferding in Austria, and found his grandfather's birth and baptismal records. As a third-generation Austrian American, he felt at home in Europe, easily and eagerly absorbing its history, art, and architecture. The young historian's time there gave him a perspective that most Asian specialists lack: a comparative view of Europe, Japan, and China, both contemporary and ancient.

> The lands of Northern Europe are of a size and age more comparable to Japan, and the past hangs heavy throughout Europe, as it does in China and Japan. At that time, internal unrest and international rivalries were severe in Europe, as they were in East Asia, but not in the United States, where the depression made Americans retreat further into the isolationism that had followed World War I. I have always felt that my ability to look at East Asia from two very different parts of the Occident permitted me a broader view of the area than most of my colleagues had, just as my study of both China and Japan—a luxury denied most students in this age of growing specialization—has given me a sharper perspective.[34]

Here we can see the origins of Edwin Reischauer's "modernization theory," in which he found common elements in the development of Japan and the nations of northern Europe. Even more important, as is evident in the next chapter, he viewed the civilizations of ancient China and Japan as at least as significant and important in world history as the civilizations of Greece and Rome. No scholar, Japanese or foreign, had to this point taken a comparative approach to the study of feudalism. Previous scholars had consigned Japan to the fringes of civilization—a small outlier, an exotic and unique island offshoot of a superior and dominant Chinese culture. For the first time, a Western scholar would view Japan's history as worthy of serious study. This attribution of equality or even superiority to East Asian culture and civilization may not seem extraordinary today, but it was a revolutionary approach among Western scholars of Reischauer's day and marked him as a pioneer in the field.

3

On the Trail of Ennin

As Edwin Reischauer's train rolled slowly across Siberia toward Japan in the spring of 1935, his life was full of hope and promise. His financial support from the Harvard-Yenching Institute for two more years of graduate study was secure. His parents and his fiancé, Adrienne, awaited him in Tokyo, a city that he still considered home. He looked forward to his marriage and to sharing his life with Adrienne in Kyoto and traveling with her to China and Korea. At last, he would get started on his doctoral thesis, which would assure him of a faculty position at Harvard and a lifetime of teaching and writing on subjects he loved. He had been bored and depressed by the long dark winter in Europe and eagerly anticipated the sunny, familiar climate of Japan.

Reischauer had firsthand experience with the ominous political turmoil in France, Germany, and Austria: riots, street demonstrations, and harsh police brutality. He was in Germany when Adolf Hitler and the Nazis were consolidating power and was disgusted by German students saluting the Nazi flag in Berlin. But nothing quite prepared him for the tumultuous days that lay ahead in Japan. He had grown up in the relatively stable 1920s, but Japan's fragile democracy would lurch in the next two years toward militarism and a kind of fascism.

The Great Depression had shattered the nation's economy, leaving desperate poverty in the farms and fishing villages outside the large cities. Political assassinations by young right-wing fanatics would multiply. Political parties and constitutional government would wither in the face of military power. There would be a coup d'état attempt in Tokyo on February 26. 1936. His older brother, Robert, his hero and mentor, would die from a bomb wound in Shanghai in July 1937. In the same month, Japan would invade China, resulting in a full-scale war. Relations between his two homelands, the United States and Japan, would steadily deteriorate, setting the course that would lead to Pearl Harbor in 1941.

And yet, arriving in Tokyo in 1935 after eight years of absence and reuniting with Adrienne and his parents, he experienced a joyful homecoming. His marriage to Adrienne Danton took place in a ward office in Tokyo on July 5. His parents then left for Karuizawa, and the newlyweds enjoyed their honeymoon in the home where he was born. Starting married life in the tense and alien culture of Japan of the 1930s would not have appealed to every young American bride, but Adrienne was exquisitely suited to her new life. Her ability to read Chinese characters helped her learn to read Japanese texts. With her master's in fine arts from Radcliffe, she took up the study of Japanese art and began translating a Japanese text on art history.

The Japan that the young couple encountered was a nation frantically mobilizing for war. Following the New York Stock Market crash of 1929, international trade had collapsed, and Japan, far more dependent on raw materials from abroad and on foreign markets for its exports of silk and other luxury products, was hardest hit by the worldwide depression that ensued. The economic crisis at home weakened liberal party government and moderate pro-Western forces, and strengthened the hand of the military leaders and nationalist elements who pushed for expansion abroad to gain control of markets and raw materials. A series of assassinations from 1930 to 1936 led to the end of democratic government and the rise of a military state.

The Japanese Kwantung army had overrun Manchuria in 1931 after a trumped-up "incident," and the Japanese government quickly turned Manchuria into a puppet state in 1932. U.S. secretary of state Henry L. Stimson announced a "nonrecognition policy" toward any Japanese conquests in violation of the Kellogg-Briand Pact of 1928 and the Nine Power Treaty of 1922. But the United States confined itself to words and took no action. After being condemned by the Lytton Commission of the League of Nations, Japan walked out of the League of Nations in 1933. The Kwantung Army consolidated its position in Manchuria and looked for opportunities to invade Inner Mongolia and northern China. Such an opportunity arose in July 1937 in the Marco Polo Bridge Incident, and from this point until the end of World War Two in 1945, Japan was a nation relentlessly committed to war.

The Japanese government mounted a strong propaganda offensive to mobilize popular support for the war in China. Military officers were assigned to every school. Pictures of the emperor were everywhere, and the national anthem ("Kimigayo") was played on all important occasions. Newspapers, magazines, and radio offered stirring accounts of great military victories. Government propagandists played up the dangers of an expanding Soviet Union on the mainland. Their message was that Japan was a resource-poor state; it stressed Japan's "disadvantage in a world of unfairly critical 'have' nations, and the history of Western aggression and exploitation that began with Perry's black ships."[1] Patriotic societies sprang up to encourage support for the war, for the "national polity" (*kokutai*), and for a "Showa Restoration" that would rid the nation of "corrupt" politicians.

Japan's universities were swept up in the nationalist frenzy. In 1935, just as the three friends from Harvard days, Hugh Borton, Charles Burton Fahs, and Reischauer were seeking to enroll in Tokyo Imperial University, one of the university's most influential constitutional scholars, Professor Minobe Tatsukichi, came under attack by right-wing intellectuals. Minobe had written that "because the Emperor's role was defined in the constitution, he was an organ *within* the state structure, rather than a sacred source of legitimacy that stood outside and above the state." For making this statement, he was accused of writing treasonous works and censured by both houses of the Diet. He had allegedly slandered the emperor (*lese-majeste*) and was harassed into resigning from the House of Peers, where he was an appointed member.[2]

It was in this superheated atmosphere that Edwin Reischauer succeeded in enrolling in the elite Japanese university in 1935. Armed with an introduction from his Harvard mentor, Professor Elisseeff, he was accepted as a special research student by Professor Tsuji Zennosuke, whom he described as "the rather conservative and nationalistic head of the Department of Japanese History in the Faculty of Letters." "So far as I know," he remembered, "I was the only Occidental student at the university at that time."[3]

Surprisingly, in this charged milieu, studying at Tokyo Imperial University proved to be reasonably safe for Western graduate students in the mid-1930s. Even as the nation slid toward war, and as key political and business leaders were assassinated by right-wing fanatics, individual Japanese citizens largely maintained a veneer of courtesy toward Caucasian foreigners. Yet Japanese government agents were vigilant in monitoring foreign residents' activities. Reischauer's close friend Hugh Borton describes being followed by Japanese agents during a trip through East Asia that ended in Tokyo: "One day [a local policeman] stopped our cook as she was passing by and casually remarked that he understood we had recently returned from a trip to China and Korea. Such an experience was common among foreigners in Tokyo."[4]

British historian Richard Storry, at the time a young teacher at Otaru Commercial College in Hokkaido, relayed similar feelings to his parents in Britain in November 1937. In a letter deliberately sent from outside Japan, he criticized Japanese actions in China but noted that "I dare not say so in my normal letters as police surveillance in this country reaches incredible dimensions: the land is stiff with police spies who keep the closest watch on all foreigners." But Storry also wrote in August 1937 that "England now is thoroughly unpopular, although everybody is personally as friendly as ever." Two months later he stated, "I have been and am treated well; even with this trouble on, the Japanese students are most friendly and my acquaintances are, if anything, more kind and generous to me than before."[5]

Hugh Borton had a similar experience. Writing in 1935 after an absence from Japan of four years, he noted that "the people, in their resentment that the world community did not accept them as equals, had acquired a self-confidence bordering on haughtiness." But in his personal dealings with fellow students, he felt little or no hostility. "Although there were clear signs of Japanese ultra-nationalism all around us, we suffered no personal harassment and our life in Tokyo was most pleasant." As a foreign graduate student at Tokyo Imperial University, he reported that "in spite of the increased nationalist feeling around us, none of us experience any animosity from the students or faculty." Even during the coup attempt in February 1936, Borton wrote, "we were impressed . . . by the fact that even though we moved about in the center of the city just hours after the coup attempt, we experienced no antipathy toward foreigners throughout the affair."

Borton also recalled, however, that "professional Americans competing with Japanese found their lives more difficult." Dr. Herbert Bowles, "born in Tokyo and fully bilingual . . . had received his medical and surgical training in the United States. He had returned to Tokyo as a skilled surgeon, on appointment to the staff of St. Luke's hospital, where he expected to remain for some time. Then he suddenly decided to return to the United States; one night he told us in confidence the reason for his decision. While he was performing an operation, a Japanese nurse, on instructions from her superiors, had refused to give him the instrument he requested, placing him in an intolerable position."[6]

Borton's most telling reminiscence was of a conversation with Professor Tsuji Zennosuke of Tokyo Imperial University, who would also become Reischauer's faculty advisor. In 1935, Tsuji examined Borton orally in Japanese on his knowledge of Japanese history. Afterward, Borton recalled, "I asked him if he did not think it presumptuous for an American with only a partial command of the language to specialize in Japanese history. He responded immediately, 'As a foreigner, you can write about Japanese history in a way I am not able to do. You should not let anything interfere with your plans.'"[7] Tsuji was of course referring to the state Shinto mythology that Japanese historians faced prior to 1945. Official Japanese history began with the Sun Goddess, Amaterasu Omikami, who spawned an unbroken line of emperors down to Hirohito; any questioning of this myth could become a case of *lese-majeste*. Marxist and other dissenting historians were ruthlessly punished.

That is why, after 1945, when the emperor avowed his humanity, there existed a tabula rasa in which Japanese and foreigners alike could for the first time write the history of a nation whose citizens had been kept in the dark for centuries. It gave historians such as Borton and Reischauer an opportunity to serve as pioneers, and it liberated Japanese scholars to test new interpretations and theories.

Reischauer could not have been unaware of the ugly side of Japanese nationalism in the 1930s, and he must have recoiled at the suppression of liberal thought in the universities. One after another liberal or left-wing intellectual went through a "conversion," or *tenko*, to the new nationalism and publicly repented his erroneous thinking. In Korea in 1937, he would see for himself the arrogance and cruelty of the Japanese military occupiers. Yet in his autobiography he glosses lightly these negative aspects of Japan, and his later accounts of the 1930s would portray this period merely as a tragic aberration in Japan's march toward modernization and democratic government.

Other scholars, such as E. H. Norman, Reischauer's tennis-playing friend from Karuizawa days, would adopt a very different view. They saw the Japan of the 1930s as a reversion to form, a continuation of the pre-Meiji state, with remnants of feudalism and militarism reappearing in a nation that had never truly modernized or had only undergone a "partial revolution" in the Meiji Period (1868–1912). They would argue later than Japan had never really accepted democratic government, that "Taisho democracy" was a sham, and that the ruling classes, led by the militarists, were always destined to prevail. This difference of opinion would lead some of Reischauer's critics to charge that he was being too soft on (or naive concerning) Japan, or, worse, that he was a Cold Warrior agent acting for American imperialism.[8]

Reischauer disagreed with Norman's view: he would argue later that "the recrudescence of military sentiment and the abandonment of parliamentary government in Japan are often portrayed as a simple return to earlier Japanese patterns and a revival of feudal tendencies, but such an interpretation misses the real significance of what happened in Japan. The military officer was no *samurai*; in fact, in the new society he represented the lower classes more than the privileged classes of wealth and aristocratic birth. In the army there was far less place for hereditary prestige and power than in either business or politics, and in this sense the army was further from the feudal past than the rest of Japanese society. The younger officers of the army and navy, with their rural distrust of the cities and big business, were scarcely defenders of the *status quo*; nor were they advocates of a return to an earlier economic balance."[9]

If these conflicting interpretations had been simply academic quarrels, they would probably have long been forgotten or consigned to graduate Ph.D. dissertations. Instead, they would become fundamental to the postwar debate over how the U.S. occupation should be conducted. If, on the one hand, Japan required a social revolution before it could become truly egalitarian and democratic, then the emperor should have been treated as a war criminal, and many of the leaders who emerged in postwar Japan should have been barred from power. Labor and left-wing parties should have been allowed free rein to carry out their programs of social upheaval. If, on the other hand, parliamentary democracy had strong roots in prewar Japan, only to be undermined by the Depression and hijacked by the military, then a very different, more benign occupation was required. Despite the sinister political events that marked his time in Japan in the 1930s, Reischauer never lost his faith in the ability of the Japanese people to adapt to democratic rule. This faith would lead him to play a role in shaping the short, benign occupation and in retaining the emperor on the throne, although in a symbolic role.

The American media during this period adopted mostly a virulent, racist view of Japan. Led by such "pro-Chinese" figures such as Henry Luce, publisher of *Time* magazine, and Pearl Buck, who wrote novels such as *The Good Earth*, portraying Chinese peasants in the most sympathetic terms, the media depicted the Japanese as cruel, mindless militarists fanatically obeying the emperor's commands. Luce's *March of Time*, a new documentary news segment that appeared in movie theaters before the main attraction, reinforced these images; it showed Japanese soldiers bayoneting Chinese civilians near Nanjing in 1937–38. The old specter of a threatening "Yellow Peril" was revived. In the mythology fed to Americans at this time were the notions that Japanese pilots had poor eyesight and that Japanese aircraft were flimsy; both conceits disappeared after the raid on Pearl Harbor.

How could Reischauer, after living through this painful era, have maintained his optimistic view of Japan and the Japanese? One possible explanation is that he had no personal confrontations with the fanatic rightists. Despite the growing hostility toward America among many Japanese, "never once did I or the members of my family feel the slightest sense of animosity among Japanese toward us personally, and our relations with our Japanese friends remained as warm as ever."[10] His contacts in Japan were mainly friends of his family: Christian, Western-educated liberals and intellectuals who deplored Japan's trend toward militarism. One might even argue that his happy childhood in Tokyo cosseted by adoring Japanese nannies predisposed him toward the most benign interpretation of Japanese behavior.

Later in his career as an historian, he emphasized the record of the political parties in Japan's fledgling parliamentary democracy. In the crucial elections of February 20, 1936, voters gave the political parties close to 78 percent of the vote. He later wrote that "millions of Japanese, very possibly the majority, were not in sympathy with what was happening."[11] In this interpretation, the militarists took advantage of world events and depression at home to usurp power and lead an unwilling nation into a hopeless war.

Whatever the explanation, Reischauer at this point revealed his extraordinary talent for compartmentalizing his life, for tuning out all extraneous background noise, and for honing in with steely concentration on his intellectual goals: he had come to Japan with a burning desire to study texts from early Chinese and Japanese history, which would lead to a career as a specialist on T'ang Dynasty China. A professor of Chinese studies in Paris, Paul Demieville, had suggested that he translate the diary of an obscure Japanese Buddhist monk, Ennin (posthumously named Jikaku Daishi), who had traveled to China from AD 838 to 847. Ignoring the political turmoil around him, Reischauer plunged joyfully into one of the most difficult and demanding research projects ever undertaken by a foreign scholar in Japan.

A less dedicated scholar might well have chosen a topic that could have been pursued in comfortable libraries and classrooms under the guidance of a helpful faculty advisor. But this was not his style. His research would take him to Tokyo, Kyoto, war-torn China, and occupied Korea, following in Ennin's footsteps. For the next twenty years, with the interruption of five years in World War Two, the research for and writing of *Ennin's Diary* and a companion volume, *Ennin's Travels in China*, would consume large chunks of his time, until finally they were published in 1955.[12]

Consider the self-confidence—even chutzpah—of this twenty-five-year old American graduate student who discovers a Japanese document that is more than one thousand years old, written by a Buddhist monk whom few Japanese or Chinese had ever heard of—a student who moreover claims that "a great historical document of this sort, although medieval in time and Far Eastern in place, is a part of our common human heritage, with significance beyond these limits of time and space. It is the report of an important traveler in world history and an extraordinary, firsthand account of one of the way stations on man's long and tortuous journey from his lowly, savage beginnings to his present lofty but precarious position."[13] This description clearly suggests that he was a scholar of broad brush strokes and large vision, showing the first signs of the bold approach that would characterize his approach to writing history.

Only a tiny handful of scholars in Japan and China were interested in Ennin's diary in the 1930s. Reischauer's English translation in 1955 sparked such a surge of interest that today Ennin is widely revered and studied in both countries. A Japanese edition of *Ennin's Travels in Tang China* appeared in 1963, and it was later published in French and German.[14] A paperback edition published in 1999 by Kodansha went through eleven editions and had sold 12,700 copies by March 2009.

In his preface to the Japanese edition, noted scholar of Buddhism Nakamura Hajime praised the work as reliable and authentic. "[Reischauer] gives a wonderfully vivid depiction of Ennin and the people surrounding him, and succeeds in shedding light on the psychology of the leading characters from 1,100 years ago. . . . This work is informed by the author's sympathetic understanding of the actual circumstances of Buddhism in those days."[15] Shiba Ryotaro, an immensely popular writer of historical novels, wrote that "it was only since the publication of Dr. Reischauer's English translation that this travel journal, *Ennin's Diary*, has come to be recognized as an asset to humanity."[16]

Richard Dyke, a Harvard Ph.D. who studied with Reischauer in 1967, has read over the diary several times and, with Virginia Anami, wife of Japan's ambassador to China from, 2001 to 2006, has organized trips to China to retrace Ennin's footsteps.[17] He calls Reischauer's translation "an amazing piece of meticulous scholarship. The puzzle is how he could have pulled this off in the 1930's. Today, a scholar of Japanese or Chinese has the advantage of libraries full of dictionaries and multi-volume sets of books with glosses and footnotes and commentaries. Even with these detailed roadmaps to the classical literature, reading classical Chinese and Japanese is a challenge. . . . The amazing thing about Reischauer's translation of the Ennin Diary was that the tools which today's scholars use had not yet been invented. . . . He was a pioneer in every sense of the word."[18]

Ennin was indeed a formidable character. Shipwrecked as he crossed the dangerous waters from Kyushu to the mouth of the Yangtse River in 838, he made it to the Chinese shore and spent the next nine years undergoing almost unbelievable hardships. In his diary, he records his dealings with Chinese officials, Korean merchants, and Buddhist monks, and describes in detail festivals, taboos, myths, and the persecution of Buddhism as he travels through T'ang China.

What prompted Reischauer to tackle such a demanding project at a time in life when many graduate students usually focus on marriage, children, family, and career steps? We can speculate that his father's research and writing on

Buddhism may have whetted his appetite. But he chose to place Buddhism in a broader historical context: he noted that Ennin's diary is the "not only the first great diary in Far Eastern history; it is also the first account of life in China by any foreign visitor." Furthermore, it is "one of the most important documents of history, a primary source unique for its time, describing in rich detail a nation and a people then in the forefront of world history."[19]

The technical difficulties of translating Ennin's ninth-century hand-written Chinese characters were horrific. Ennin wrote in cursive Chinese characters, but his grasp of the language was not perfect, nor was his handwriting always legible. He wrote in a mixture of colloquial and classical Chinese whose meaning and pronunciation were different from modern Chinese. Reischauer worked with a monk of the Tendai Sect (the same sect as Ennin's) named Katsuno Ryushin, who could translate the Chinese only into modern Japanese, which Reischauer would then have to turn into literate English. Moreover, he worked not only from a 1918 printed version of the diary, but also from a 1926 photographic reproduction of a copy of Ennin's manuscript written in small characters by the shaky hand of a seventy-two-year-old monk in 1291. The latter text had Japanese phonetic text (*kaeriten*) along with the original Chinese characters. Worm holes obscured parts of the text. Number and tense were not specified in the original Chinese but had to be added in the English. The entire diary contained about seventy thousand Chinese characters, which ran to 409 pages in the English translation.

As Reischauer wrote in his preface to the diary, "The translator of this diary ideally should have a deep understanding of such widely separated fields as Buddhist theology, T'ang political administration, Korean history, Far Eastern diplomatic relations, Shinto mythology, Chinese historical geography, ninth-century maritime navigation, and a host of other equally complicated and sometimes esoteric subjects."[20] An example of his meticulous research along these lines is a letter he wrote to an astronomer at Harvard: "Dear Professor Shapley: If it would not be too difficult, I wonder if one of the members of your department could tell me what comet was visible in China in 837 and 838."[21] There is no record of Shapley's reply, but Reischauer was able to confirm that Ennin did indeed accurately report on the comet. "Coming as it did shortly after the close approach to the earth by Halley's comet in the spring of 837, the comet of 838 was identified by the Chinese as a reappearance of that spectacular heavenly body and occasioned considerable excitement."[22]

"*Ennin's Diary* was an immensely impressive work," according to Donald Keene of Columbia University, himself perhaps the greatest Western translator of Japanese to English of his era. "Ed must have mastered at least five thousand

Chinese characters. There are at least a thousand footnotes. It is a pleasure to read—a superb piece of work. If he had written nothing else, this alone would have assured him a place among the leading scholars of China and Japan."[23]

In the course of his laborious translation, Reischauer clearly came to admire his subject: "As the greatest churchman of his day, [Ennin] apparently remained as simple in his faith, as fully devoted to his work, and as blameless in his relations with others as he had been as a humble pilgrim and eager traveling scholar." Reischauer viewed him, finally, as "a major figure showing a rare balance between energy, intellect and character—a man of outstanding ability, as saintly in conduct as he was determined in action, and driven throughout by a strong unswerving faith in his religion. . . . He was one who through the strength of his own determination and the inspiring example of his character led his fellow men in the less spectacular but perhaps more difficult task of developing the new lands which others had discovered."[24]

Does his portrait of Ennin reveal a clue to Reischauer's own personal goals and ideals? Though never religious in any orthodox way, he would become a man of powerful energy, intellect, and character. And at the end of his life, as we shall see in chapter 11, he was more affected by Buddhist imagery than by any of the Western religions. He would combine intellectual self-confidence, bordering on arrogance, with unlimited energy, but also with humility in his relations with others. This unusual combination of supreme self-assurance and energy, tempered by personal modesty, would become evident both in his academic life and in his government service and would win him devoted friends as well as critics throughout his career.

Later, as ambassador, Reischauer went out of his way to pay homage to Ennin. In April 1963, with his wife, Haru, he spent two nights as a guest of the Enryakuji Monastery on Mount Hiei and participated in the ceremony for the 1,100th anniversary of Ennin's death. He and Haru marched up to the altar and presented flowers and a copy of his books to Ennin's picture.[25] The following March he visited two of Ennin's reputed birthplaces in Tochigi Prefecture.

Robert Scalapino, who studied under Reischauer at Harvard and who himself became a major figure in East Asian studies at the University of California at Berkeley, thought that "Reischauer's major contribution as a scholar was his ability to see the big picture. He was an excellent synthesizer of knowledge, capable of large formulations."[26] Marius Jansen, another of Reischauer's students who became a giant in the field of Japanese history, said that Reischauer was "unfailingly adventurous" and spoke of his "Olympic level of generalization."[27]

What were these large formulations? In tackling Ennin's diary, Reischauer revealed four of his deepest scholarly convictions. First, he believed that T'ang

Dynasty China (AD 618–907) was far superior to European civilization of the time and that it was worthy of serious study by Western students. He would later assert that "China during the seventh century towered high above all other political units of the time. During the Han Dynasty (206 BC to 220 AD) China had drawn abreast of the Mediterranean world. Now it was starting on what was to prove to be a millennium of preeminence as the strongest, [the] richest, and in many ways the most culturally advanced country in the world."[28] He notes that the Chinese discovered the technology of printing with movable type more than three centuries before the Europeans did with printing of the Gutenberg Bible. The T'ang rulers had established a stable, dependable bureaucracy, a merit-based examination system for recruiting talented bureaucrats, a genius for organization, and an extraordinarily sophisticated literature.

In this vein, Edwin would argue that Ennin, as a Buddhist who could speak and read some Chinese, was a far more reliable and sympathetic observer than Marco Polo, who would visit China four centuries later. The comparison with Marco Polo was revealing: Edwin treats Ennin, an Asian (or "Asiatic" as they were then called), as the equal or superior of the Venetian adventurer—a startling assumption for a Western scholar of that time.

A second formulation involved Japan's ability to import Chinese and (later) other cultural influences without losing its basic national identity. Ennin and other Buddhist travelers to China brought home not only religious knowledge, but important information about governance, city planning, language and literary skills, and bureaucracy. From this approach, Reischauer would later trace the foreign influences that affected modern Japan and would describe in fascinating detail how subsequent generations of Japanese filtered the foreign influences that would buffet them when the Western powers began to approach from the sixteenth to the twentieth centuries.

Third, he came to reflect in 1937 on how deeply ignorant his fellow Americans were about East Asian history and culture, even as the United States was hurtling toward a bloody war with Japan and would soon be fighting Chinese troops in the Korean War (1950–53). One can see him resolving to devote the rest of his life to the mission of educating Americans, especially policymakers, about the importance of Japan, China, and Korea.

Finally, we can see in his portrayal of Ennin the origins of his deeply held belief that individuals *can* make a difference in history. This may not seem to be a startling insight today, but in the intellectual climate of Harvard and other universities of his day, a prevailing orthodoxy was that human history is determined by large, impersonal forces over which individuals have little or no control. This notion was, of course, a fundamental tenet of Marxism, but it also had roots in the works of Sigmund Freud and Albert Einstein. Reischauer would have none of it. It was clear to him that Ennin had played a critical role in transmitting Buddhism and other facets of T'ang civilization to Japan. It is just possible that Reischauer's plan to bring East Asian civilization to the attention of his fellow Americans grew out of his deep admiration for Ennin.

In his lectures at Harvard, he would praise the role of individuals in Japanese history. Two of the individuals he admired most in modern Japan were Shibusawa Eiichi, an entrepreneur and business leader born in 1840 who played a central role in establishing modern industry in Japan and Hara Kei (Takashi), prime minister from 1918 to 1921 and a chief architect of party government in Japan. Other favorites were Fukuzawa Yukichi, founder of Keio University; Itagaki Taisuke, political leader; and Okuma Shigenobu, prime minister and founder of Waseda University. He was also fascinated by Minamoto Yoritomo, Nichiren, Hideyoshi, and Ito Hirobumi. His belief that individuals can affect history was so evident to his colleagues at Harvard that they titled a volume in his honor on the occasion of his sixtieth birthday *Personality in Japanese History*.[29]

Edwin and Adrienne Reischauer enjoyed one of the happiest and most carefree years of their lives in Kyoto from the summer of 1936 to the summer of 1937. They lived in Japanese style, studied Japanese, wore *yukata* in the summer, slept on *tatami*, and huddled around a charcoal hibachi on cold winter nights. They hiked and bicycled through the countryside, visited temples, museums, and bookstores, and behaved much like normal graduate students. They were determined to ignore as much as possible the turmoil in Japan and China. At last, Edwin could begin his research for his Ph.D. dissertation. His study with several Japanese professors in Tokyo and Kyoto left him with warm friendships and a real appreciation for their generous guidance.

Edwin also helped Adrienne translate a book on Japanese art history. In addition to working on Ennin's diary, he translated eleventh- to the thirteenth-century Japanese texts, some of which were later published by Harvard. He studied Japanese cultural history at Kyoto Imperial University and was tutored in contemporary Japanese language, calligraphy, and tea ceremony. Adrienne studied flower arranging. In short, it was the kind of total immersion in Japanese life that Edwin had missed as the isolated son of a missionary in Tokyo, and he clearly loved it.

The home they rented in the northern part of Kyoto turned out to be situated next to a vacant lot owned by a member of the *burakumin* (outcast) community, which caused other citizens to avoid building there. In one of his rare criticisms of Japan, he would write later, "This was a good example of the cruel and senseless prejudice other Japanese hold for this small outcast element in their otherwise extremely homogenous society."[30]

Their idyllic sojourn in Kyoto ended when word arrived that Robert Reischauer had tragically died in Shanghai, the result of a stray Chinese bomb landing near the lobby of the hotel where he was staying. A thirty-year-old instructor at Princeton and one of the rising stars in the field of Japan studies, Robert had organized a study tour of East Asia for fifteen students. Fighting had broken out between Japan and China on July 7, 1937, and as Robert was checking the group into a hotel in Shanghai on August 14, a bomb landed nearby, blowing in the plate-glass windows of the lobby and shearing off one of his heels. Bleeding profusely, he went into shock and died on the way to a hospital.[31]

Edwin made all the arrangements for Robert's funeral in Tama Cemetery in the western suburbs of Tokyo. The shock to the Reischauer family was profound, and the incident altered Edwin's entire career. Robert had already published a two-volume reference work on ancient Japanese history and was working on a shorter book, *Japan: Government– Politics*,[32] which was published posthumously in 1939. It was he who his family and contemporary scholars felt was destined to be the superstar on modern Japan, whereas Edwin was to specialize on early Japan and China. "If [Robert] had still been alive when the war broke out with Japan," Edwin wrote later, "it would have been he rather than I who would have been pushed into various positions involving modern affairs."[33]

Reischauer's love and admiration, almost hero worship, for his older brother, coupled with his innate competitive instincts, were to shape the rest of his career. He would name his first and only son, born on January 18, 1941, Robert Danton Reischauer.[34] He clearly believed that Robert was the superior scholar and teacher. "He was not only a brilliant scholar, but had a great deal of charm and a distinct histrionic flare," he would recall.[35] Yet Edwin also accepted the challenge of living up to Robert's memory and reputation. It was a heavy burden, yet he viewed it as his destiny, and so, as a driven man, he plunged back into his research, heading for Korea and China.

For the next two months, Edwin and Adrienne lived in Seoul and traveled extensively throughout Korea. Reischauer came face to face with the "spiritual cruelty" of the Japanese occupation and became a sympathetic supporter of Korean national aspirations. He did note, however, that despite its brutal occupation, Japan's investment in Korea, when compared to that of European powers in their colonies, was proportionally much larger.[36] Never one to waste precious time, he teamed with an American Korea specialist, George McCune, to create a system for romanizing the Korean language. The McCune-Reischauer system remains to this day the standard in the field.

When Edwin and Adrienne lived in Beijing for seven months, he was appalled at the poverty around him. After observing the rickshaw men in the streets of Beijing, he wrote, "I found that I simply could not endure having these pathetic fellow human beings haul me around, and I was constantly revolted at the sight of Chinese and foreigners lolling back in apparent pleasure as other men literally coughed out their life blood serving them as beasts of burden."[37] It was in this period that Reischauer had his closest look at the ravages of Western imperialism, and it would deepen his sympathy for its victims throughout Asia for the rest of his life. Realizing that he would be teaching second-year Chinese back at Harvard, he plunged into the study of spoken Chinese, but never felt fully comfortable in the language.

In the summer of 1938, his fellowship expired, and he and Adrienne embarked for the United States and for the new challenge of teaching at Harvard. En route, they learned that Adrienne was pregnant with their first child. In June of that year, Edwin O. Reischauer received his Ph.D. from Harvard, and that fall he was appointed an instructor in the Department of Far Eastern Languages.

The Scholar at War

Edwin and Adrienne Reischauer returned to Harvard in the late summer of 1938 after five tumultuous years in Japan, China, and Korea. After watching the country of his birth go to war with China, losing his brother in that war, traveling far from family and friends, living in unsanitary, unheated homes, they rejoiced at the peace and tranquility of Harvard's small intellectual community. Adrienne gave birth to their first child, Helen Ann Reischauer, the following year on February 23. The young couple settled into a cozy home on Hawthorn Street near Harvard Yard, expecting for the first time to live a more or less normal life. In January 1941, their second child, Robert Danton Reischauer, was born. Anticipating this new arrival in the summer of 1940, the family had moved into a larger home on Longfellow Road, near Mt. Auburn Hospital.

The young scholar who came back to Cambridge was supremely confident, competitive, and ambitious. He was impatient with the details of academic life and had no stomach for faculty politics. He was a keen observer of his colleagues and quickly sized up them up as straightforward or phony. He hated pretense and hid behind a self-deprecating persona. He loved sports and competed fiercely in softball and tennis. Most of all, he had a steely capacity to concentrate on his research and writing and to educate himself on foreign-policy issues.

For the moment, Edwin and Adrienne could try to ignore the looming wars in Europe and Asia that would once again bring turmoil to their lives. Reischauer could at last complete his Ph.D. dissertation and get about the work of teaching Americans about Japan and China. "No one was more concerned than I over the dangerous situation abroad, but I viewed it more as an onlooker than as a participant. I did not think anything I could do would help to overcome the disastrous lack of international understanding in the United States as well as in Asia and Europe, and so I stuck resolutely to my long-range goal of getting East Asian studies established at Harvard as a first step toward increasing knowledge between the West and Asia."[1]

Life in Cambridge during the days just before war engulfed America was eerily calm and pleasant. The Reischauers joined an intimate community of like-minded scholars and students. Each work day began for Reischauer with a walk to Boylston Hall in Harvard Yard, then headquarters of the Harvard-Yenching Institute. Colleagues in East Asian studies included Arthur Wright (history), James Robert Hightower (Chinese literature), and John Pelzel (anthropology), all of whom would go on to become distinguished scholars in their respective fields as well as personal friends. It was at this point that the Reischauers also met John King Fairbank and his wife, Wilma, a turning point in the careers of both men, as we shall see in the next chapter. The Fairbanks in turn introduced the Reischauers to others in the community. These were stimulating times for a young scholar: evening discussions at the apartment of Alfred North Whitehead, the renowned English philosopher, visits to the Japanese collection at the Museum of Fine Arts in Boston, and concerts by the Boston Symphony Orchestra. "Life in Cambridge was pleasant, and we fitted into it with ease," he would later recall.[2]

Reischauer completed his doctoral dissertation—a translation of one-quarter of the Ennin diaries with commentary—and received his Ph.D. in June 1939. He then joined the Harvard faculty as an instructor, teaching two second-year Chinese-language courses. He had only three students, two men and one woman, but had to teach them separately because women were not permitted to take classes with men at that time! Later in 1939 he was also permitted to teach Japanese—his first love—and with Elisseeff began to prepare several new texts to update the nearly useless existing texts.

America's lack of interest in and knowledge of East Asian affairs in the 1930s were appalling. The Great Depression of the 1930s and the inward-looking spirit of isolationism blinded most Americans to the threat that was approaching from Asia. The nation had no centralized intelligence service at this time to provide early warning: "Gentlemen do not read each other's mail," Secretary of State Henry L. Stimson had famously growled in 1929.

What coverage there was of Japan in the media was almost entirely negative. Led by Henry Luce, the son of American missionaries to China, *Time, Life*, and *Fortune* magazines turned virulently against Japan in the wake of Japan's conquest of Manchuria in 1931. *Time* had no problem using racist images against the Japanese while supporting the Chinese: "With its slanty eye cocked on China, all Japan trembled with patriotic fervor last week. General elections were coming, the budget was unbalanced, the yen was falling, Government bonds were off. But about such things few subjects of the Emperor cared when Japanese arms were carving out world headlines in Shanghai, Nanking, Harbin. Flags fluttered from every Tokyo home. Troops drilled in every barracks. Full of martial memories, reservists tramped back and forth to business, pretending their umbrellas were guns. Proud Japanese fathers lectured their sons on the honor of dying for Nippon."[3]

American missionaries in China and back home in America were painting a picture of Chiang Kai-shek and his wife, a Wellesley graduate, as the last best hope for Christianity, capitalism, and democracy in China. Elite opinion in America was hopelessly ignorant of Asian affairs. Wealthy businessmen and lawyers in the foreign-policy establishment who routinely traveled to Europe, hardly ever visited Japan or China and had little access to accurate reporting from East Asia. To the extent they had any views at all about East Asia, these views were often based on anecdotes and family lore.

President Franklin Delano Roosevelt's pro-China sympathies probably came from his grandfather, Warren Delano, who had been a partner in Russell and Company, the leading nineteenth-century American trading firm with China. Roosevelt grew up in Hyde Park, New York, surrounded by Chinese furnishings, stamps, vases, and a bronze Chinese bell. He also found ominous the words of a Japanese fellow student at Harvard who had told him of Japan's "schedule," drawn up in 1889, for a one-hundred-year program of expansion that would absorb Korea, Manchuria, Jehol, Australia, New Zealand, and Hawaii.[4]

Against this background, only a tiny handful of American experts could offer informed commentary on Japan. The universities were hopelessly lacking in regional expertise. In 1935, a Japanese professor, Takagi Yasaka, published a survey of Japanese studies in the United States for the Institute of Pacific Relations, a left-leaning think tank based in New York City. As recounted by the historian Marius Jansen, Takagi found that "there were a number of courses in international relations in which Japan figured, but most of those were taught by China-oriented specialists. There was one chair, recently established at Stanford, but held by a man who did not read Japanese. . . . Harvard had recently decided to give course credit for work in Japanese offered by a visiting professor of religion; Columbia, more cautious, was willing to honor only one such course." Takagi did note five younger scholars of Japan who spoke excellent Japanese and who might play a role in the future: Gordon Bowles in anthropology, Burton Fahs in political science, Hugh Borton in history, and two young historians named Reischauer at Harvard.[5]

The military was in no better shape. Jansen related that in 1941 "the United States Navy set about building a file of people who were supposed to have knowledge of either Chinese or Japanese. Of the 600 they found, only 56 people were judged on closer examination to have enough background knowledge of Japanese to justify further training."[6]

Surprisingly, *Harper's Monthly Magazine*, an intellectual journal with a circulation of a little more than one hundred thousand readers, ran a series of reasonably well researched articles between 1936 and 1940 aimed at sophisticated readers. One of the best of these articles was by Edwin's brother, Robert Karl Reischauer, published in 1936, the year before he died. Describing the ancient struggle in Japanese history between civilian and military rulers, he provided a derisive portrait of Japan's new military leaders:

> The militarists argue that they are the spiritual successors of the glorious samurai. They are incorruptible, one hundred percent patriotic, idealists who have earned the right to control the destinies of a country they have saved by their strong arms from being crushed by Russia and other Western powers. The civilians are simply the successors of the despised tradespeople [*sic*] and ignorant farmers. Business men [*sic*] have no ethics. They put selfish private interests above patriotism. Their pursuit of money makes them crass materialists without a touch of idealism, and their entrance into politics spells corruption and moral decay. Hence Japan is doomed if her destiny falls into the hands of such vultures. Only with the pure-hearted militarists in control can Japan hope to have a glorious future.

He then goes on to describe the thinking of Japan's civilian leaders, who argued that Japan's future depended on how it solved its economic problems:

> Successful business men and competent farmers understand these economic questions best and are the only ones who can answer them; that it is the phenomenal growth of Japanese industry and commerce that has made her great army and navy possible; and that Japan will prosper only when her destiny is controlled by the brains and wealth of her powerful civilian capitalists. Should the government be conducted by ignorant, narrowminded [*sic*] militarists, whose knowledge of economics is negligible if not downright fallacious, whose international outlook is limited to the

strategy of naval and land warfare, who may possibly be "simple-hearted" but are undoubtedly "simple-minded" when faced with domestic and international problems, then indeed Japan's days are numbered and nothing but chaos lies ahead.[7]

In the chaotic conditions of 1936, when a coup d'état attempt by young army officers in central Tokyo paralyzed the capital for three days, what was an ordinary Japanese to do? Robert Reischauer, who clearly knew firsthand the thoughts of many of his old friends in Tokyo, wrote: "It behooves everyone to speak softly, eye his neighbors with suspicion, take no definite course of action, and voice no sentiment except that he is consumed with loyalty and devotion toward the Emperor, and that everything he has said or done has been for the eternal glory of the Imperial Family and the everlasting prosperity of Great Japan."[8]

A close reading of this statement reveals two important judgments Robert made—judgments that Edwin would come to share over time. First, he rejected the notion that the entire nation had been brainwashed into blind devotion to a divine, godlike emperor. Rather, he suggested, many ordinary citizens were hunkered down in a survival mode, waiting for the storm of fanatic ultranationalism to pass. These folks did not buy into the notion of a divine emperor, but simply feared the consequences of openly expressing any skepticism. The elections of 1936, in which the parties won large a large majority, even at a time of assassinations and growing military power, showed that the voting public still had faith in the civilian rule. The two main parties in 1932 won 447 of 466 seats in the Diet, and in April 1937 they carried 354 seats. Robert's other clear conclusion was that the military rulers who seized power in Japan were "simple-minded" fools who were leading the nation to a disastrous outcome.

It would clearly have been foolhardy for a foreigner whose parents lived in Tokyo to voice such heretical notions too loudly. For this reason, Robert's indictment of the militarists was somewhat veiled; he doubtless worried that Japan's zealous thought police might contact and grill his family's friends and acquaintances in Tokyo as a result of his indiscreet observations. We know that his parents remained in Tokyo until 1939, wrote weekly letters to Edwin, and were clearly in touch with their Christian and intellectual contacts at Meiji Gakuin University and elsewhere.

As noted earlier, this question of how the Japanese people viewed their emperor would become a crucial issue when American leaders discussed "unconditional surrender," the Potsdam Declaration, and the occupation of Japan. Was the emperor part of the problem or part of the solution to Japan's blatant militarism? Robert Reischauer's view, which Edwin pushed forward after Robert's death, would prevail. The emperor would be allowed, under the new constitution of 1947, to remain on the throne as a "symbol of the unity of the Japanese people." The military establishment would be disbanded and discredited. The brothers' faith in the common sense of the ordinary Japanese citizen, with General Douglas MacArthur's muscular assent, would prevail in policy councils.

Robert Reischauer's trenchant reporting from Tokyo in *Harper's Monthly Magazine* came to an end with his tragic death in Shanghai in 1937. But *Harper's* continued to publish a series of articles by a few thoughtful observers of East Asian affairs; these articles would set the stage for policy discussions about Japan in the late 1930s. It is impossible to weigh Edwin Reischauer's radical policy positions without a brief look at the ideas floating in the air at this time.

First, there was the argument that Japan had never escaped from its feudal past. In 1937, Nathaniel Peffer, a professor of international relations at Columbia University with a deep interest in China, wrote:

> For Japan is now in its ascendancy. It is among the great of the world, its words inspiring respect and its acts fear. It has the third biggest navy. It can defy the mandates of the world and proceed toward hegemony over half a continent. It can force the most highly industrialized countries to throw up unprecedented barriers in a panic lest cheap Japanese goods capture markets at the threshold of the most efficient Western factories. Nevertheless its lot is far from enviable. In fact, if one can put aside for the moment a general irritation at Japanese aggressiveness and a fear of the effect of an irresponsible militarism on the precarious balance of international relations, Japan is rather to be pitied. There is indeed something pathetic in the bewilderment of its people. . . . Conscious of their eminence and proud of their achievement, they are at the same time frightened. That there is something wrong they know, but what and why they do not know.

Peffer goes on to argue that although Japan possessed the veneer of a modern nation (railways, telegraphs, textile mills), it had changed little from its feudal past: "Japan had donned an extra outer garment, but the body and spirit were the body and spirit of medieval Japan."[9] This argument, too, would later become a central issue for occupation planners. Did the old feudal order carry out the Meiji Restoration and subsequent industrial progress and thus continue itself, or did the Taisho Era (1912–26) auger in a new era of parliamentary democracy and modernization? If the former view were correct, then Japan would require a thorough social upheaval to purge the old order. Edwin Reischauer would adopt the latter view, but it was by no means the conventional wisdom of his time.

Another influential voice was that of Eliot Janeway, an economist, journalist, author, and advisor to the Roosevelt administration. Deeply sympathetic to China, Janeway warned against selling oil and scrap iron to Japan long before the Pearl Harbor attack:

> Japan is the one nation in the world whose aggression we fear. Japan is the unashamed attacker of the country [China] with whom we sympathize, whose magnificent defensive stand we admire heartily. In this attack have occurred atrocities—the bombing of universities, for example—which shock the world.
>
> American industry is selling Japan the goods which permit her to do this and to rear grandiose schemes for continuing to do this on a scale so huge that all Western Asia [*sic*] will be reduced to the level of the Japanese subjects in Korea.... The Japanese menace is made possible by American exports.[10]

Other influential advisors to President Roosevelt would soon take up Janeway's call to end sales of oil and scrap metal to Japan. In July 1939, the United States gave notice of its intention to abrogate the Commercial Treaty of 1911 with Japan, thereby permitting the embargo of U.S. exports to Japan. The embargo was finally imposed in the summer of 1941, following Japan's joining the Tripartite Pact with Germany and Italy in September 1940 and its invasion of the French colony of Northern Indochina (North Vietnam).

John Gunther, the indefatigable American journalist who roamed the world and wrote books purporting to tell the "inside" story of each nation he visited, traveled extensively in Asia in 1937–38 and published a long piece on the emperor of Japan in 1939. Gunther explained that most, but not all, Japanese revered their emperor: "The veneration, the indubitable awe, with which loyal and patriotic Japanese—which means a very considerable proportion indeed of the Japanese nation—hold the Emperor is a phenomenon unique in contemporary politics."

But after outlining the history of the Chrysanthemum throne and the life of Emperor Hirohito, Gunther added: "When you ask an intelligent, modern-minded Japanese, a research student in biology for instance, or a political journalist who went abroad to school, if he believes the Emperor of Japan to be divine, he will probably reply—if the door is shut—that he does not." This judgment echoed Robert Reischauer's in 1936.

Gunther concluded: "Japan is ruled, not 'by' the Emperor, but in the name of the Emperor. The Emperor is a man, as we have seen; he is a God, as we have seen; he is a symbol, as we have seen; he is an embodiment, a projection, of a conglomerate mass of theories and traditions and influences; but he is *not* a dictator. He is no Peter the Great, no Stalin, no Cromwell, no Mussolini."

Toward the end of his article, Gunther ventured to say that "it is not correct to assume that the Japanese army alone and exclusively, even now, influences the Emperor." Persuaded, perhaps, by the views of the American ambassador to Japan, Joseph C. Grew, he called Prince Saionji Kimmochi, the elder statesman (*genro*), a "profound liberal and democrat." He also listed Count Makino Nobuaki (the "Elihu Root of Japan") and Matsudaira Tsuneo, Imperial Household minister, as liberals, and Count Yuasa Kurahei, the Lord Keeper of the Privy Seal, as closer to the emperor than any man in Japan. This group, he suggested, could be expected to be more reasonable, more willing to negotiate, than the top army brass.[11] It was the existence of this group that led Grew and other Japan experts to cling to hope for peace in the tense days leading up to Pearl Harbor. To a large extent, Reischauer would ally himself with their views.

By April 1940, as Japan and the United States were hurtling toward their fateful confrontation, most opinion leaders were calling for tougher measures against Japan. Nathaniel Peffer in *Harper's Magazine* once again insisted on a complete embargo on U.S. exports to Japan and heavy duties on imports from Japan. Calling then current U.S. trade policies "absurd," he argued that Japan, weakened by its stalemate in China, would be deterred from further aggression by a series of escalating American threats. If necessary, America should take the lead in imposing a blockade of the Japanese islands to force the evacuation of Japanese troops from China.[12] Peffer's view was gaining traction in Washington.

Such was the climate of opinion in America when Reischauer was invited to join the Division of Far Eastern Affairs of the U.S. State Department in the summer of 1941. At this juncture, a small handful of diplomats and academic experts worked desperately to head off war. Japan was bogged down in China, but unwilling to retreat. "That I, a fledgling scholar of early Chinese and Japanese history, should be asked for by the State Department showed how scarce American experts on Japan were at the time," he would recall.[13]

Reischauer found himself, at thirty-one, the youngest and lowliest of the fifteen officers in the Division of Far Eastern Affairs. His first, rather menial task was to send a weekly report to Ambassador Grew summarizing American press opinions on Japan. Because the division head, Maxwell M. Hamilton, was in poor health, real power over U.S. policy in East Asia was then exercised by Stanley K. Hornbeck, a former Wisconsin and Harvard professor who was special assistant to Secretary of State Cordell Hull. Hornbeck's assistant was Alger Hiss, who would in 1948 be charged with being a spy for the Soviet Union and convicted of perjury in 1950 in connection with that charge. Hornbeck was well known for his pro-China, anti-Japanese views, and Reischauer thought he had a "prickly personality, apparently quite sure that he alone could steer American relations with Japan and China. I remember being thoroughly irritated when he called me in to criticize the style of my press reports to Grew. Perhaps this was because of his undisguised bias against Japan, or perhaps because he felt that the young instructor from Harvard needed to be put in his place."[14]

Undaunted, Reischauer immediately began to assert his views about Japan policy with extraordinary self-confidence, even though they ran counter to the overwhelming tide of popular and elite opinion. The critical issue was whether the United States should cut off oil and scrap iron to Japan. The Far Eastern Division was about equally divided on the question. Reischauer boldly argued against an embargo on the grounds that such a move would precipitate a violent reaction in Tokyo and would lead to a war for which the United States was not yet prepared.

We know now that Reischauer got this exactly right: the Japanese military leaders understood that a U.S. embargo would leave them with only about a two-year supply of oil. Unless they could conquer the Dutch East Indies (Indonesia) and gain access to its rich oil supplies, Japan would be forced to withdraw from China and to accept a humiliating loss of its great-power status. To ensure success, they would have to cripple American and British naval power in the Western Pacific by launching a surprise attack on Pearl Harbor and by capturing or disabling the British naval base at Singapore. The United States was unprepared for such an attack.

How could Edwin Reischauer have arrived at this position when most American policymakers thought the embargo would head off war and bring Japan to the bargaining table?[15] There are two possible answers. First, he probably understood from living in Japan the psychology of Japan's military leaders: humiliating them, causing loss of "face," could well lead to an explosive response. They were more likely to strike back against their enemies than to risk the loss of all they had gained since 1931. This judgment would be an intuitive one based on his understanding of Japanese history and the code of its warriors. Second, Reischauer was convinced that there existed a peaceful element within the ruling circles in Tokyo and that a direct appeal to this group with a reasonable negotiating position could prevent war. Here he doubtless assumed that some remnant of Japan's "Shidehara diplomacy," referring to a period in the mid-1920s when Japanese foreign minister Shidehara Kijuro tried to cooperate with the Western powers and took a conciliatory attitude toward China, might still prevail.

Reischauer's summer in Washington and first experience with the State Department transformed him from a quiet scholar of ancient China into an active, impassioned policy advocate. Before returning to Cambridge, he typed out an eighteen-page memo, mostly single-spaced, marked "Strictly Confidential" and submitted it to his superiors. The document, entitled "The Adoption of Positive and Comprehensive Peace Aims for the Pacific Area," was never published or even taken seriously, but it was an amazing departure from the conventional wisdom of the day.[16]

In essence, he asked how America could oppose twentieth-century Japanese imperialism while continuing to support nineteenth-century European and American imperialism. In effect, he was comparing the U.S. conquest of the Philippines, the British seizure of Hong Kong, Malay, and Singapore, the Dutch conquest of Indonesia, and the French conquest of Indochina with what Japan was doing in Korea and China. He wrote: "We have demanded that Japan abandon steps already made towards the fulfillment of its programs . . . but in return, what have we offered? Certainly nothing definite and constructive . . . in fact, nothing more than implications that Japan's *legitimate* claims and aspirations may be considered if and when Japan abandons her present program. Can we hope for any peaceful solution of the present Far Eastern situation until we have a comprehensive, concrete and fair alternative program?"

Notice Reischauer's use of the word *legitimate* with respect to Japan's claims and aspirations. There could not have been more than a handful of Americans in 1941 who viewed any of Japan's claims as "legitimate" or who believed that Japan should be treated as an equal with the Western powers. But here he wrote as an historian with a longer view and revealed his intense resentment of colonialism and racial inequality—an anger noted in chapter 1. "Are we prepared," he asked in perhaps his most eloquent statement, "to oppose and even to fight Twentieth Century imperialism while tolerating and actually maintaining the injustices of Nineteenth Century imperialism?"

Reischauer's confidential memo went on to insist that American peace aims should be proclaimed: equality of all peoples and nations in the Pacific area; complete sovereignty and territorial integrity for all nations; equal access for all to the products of the area (i.e., no exclusive economic spheres), and preparation of all the colonies for self-government and independence.[17]

Consider how revolutionary, and perhaps naive, this proposal was at a time when the U.S. government was doing its best to prop up the British, French, and

Dutch against the Germans. How could the United States call for the independence of these countries' colonies at this critical moment? The ideal of racial equality with the Japanese must have struck many Americans as preposterous: throughout their history, Americans had mindlessly conquered Native Americans and Mexicans and still tolerated Jim Crow discrimination against the African American descendants of slaves. How could they view Japan as an equal?

In the U.S. government, it is usually wrong to be right too soon. "My State Department colleagues, regarding what I had written with condescension, quickly pigeon-holed it," Reischauer recalled. "But in terms of the thinking of the time, I was light-years ahead of most other people. Who could envisage the disappearance of the British, French and Dutch empires?"[18] It happened within the next two decades.

To what extent a peaceful element actually existed within the ruling circles of Japan and whether it could have carried the day against the well-entrenched army generals remain a matter for speculation. But Reischauer was not alone in his belief in this outcome. Although Reischauer could not have known it, Ambassador Joseph Grew was in the summer of 1941 engaged in secret talks with Prime minister Konoe Fumimaro about a possible summit meeting between Konoe and Roosevelt either in Honolulu or Juneau, Alaska, aimed at heading off the war. Roosevelt trusted Grew, who had graduated two years ahead of him from the elite Groton boarding school in Massachusetts and from Harvard, and the idea allegedly captured his imagination. Konoe, a member of one of Japan's most noble families (*kuge*), claimed to have the secret backing of the emperor and key military advisors.

But as the secret plan moved forward, Stanley K. Hornbeck intervened. Any summit meeting would have to be preceded by a specific agreement by Japan to pull back from China, Indochina, and the Axis Pact and by consultations with the Chinese Nationalist government as well as the British and the French, he argued. Konoe, however, thought that this agreement would be fatal to his plan. If the summit meeting became known in advance, he would risk being assassinated by right-wing fanatics. But if he could conduct secret talks with Roosevelt and bring home a face-saving set of agreements, he might win over the emperor to his initiative, trump the war faction, and win a lasting peace with the United States.

Robert A. Fearey, Grew's private secretary in 1941, wrote fifty years later:

> Until the day he died, Ambassador Joseph C. Grew, who served in Japan from 1932–1941 and was the most experienced U.S. diplomat of that era,

> believed that Washington's handling of the U.S.-Japan negotiations preceding the Pearl Harbor attack was unimaginative and inflexible. Grew thought that Washington gave short shrift to the embassy's carefully considered reports, analyses and recommendations centering on Japanese Prime Minister Konoe's proposal that he and President Roosevelt meet face-to-face in Honolulu in a direct effort to achieve a settlement of all outstanding issues. If the meeting had been allowed to take place, he believed, the Pacific War might have been avoided.[19]

Hornbeck, ever mindful of China's interests, used an old State Department ploy against Grew: he was quoted as saying that "Grew had been in Japan too long, that he was more Japanese than the Japanese, and that all one had to do with the Japanese was to stand up to them and they would cave."[20] (Ironically, the charge of being too close to the Japanese would also be leveled against Reischauer forty-five years later.) Hornbeck's view prevailed with Secretary of State Cordell Hull and ultimately with President Roosevelt. The summit plan fell through, and the Konoe cabinet was replaced by that of General Tojo Hideki on October 18, 1941. On November 26, 1941, Hull presented Japan with a full restatement of the American position: withdrawal of Japanese forces from China and French Indochina, sole recognition of the Chiang Kai-shek government in Chungking (today's Chongqing), and abrogation of the Tripartite Pact with Germany and Italy. Tojo, already committed to the surprise attack against Pearl Harbor, chose to view this restatement as an ultimatum. Japan attacked Pearl Harbor eleven days later.

Grew would be repatriated from Japan in 1942 and would head up the small group of Japan experts in the State Department who supported retention of the emperor and a benign, liberal occupation. The group included Eugene Dooman, former deputy to Grew in Tokyo who was fluent in Japanese; Hugh Borton; and Robert Fearey. Even though Reischauer was a uniformed officer in Special Branch, he was able to meet unofficially with these State Department planners during the war and would come to associate himself with their views.[21]

Grew wrote in 1942 that "the Japanese people have strong traces of zealotry and fanaticism in their individual and national thinking, but they did not yield to their present totalitarianism without reluctance. They were seduced by their rulers—particularly by the military chauvinists—over a period of many years. It is terrible to consider the corruption of a people by its own leaders, its own government." This line of thinking led him and other Japan specialists to the position that once the militarists had been defeated and disbanded, the "good Japanese" would return to their former ways: "The Japanese people have great cultural assets with which they could continue to contribute to the happiness and civilization of mankind. But they have—particularly in recent years—been led along a road of militarism and overweening extremist ambition which have directed Japanese civilization into a blind alley of potential ruin. We and our allies of the United Nations can free those people of Japan who yearn in secret merely to be allowed to pursue their normal beauty loving lives in peace, in their own homes, and in their own cultural surroundings."[22]

But Grew's views, largely shared by Reischauer, were strongly opposed by Stanley K. Hornbeck. The "Japan hands" viewed Hornbeck as a curmudgeon and an anti-Japanese bigot, but his views on postsurrender Japan carried weight with Secretary of State Cordell Hull." Hull, a native of Tennessee, held typically southern attitudes on racial matters and was inclined to be anti-Japanese. Hornbeck and the "China hands" argued for a punitive occupation of Japan and an end to the reign of the imperial family. By 1944, however, Grew and Dooman appeared to have the upper hand in planning for Japan's occupation: it should be benign and short, and the institution of the emperor should be retained. The battle over "unconditional surrender" and the future role for the emperor had begun in earnest.

Back at Harvard in September 1941, Reischauer began to go public with his views on policy. In an October 28, 1941, column headlined "Ideal Answer Is Not War," in the *Washington Post*, he warned, after rejecting any idea of selling out China, that war with Japan would not be easy: "fighting Japan in her own waters, where she would have the support of land defenses and planes and where she might stall for many months, avoiding any major battle," would make no sense. He also disparaged the idea that Japan's military clique should be discredited. "Given Far Eastern psychology, military defeat would be a disgrace, always remembered, always demanding revenge." Instead, the U.S. should "offer the Japanese some fair alternative while condemning their present expansionist policy." He proposed that the United States offer them a

> just economic order in which Japan can live prosperously. This means applying the Atlantic Charter to the Pacific, opening up the resources of Southeast Asia and the Americas to Japanese trade. . . . It is my belief that Japan would respond to this combination of pressure and a positive offer. The central block of her rulers is more hard-headed, more realistic than is often thought. The group about the Emperor, the top admirals, and many generals are not hostile to compromise. It is not the fire-eating few who

> are dominant. If we keep increasing our military power, the day may well come when the Japanese Government will be ready to accept our offer.[23]

Such a course was never tried and probably would not have worked, given what we know today. Forty days later, Pearl Harbor was attacked, and Reischauer's world changed forever. Fortunately for the family, his parents and his sister, Felicia, were now living in the Los Angeles area. A year earlier, A. K. Reischauer had suffered from a serious ulcer condition and had returned to the United States in February 1941 for an emergency operation. He and his wife were in the United States at the time of Pearl Harbor and thus escaped the fate of so many Americans who were trapped in Japan and only later repatriated. The family later moved to New Jersey and spent the duration of the war there.

Reischauer began at this point to involve himself seriously in public-policy debates, using his special knowledge of Japanese history and culture. Twelve days after the surprise attack, the young scholar warned the American people against overconfidence. "I recognized as race prejudice the popular belief that Japanese were mere imitators who might be able to defeat other Orientals like the Chinese but would not stand up to Western armies," he wrote later.[24] In an article cosigned with a newsman named J. C. Goodbody, he warned: "A tremendous struggle lies ahead of us in the Pacific. The Japanese are a virile, intelligent people of some 70 millions. Their land is relatively poor, the standard of living low, and the natural resources of the Japanese are limited in comparison with those we possess. But the Japanese on their side have strategic advantages in shorter lines of communications; they have a strong military tradition; and above all the Japanese people possess a high degree of self-discipline and group discipline which gives them great powers of endurance."

The article goes on to explain the exalted role of the military throughout Japanese history, the role of discipline in Japanese life, and the importance of self-sacrifice in the Japanese ethical system. Most significantly, the article calls for a "sane attitude" toward the Japanese people: "We are at war with the Japanese Government and its militaristic leadership. We must never forget that there is an extremely strong pro-American sentiment in some sectors of Japanese opinion—even if for many years there has been little pro-Japanese sentiment in the United States. There is no need for a cultural, emotional or intellectual program. When the day comes to discuss peace, American public opinion during the war may be a very important factor."[25]

Another of Reischauer's concerns was the treatment of Americans of Japanese ancestry. He could foresee the prospect of a cruel roundup and internment of the West Coast Japanese population, and he knew how unjust it would be. Calling them patriotic Americans, he insisted that "every community must treat them with respect—in fact with more sympathy and understanding than ever before."[26] This warning, of course, went unheeded, and a shamefully cruel internment policy placed a dark blot on U.S. history as more than 120,000 loyal Japanese Americans were hauled off to concentration camps far from their homes and farms on the West Coast of America. A federal commission concluded in 1983 that the mass incarceration of persons of Japanese ancestry without due process of law was not justified by military necessity: its true causes were "race prejudice, war hysteria, and a failure of political leadership."[27] The U.S. Congress in 1988 passed and President Reagan signed the Civil Liberties Act, providing for an indemnity of twenty thousand dollars to each of the surviving Japanese who were uprooted from their homes on the West Coast and thrown into concentration camps.

Reischauer also argued in 1942 that Japanese Americans should be allowed to prove their loyalty to the United States by forming units in the U.S. military. "This would help play down the racial overtones of the war and prove that we were not intent on fighting the Japanese people but only their military masters."[28] This insight was prophetic; the 442d Infantry Regimental Combat Team, composed mostly of Japanese Americans whose families were incarcerated, became the most highly decorated unit in U.S. military history, noted for its heroism in Italy, France, Germany, and northern Africa.

In addition, Reischauer wrote two policy memos in December 1942 that offered advice on psychological warfare and surrender propaganda. "I urged that surrender propaganda be limited to situations in which the Japanese soldiers faced certain destruction, that it should be aimed solely at the commanding officers; and that, instead of emphasizing self-preservation, it should stress the saving of the lives of the soldiers under their command for the postwar service to their country."[29]

This advice reveals Reischauer's belief in the selflessness and patriotism of Japan's officer corps and in the well-disciplined obedience of their troops. An appeal to their instinct for self-preservation would fall flat, he felt. It would be more effective to urge them to act on their deeper love of country and concern for its future welfare. He once again assumed, contrary to prevailing opinion, that there existed "a few hundred intelligent and well-informed leaders in Japan" to whom radio propaganda should be addressed. Give them "reliable war news, full texts of official documents, and serious cultural features," he argued, so that they "would be influenced by rational arguments about the impossibility of Japanese victory and reasonable proposals for a postwar world order."[30] At a time when official American propaganda was portraying Japan as a nation of fanatic militarists, this faith in the rationality and common sense of at least some Japanese leaders ran against the tide.

Reischauer's assertion that there existed in Japan a strongly pro-American element swam against the tide of accepted opinion. Most foreign observers at the time wrote of a nation in triumphant lockstep with its leaders. Even the great British historian of Japanese culture, Sir George Sansom, thought that the militarists had substantial support from the Japanese people:

> To suppose that a military clique has ruthlessly overruled a substantial civilian opposition to its domestic and foreign policies is to misunderstand the political development of Japan. In all government departments . . . there was, for some years before the Manchurian affair of 1931 and increasingly thereafter, an influential body of officials, especially in the middle and junior ranks, who were thoroughly imbued with totalitarian thought. Behind them was a numerous class of salaried workers and small property owners from whom they largely sprang; and to many of these a belligerent national-socialist regime seemed to offer peace and profit.[31]

Reischauer worried throughout the Pacific War that harsh American propaganda would embitter the American people against the Japanese people for decades to come and lead to a vindictive occupation. Indeed, the propaganda film *Know Your Enemy—Japan*, produced by Frank Capra in 1945 for the U.S. War Department, was a masterpiece of propaganda and blatant racism, appealing to all the English-speaking world's dominant clichés about the Japanese enemy, as John Dower has eloquently pointed out in *War Without Mercy*. The film reinforces "the impression of a people devoid of individual identity. The narrative referred to 'an obedient mass with but a single mind.'" Capra's portrayal of

> the collective will which moved the Japanese was shown to be fantastic and fanatic—riddled with the ghosts of history and dead ancestors, taut with emotional tensions, and fired by blind and relentless nationalistic ambitions. Writ small, the Japanese soldier epitomized this. Trained from birth to fight and die for his country, he was a disciplined, proud and able fighter on the battlefield—and also given to "mad dog" orgies of brutality and atrocity. Writ large, nothing better illustrated the insanity of the collective Japanese mind than the current war, for Japan's single, unified ambition was described, as in the earlier Army films as being nothing less than to rule the world.[32]

By 1945, leading voices in Washington, including Secretary of State James Byrnes, Undersecretary Dean Acheson, and Secretary of the Treasury Henry Morgenthau were outspoken advocates of a punitive policy toward a defeated Japan. The villain in this scenario would be Emperor Hirohito, who would be treated as the equivalent of Hitler or Mussolini. From 1942 on, Reischauer worked tirelessly to educate American policymakers about the nature of the emperor system in Japan. In a memo dated September 14, 1942, to U.S. State Department planners, he wrote:

> That the Emperor is not responsible, all the [Japanese] people know full well, and to repudiate him would be no more satisfactory than to blame the flag. Actual leadership in Japan tends to remain anonymous, there is no party to be blamed, and there are few, if any, prominent individuals who could serve as scapegoats. The Army would be the only institution which could be singled out as the false leader and evil genius, but almost the whole nation is now identified with the army in one way or another, and with their long tradition of respect for the military man, the Japanese would derive no satisfaction from attacking their army. In fact, military defeat might well serve to strengthen rather than to overthrow military dictatorship in Japan.

Suggesting a carefully planned strategy to win the cooperation of the Japanese people, he argued that "Japan itself has created the best possible puppet for our purposes, a puppet who not only could be won over to our side, but who would carry with him a tremendous weight of authority. . . . I mean, of course, the Japanese Emperor. . . . There is good reason to judge from his education and from the associates he has had for the greater part of his life that, as things are measured in Japan, he is a liberal and a man of peace at heart."[33]

Leftist critics in Japan later attacked Reischauer for his use of the phrase *puppet regime* when Americans were supposed to be fostering democracy in a new nation-state. But they missed the point that Reischauer, as a skilled communicator, was writing not as a scholar, but rather in a style designed to persuade bureaucrats and policymakers in Washington. His true feelings about the emperor are better revealed in a subsequent private letter to his family in January 1945. Adrienne's parents, the Dantons, who had lived in China for several years, apparently let Reischauer know that they disagreed with a policy of leniency toward the emperor. In his impassioned (handwritten) reply, he lamented: "I still feel much distressed about the family (Danton) view not because of them individually but because it is the decidedly prevalent view of most reasonably well informed people, particularly those with some knowledge of the Far East." Citing the contrary views of experts he respected, including his parents, Sir George Sansom, Burton Fahs, Hugh Borton, John Embree, and his old mentor, Serge Elisseeff, he wrote that "the people who really know Japan best are pretty well united in their hands off the Emperor attitude."

> The chief reason is that insofar as the Emperor is godlike he *cannot* be dethroned, whatever we may wish to do about it. The person of the Emperor is not important. The concept is the important thing. Our dethroning of an actual Emperor would make the Japanese cherish the concept of the Imperial throne all the more. And the concept is very much harder to attack than the person. In fact, a rash move like that would saddle the Japanese possibly for centuries with all the evils of the Imperial throne. All Japanese would be for it if they thought an outsider was trying to take it away. The only way in which the evils of the Imperial throne can be abolished in Japan is by debunking and not by dethroning, and debunking becomes impossible when the Emperor is martyrized.

In a passage sure to create controversy later on, Reischauer concluded that "in the past two decades it was the throne (more in the persons of the advisors rather than in the person of the Emperor himself) which has been the chief opposition to militarism. Are we to take the institution which in the past has acted as the best check to rampant militarism in Japan, and attempt to abolish it?" Clearly, in Reischauer's mind, the emperor was no puppet.

At the end of his letter, Reischauer added, "Actually I have some hopes that the Emperor (who from all we know is probably as much of a liberal as is to be found anywhere in high places in Japan) will repudiate the actions of the military in bringing about this war, and thus start Japan on the road to a fairly rapid rehabilitation. . . . I certainly see no other institution or person who will emerge in even a matter of decades to lead Japan back to a respectable position in the family of nations, and if she does not come back there soon we shall be saddled with a long time job of running the country or at least controlling it closely."[34]

With hindsight, it is easy enough to recognize the wisdom of Reischauer's advice, particularly in light of the bungled U.S. occupation of Iraq beginning in 2003. This view of the emperor as a force for peace became crystal clear on August 30, 1945, when General MacArthur landed peacefully at Atsugi without a shot being fired, and the entire nation followed the emperor's injunction of August 15, 1945, to surrender, "enduring the unendurable and suffering what is insufferable."

The war brought new and drastic challenges to Reischauer's life. After working frantically with Elisseeff to prepare a Japanese-English dictionary of scientific terms, he found himself in February 1942 teaching Japanese to a Harvard class of about one hundred students—up from the five or ten who had enrolled the previous year. In the summer of 1942, the U.S. Army Signal Corps asked him to set up a school in Washington for the training of translators and cryptanalysts for work on Japanese coded messages. His growing family of four moved to a small home in Arlington, Virginia.

The work was highly classified, and Reischauer was subjected to an intense security investigation, which took considerable time. "I began to think I had failed the test," he recalled, "because I had told my first questioner that all Japanese were by no means evil and militaristic, and that many were fine, honest, peace-loving people."[35]

His clearance eventually came through, and he settled into his new job in Arlington Hall, a former girls' school, where the Signal Corps conducted its decoding activities. Security was tight: the building was surrounded by three circles of barbed-wire fencing, and those who worked inside were sworn to lifetime secrecy. Reischauer's own account of this period contains about as much information as we are likely to get about his classified work, and I need not repeat it.[36] His service consisted of two phases: the first was as a civilian instructor of Japanese language to train the men who would translate intercepted Japanese messages, and the second as a uniformed major and then lieutenant colonel in Special Branch, where intelligence experts tried to make sense out of the massive volume of intercepted messages in a program code-named "MAGIC."

What is interesting about his own account of this period is his single-minded dedication to winning the war for America in spite of his love for the Japanese people. If he had the slightest qualm about helping to send Japanese merchant ships and their crews to death, he never revealed it.

> The war might have raised questions for me as to where my true loyalties lay. I had been born and raised in Japan, which had been my home for more than half of my life. I respected and liked the Japanese as individuals as well as much about their culture and country. But I had always felt myself to be one hundred percent American and had no doubt in my mind that Japan was basically in the wrong in the war. Within Japan I deplored the military rule that had blotted out the promising start made toward democracy and led to ruthless aggression abroad. Despite the validity of Japan's condemnation of Western imperialism in Asia and the unjustified racist treatment of Japanese in America, Japan's acts of aggression in China

> and now Hawaii could in no way be justified. The Japanese war machine, I felt, had to be stopped for the sake of world peace and in the long run for the Japanese themselves. I took all this so much for granted that I do not remember even needing to ponder over it.[37]

Reischauer spent about a year setting up the new school, drawing on the Japanese-language talents of two former Seventh Day Adventist missionaries to Japan and the son of a missionary. He recruited about fifty to sixty students from his classes at Harvard, as well as others from Columbia and Yale. They served as enlisted men in U.S. Army uniforms for the first two years of the war, but were promoted to second lieutenants in 1944. Among his Harvard students, Howard Hibbett would go on to become a brilliant professor of Japanese literature at Harvard, and Benjamin Schwartz would also become an immensely popular scholar of Chinese thought at Harvard.

Howard Hibbett remembers Reischauer as a demanding teacher in his seminar of eight students. Their task was to learn to read intercepted Japanese diplomatic cables from *romaji* texts. Once the students mastered enough relevant vocabulary, they would work in a large room handling incoming messages twenty-four hours a day in 3 eight-hour shifts. They got off on Wednesday afternoons and often played softball (Reischauer was an enthusiastic participant) or swam at the Wardman Park Hotel pool in Washington. They used code names rather than real names for each other. Reischauer's was "Ree-us." Ben Schwartz used to sing the Japanese army song, "Gunka, Sen'yuu" (Comrade in Arms),and once created a large wall poster in *kanji* that read "Dai Towa Kyoei Ken." (which means "Greater East Asia Co-prosperity Sphere," the creation of which was Japan's alleged reason for going to war).[38]

The school Reischauer set up in Arlington Hall and the subsequent code-breaking operation, MAGIC, drew on an extraordinary group of men who would go on to stunningly successful careers. Among them were John Paul Stevens, who at this writing is an associate justice of the U.S. Supreme Court; Burke Marshall who would become assistant attorney general in the Kennedy administration and a champion of the civil rights movement; Bayless Manning, who would become dean of the Stanford University Law School and later president of the Council on Foreign Relations in New York; Sumner Redstone, who would become the billionaire head of Viacom, a major communications firm; and Henry F. Graff, who was to become a distinguished professor of history at Columbia University.

Sumner Redstone had been one of Reischauer's Japanese-language students at Harvard. He had earlier taken twelve years of Greek and ten years of Latin and was clearly adept at languages. "Professor Reischauer motivated and prodded us to great heights," he would later recall.[39] Reischauer obviously recognized Redstone's talents and summoned him to Arlington Hall. Redstone claimed that after studying at Arlington Hall, "I knew more *kanji* (Chinese characters) than the average Japanese." He recalled Reischauer as "young and aggressive but compassionate. He was always interested in our personal problems. He was extremely self-assured, and never showed the slightest softness toward the Japanese, despite his upbringing in Japan. In fact, he was incensed by their attack on Pearl Harbor."[40]

Henry Graff recalled Reischauer as a young, rather nervous instructor who jiggled the keys in his pocket while he lectured. But he was a "great man, with a remarkable wealth of information about Japan. There was a grace about him, especially in the stylish way he wore his uniform. He knew the best restaurant on the Ginza and taught us much about the Japanese people. Some element in what he was doing was to make up for the death of his brother, I thought."[41]

Reischauer took pride in training several hundred future officers. "I am proud to say that, so far as I know, none of them ever showed any special animosity toward Japan and most became more sympathetic and understanding because of their extensive study of the country."[42]

In August 1943, he was commissioned as a major in the intelligence section of the army's general staff and assigned to the top secret group called Special Branch—the unit in charge of analyzing all intelligence derived from intercepted messages. This unit produced MAGIC—the critical intelligence that went straight to the president and his top advisors. Reischauer served as liaison between Special Branch and his former Japanese-language school at Arlington Hall. In December 1944, he was promoted to lieutenant colonel. Wearing the uniform and working closely with high-ranking army officers—understanding their mindset—would prove to be valuable experiences when he became ambassador in 1961.

Henry Graff recalled a time in 1945 when some of his fellow cryptanalysts started mentioning plutonium and referred to a secret project to develop a new and deadly weapon in Alamogordo, New Mexico. Graff recalled bringing up the subject with Reischauer, who told him, "I don't want to hear another word about this."[43] Reischauer's published memoir contains no mention of this conversation, but in the unpublished manuscript version of the memoir he recalled that "although [the atomic bombs] remained a well kept secret, one of my young officers at Arlington Hall, by pretending to know more than he did, had gotten wind of the so-called Manhattan Project. He used to bother me by bringing in evidence, such as the ban on publicity about certain to me unknown elements, such as uranium, to prove that an atom bomb was in fact being built. I would brush him off, being much too busy for such nonsense, but one morning I was called into the Central office of Special Branch together with about five other officers, and told about the dropping of the bomb on Hiroshima."[44]

Reischauer was at first dismayed by this horrific turn of events. From his reading of intercepted Japanese messages, he believed that Japan would surrender in about three months, probably in November 1945. But his reading of subsequent research made him less certain about this outcome:

> The various alternative proposals for demonstrating the capacities of the bomb without using it on a populated target would probably have been ineffective. Even with the two atom bombs dropped on Hiroshima and Nagasaki and the invasion of Manchuria by the Soviet Union, which was launched between the two bombings, it was touch and go whether the Japanese military would permit the civilian government to surrender. Without the dropping of the bomb, the military would probably have insisted on fighting on, leading to hundreds of thousands of American casualties, the death by starvation if not in the fighting of many millions of Japanese civilians, and the virtual destruction of the Japanese nation. . . . [T]he Soviet Union would probably have occupied the whole of Korea and possibly part or all of Japan, creating an entirely communized Korea and a Japan resembling either a Soviet-dominated Poland or a divided Germany.

He added, "I also wonder whether people generally would have come to realize the horrible potentialities of nuclear weapons if one had never been used in war."[45]

But he drew a firm distinction between the bombing of Hiroshima (August 6) and the bombing of Nagasaki. "If there was some possible justification for the first atomic bomb, however, there was none for the second, dropped on Nagasaki on August 9," he wrote. "The top American authorities did agonize over the decision to use the first bomb but seem to have given the second little if any thought, snuffing out some 70,000 lives almost inadvertently."[46]

Some accounts of this period credited Reischauer with sparing the ancient capital of Kyoto from conventional or nuclear bombing or both by the U.S. Air Force. Others credited Langdon Warner. Reischauer was careful to put these rumors to rest. Drawing on a lifetime of research by Professor Otis Cary of Doshisha University in Kyoto, he confirmed that credit for sparing Kyoto in 1945 must go to Henry L. Stimson, secretary of war at the time. Cary discovered that

Stimson had enjoyed a honeymoon in that city in 1925 and could not tolerate the thought of its destruction.

Several opportunities to go to Japan were offered to Reischauer at the end of the war. He was invited to join a Strategic Bomb Survey to assess the results of the U.S. bombing attacks against Japan. But the arrival of his third child, Joan, on June 9, 1944, made him reluctant to leave his young family. He was offered a position in the Counter Intelligence Corps, but he felt that the corps was no more than a high-level police force, and because he planned to spend the rest of his life as a student of Japan, he did not want to be branded as a "police spy." There was also an opening on the staff of the political advisor to General MacArthur and later as chief historian of the occupation, but he turned down both jobs. MacArthur, he thought, was "too egotistical to tolerate a reasonably balanced account."[47]

The real action on Japan policy was taking place at the State Department. Joseph Grew and the "Japan hands" retired at the end of the war, and the Division of Far Eastern Affairs was taken over by John Carter Vincent, a pro-China career officer. Reischauer became his deputy in November 1945 and at last had a direct hand in the policymaking process. At this point, Reischauer and Hugh Borton were the only two Japan specialists left in the Sub-Committee for the Far East of the State-War-Navy Coordinating Committee (SWNCC). A crucial question at this point was whether to try the emperor as a war criminal, force him to abdicate, or use him to further the occupation goals of democratization and demilitarization. The press and public clamored for revenge for Japan's unprovoked sneak attack against Pearl Harbor; the emperor was a perfect scapegoat.

The public mood in America in 1945 was hell bent on revenge and almost totally ignorant of the realities in Japan. Respected columnist Marquis Childs wrote on August 17, 1945: "It is psychologically almost impossible for the Japanese people to face the fact of defeat. . . . The few Westerners with a little knowledge of Japan . . . do not see how any Japanese could have approached the Son of Heaven to tell him the nation was defeated and he would henceforth have to carry out orders given by an American commander. That is contrary to everything in the Jap character."[48] *Time* magazine added: "Docile Japs? Would the regimented, superstitious, uninformed Japanese docilely obey their Emperor? Washington experts were divided: most of those who knew Japan in the comfortable 20's thought that they would. Some even said that the Japanese were not a warlike people. Those who had met the Japanese in battle differed."[49]

A measure of the public hostility to the Japanese people can be seen in the plea for them by a gentle former missionary to Japan, Willis Church Lamott, who was moved to write: "We cannot exterminate the Japanese people. . . . We shall have to live with them as fellow members of the human race for some time to come." Then, in an extraordinary passage, he mentioned the kind of images of the Japanese people that wartime propaganda had created in America: "In the first place, we should remind ourselves that there is nothing in their blood that makes the Japanese a warlike, cruel, cunning, unreliable, crafty and generally loathsome people. We will never get anywhere in dealing with them until we stop thinking of them as being, racially, subhuman devils, monkeys without tails, or something slimy that crawled from under a rock."[50]

President Roosevelt had announced the policy of unconditional surrender at his meeting with Prime Minister Winston Churchill at Casablanca in January 1943. As the war ground to a halt in July 1945, Japan was desperately seeking a way to end it, and Grew and the Japan hands urged President Roosevelt to modify the demand for unconditional surrender and to declare publicly that the emperor would be retained after surrender as a means of strengthening the peace faction in Tokyo. Instead, the Potsdam Declaration of July 26, 1945, was vague on this point, stating only that the emperor's future would be decided according to the will of the Japanese people. This ambiguity, of course, only strengthened the pro-war army generals who wanted to keep fighting to the bitter end. The Japanese government ignored the Potsdam Declaration with a policy of *mokusatsu* (killing by silence or ignoring), and with the atomic bombings of Hiroshima and Nagasaki, the entrance of Soviet Union into the Pacific War ensued, leading to Japan's surrender on August 15, 1945. Japan accepted the terms of the Potsdam Declaration with the understanding that the imperial institution would be saved. But President Harry S. Truman, in his statement to the press on August 15, 1945, declared unequivocally that Japan's surrender was "unconditional." So the future of the emperor and the throne was still up for grabs.

Borton and Reischauer were able to convince John Carter Vincent that the emperor should be retained, but the War and Navy Department members of the Sub-committee for the Far East argued that the emperor should be tried and punished as a war criminal. On September 25, the U.S. Congress debated a resolution (never acted upon), declaring it to be "the policy of the United States that Emperor Hirohito be tried as a war criminal."[51] Dean Acheson, now undersecretary of state, agreed. On January 21, 1946, the Australian government proposed to the War Crimes Commission in London that Hirohito and sixty-one other Japanese leaders be charged as war criminals. Far harsher measures were also in the air: Captain Harry L. Pence, a naval officer, advocated "the almost total elimination of the Japanese as a race."[52]

The debate in Washington finally reached a deadlock, and, in a document dated November 30, General MacArthur, as supreme commander of Allied Forces in Japan, was empowered to make the final decision. MacArthur decided to retain the emperor as a symbol of the unity of the Japanese people based on three factors: first, the arguments put forward by the Grew-Borton-Reischauer position; second, the success of imperial palace insiders' attempts to present the emperor as a pacifist who was willing to cooperate; and third, MacArthur's quixotic personal goal of advancing Christianity in Japan with the emperor's help.[53] This outcome was Reischauer's first concrete input into shaping policy toward Japan, and he loved it.

Reischauer also helped draft a plan in 1946 for the disposition of the Ryukyu and Kuril Islands. He thought Soviet-occupied Habomai and Shikotan should be returned to Japan, but the Russians were in no mood to give up anything. They had earlier aspired even to occupy Hokkaido. The Russians continue to hold these islands, a fact that has blocked the full resumption of peaceful diplomatic relations between Japan and Russia to this day. Reischauer's efforts to implement a four-power, five-year trusteeship for Korea similarly failed when a vast majority of Koreans protested against the delay in independence. "It is ironic that the United States, though it expended great efforts in preparing for the future of its enemy, Japan, made virtually no preparations for the future of a friendly Korea it was liberating from thirty-five years of Japanese rule," he later commented.[54]

It is easy to push out of sight what could have happened to Japan if the Russians had entered the war a few weeks earlier, occupied Hokkaido, and behaved as they did in East Germany. Occupations have been cruel affairs throughout history: rape, torture, revenge, death from hunger and disease, homelessness, disappearance forever of millions of losing troops are the rule, not the exception.[55] The occupation of Japan stands today as an extraordinarily successful case of a military imposition of constitutional democracy on a conquered nation.[56]

By 1946, after almost a year in the State Department, Edwin Reischauer felt a different ambition gnawing at him: the dream of educating the American people about Japan and East Asia through writing basic texts, training a new generation of Harvard students and scholars, and voicing his views about policy in the media and in a variety of public forums. His first step had been taken: *Japan: Past and Present* was published by Knopf in 1946. As noted in chapter 1, this book presented the first comprehensive look in English at the Japanese people through their history, culture, and political system. But it went far beyond that, to challenge the ugly stereotypes of the Japanese people ("Japs") that had been ingrained in American minds since 1905 or even earlier. This project was bold, even revolutionary, but Reischauer now had the confidence and skill to undertake it. Harvard would be his platform for the next fifteen years, until President John F. Kennedy appointed him U.S. ambassador to Japan in 1961.

5

A Time of Large Ideas

The period following World War Two was a time of surging optimism in America, of high expectations and faith in the power of large ideas to reshape the world. U.S. military and industrial power had defeated the forces of aggression and had created the conditions for a better world order. The United Nations, launched in 1945, seemed full of promise. The stage was now set for triumphant American leaders to imagine and craft new and better ways to secure world peace and prosperity.

Ambitious and idealistic scholars took it upon themselves to understand and explain America's ascendancy and to forge programs that would foster the spread of freedom and block the rising power of the one remaining enemy: Soviet-style communism. There has probably never been a time before or since that "public intellectuals," as they came to be known, would have such an opportunity to affect policy, either by joining the government or through the force of their ideas or both. The zeitgeist was that social science could save the world and that enough of their fellow citizens would be rational enough to accept their nostrums. It was their good fortune that a young Harvard graduate named John F. Kennedy, who enjoyed the company of intellectuals, was preparing in 1958 to run for president.

The epicenter of this ferment lay along the banks of the Charles River in Cambridge, Massachusetts, on the campuses of Harvard University and the Massachusetts Institute of Technology (MIT). McGeorge Bundy, who in 1953 at the age of thirty-four had become the youngest ever dean of Harvard's Faculty of Arts and Sciences, was perhaps the most prominent figure in this new world. He combined impeccable establishment credentials (Groton Academy and Yale

University) with supreme intellectual confidence. He would become President Kennedy's national-security advisor in 1961, a position that enabled him to support Reischauer's appointment as ambassador to Japan.

"Bundy was a triumphantly successful dean," according to Geoffrey Kabaservice. "Professors later recalled that his 'natural assurance, crisp style, mastery of precise language, impatience with fools, and extensive curiosity allowed him to be both an imperious and an extremely popular member of the faculty; at faculty meetings, he was something of a tamer lionized by his dazzled lions.'"[1] Kingman Brewster, who taught at Harvard Law School from 1950 to 1960, was a member of Bundy's circle. He would become president of Yale University and later ambassador to the Court of Saint James. The two were leading members of what Kabaservice would call "the liberal establishment" that came to power in the 1960s.[2]

Bundy and Brewster were also members of the Friday Evening Club, a group that originated in a joint university-government collaboration beginning in 1950 when the State Department asked MIT to help overcome the Soviets' jamming of Voice of America broadcasts into Russia. This project brought together scientists, technicians, social scientists, philosophers, poets, and practitioners of international relations such as George F. Kennan, which in turn led to the creation of the Center for International Studies at MIT, supported by the Ford Foundation and the Central Intelligence Agency (CIA).

The Friday Evening Club, which Bundy called "a self-important little dining club," met for drinks and dinner on the first Friday of the month and included intellectuals who went on to achieve international prominence. Seven Harvard faculty (including an art historian, a psychologist, a physicist, a sociologist, and an historian) and four MIT faculty were founding members. The inventor of the Polaroid camera, Dr. Edwin Land, was also among this group, and Wassily Leontief, the Harvard economist, joined in the first year. No new members were admitted after that. Prominent speakers at their dinners included Walter Lippmann, Robert Oppenheimer, and Alfred Kazin. These dinners continued for fifteen years until the club broke up over the issue of Bundy's role in the Vietnam War.[3] These men doubtless saw themselves as "masters of their universe."[4]

When in 1958 John Kenneth Galbraith, a fifty-year-old liberal economist, published *The Affluent Society*,[5] it quickly became a best-seller. In it, he scolded America for ignoring the public sector, tolerating the poverty of its lower classes, and failing to invest in social capital. Galbraith was one of the first economists to note that more people died in America of too much food than of too little. The book became an instant bible for liberals and the Democratic Party, and came to the attention of John F. Kennedy, who appointed Galbraith ambassador to India in 1961.

Arthur M. Schlesinger Jr., the historian who had won a Pulitzer in 1946 for his brilliant book *The Age of Jackson*, was forty-one in 1958. Having written speeches for the campaigns of Adlai Stevenson in 1952 and 1956, and having helped found the liberal (anti-Communist) organization Americans for Democratic Action, he was now turning his attention to the incipient presidential campaign of John F. Kennedy. Like Bundy, he would go to Washington as a special assistant and speechwriter for President Kennedy.

"Cambridge in the 1950's was a wonderfully social place. Not to mention well lubricated. Galbraith and Schlesinger were both regulars at a Sunday evening cocktail hour at the home of Bernard DeVoto, a Mark Twain scholar. . . . He [DeVoto] worshipped martinis," a *Washington Post* article remembered in 2006.[6] The two scholars, Galbraith six feet eight inches and Schlesinger five feet eight inches tall, grew close to John F. Kennedy over regular lobster stew dinners at Locke-Ober restaurant in early 1960.

Richard Neustadt, a Harvard Ph.D. in 1951, was perhaps the most influential of the political scientists. His book *Presidential Power*, published in 1960, led to his appointment as an advisor to Presidents Kennedy and Johnson. He would later become a founder of the Kennedy School of Government at Harvard.

Among the other Harvard luminaries in 1958 was a young instructor named James H. Billington, who lectured to standing-room-only undergraduate classes on Russian history. He would go on to become librarian of Congress in 1987, perhaps the most prestigious position in government for any intellectual. Also lecturing on international relations at Harvard were Zbigniew Brzezinski, who would become national-security advisor to President Jimmy Carter; and Henry Kissinger, who would hold the same job for President Richard Nixon before becoming secretary of state. Hans Morgenthau, a professor at the University of Chicago, offered seminal lectures at Harvard Summer School on realpolitik theory and balance-of-power politics.

At MIT in 1958, Paul A. Samuelson, forty-three, was writing and rewriting the mainstream economics text that would inform the next several generations of college and graduate students. He was awarded the Nobel Prize for his work in 1970.

Also in 1958, Samuelson's colleague at MIT, a forty-two-year-old former Rhodes scholar named Walt Whitman Rostow was writing *The Stages of Economic Growth: A Non-Communist Manifesto*, which served as a guide for U.S. foreign-aid programs for the next decade. In the introduction to this book based on a series of lectures Rostow had given at Cambridge University in England, he explained that "I found Marx's solution to the problem of linking economic and non-economic behavior—and the solutions of others who had grappled with it—unsatisfactory, without then feeling prepared to offer an alternative."[7] He outlined in 167 pages what he viewed as the five stages of economic growth: traditional society, preconditions for take-off, the take-off, the drive to maturity, the age of high mass consumption, and beyond consumption. The trick was to identify which stage a nation was in and then to provide aid appropriate to its condition. Rostow would come to Washington as deputy special assistant to the president for national-security affairs, reporting to McGeorge Bundy in the administration of President John F. Kennedy in 1961.

With supreme self-confidence, this new generation of American scholars took positions of unaccustomed leadership. Many of them made lasting contributions to the intellectual capital of postwar America. In the case of Bundy and Rostow, however, their toxic combination of intellectual arrogance and profound ignorance of Asia led to the quagmire of Vietnam. As President Lyndon B. Johnson's top national-security advisor, Bundy thought the defense of South Vietnam was vital to preventing the spread of Communist Chinese influence and power throughout Southeast Asia. And he believed that American military power could prevail anywhere in the world. Secretary of State Dean Rusk shared this faith and subscribed to the "domino theory," which held that if the Communists prevailed in Vietnam, the other nations of Southeast Asia would soon follow. He also believed that Chinese Nationalist Regime of Chiang Kai-shek on Taiwan represented the future for China. Neither man had ever spent a night in an Asian village. Neither spoke an Asian language. Neither understood the power of nationalism in the former French colony. As a result, 58,209 young Americans tragically lost their lives, and 153,303 others were wounded. The victorious Communist North Vietnam would ironically later serve as a bulwark against the spread of Chinese influence in the region.

In this highly charged atmosphere, two young scholars, John K. Fairbank and Edwin O. Reischauer had a radically different but equally large idea. It involved humility rather than hubris. They set about instead to cure America's ignorance of East Asia by creating the new field of East Asian studies at Harvard. They were not members of the establishment, and they were not close to the group around John F. Kennedy. (Reischauer's rise to prominence in Washington would not come until the fall of 1960.) Their goal in this period of large ideas was to educate a wider American public and to have an impact on U.S. policy in East

Asia by enlarging America's consciousness of East Asian history and cultures. Instead of trying forcibly to remake the world in America's image, they sought to open American minds to the possibility of coexistence—even respect—for these ancient civilizations.

Their first task was to secure a place for East Asian studies in Harvard's curriculum. The need seems obvious enough today, but in 1947 Chinese history was lodged in the Department of Far Eastern Languages, and, like Latin, Chinese was still taught as a dead language. Graduates emerged who could speak no Chinese in its modern form. There was no course on Japan's modern history. No scholars claimed to know the language or culture of modern Japan and China. Arthur Waley, the great British orientalist who translated *The Tale of Genji* (1921–33), famously refused all opportunities to visit modern Japan.

To establish the field, Reischauer and Fairbank needed to create a comprehensive text on Japanese, Chinese, and Korean history. Nothing existed in the English language that would serve their purpose. Japan until then had been treated as an alien land, an exception to all known patterns of history. "Up until then we had only James Murdoch of an older generation, and George Sansom, whose approach to history was largely cultural," recalled Harvard historian Albert M. Craig. "Ed Reischauer created an historical framework. He included politics, economics, culture and religion, and showed how they all fit together. No one in the Japanese field had done anything quite like it."[8] Reischauer and Fairbank made no apology for approaching their topic through the study of history: "To approach [the East Asians] through their history is to look at them as they see themselves, which is the first requisite for understanding."[9]

They also announced their interest in reshaping U.S. foreign policy: "For Americans," they wrote, "the most important facts about East Asia are, first, its vast size, particularly in population; second, its growing power; and third, the cultural gap that lies between East and West." They pointed to the irony of recent U.S. military involvement in the region: "The wars we have fought in East Asia illustrate the rapidity of change and also the complexity of the problem we face," they wrote in 1958. "In World War II we fought Japan partly in defense of China; five years later in Korea we fought China partly to defend Japan. . . . [W]e must achieve between ourselves and the peoples of East Asia mutual respect, a willingness to cooperate, and a certain meeting of the minds."[10]

These ambitious goals were challenging enough in themselves, but they were made more difficult by events then unfolding in China. The nation was wracked by civil war—a war that Mao Zedong and his Communist Party won in 1949. This outcome produced in Washington the ugly period in which Senator Joseph McCarthy would ask "Who lost China?" and accuse America's top China experts of being Communists or sympathizers with communism. Fairbank, who had been openly critical of the losing Chinese Nationalist regime, was harassed. He testified before the McCarran Committee in 1952 in an effort to clear his name, but Reischauer noted that "the wounds lingered on. . . . John showed the effects of his ordeal for some years."[11]

Japan presented a different set of problems. Its history was a tabula rasa for Americans. Prewar histories written by Japanese scholars had focused on "official" versions, with the emperor at the center of all activity, and were now useless. Japanese historians who rushed in to fill the void after Japan's surrender were largely influenced by Marxist theory. A few brave Marxists in prewar Japan had stood up to the right-wing fanatics and militarists. Some had been jailed and were now seen as heroes. Others felt a sense of guilt because of their prewar silence or because they had actually converted (*tenko*) to the nationalist fever of the day. In the postwar period, influential professors and writers at leading universities and in literary circles found that Marxist theory provided an easy explanation of the causes of war: capitalism was to blame.

An additional hurdle for any historian of Japan in 1947 was formed by the caricatures of Japanese people that had hardened in many Americans' minds. Wartime propaganda had portrayed Japanese soldiers as subhuman fanatics and their culture as full of imported imitations from China and the West. In the brutal fighting for uninhabited islands in the Pacific War, 100,997 Americans had died, and 291,543 more were wounded.[12] Americans were scarcely prepared for a balanced view of the Japanese that would include an appreciation of their culture. Reischauer must have been keenly aware of the ugly stereotypes and of his readers' prejudices when he sat down to write a history of Japan.

The only book in 1947 approaching a general history of Japan in English was Reischauer's *Japan: Past and Present*, the short account he had dashed off in two months in 1945. This book became the seedling for all his subsequent writings on Japan. It was a start, but it needed amplification involving much further research. He plunged happily into this research; at last he was embarking on the project that had brought him to Harvard in 1931.

Reischauer's collaboration with John K. Fairbank had begun in 1939. From the start, it had involved both intellectual synergy and intense competition. Reischauer would recall being asked to teach a new course called "Chinese 10" in 1939. "The first year John Fairbank's name was added to mine as an instructor, perhaps to afford a backup in case I proved unequal to the assignment. I do not remember him taking much part, but from this time on we began to exchange guest lectures in each other's courses." He remembered that he had an amazing thirty-five students in his class in the spring of 1940. "This was a good showing, since Fairbank in his fourth year of teaching the more obviously relevant modern end of East Asian history was drawing no more than 75 students."[13] Already the rivalry had begun.

Starting in 1947, the two historians cobbled together a year-long course that came to be called "Social Science 111," quickly dubbed "Rice Paddies" by their students. They wrote the basic texts, *East Asia: The Great Tradition* (739 pages) and *East Asia: The Modern Transformation* (955 pages), that would transform the field of East Asian studies in America and the world.[14] For the second volume, Albert M. Craig, who had studied under Reischauer and was himself a pioneering scholar of the Meiji Period, joined them, filling in for Reischauer when the latter served as ambassador to Japan from 1961 to 1966.

In the years before these volumes were published, students were handed purple mimeograph drafts of the chapters that would go into the books. These mimeos became the "bible" on East Asian studies for several generations of students at Harvard and elsewhere. The official enrollment for the course in 1950 was 265 students, and 70 more audited. Attendance peaked at 520 at the height of the Vietnam War in the late 1960s. Students had to be turned away during this period due to a lack of teaching assistants to handle breakout sections of 12 to 17 students.

"In planning our contributions," Fairbank would recall, "listening to each other lecture and revising each other's manuscripts, [Edwin and I] tried to winnow out the gist of what *we thought the American public ought to know* for a perspective on East Asia. The fruitful miscegenation of social science and history in Area Study was of course already under way like a common law marriage, but we persisted in feeling that history is essentially a story, a narrative with analysis subordinate. Once started we both kept on writing the story of Japan and the story of China."[15]

The two professors developed dramatically different speaking styles that drew students from many departments, including upperclassmen who took the course as an elective. "There was the most electricity, the most energy, of any course I took at Harvard," one of their students recalled.[16] Fairbank had an elliptical speaking manner and a dry, caustic wit. In a lecture on Tibet, he would show a slide of a yak. "This is a yak," he would announce in a deadpan voice. Reischauer recalled that Fairbank "spoke somewhat slowly, with a great deal of dry humor and a somewhat ambiguous cynical tone, whereas I talked with machine-gun rapidity and much verve and earnestness."[17]

Michael J. Smitka, who became a Japan expert and professor of economics at Washington and Lee University, had no intention of specializing in Japanese studies until he took this course. "I was a freshman in the fall of 1971, Nixon was heading for China, so I thought I might as well learn something about Asia," he recalled. "Reischauer was full of energy, with spring-loaded knees so that he bounced to and from the podium whenever he emphasized a point. His enthusiasm was contagious. It changed my career."[18]

Orville Schell, the distinguished journalist and China scholar, recalls that he "stumbled into Rice Paddies as a sophomore at Harvard in 1959–60 quite by chance. I had never studied Asia at all. My sister was also at Harvard and we wanted to take one course together. This was the only one where our schedules meshed. It was like walking into an atomic reactor. The quality and density were tremendous. The course was vivid. Reischauer was very patrician, always in a suit and tie, and stood ramrod straight. He took titanic positions. It changed my life, and I enrolled in the intensive Chinese-language course at Stanford the following summer."[19]

By the late 1950s, Reischauer and Fairbank had become campus celebrities. Reischauer covered the period from the birth of Chinese civilization to the late T'ang (A.D. 618–907) and Sung (960–1279) dynasties up to 1279. Fairbank covered the Yuan, Ming, and Ch'ing dynasties, from 1279 to 1911. Reischauer also lectured and wrote on traditional Korea and Japan from its earliest days through the Tokugawa Era. Harvard had become, by the late 1950s, the American mecca for East Asian studies.

"I was an educational missionary," Reischauer admitted later. "I accept that and call myself that. For that matter, every person in our field who's a good teacher is almost automatically a missionary of that type. Even John Fairbank admits to being a missionary in that sense, because we have a feeling that Asia is something that must be studied. We must know more about this and we've been working for that all our lives."[20]

Fairbank agreed: "This urge to spread the word I can only attribute to a missionary impulse (I notice Ed Reischauer has it too), more rife in America than elsewhere. I suspect many people in older societies find it slightly crazy, wondering how we can be so energetic about it except as greed or a power drive or fanaticism moves us. Perhaps it is best understood as academic entrepreneurship, a pale reflection of the concurrent expansion of corporate capitalism."[21]

Students were struck by Reischauer's eloquence and wit as a lecturer. He was a natural speaker; his words seemed to flow in an elegant and effortless way, just as he wrote. A former student commented that "his brilliance was in making complex matters seem simple." Not only was Reischauer articulate, but he also combined energy and passion in a most attractive way. He understood, I think, that passion is the pith of eloquence. Audiences responded enthusiastically and learned from him.[22] "Studying Japanese history with him was a positive pleasure," recalled Albert M. Craig, one of his students in 1953 and a colleague beginning in 1959. "I remember his skill at fielding students' questions: he was immensely learned but could phrase a response in terms that even beginning students could easily grasp.... I recall his exceptional generosity with students.... He would sometimes complain: 'Why does so and so keep coming to see me?' The answer was that, despite his busy life, he gave them time and help and sympathy. They recognized in him a special quality of kindness."[23]

His kindness was not confined to the classroom. Craig remembered a time when a Japanese sailor was hospitalized in Boston, alone without friends or relatives. Reischauer went to visit him. Teruko Craig, Albert's wife, remembered a time when Reischauer was parked in his car outside the post office in Belmont when a woman with a child in her car bumped into him from the rear. Reischauer leaped out of his car and asked the woman if she and the child were all right.

"Reischauer was a private man," Craig recalled. "No one knew all aspects of him. But he was a completely straight arrow, totally trustworthy. If he said something, he meant it."[24] He disliked stuffed shirts and had a wicked sense of humor that he unveiled only to his family and closest friends. A glimpse of his personality can be seen in a letter from Kyoto to his parents in which he described the academic colleagues who were part of his five-man Cultural Science Mission to Japan in 1948:

> They range from 53–57 in age. Martin, the eldest, is a political scientist from the U of Washington—short, fat, and bald, but with quite an eye for the girls yet senatorial sounding in speech, able to make a simple thing seem complicated, shallow in thinking but jovial—a good stuffed shirt front man, with a semi-specialist's interest in and appreciation of Japan. Brady, next in age, is a tall, handsome English professor from Kentucky—essentially a comic actor in his love of tall speech and his sentimentality, but absolutely forthright and honest in his attitudes—not one inch of stuffed shirt to him, but he had the aesthete's love of spending time pleasantly down to the point where he probably gets little accomplished. Luther W. Stalnaker, professor of philosophy and Dean of Drake University, is small, baldish but benign looking. He is probably more of a living philosopher than a creative one. He exudes kindness and cheerfulness—is as wise and understanding as he looks—in fact is in all ways an admirable man, and what is more, a highly likable one at the same time.... [Glen]

> Trewartha, authority on Japanese geography and head of the geography department at Wisconsin, is smallish, white-haired and handsome. He is a hard driving scholar, always typing up his notes, utilizing every moment to amass factual data, obviously a man of the highest moral qualities, an ideal husband, father, citizen, but cut and dried in his attitudes, obstinate in his views, narrow in his interests (he did not enter the Horyuji when we finally got there, but wandered off to take pictures of Japanese agriculture), and all in all thoroughly disliked by the other three—a stuffed shirt, aesthete and philosopher, alike. . . . The fifth man of our group is tall, thin and homely—but we'll let it go at that.[25]

"Reischauer was a great popularizer and synthesizer," recalled John Curtis Perry, one of his students who went on to become a much admired professor at the Fletcher School of Law and Diplomacy. "He had the courage to be a generalist—that was his genius—and we won't see his like again, I'm afraid. His range of interests and erudition extended through all phases of Japanese civilization, and that was balanced by his profound knowledge of early China. He was awesome and we revered him, but we jokingly referred to him as 'Oomi,' from early Japanese history."

Reischauer's role as a teacher left its mark on many who would come to be leaders in the field. "His enthusiasm, his articulateness, his ability to express complex ideas in a simple and engaging fashion was marvelous," Perry reminisced. "He paid attention to precise expression. His army experience ensured that Reischauer would never become a conventional professor in a small parish. His parish was universal. He was not embarrassed to write for the *Readers Digest*, for example, to appeal to a large number of people. His colleagues at Harvard were very sniffy about that—feeling that it somehow compromised your professional dignity to do those things. But that's not how he saw his role, and that's why he was so important, because he did reach far beyond Harvard."[26]

"There was the extraordinary clarity of mind, the sharpness of intellect, and the vitality of presence," Marius Jansen remembered. "Then and later he took his work seriously, but not himself. In those postwar years he was carrying the work of several people; teaching language, lecturing in the survey course, working over drafts with graduate students, in a crowded and noisy office, and revising his materials on early Sino-Japanese relations for the wonderful study of Ennin's pilgrimage. . . . What distinguished Ed's conversation then and after was that it was so open, down to earth, and full of common sense. He abhorred pedantry and obscurity."[27]

Reischauer quickly developed a reputation as a caring, accessible teacher who, unlike many full professors, graded papers himself. Robert Scalapino recalled asking Reischauer to be on his Ph.D. thesis committee at Harvard in 1946. "I then came down with polio, entered a hospital for two months, and then recovered in bed at home for four months. Though I had never formally studied under Ed, I will never forget that he visited my home twice while I was sick. He was a remarkably nice man. I shall always be grateful."[28] Scalapino went on to become a leading American scholar of East Asia at the University of California in Berkeley.

Peter Grilli, who grew up in Tokyo and was a freshman at Harvard in 1959, remembered being lonely and far away from his parents on his first Thanksgiving away from home. Reischauer invited him to his home for dinner, noting that he too had felt lonely in his freshman year at Oberlin, away from home for the first time.[29]

Benjamin I. Schwartz, who studied Japanese language with Reischauer during World War Two and later became a faculty colleague at Harvard, viewed him as the "quintessential American liberal in the best sense of that term—full of an essential optimism and a resolute 'can do' spirit. At a time when there were suspicions that the Japanese language was an infernal, impenetrable mystery inaccessible to the Western mind, he convinced us that we could do whatever we had to do. At a time when the Japanese were thought of not only as the enemy but as the weirdly inaccessible Other, he convinced us that they could be understood in universal human terms. He never appealed to the exotic nature of his object of study."[30]

Cutting through a maze of detail to get to the heart of the matter was perhaps his most impressive skill. Albert Craig recalled that he, Donald H. Shively, and Reischauer offered a research seminar to six to twelve doctoral candidates in Japanese studies each year for twenty years, beginning in 1966. Each week a student would describe his research and present a draft chapter of his dissertation. Shively would focus on the scholarly organization of the paper: theoretical assumptions, references, bibliography, footnotes, and the like. Reischauer, who disliked "any sort of bibliographic chore,"[31] would listen and even on subjects on which he had no knowledge would ask the question that would go to the core of the issue and clarify the problem.[32]

James W. Morley, a distinguished professor at Columbia for many years, remembered a conference in January 1968 at Hakone, Japan, where a group of Japanese and American scholars held their sixth and final conference on the modernization of Japan. They tried to reach a common understanding of why Japan had taken a disastrous turn in the 1930s and 1940s. He recalled:

> After a number of learned papers had been presented on various aspects of Japan in the period, we were, I am afraid, breaking up without much of an answer. Each of us was caught up into much detail. Ed was in attendance, participating in the discussions, but he presented no paper. We had asked him, instead, to say a few words at the end—and in those few words he did what none of us had been able to do. He addressed the overall question directly: 'What went wrong?' And without notes, speaking freely, he rose above the detail, placing our problem in perspective, and at the end boiling the discussion down to its essential elements, and achieving a clear consensus that all could accept.

All in all, Morley summed up, "[Ed] was an extraordinary practitioner of the historian's highest art, the ability to see the wider meaning of events."[33]

Kent Calder, Reischauer's last Ph.D. student from the government department, remembers taking his course on Japanese politics in the fall of 1971 and being handed three large preliminary syllabi, providing the Meiji Constitution, the 1947 Constitution verbatim, the evolution of the franchise and electoral system, election returns since 1946, and a list of all the prime ministers of modern Japan. "He was always writing on the board, sometimes in Chinese characters (*kanji*) also—mainly names of those whom he considered important historical figures, many back in the years of Taisho Democracy, in which he had quite a bit of interest. The roots of democracy since Meiji, the idea that the Occupation had much to build on, a contempt for the parochialism of the military, and a belief in the abiding good sense and moderation of the Japanese people were some major ideas that I took away."[34] "In one way or another," stated historian Kenneth B. Pyle in 1997, "directly or indirectly, Edwin Reischauer is the father of all of us Americans engaged in Japanese studies."[35]

Students came to be fascinated by the interaction between Reischauer and Fairbank and often took sides in what they viewed as an intense rivalry between the two giants in the field. Fairbank was three years older and the more sophisticated in academic politics. He wrote that "on our first meeting I recall Ed's look of oriental inscrutability, dead-pan, as if thinking, 'Who is this Fairbank and what does he want?' No doubt I looked just as inscrutably at him, having had some practice at it myself. . . . We at once found a common bond in *our desire to educate the American public*. My life would have been quite different without him as a colleague." Fairbank felt that he and Reischauer, as two ambitious young academics in parallel fields, had a sort of sibling rivalry.[36]

Reischauer knew that students "circulated rumors of a deep animosity existing between us," but he denied it. "In actuality, our collaboration could not have been more harmonious." He was "my closest colleague and a lifelong friend."[37] But an associate who knew both men well remembered Reischauer muttering, "I wouldn't trust Fairbank as far as I could throw him." Basically, they got along pretty well by not interacting very much, another colleague recalled. "There was both collegiality and rivalry; mostly the rivalry was felt on Fairbank's side," according to Howard Hibbett, a friend of both men. "Fairbank was jealous of the money that he thought should have gone to Chinese studies that instead was directed by Ed into Japanese studies."[38] And Fairbank could never forgive Reischauer for becoming ambassador to Japan while he stayed home at Harvard.

Behind this rivalry were the following facts: Fairbank apparently could not quite forget that Reischauer had been born in Japan and could claim earlier and more authentic firsthand knowledge of Asia. Further, Reischauer had specialized in early Chinese history and had language skills and knowledge of the T'ang Dynasty that Fairbank, the great sinologist, would never achieve. In later years, Reischauer would influence U.S. policy toward Japan, whereas Fairbank was always on the sidelines in matters of China policy.

Fairbank shared some of Reischauer's religious background. His grandfather was a Congregational minister in the Midwest, and his great uncle was a missionary in India. But here the similarity ended. Fairbank grew up in a nonreligious, relatively wealthy family in Huron, South Dakota, graduated from Phillips Exeter Academy, the elite boarding school in New Hampshire, and from Harvard. He then won a coveted Rhodes Scholarship to Oxford University, completing a D.Phil. in Chinese studies, focusing on British-Chinese relations in the nineteenth century. Fairbank the historian tended to look down on the American missionary enterprise in East Asia of which Reischauer's family had been a part. In fact, the antimissionary posture of students and scholars at Harvard in this period was overwhelming. Reischauer, as we have seen, steadfastly defended his parents' chosen mission.

Fairbank exuded self-confidence born of a happy, prosperous American childhood in the Midwest, whereas Reischauer felt obliged to assert his credentials as an American. Fairbank became a Rhodes Scholar—something Reischauer tried and failed to achieve. In later years, Fairbank took on a rather imperious air as undisputed leader in the field of China studies with dozens of worshipful disciples scattered on campuses around the world. Reischauer, the more humble and accessible of the two, would come under attack from succeeding generations of students in the field.

James C. Thomson Jr., a "Mish-kid"—the slang term for a child of American missionaries to China—who studied under both men and was a Fairbank disciple, thought their differences as historians were profound. "Fairbank confronted the tragedy and irony of the human condition, especially in the 20th Century, and was deeply pessimistic about the future. Reischauer was more of a Manchester liberal of the 19th Century variety, always upbeat about the future," he contended.[39] John Curtis Perry agreed: "Reischauer was an optimist. His enthusiasm and success were due to this optimistic view that the most intractable problems in international relations could be solved by good sense and good will, with people thinking together."[40]

Fairbank was the consummate academic politician, helping to find money for scholarships, directing the study of his Ph.D. students into areas that interested him, and finding academic jobs for his disciples after they graduated. He had an enormous ego and a desire to control his students. Reischauer, by his own admission, "was more of an intellectual loner": "I enjoyed my teaching and loved my research work and writing, but I hated the busy work of letter writing, phone calls, committee meetings and the like."[41]

Reischauer did admit there were two points of friction. First, thanks to his position as director of the Harvard-Yenching Institute,[42] Reischauer had a sizable amount of fellowship money at his disposal, which annoyed Fairbank and those experts who saw China as the center of the universe. Second, Reischauer resented Fairbank's "forceful leadership, or domineering ways as some saw them." He steered East Asian projects into his own field of nineteenth-century Chinese history, a habit that others jokingly called "guided democracy."[43] In his most frank appraisal, Reischauer confided to his daughter, "He really is a wonderfully warm and humorous person—as well as a very hard, calculating and opinionated one—a confusing combination."[44]

Whatever their differences, the collaboration of these two very different historians would far outweigh any personal or philosophical differences. Their first small but important accomplishment was to create and recognize their field of study as "East Asia." This recognition, Reischauer later recalled, "marked the first step toward the eventual adoption of East Asia in place of Far East, which John and I managed to engineer after the war. 'Far East,' we thought, implied a Euro-centric concept of the world, which we were determined to get away from."[45] The U.S. State Department and the rest of the U.S. government, as well as the Association for Asian Studies, would eventually follow suit. Reischauer's deep contempt for European colonialism lay behind this shift.

Their most lasting achievement was to make respectable, once and for all, the study of contemporary East Asia not just at Harvard, but throughout America.

Their graduate students went on to head up relevant departments at all the major universities. The list of scholars (in alphabetical order) who were their students or colleagues reads like an all-star team in the field: George Akita, professor of history at the University of Hawaii; Jackson H. Bailey, professor of history at Earlham College; Kent Calder, professor of East Asian history at Johns Hopkins School of Advanced International Studies; Albert M. Craig, professor of history at Harvard; Peter Duus, professor of history at Stanford; John W. Hall, professor of history at Yale; Howard S. Hibbett, professor of Japanese literature at Harvard; Akira Iriye, professor of history at Harvard; Marius B. Jansen, professor of history at Princeton; Tetsuo Najita, professor of history at the University of Chicago; John C. Pelzel, professor of anthropology at Harvard; John Curtis Perry, professor of diplomatic history at the Fletcher School of Law and Diplomacy, Tufts University; Henry Rosovsky, economist and later dean of the Faculty of Arts and Sciences at Harvard; Robert K. Sakai, professor of history at the University of Hawaii; Thomas C. Smith, professor of history at Stanford; Donald H. Shively, professor of history and literature at Harvard; Conrad Totman, professor of history at Yale; George M. Wilson, professor of history at Indiana University; and Ernest Young, professor of history at Michigan University.

Another major achievement, given the temper of the academic world of their day, was to tell the story of East Asian civilization free of the ideological systems that were popular at Harvard at the time. The two agreed that history was a narrative about what happened and why; it was not a tale of large impersonal forces shaping human events. History was made by individuals, groups, and nations reacting to their environments and to events. It was full of contingency and random forces. At a time when the theoretical work of Karl Marx, Max Weber, and Emile Durkheim were much discussed among historians at Harvard, Reischauer and Fairbank stuck to their conviction that history should be free of abstract theory.[46] "Ed was by no means an ideologue," Perry commented. "He had no specific interpretive framework. The most descriptive word for his kind of history would be empirical. History was a story waiting to be told. He once remarked, 'After all, you can't make it up.'"[47]

Reischauer's critical views of both the theory and practice of Marxism and communism would become controversial in the late 1960s. I return to this topic in chapter 10, but suffice it to say here that he was an unabashedly liberal critic of communism. From his reading of history, he believed that Karl Marx's theory based on dialectical materialism— class struggle—that societies moved by immutable laws from feudalism to monopoly capitalism to a "dictatorship of the proletariat" was nonsense and bore no relationship to the actual course of human history. Further, he thought that the practice of communism in the Soviet Union under Joseph Stalin in the 1930s was abominable.

In the spring of 1938, while Reischauer was living in Beijing, he received a visit from an old friend from his days in Paris, Arthur Billings, who had spent the previous two years in Moscow. "Billings was a confirmed Socialist, a staunch pacifist, and a man of unbounded kindness. Because of his doctrinaire leftism, I found his gloomy report on the Soviet Union all the more convincing. He had lived there for more than two years, deeply immersed in Russian society and speaking the language fluently. His constantly repeated summation of his experiences was that the Soviet Union made a 'mockery' of all he believed in. It was probably in large part because of what I learned from Billings that I never fell into the trap that engulfed so many liberally minded Americans in the 1930's of converting their disapproval of fascism, Nazism, and militarism into admiration for the Soviet Union."[48]

At Harvard in the 1950s, however, Marxism as a theory was widely studied and often admired. Among students of China, Mao Zedong was regarded as something of a hero. Reischauer was having none of it, but he was equally opposed to the wild allegations of "Communist sympathy" by the Senate demagogue Joseph McCarthy, Republican of Wisconsin. When McCarthy named Reischauer's old friend from Oberlin, John S. Service, who was an expert on China in the Foreign Service, a Communist sympathizer, Reischauer was enraged and wrote to Service:

> Dear Jack:
>
> This is just a line to assure you that all your friends are still standing behind you. Senator McCarthy has so discredited himself by his broadside and unsubstantiated charges that no thinking person can pay any attention to them except to be irritated at his willful squandering of the time and nervous energy of valuable people in the government. I realize how hard this is on you personally, and I admire the way you have stood up under so many unjustified attacks. I should be glad to do whatever I can to help and in the meantime hope this letter, added to the many others I am sure you are receiving, will give you some encouragement.
>
> Please do not bother to acknowledge this. You need to save your efforts for more worthwhile matters.
>
> Yours sincerely, EOR.[49]

Robert N. Bellah, the distinguished sociologist at the University of California at Berkeley, had a somewhat less flattering view of Reischauer's stance on McCarthyism. As an undergraduate student at Harvard, he had been a Communist Party member from 1947 to 1949, and then was a graduate student in the Department of Far Eastern Languages from 1950 to 1955. In a February 2005 article in the *New York Review*, he charged that Dean McGeorge Bundy in 1954 had threatened to deny him a Harvard fellowship if he refused to answer the FBI's questions about his Communist associations.[50] He said that Reischauer had urged him to speak with "complete candor" (which Bellah took as a coded signal for naming names). He had concluded that Reischauer was in Bundy's camp. "Perhaps even in 1954 Reischauer had ambitions that might be compromised if he didn't cooperate with what Bundy wanted."[51]

Whatever may have happened in Bellah's case, Reischauer was a lifelong Jeffersonian liberal and was disgusted by McCarthyism in all its forms. He rejoiced at the election of Truman in 1948 and voted for Adlai Stevenson twice, in 1952 and 1956. He was an enthusiastic supporter of John F. Kennedy in 1960. "I never voted for a Republican in my life," he once told me. Ironically, as we shall see in chapter 10, during the anti–Vietnam War movement of the late 1960s, younger scholars of Asia would brand him as a Cold Warrior and a defender of American imperialism in Asia. The accusations stung.

If Reischauer treated history as a story, it is important to examine the assumptions that guided his selection and arrangement of facts. These core beliefs would inform his interpretation of Chinese and Japanese history and would later serve as the basis for his consideration of policy issues. His starting point was his unconcealed admiration for ancient Chinese culture. It would be impossible to capture in a few words the flavor, breadth, and depth of his prose in *East Asia: The Great Tradition*, but a few examples illustrate the point:

> China during the seventh century towered high above all other political units of the time. During the Han dynasty China had drawn abreast of the Mediterranean world. Now it was starting on what was to prove to be a millennium of pre-eminence as the strongest, richest, and in many ways most culturally advanced country in the world. (p. 170)

> Nothing produces change more inevitably than growth, and growth in population, production, trade, culture, and institutions takes place more easily in peaceful times than during periods of disruption. This is what happened during the T'ang. (p. 184)

During his stay in China between 838 and 847 the Japanese diarist Ennin described a prosperous and well-ordered society with a degree of bureaucratic meticulousness and centralized control that probably was not matched in other parts of the world until much later times. (p.192)

The triumph of the civilian as opposed to the military point of view was one of the chief characteristics of the new urban culture.... But by the Sung there had appeared the overwhelming emphasis on civil accomplishments, and the undercurrent of pacifism that have since been characteristically associated with Chinese civilization. There was a growing disregard and even contempt for martial life and prowess that was not unlike the attitudes that appear to be in the ascendant in modern urban societies of the Occident. Military service, it was felt, was only fit for the dregs of society; or, as the Chinese put it, the best men were no more to be used for soldiers than the best iron for nails. (p. 223)

Such favorite Sung wares as the lustrous green celadons, the delicately figured white porcelains, and the roughly shaped rich brown *t'ien-mu* ware . . . are often regarded as the finest works of the potters' art ever produced anywhere in the world. (p. 226)

Of all civil accomplishments in a now essentially non-military culture, writing, including its expression in the art of calligraphy, was the most prized, and remained so until the contemporary period. (p. 228)

Printing was a purely Chinese invention which put scholarship and learning on a new level in East Asia, just as it was to contribute to an even more thorough transformation of Western society a few centuries later. It is perhaps significant that printing and paper, the two technological underpinnings of the literate aspects of modern civilization, were both contributed by China, the literary civilization par excellence. (p. 231)

The ideal Confucian type that had evolved by the Sung was that of the 'universal man' who was scholar, poet, and statesman all at the same time, and possibly a philosopher and painter as well. (p. 235)

For the successive generations of Chinese who lived during this long period, the high degree of political, social, and spiritual stability which they enjoyed was probably preferable to the constant turmoil of life

> and thought during these same centuries in Europe. We moderns, living in the notably unstable world civilization that has grown out of the rapidly changing culture of the West, may also look with envy at the peace and stability of China between the thirteenth and nineteenth centuries. (p. 241)

Noting the Chinese "characteristic genius for organization" (p. 161) and "dependable bureaucracy" (p. 163), he argued that the T'ang Dynasty's examination system led to a civil service merit system that "was to prove one of the greatest achievements of Chinese civilization and that was to produce most of the great political leaders of the next thirteen centuries" (p. 165). He praised "the essentially non-aristocratic and more egalitarian society of the late Sung" (p. 220) and "a bureaucracy chosen by intellectual standards" (p. 222).

Writing of the "very perfection that Chinese culture and social organization had achieved by the thirteenth century," Reischauer concluded, "In retrospect, the Chinese have every right to view with pride the stage in their civilization in which they created a society so perfect within its own guiding ideals and technological limits that it achieved a degree of stability no other high civilization has ever been able to approach" (p. 242).

Implicit in this last passage is the notion that Chinese civilization, having known greatness in the past, might some day return to its former glory. It is of some interest to note that, as Reischauer was educating his students on China's noble past, he was also an early and steadfast advocate of recognizing the new Communist regime after it consolidated power in 1949. Expressing this opinion took some courage because Americans and Chinese were engaged in a hot war on the Korean Peninsula from 1950 to 1953. For advocating recognition, he was ostracized from his role as an informal advisor to the State Department in 1950. It would be twenty-one years before his erstwhile Harvard colleague, Henry A. Kissinger, showed up in Beijing to prepare the way for a rapprochement between the United States and Communist China.

Reischauer's portrait of early Japanese history was strikingly original. Several broad brush strokes serve to illustrate his effort to situate Japan within the main currents of world history. For the first time, Japan was treated as an "ordinary nation," subject to the same kinds of influences and forces that prevailed in Europe.

He tried to explain in *East Asia: The Great Tradition* the factors in East Asian cultures and especially in Japan that led to higher rates of literacy and an emphasis on education:

> In East Asian civilization the written word has always taken precedence over the spoken; Chinese history is full of famous documents—memorials, essays and poems—but lacks the great speeches of the West. The magic quality of writing is perhaps one of the reasons why the peoples of East Asia have tended to place a higher premium on book learning and on formal education than have the peoples of any other civilization. It is no mere accident that, despite their extremely difficult systems of writing, literacy rates in East Asia run far higher on the whole than in the rest of the non-western world (and in the case of Japan even surpass those of the West). (p. 43)

He argued that the pattern of Japanese history had more in common with the history of European nations than with the history of China. "Feudalism in Japan is an outstanding example of this. So also is Japan's more rapid modernization during the past century, which has produced closer parallels to the political, economic and social phenomena of the contemporary Occident than are to be found in China or anywhere else in Asia" (p. 450).

Reischauer had no patience for the oft-repeated Japanese assertion that Japan had a *unique* national character. There were perfectly logical reasons for Japan's distinctive history, such as language and cultural substructures, but national character was not one of them. Isolation from the mainland (whereas England was only twenty-one miles from the European mainland, Japan was 115 miles from the Asian) was a factor. Protection from military pressure by surrounding seas was another. Free from foreign conquest, change came slowly and primarily from internal evolution rather than external pressure.

Another key point was that the Japanese are not mere imitators of foreign cultures: "The consciousness of borrowing from abroad has also fostered the myth, both in Japan and elsewhere, that the Japanese, in contrast to other peoples, have been a nation of borrowers, although the truth seems to be that, just because of their isolation, they have independently created a larger part of their own culture than has any other nation of comparable size and cultural development" (p. 452).

He contended that Japan's rugged terrain of narrow river valleys and rugged hills probably kept it from having the kind of centralized rule found in China.

The Shinto religion, he asserted, "lacking any moral sense of guilt or sin, is an essentially cheerful, sunny religion. Unlike the Koreans, who came to concentrate on the menacing aspects of nature, the Japanese emphasized its beauty and bountifulness" (p. 473).

The most original (and controversial) of his assertions concerned his comparison of Japan's history with Europe's. "Japan's early feudalism had much in common with that of Europe; both experienced a time of ardent faith and high religious fervor. As in feudal Europe, Japan went through a time of continual warfare" (p. 556). "Japan's developing feudal system actually proved to be a great stimulus, rather than a check, to the economy" (p. 557). During the middle and late Ashikaga period (1336–1573), Japan passed through the stage most like that of high feudalism in the West (pp. 574–75).

He was directly confronting the Marxist orthodoxy when he found redeeming aspects in feudalism, as we shall see in chapter 10. He found that "the early feudal system had given the lower classes a more secure and prominent position in society than they had ever enjoyed before. The growing military role of the foot soldier in the fifteenth and sixteenth centuries and the tendency of the village aristocrats to side with their fellow villagers now gave the common man a measure of political power for the first time in Japanese history" (p. 576). Instead of comparing Japan's problems in modernization to the advanced countries of Europe in Marxist terms, he used nineteenth-century China as a yardstick and viewed Japan's social and economic modernization and remarkable progress toward democracy as "an amazing success story that required more explaining than its less surprising failures," according to his memoir.[52]

As he explained in his memoir, "When I had written *Japan Past and Present* just after the end of World War II, I had been much under the influence of the dominant Marxist interpretation of the day. With my new insights, I began to emphasize the intellectual diversity and entrepreneurial vigor of the late Tokugawa period rather than its social stratification and political decline, the positive aspects rather than the repressive measures of the new government created by the Meiji Restoration, and the successes rather than the failures of parliamentary development and party government in Japan. This interpretation I injected bit by bit in the later editions."[53]

And in *East Asia: The Great Tradition*, he wrote, "Thus by the middle of the sixteenth century political and social realities had moved far beyond the situation usually pictured as high feudalism in Europe. And once again the movement was in the same general direction as that taken by European society—in other words, toward the centralization of political power that characterized Europe in early modern times. In fact, when the Europeans first arrived in Japan, in the sixteenth century, they found political and social conditions which were completely understandable to them in terms of the sixteenth-century Europe they knew" (p. 578).

The broad outlines of Chinese and Japanese history that he and John Fairbank drew became an essential narrative for students of East Asia in the period from 1950 to 1975 and served as the starting point for many specialized works in the field. It may not be an exaggeration to suggest that they helped pave the way for America's readiness to recognize Communist China in 1972. Reischauer's advocacy of recognizing Communist China from 1950 on certainly turned out to be a major factor leading to his appointment as ambassador to Japan, as we shall see in chapter 7.

6

A Family Tragedy and a New Start

Edwin Reischauer characterized the period from 1945 to 1960 as his "Golden Years at Harvard."[1] They were indeed golden in terms of his scholarship, teaching, and writing, but they were also years of deep personal tragedy. He would watch his wife die of heart disease in 1955 after six agonizing years of illness, and his mother would suffer a series of strokes that left her incapacitated and led to her death in 1956. He had to take care of his aging father and deaf-mute sister, Felicia, after he brought them to live in nearby Belmont, Massachusetts. August Karl Reischauer had retired in 1952 at the age of seventy-three from a teaching job at the Union Theological Seminary in New York. Edwin would also have to deal with his own severe health problems while raising three energetic children. He was ravaged by severe migraine headaches and atrial fibrillation. That he could look back on this period as "golden" reveals again his ability to compartmentalize his life, shut down his emotions, and take refuge in scholarship. An intensely private man, he was unable to share grief with friends. If a colleague ventured to ask a question Reischauer deemed too personal, he would deflect it with a joke or with a serious comment on his current research. In his later years, he paid a heavy price for this emotional isolation.

His professional career, however, did seem "golden." In 1950, at the age of forty, he achieved the title of professor of Far Eastern languages with tenure at Harvard.[2] By the mid-1950s, he was indisputably America's leading expert on Japan. In 1955, he was elected president of the Far Eastern Association, the national organization of scholars in the field.[3] Two years later he succeeded Serge Elisseeff as director of the Harvard-Yenching Institute. His book *The United States and Japan*, published in 1950, was given a front-page review in the *New York Times* book review section and became the standard work on the subject.[4]

Beyond these academic distinctions, he achieved national prominence in the popular media, churning out a steady stream of magazine and newspaper articles, book reviews, and prefaces to the works of other writers. He lectured at the National War College and to foreign-policy groups. He became a close friend and advisor to John D. Rockefeller III on several important cultural initiatives in Japan (discussed more fully later).

His fame was also spreading in Japan. From 1950 to 1952, he wrote a series of six articles for the newspaper *Mainichi Shimbun*, all of which were carried at the top of page one. In the first of these articles, he assured Japanese readers that the United States shared their interest in economic development. He wrote that the future of democracy in Asia depended on its success in Japan.[5] He relished his role as interpreter of American thinking to Japanese readers and of Japanese thinking to American readers. For example, he wrote in 1952 that "the Japanese and American people can congratulate themselves for having completed without serious loss of amity or mutual respect the most difficult relationship that can exist between two nations—war and occupation." But, he added, the average American, unaware of the grave economic and social problems that the Japanese faced, "is puzzled and a bit indignant that Japan, which he well knows was recently a major military power, must now depend on him for so much of its own defense."[6] His office at Harvard soon became an obligatory stop for visiting Japanese scholars, journalists, and students.

When *Mainichi* offered to pay him 120,000 yen for the articles, Reischauer demurred. "I would have scruples about receiving payment from a country which is still not fully back on its feet economically. I wonder, therefore, if you would be good enough to divide this money and any further payments . . . between two educational institutions with which my parents were closely associated during their life in Japan." He asked that three-quarters of the money should go to Tokyo Joshi Daigaku and the rest to Nippon Roa Gakko (Japan Deaf Oral School), the two institutions his parents had founded.[7]

As the newly established democratic government in Japan took root in the 1950s, Reischauer came to champion the nation as "a psychological factor of the greatest importance in the battle for Asia." The first task was to convince the Japanese that they had this potential: "This will require a great deal more intellectual honesty and daring than Japanese leadership has shown of late. The Japanese will also have to abandon their own snobbish disregard of Asia and pay much more attention to the psychology and problems of their neighbors. . . . It cannot be hoped that the peoples of Asia will look to Japan for aid or leadership unless the Japanese first look to Asia with sympathetic interest and sound understanding."[8]

In 1957, his fame as a scholar brought him an offer to be a candidate for president of his alma mater, Oberlin. He had no trouble deciding to turn it down. "A college presidency was the sort of diffuse administrative job that did not interest me in the slightest," he wrote later.[9] Oberlin did nevertheless award him his first honorary degree, a doctorate of literature in 1957.

Reischauer also somehow found time for "golden" moments with his children. From 1946 to 1952, the family shared a two-family home on Divinity Avenue on the Harvard campus with other faculty members and their families. The Reischauers took summer trips to the beaches of Cape Cod and to the mountains of New Hampshire. Reischauer loved to square dance with his daughter Ann, play softball and tennis, and swim with his children. In 1950, the Reischauer children, Ann (eleven), Bobby (nine), and Joan (six), were surrounded by a pack of same-age neighboring children, including those of Arthur M. Schlesinger Jr. In spite of his heavy schedule of writing and teaching, Reischauer delighted in playing games of every sort with this gang of kids. Bobby Reischauer, at eighteen, would remember those days with his father in a mock-serious high school composition that well captured his father's personality:

> Mr. Reischauer [a tongue-in-cheek reference to his father] has been considered as "one of the gang" for as long as I can remember. As we grew up and our interests changed, so, it seemed, did his. Since his working hours paralleled the time we were employed exercising the three R's, he was always free when we were.
>
> Probably the most famous of his accomplishments was the parking-lot baseball league. On every available afternoon in the summer and on weekends during the school year, "Mr. Reischauer," using his incredible sense of judgment, would divide the odd assortment of athletes who had gathered under the shady elms of Divinity Street, into two equal teams. These players ranged from the local urchins, both boys and girls, to a passing Harvard or Radcliffe student. On rare occasions, several professors from these famed institutions could have been found chasing flies across the dusty parking lot. On the mound serving as umpire and pitcher for both teams was "Mr. Reischauer." The whirling sphere, a tennis ball, crossed the plate according to the batters' ability and temperament. The arrogant youngster after blasting a home run high off the Peabody Museum invariably went down swinging his next two trips amid the jeers of the opposing team

> [and] his own pleas for justice. Miraculously enough almost all the games ended in a dead tie or a one run victory.

Bobby goes on to recall trips to the beach with his father driving, providing games, and songs to pacify the children in the back seat. He recounts how his father loved to play board games of all kinds—Monopoly, Clue, Parcheesi (a game similar to backgammon)—and card games. He usually won. "It even became a feat to beat him with two moves for every one of his. In our eyes he loomed as the unbeatable card shark, a dice artist, and controller of the fates." In a conclusion that would warm any father's heart, the eighteen-year-old Bobby wrote: "When I look back on my youth, the baseball, the trips to the beach, and the rainy-day games, I often wonder why 'Mr. Reischauer,' whenever he was approached by an adult trying to persuade him to be a Den Father or a Big Brother, always answered scornfully that he had no time to play with kids. I also find it hard to tell whether 'Mr. Reischauer' or we enjoyed our childhood more; but one thing's for certain—we shared it."[10]

In a later recollection, Robert would recall, "My father was not a man with a small ego, but he was not domineering. At the dinner table, we played lots of geography and history games. We would go around the table, for example, naming the states that formed the perimeter of the United States. Joanie would start with Maine, and we would go all the way around to Oregon and Washington. The hero was of course my father, who knew all the capitals of the states and countries."[11]

Joan Reischauer Simon, youngest of the three, remembers her father fondly as a "fun guy" to be with. "My father thought he was a riot. Don't we all? He thought he had a great sense of humor. He wasn't a stern father. When there was a last piece of dessert on the table, he would compete for it with the rest of us, calling for a round of *jan-ken-po* (rock-paper-scissors). There was a piece of my father that never grew up. He knew his responsibilities but he loved to play games—croquet, board games, outdoor games, whatever."

Joan marveled at his power of concentration.

> He would be writing his book on the Ennin diary on a yellow legal-size lined pad in the open dining room. He was always jingling the keys in his pocket while he worked. My mother would come in and take the keys away from him. The kids would be running in and out, and I never remember him telling us to be quiet. He was so much in his own head that he could just shut out the world. I remember going to the Schlesingers' house and Arthur coming down from his third floor study say-

ing, "I'm working, you guys have to be quiet." I never remember that with my father. When he did relax, he always had to be doing more than one thing at once: on a Saturday afternoon, he would read a newspaper, watch college football on TV, and listen to the Harvard game on radio.[12]

It was this same almost inhuman power to compartmentalize his personal and professional life that enabled him to cope with personal suffering. Adrienne had contracted a severe case of diphtheria as a teenager in China that left her with an intermittent blockage of the heart. Winburn T. Thomas, a missionary friend who visited the Reischauers in the fall of 1949, noticed her frail health even then, when she was only thirty-eight. In January 1951, while she was having lunch with her children, her heart stopped beating for a few seconds, and she fell to the floor. Her heart started up again, but she felt miserable for the next few days. Reischauer's own words best describe what happened next:

> She had developed a heart block, which meant that her heart was cut off at times from the rest of her nervous system, not responding to exertion and leaving her out of breath even when she simply walked upstairs. Her condition remained poor. A second complete stoppage of the heart occurred about six months later, and thereafter they became gradually more frequent. I accidentally discovered that I could get her heart going again by giving it a good thump. Over the next few years I revived her in this way probably close to a hundred times. Each attack left her semi-dazed for several hours and in great distress for two or three days. The doctors hospitalized her repeatedly but could do nothing for her. A pacemaker, which had already been developed in the laboratories at that time but had not yet come into general use, could have cleared up her problem easily, but neither we nor the doctors knew of this possibility.[13]

The six years of Adrienne's fatal illness took its toll on everyone in the family. Bobby, age fourteen at the time of her death, remembers coming home from school on four or five occasions and finding his mother passed out on the floor. "We had instructions about sticking a thing in her mouth so she wouldn't choke on her tongue, and who to call. She would end up being in bed for a month or two afterwards. This was a very difficult time for my father."[14]

During the last year of Adrienne's life, as she was bedridden, Reischauer did all the cooking, cleaning, shopping, and driving for his family. "These were grim years," he would recall, "but they were wonderful years that brought the two of us very close together. She remained marvelously cheerful to the end. In every hospital where she was placed, she almost immediately became the center of life on the whole floor. At home our children and their friends would gather almost nightly to play cards with her and me on our bed."[15]

Adrienne died on January 17, 1955, while Edwin was teaching at Harvard. Though not a surprise, her death came as a terrible shock. There is no question that Adrienne was the love of his life, the one person who knew all aspects of his personality, who helped him fulfill his potential. So sacred was their relationship that soon after her cremation (there was no memorial service), he burned the daily love letters they had exchanged as graduate students in Europe from 1933 to 1935. "I felt as if my whole internal wiring system had been burned out," he wrote. "Adrienne was a wonderful person, cheerful, effervescent and bubbling with *joie de vivre*. At the same time, she was endlessly thoughtful of others, and this combination of qualities made her immediately beloved by anyone she met. She was also a person of strong principles and incredible bravery in the face of great physical suffering. When she saw fit, she could give me a good tongue lashing for my thoughtlessness of others or my blind concentration on my studies, perhaps knocking off some of my more offensive rough edges. I was indeed privileged to share two decades of my life with such a wonderful person."[16]

"People who knew them best thought they had a spectacular marriage," their son Robert would later recall. "They viewed my mother as someone who made my father as close to human as possible. She was the person with the better judgment and the social skills. He was something of a machine, very career-oriented."[17]

On learning the sad news, missionary Winburn Thomas wrote: "We have been saddened that Adrienne passed away. . . . I had been worried about her since we visited your home in autumn of 1949. . . . I helped your mother out to the car in the summer of 1934 when she left for the mountains after her nervous breakdown. We were shocked by the death of Bob [Reischauer's brother] back in the summer of 1937 as by the death of few other persons. We know from these experiences how you Reischauers bear up under trouble. We know that you are taking this with the same fortitude and trust."[18]

Helen Oldfather Reischauer, Edwin's mother, died at age seventy-six on March 22, 1956, after a series of debilitating strokes. At this time, Edwin and his three children were in Japan on sabbatical leave. Her death came as another severe blow. Helen's health had never been robust. She had apparently suffered a nervous breakdown in Japan in 1934, perhaps brought on by her fruitless effort to find a solution to Felicia's deafness and by the rigors of missionary life in an increasingly nationalistic land. She began to suffer a series of small strokes in 1952 and could do little more than sit in a chair and smile after that.

Helen Reischauer, according to her granddaughter Joan Reischauer Simon, was the driving force in the family. It was she who pushed her husband to found Tokyo Joshi Daigaku and Nippon Rowa Gakko. Edwin never seemed to get over the feeling that his older brother, Robert, was his mother's favorite and that he somehow never quite measured up in her eyes. This uncomfortable feeling doubtless motivated him to strive even harder to get to the top of his profession.[19]

As if the deaths of his brother, wife, and mother were not enough, Reischauer battled serious health problems of his own. As a lecturer at Harvard, he gave the appearance of a man in his prime, fit and full of energy. In fact, he suffered from almost annual bouts of flu and viral pneumonia. And starting in the 1930s, he suffered from monthly attacks of agonizing migraine headaches. Each attack would last for about three days, forcing him to lie in bed in darkness. They peaked in 1950 and gradually tapered off around 1960. In a letter to Takata Ichitaro, foreign editor of *Mainichi Shimbun*, he wrote, "I am far behind due to protracted illness in December 1951."[20]

Few persons outside of his immediate family knew of these problems, and Reischauer, with his hair-shirt missionary upbringing, soldiered through them with an appearance of good cheer. Amazingly, the years from 1950 to 1955 were his most productive as a scholar. Despite Adrienne's illness and death, he was able finally to complete and publish his two books on Ennin as well as *Wanted: An Asian Policy* in 1955. "I put away my Ennin studies with regret, feeling that I was bringing to an end a whole phase of my life and also saying farewell to an old friend."[21] He would admit only later, in a letter to his daughter Ann, "I don't deny that I had a breakdown of sorts in the spring and summer of 1956."[22]

We have seen that Reischauer thoroughly enjoyed his time in the policy world as an advisor at the State Department in 1945–46. Even after returning to Harvard, he stayed in close touch with the Far Eastern desk at the State Department and with developments on the ground in Asia. In 1948, he was invited to join four other American scholars on a four-month Cultural Science Mission (Jimbun Kagaku Komon Dan) to study postwar conditions in occupied Japan. This trip was his first brush with postwar Japan, and the sight of American occupiers living in luxury while his old Japanese friends struggled with hunger and poverty disgusted him. Deploring what he called "the corruption of conquest," he later observed that

> [t]he most subtle but perhaps the most persistent problem of the occupation was the inevitably corrupting influence of any occupation on its members. Living under conditions of great luxury by postwar Japanese standards, they inescapably constituted a class set apart—a superior breed of conquerors. They enjoyed the use of the Japanese telephone network without charge. All the best hotels, the best private homes, the best trains, the best facilities of every sort were theirs by right of conquest.... To parallel his greatly augmented prestige, the average American in Japan enjoyed vastly more power than he ever had before, and was likely to have again. He was always right, and the Japanese officials always wrong.[23]

The mission gave Reischauer an opportunity to catch up with many old friends of his family, and he received something of a hero's welcome when he offered lectures in Tokyo. The highlights of his visit were meetings with the emperor and General Douglas MacArthur. The emperor, he thought, "seemed nervous and fidgety, but dutifully asked each of us appropriate questions, while punctuating the conversation with 'Ah, so' ('Oh, is that so?'), spoken in a high, squeaky voice."[24]

Reischauer had only one chance to meet and observe MacArthur in action, over a two-hour lunch at the American Embassy residence in Tokyo on December 3, 1948. He was far more impressed than his later account admits. Over pheasant and chocolate parfait, the supreme commander spoke with "power and grandiloquence as we sat on the edge of our chairs," Reischauer breathlessly wrote his family. "He waxed eloquent, speaking with emotion and force, as if we were a myriad crowd, grouped round his dais, and we listened almost open-mouthed. The two most impressive aspects of the general are his idealism and his breadth of view. He is convinced that the ideals of democracy and Christianity will sweep all else before them in Japan. A thousand years from now, when only a line in history books is devoted to this recent war, a whole paragraph will say that at this time the ideals of democracy and Christianity came to Japan from America to become the foundation of all future civilization."[25]

Reischauer's worshipful appraisal would change within a few years. The general's insubordination to President Truman during the Korean War and his overweening egotism and ambition to be president would temper this glowing account.[26] But Reischauer gave him high marks for his conduct of the early occupation years. Reischauer noted that MacArthur admired the self-respect, industry, and sincerity of the Japanese people, and he confessed that "I was in complete agreement with his major statements, and found that he had the facts at his fingertips." "All in all it was as fascinating a two hours as I have ever spent. One cannot help but come away from MacArthur with a feeling of the greatness of the man. Whether or not one may agree with his policies, (and I agree with almost all of them), one must admit that here was a man who could recognize the magnitude of the historic role thrust upon him, and who has been able to do his work in a broad global and long historical setting."[27]

Reischauer generally believed that MacArthur's occupation had been a success. To its critics, he replied: "One can speak of failure in Japan if one's standard of comparison is Utopian. A fairer comparison would be to the real alternatives—political or economic colonialism, the re-creation of Japan simply as a military ally, a mechanical program of political reform without regard to basic economic or social conditions, a confusion of policies, or perhaps no clear policy at all. As measured against the real possibilities, our occupation of Japan has been a remarkable success."[28]

Reischauer, however, invariably gave most of the credit to the Japanese people themselves rather than to the occupiers for making democracy work. He was more optimistic about Japan's political future than most observers at the time. "I based my optimism on Japan's spontaneous growth toward democracy in the years before 1931."[29] As always, he admired the ordinary citizens who had to put up with military government and praised "the simple earnest, beauty-loving little people of Japan." He pointed to their "simple dignity and serenity that is hard to match."[30]

Regarding the rest of East Asia, though, his concern grew by the day. He agreed with President Truman's policy of intervening in Korea in June 1950 and even of U.S. troops crossing the thirty-eighth parallel and attempting to unite all of Korea. Like most policy planners, he did not anticipate the massive Chinese intervention in October 1950 that would drive U.S. forces back to the thirty-eighth parallel and end in a truce that lasts to this day. At this point, he changed his mind and became highly critical of MacArthur, who claimed to understand the Oriental mind: "No one actually was less prepared to understand the thinking of Asians than MacArthur, with his unparalleled arrogance and outmoded concepts of Asia," he commented later.[31]

Shortly after the Communist victory in China in October 1949, Reischauer was called to a meeting with General George Marshall and other top officials at the State Department to consider how the United States should respond. He advised that the United States should coordinate its actions with other nations, such as India, and favored early recognition of the new government in Beijing. Another professor at the table, Kenneth W. Colegrove of Northwestern University, later denounced Reischauer as being pro-Communist for taking this position.

The virulent campaign to find Communist sympathizers or spies in the State Department, kicked off by Senator Joseph McCarthy in February 1950, would make it virtually impossible for Reischauer or any other liberal Harvard professor formally to serve as a consultant on East Asia to the State Department for the rest of the decade.[32]

Nevertheless, there was one last chance. Early in 1950, Reischauer was summoned to meet with Secretary of State Dean Acheson to discuss a proposal to offer Japan less than a full peace treaty, a plan that would essentially continue the U.S. occupation. Reischauer strongly opposed this idea on the grounds that Japan was ready for full sovereignty and would react badly to anything less. In April 1950, John Foster Dulles was charged with preparing the peace treaty. In June of that year, the Korean War broke out and earlier plans for a partial peace treaty were abandoned. When in September 1951 the United States, Japan, and forty-seven other nations finally signed a peace treaty, but the Soviet Union and China boycotted the treaty, Reischauer felt this outcome was better than the partial treaty that had been proposed in 1950.

Despite the hot war that broke out between U.S. and Chinese troops in October 1950 in Korea, Reischauer never wavered and for the rest of the decade consistently argued in public and private forums that China and the Soviet Union, who had formed an alliance in 1950, would split and that recognition of China would hasten that split.

Far from walking away from Japan policymaking, however, he served as a consultant to the Ford Foundation in 1952–53. In one of his most complete surveys of the Cold War in Asia written for the foundation, he argued for sending Western experts in the fields of law, economics, government, history, philosophy, science, literature, and religion to Japan in order to "promote Japan's participation in the non-Communist world of ideas."[33] Contending that the West would lose if it relied only on its military or economic might, he insisted that the United States should engage Marxist dogma on the crucial battleground of ideology. The government alone could not do the job; the American private sector, especially its foundations, was best equipped to meet the challenge. As he stated in this memo,

> In part the problem is one of education in the broadest sense. More serious than Asia's all too obvious physical poverty is its intellectual poverty. In most parts of Asia there are far too few people trained or being trained for leadership, and, what is still more dangerous, the knowledge of even this group is often extremely superficial. Their approach to their own culture and problems tends to be emotionally biased and intellectually doc-

> trinaire; their knowledge of the outside world often is absurdly distorted. In their ignorance and confusion, the disordered profusion of Western experience and knowledge tends to be confusing. In the desperation of their plight, the neatly packaged dogmas and extravagant but ostensibly guaranteed promises of Communism have a strong appeal. It is for this reason that the minds of almost all Asian intellectuals tend to stray down the carefully marked channels of Marxism.

Drawing on his experience in intellectual exchanges at the Harvard-Yenching Institute, he warned in this same memo: "If we are to defeat Communism in Asia, we must bring to our effort the big guns of theory, in other words, the great concepts and beliefs that impel men to action. The case of China is all too clear. One side was equipped with the heavy artillery of big ideas, while the other fought with the rusty swords of factional loyalty. But these guns are not easy to make. Our own intellectual facilities of the West perhaps are not up to the task of casting them alone. For this we need the help of the intellectual resources of Asia wherever these are available, which today is primarily in Japan." Reischauer urged that Japanese and Western scholars should work together to produce a deep study of the Far East and that this effort could produce a philosophy of history that could challenge Communist dogma in China: "We are still entirely on the defensive in our approach to China. Perhaps our first step in going over to the offensive should be the preparation of a platform of theory on which the disenchanted Communist can find new footing when the false theories of Communism begin to crumble from beneath him."[34]

This was Reischauer at his most visionary. The ideal of creating a new philosophy of history to which Japanese, Chinese, and Western leaders could rally was perhaps impractical, but his conviction that Marxism would crumble in China seems prescient today, and his faith in the training of a new generation of Japanese and American scholars in East Asian history has been vindicated. The Ford Foundation accepted at least some of his vision when it launched its Foreign Area Training Fellows Program in the mid-1950s. This program nurtured a generation of young scholars who today populate the East Asian studies departments of many American universities.

Starting in 1953, Reischauer became highly critical of the policy of John Foster Dulles, secretary of state under President Dwight Eisenhower. Dulles was a grim, humorless lawyer from the elite New York firm of Sullivan and Cromwell and an extreme hater of what he called "Godless communism." Reischauer thought religion should not dictate the making of foreign policy, and in the summer of 1954 he sat down to write a powerful critique of U.S. policy in East Asia. It was published in January 1955 as *Wanted: An Asian Policy.*[35] For his first major policy statement, it was a passionate critique of what he viewed as "American blundering in East Asia." Today, the book reads like a commonsense primer, but in 1955 it was a radical departure from conventional wisdom.

In a preface written in October 1954, he stipulated modestly that "the greater part of this book extends far beyond my professional competence," but quickly added that there is no reason to leave the subject "entirely in the hands of those [read Dulles] who have no specialized competence whatsoever" (p. viii). Alternating between the tone of an angry Old Testament prophet and a patient high school teacher, he laid out the issues facing America in Asia.

Noting that the defeat of the Nationalist government in China had been a traumatic experience for the American public, he wrote: "We have approached some of our problems hampered by the chip-on-the-shoulder attitude of the weak rather than with the breadth of vision and understanding tolerance of the strong" (p. 6). Of Senator McCarthy's intemperate accusations, he added, "It would be hard to find a historical parallel either to the defeat we suffered in China or to the crippling aftereffects it has produced" (p. 6).

Looking at Asia as a whole, he noted the irony of America's position: "We expect friendship from the Chinese and they turn on us with hate. We expect hate from the Japanese and they turn to us with admiration and trust. We expect sympathy and trust from the Indians and they look upon us with suspicion and fear. In Asia at best we are skating on a very thin ice of mutual understanding over deep and unknown waters" (p. 9).

Dismissing Senator McCarthy's charge that America "lost China" due to treachery in our government, he explains that the Communist triumph in China did not result in what Americans did or did not do. The United States was wrong to think during World War Two that the Chinese Nationalist government would play a large role in the defeat of Japan, that it could be one of the five major powers in the postwar era, or that it could be persuaded to become a democracy while fighting a civil war.

Regarding Korea, he wrote, "we find an even more glaring case of ignorance leading to catastrophe" (p. 14). American planners in the wake of Japan's defeat paid little attention to that Japanese colony, and the division of the nation at the thirty-eighth parallel "was conducted by persons with no clear understanding of the circumstances under which the line had been drawn" (p. 14). This statement was a clear reference to Dean Rusk, who would become President Kennedy's secretary of state. Though Reischauer almost always avoided ad hominem attacks against his critics, he made an exception for Rusk. The two men mistrusted and disliked each other, as we shall see below. "Until the outbreak of war," Reischauer continued, "our ignorance of Korea was only matched by our indifference" (p. 15). It should be noted that Dean Rusk was assistant secretary of state for the Far East in 1950–51.

In case anyone missed the reference to Rusk, Reischauer returned to the subject a few pages later: "It is all too easy to condemn those who represented American policy in Korea in the early postwar years, but the real blame lies with all of us Americans for having sent such ill-prepared and unguided men to a task that called for the highest degree of skill and tact" (p. 20). In sum, "there was every reason to fear that a feeble and chaotic Korea would be a weak spot in the postwar world order, if not a serious menace to world peace. And yet what did we do to prepare for this situation? Absolutely and literally nothing" (p. 17).

What was the solution to our ignorance of Asian realities? Reischauer thought the answer was twofold: train a much larger body of Asian specialists and educate the American public. Noting that "it is a huge jump from the broad wheat fields of Kansas to the narrow rice paddies of the Philippines, he warned that "we must develop a far larger and decidedly more expert body of specialists in whom the rightly suspicious average man can put more trust, but at the same time we must also develop a far more understanding general public. This is a stupendous task" (pp. 27–28). It was precisely the task that Reischauer had set out for himself at Harvard.

Reviewing at length the long history of Western imperialism in Asia and Asians' varied attempts to respond by modernizing and industrializing in order to catch up with the West, Reischauer concluded that the American response to the Cold War could not rest solely on military power: we had to use our "arsenal of ideas." Instead of talking to Asians about the "American way of life," he wrote, we needed to explain the "ideals and practices of democracy itself" (p. 197). The Communists represented yet another dictatorial rule by an elite group in the Asian tradition. American democracy could appeal to the ordinary Asian's desire for equality, freedom, and a better livelihood.

Reischauer was highly critical of the French colonial regime in Indochina, believing the French had warped its colony's economy to fit its own needs. He admitted that France contributed to Vietnam's awakening by investing skills and money in the nation, but he warned prophetically against the idea of using U.S. military power to prop up the French colonial regime in Saigon.

At the time he was writing *Wanted*, the French had just lost the decisive battle of Dien Bien Phu to the Vietnamese Viet Minh, and President Eisenhower had made a firm decision to keep U.S. troops out of the battle. In the summer of 1955, at the Geneva conference, Vietnam was divided into two parts, with the Communists controlling the North from their capital in Hanoi. But as the Communists expanded their influence in the South through the Viet Minh guerilla network, Eisenhower was persuaded over the next four years to send sixteen thousand military "advisors" to South Vietnam to assist the regime in Saigon. Vietnam was perceived in Washington as the next decisive battleground in the Cold War. Reischauer, writing in *Wanted* in 1954, could see the folly of sending U.S. troops to Vietnam. "Both terrain and climate would be less favorable for us than in Korea, and we should find that whatever our lines of defense might be, they could be anchored by sea power only on the east and would melt away into the jungles and mountains of the interior on the west, where the advantages would lie entirely with the Communist guerillas. And, worst of all, we should find few Indochinese willing to fight with the ardor of our Korean allies, and at our backs would be a veritable quagmire of civilian apathy or resentment" (pp. 178–79).[36]

Reischauer dismissed the idea that Soviet-style communism represented the wave of the future in Asia. "Asian nationalism is perhaps the greatest bulwark against communism and therefore the greatest immediate support of the cause of international democracy. We, instead of the Russians, should be making effective us of these tides," he wrote (p. 251). "The whole history of the Communist Vietminh revolt against the French . . . indicates that from the start it has rested more heavily on nationalism for its mass support than on Communist dialectics. Therefore, in supporting the French in Indochina, we found ourselves attempting to stem this great Asian tide" (p. 253).

Indochina, he insisted, "shows how absurdly wrong we are to battle Asian nationalism instead of aiding it." "Americans would have preferred to see Indochina a truly independent nation or group of nations rather than a colonial or semi-colonial land. We had scant sympathy for French colonialism there even if it had not been the Achilles' heel of our cause. Our failure to prevent the Indochinese situation from falling into this sorry state is another great failure of foresight, comparable in many ways to our failures in China and Korea" (p. 257).

In a final, prophetic note, he warned, "The French failure to relinquish Indochina has put a heavy burden on the United States financially and could end by costing us dearly in lives" (p. 257).

Reischauer wrote these words in the summer of 1954. *Wanted: An Asian Policy* was published early in January 1955, the month in which Adrienne died. The *New York Times* gave it a front-page review in its book review section, but then he noted, "it dropped into the pool of public opinion without raising a ripple. The nation, under Dulles' unwise leadership, was headed determinedly in the opposite direction."[37]

Understanding, as few Americans did at the time how important both Korea and Vietnam would become to American policymakers, Reischauer managed in 1958 to win a grant of two hundred thousand dollars from the Rockefeller Foundation to help establish a chair in Korean studies at Harvard, the first such chair in the United States, and to install Edward Wagner, one of his Ph.D. students, in that chair. On Vietnamese studies, he was less successful. John Fairbank found the necessary funding, but no suitable scholar could be found to fill the position—this just six years before U.S. troops would be engaged in a massive and tragic escalation in that nation.

The appalling irony would become apparent ten years later. In 1965, Reischauer would be the American ambassador in Tokyo, charged with defending a war in Vietnam that he had resolutely opposed. Dean Rusk would be secretary of state, adamantly urging President Lyndon B. Johnson to step up the war against the Communists in Vietnam. McGeorge Bundy, Johnson's national-security advisor, would be a leading hawk in the war effort. No one in the Kennedy or Johnson administrations thought to ask Reischauer for his opinion. Reischauer would refuse to criticize his nation's foreign policy while serving as ambassador, but he would resign in 1966 and later call for Rusk's resignation. He would nevertheless be attacked by antiwar activists, some of them his former students, for supporting the war.

In June 1955, Reischauer, still in shock over the loss of Adrienne, embarked on a trip to Japan accompanied by his three children. The family of four drove across the United States, stopping at the Black Hills, Yellowstone National Park, the Grand Canyon, Yosemite, and the California coast. Flying on to Hawaii and then Tokyo, they stayed in the former Reischauer home (Raishawa-kan) on the campus of Tokyo Women's University (Tokyo Joshi Daigaku). Enrolling the children in the American School in Japan, he set about a schedule of giving lectures and seminars, renewing his friendships, reading scholarly Japanese books, and conducting the business of the Harvard-Yenching Institute in Korea, Hong Kong, and Taiwan.

In his emotionally drained condition, he found solace in long conversations with Kuwabara Motoko, who had been his family's maid in 1937 and was now the housekeeper at Raishawa-kan. "My children tutored [her] two boys in English, but Motoko counseled me on life, being a font of common sense wisdom. We would talk together by the hour, and I do not know what I would have done without her those first few months."[38] Once again, as in his youth, he discovered in a Japanese woman the emotional support that was missing in the rest of his life.

At this low point in his life, however, he also had an extraordinary encounter. While having lunch at the Tokyo Foreign Correspondents Club in June 1955, he met Haru Matsukata, who was at a nearby table with the novelist James Michener. Michener introduced them. In January 1956, they married. The next chapter of their lives together was launched. They would come to share, above all else, a common mission.

Haru Matsukata, at thirty-nine, was a strong woman, noble in appearance, and aristocratic in manner. Her lineage could be traced back to the twelfth century on her father's side and to the eleventh century on her mother's side. Her father's father, Matsukata Masayoshi (1835–1924), was a financial genius and one of the Satsuma "oligarchs," or *genro*, who played a key role in building the successful Meiji state in the late nineteenth century. He served more than fifteen years as Japan's finance minister and served twice as prime minister (1891–92 and 1896–98). He lived in Japanese style in a grand home with more than twenty servants, fathered many children with his wife and concubines, and was given the noble rank of prince toward the end of his distinguished career. One reliable estimate credits him with about fifty grandchildren!

Her mother's father, Rioichiro Arai, could not have been more different. He had gone to New York in 1876 at the age of twenty to set up a business exporting Japanese raw silk into the American market. Except for annual business trips back to Japan, he lived for the rest of his life in the United States. His daughter Miyo (Haru's mother) was born in New York and grew up there and in Old Greenwich, Connecticut, "becoming at heart and in her ways, much more American than Japanese."[39]

When Haru's father, Matsukata Shokuma, a younger son of Prince Matsukata, studied briefly at Yale, he met and became engaged to Miyo. Their marriage ceremony took place in Japan, and Miyo had to make the difficult adjustment to her new life in Tokyo as part of a traditional Japanese family. Determined to raise her children as strong, independent individuals in the American style, she soon became frustrated and despondent at the strict social rules of an aristocratic Japanese family. But in 1917 she began to study Christian Science and later hired an American school teacher from California to tutor her own children in Christian Science, the English language, and other subjects. She eventually had six children, and all were educated by English-speaking governesses. Haru attended high school at the American School in Japan and then went to Principia College near St. Louis, Missouri. At college, though, she continued to feel like an outsider: "I had my share of dates and social life, but I remember looking enviously at happy couples among my schoolmates, realizing that their relationships might lead to marriage while I belonged to a different world. At times I felt almost bitter that I had been raised to be so different from other Japanese. Why couldn't I have been brought up the ordinary way, I would think, since being different didn't seem to make me a real American either?"

Graduating from Principia in 1937 and returning to Japan in 1937, Haru was a confused young woman: well educated but almost totally lacking in a sense of personal identity and purpose. Her confusion got worse as she found America and Japan hurtling toward war. The next eight years were the hardest in her life.

She studied Japanese history and art in a search for her roots and identity. "Marriage appeared out of the question. My upbringing made me feel that I could never submit to what we would now call the blatant male chauvinism of Japanese husbands." There were few careers open to Japanese women—especially those without a traditional Japanese education. She was desperately lonely. She conducted research on her paternal grandfather's life, impressed by the "Spartan virtues and steel-like willpower of the feudal society that produced him." She discovered that he had opposed Japan's aggressive policy toward China in 1915 (the Twenty-One Demands).

With the onset of war between Japan and the United States, Haru and her family left Tokyo for Kamakura, forty miles south of Tokyo, where they became farmers until the end of the war in 1945. "These were sad, hopeless years for me, and I even contemplated suicide," she admitted later.

Japan's surrender brought her no relief. At the age of twenty-nine, "after eight miserable wartime years in Japan, I was still at a loss about who and what I was," she wrote in her extraordinary autobiography in 1986. "As the years passed, my sense of aloneness deepened. I was still living in two worlds, even though these worlds were no longer at war and were beginning to become better acquainted."

With the loss of her family's fortune through the destruction of war, confiscatory laws on land and capital, and rampant inflation, Haru was forced to find a job. Being bilingual and a Christian Scientist, she became an assistant to the correspondent of the *Christian Science Monitor* in Japan and later a Tokyo representative of the *Saturday Evening Post.* This position enabled her to join the Foreign Correspondents Club of Japan, the first Japanese citizen to join and one of only a handful of women. In 1954, she was elected secretary of the club.

Nevertheless, she felt ill at ease and uncertain of her identity: "My colleagues and friends were mostly American, but I always felt a gulf between us because of their appalling lack of understanding of Japan. On the other side, I had some Japanese friends and many acquaintances who knew little of the United States and had no understanding of the basically American type of life I was leading.

Another problem was that my American friends kept coming and going. After several painful partings from dear friends, I began to shield myself from making close friendships."

At this moment, two desperately lonely humans discovered each other. Or rediscovered each other. It turned out that Haru had been in the sixth grade at the American School in Japan when Edwin Reischauer was a senior, captain of the basketball team and a big man on the campus. He knew much about Japan's history that she did not know. "He was as devoted as I to Japanese-American understanding and friendship. In short, he combined my two cultures, though in his own way. He was like the proverbial boy from next door, and after a few dates we fell in love and were married."

Edwin had no recollection of a "small fry" like Haru from their school days, but had met her younger brother, Mako, and sister, Naka, and was certainly aware of the significant role that her grandfather Matsukata had played in the Meiji Era. Their attraction to each other was instant and mutual. Reischauer had hoped to get married again, though probably not so soon after Adrienne's death just eight months earlier.

"Having had a happy marriage," he wrote, "I found being alone quite intolerable. During her fading years Adrienne expected me to remarry and would frequently question me as to what type of person I would choose, though neither of us happened to think of a Japanese as a possibility for the second Mrs. Reischauer. But Haru and I shared a mixed Japanese and American heritage and a devotion to friendship between our two countries. Except for her far wealthier and aristocratic background, she was for me much like the girl next door."[40]

The courtship proceeded at whirlwind speed starting in December 1955. After going dancing together and several more dates, Reischauer popped the question: "I hope you haven't ruled out completely the possibility of marriage," he said. Her fierce reply: " I wouldn't want to see you again if we weren't going to get married."[41]

In an ecstatic letter to his parents on December 24, 1955, he announced his engagement to Haru: "Haru is 40, not pretty, but extremely aristocratic and refined, a 100% lady, and a truly wonderful person. Having a Japanese daughter-in-law may shock you at first—but I know you'll come to feel about her as you did about Adrienne. She is very calm, matter-of-fact, wonderfully efficient—and so sweet, good and considerate and loving as one could wish. She neither smokes nor drinks—most unusual in this society." In another glowing letter to family members, he wrote that Haru was a "truly wonderful person—much like Adrienne in her thoughtfulness, straightforwardness, and complete genuineness."[42]

As for an interracial marriage, Reischauer declared, "Neither of us had the slightest sense of being of different nationality or race. My father would often ask me confidentially if we did not encounter embarrassing situations, but I could honestly assure him that none had ever arisen. Our racial difference, which must have been all too obvious to anyone else, never entered our minds, except when we jokingly reminded each other of it."[43]

The two were married on January 6, 1956, in a Tokyo ward office. Reischauer hoped to keep it secret until after the first anniversary of Adrienne's death (January 17, 1955) so that he would not appear to be acting with unseemly haste. A small wedding ceremony involving both families took place on February 4. Interestingly, Herbert Norman's older brother, Howard, a missionary in Kobe, performed the ceremony. A year later Herbert Norman would commit suicide in Cairo, hounded by accusations that he had been a Communist spy, and a later generation of academics would paint a picture of hostility between Norman and Reischauer—one that never existed for all their scholarly differences.

"At the time of our marriage," he wrote, "I was an exhausted widower of 45 with three teenage children, long neglected because of Adrienne's terrible illness and getting progressively more out of hand. Haru was a 40-year-old spinster, as they would have called her in an earlier day. It might sound like a marriage of convenience, but it most certainly was not. We were deeply in love with each other and Haru proved to be a wonderful wife, much like Adrienne in some ways, but very different in others."[44]

And in the unpublished manuscript of his memoirs, there was this note:

> [Haru] had none of Adrienne's effervescence and demonstrativeness, being subdued and quiet in a Japanese way, and, when I first knew her, she seemed a little sad from the disappointments her early life had brought her. She is not given to any outward show of affection, again in a typically Japanese fashion, and even today (1986) has not learned to call me to my face anything but "you," not even "Ed" let alone "dearest." From Adrienne I had learned to overcome my Japanese reticence and be somewhat more effusive. However, Haru gave me tremendous support, especially through the early months of our marriage when I continued to be below par both physically and psychologically.[45]

In Haru's account, "Suddenly becoming at age forty the mother of three teenagers and moving to the United States as a professor's wife posed challenges—but there were rewards as well." She admitted that "his scholarly life as a Harvard professor had no appeal for me. I had always felt that professors, because of their dullness, and diplomats, because of their stuffiness, were two types of men I could never be interested in."[46]

By all accounts, Haru, despite her aloofness, fit right into the Reischauer family. She and Ed went through a rather unusual procedure. Edwin put up his three children for adoption, and then he and Haru adopted the children, making Haru their legal mother rather than stepmother, a category they both disliked. The children, especially the girls, came to love her, and she turned out to be an excellent mother, cook, gardener, and even disciplinarian of teenagers. Of the three children, Robert was somewhat hostile to his father for marrying so soon after the death of his mother, but over time he came around. "They were clearly quite fond of each other," he admitted. "Whether it was super best friends as opposed to lovers, I don't know. There were little bits of affection. They would hold hands and exchange a little kiss. But Haru was aloof. I don't remember her ever kissing or hugging me or my sisters. She was shy. I only saw her cry a couple of times."[47]

Selma Janow, wife of American businessman Seymour Janow in Japan, knew Haru in the 1950s, before she met Edwin, and described her as "wonderfully competent. She was practical and full of common sense. She loved kitchen gadgets and became a great cook and gardener. She was very generous and inadvertently funny. She was not sophisticated or worldly. I remember her telling me that she drove Prince Konoe's son across the U.S. in the 1930s without knowing we were in a depression. Her relationship with Ed was amiable, but distant. It was not romantic. Ed was romantic and loved to dance, but she didn't."[48]

Between January, when his marriage took place, and June 1956, Ed, Haru, and their children lived in Haru's small home in Azabu, Japan. Haru continued working for the *Saturday Evening Post* while Ed worked with Matsumoto Shigeharu, a cousin of Haru's, to develop the newly established International House of Japan. This institution would become an important meeting ground for visiting intellectuals and graduate students, linking them to centers of scholarship throughout Japan.

Reischauer also helped found the English Language Educational Council, which would play a major role in helping to support the teaching of English in Japan. Both were funded in part by John D. Rockefeller III. Matsumoto and Rockefeller had become friends in the 1930s when they had studied at Yale. Rockefeller developed a keen interest in Asian culture, especially Japanese art, in the those years and served as an assistant on cultural matters to John Foster Dulles during the negotiation of the peace treaty signed in 1951. He later became the president and a generous benefactor of the Japan Society of New York. Reischauer became a key advisor and board member of that society and a close friend of Rockefeller.

It is impossible to overstate the Rockefeller family's role in introducing Asian culture to America. Almost all of the other leading families in the United States looked first toward Europe: their children learned French in school, read Victorian novels, quoted Shakespeare, and made the grand tour of European cathedrals and museums. They looked upon Asia as a backward, benighted region from which they could learn nothing. A few hardy souls got into the China trade, including the Delano family, President Franklin Delano Roosevelt's forbears, but this was for commerce, not culture. John D. Rockefeller III and his wife, Blanchette, were unique in their appreciation of Asia, its art, and other cultural treasures.

In 1956, Rockefeller asked Reischauer to give advice to his son Jay (John D. Rockefeller IV), who was then a sophomore at Harvard.[49] But Reischauer, understanding that advice is best given when sought, waited for Jay to approach him. Jay had decided even before entering Harvard that he would concentrate on East Asian studies. He took "Rice Paddies" with Fairbank and Reischauer. He also joined the elitist Fly Club, which in that era admitted no public-school graduates. By his junior year, as president of the club, he came to view its snobbery as sickening and came to Reischauer with a plea: "Help me get out of here." Reischauer quickly found him a position teaching English at International Christian University in Japan.

Soon after his arrival, Jay, twenty years old, became fascinated by Japanese culture and decided that instead of teaching English, he would immerse himself in the language. For the next three years, he studied at the International Christian University and spent six months in Kyoto. He arose each morning at 4:30 A.M., learned 3,500 *kanji*, slept on a *tatami* mat, and tried to stay warm in freezing weather in a hot tub (*ofuro*) that could barely contain his six-foot six-and-a-half-inch frame. He loved the discipline and adored his teacher, Ms. Koide, who was "tiny and tough."

Jay would of course go on to become governor of West Virginia and a U.S. senator. In an interview in 2008, half a century later, he viewed his time in Japan as life changing and considered Reischauer "one of my favorite people. He was gracious and outgoing, but always formal," he recalled. Rockefeller's Senate office wall is graced by a large Japanese screen depicting a scene from *Genji Monogatari*. He is, at this writing, the only member of the U.S. Senate with a firsthand understanding of Japan and the Japanese. He is proud to boast that in 2008, the only place where Lexus makes its auto engines outside of Japan is Buffalo, West Virginia. Of all Reischauer's former students, he is perhaps the most influential in the world of politics. Reischauer, in his unpublished memoirs manuscript, wrote about Jay with tongue in cheek, "It's always a pleasure to be able to help a deserving young man get started!"[50]

In June 1956, just a year after embarking with three unruly children on a voyage across America to Japan, Reischauer, along with his newly formed family, set off on a fifty-three-day sea journey from Kobe to Rotterdam on a Japanese freighter, stopping in Taiwan, Hong Kong, Singapore, Cairo, Genoa, Barcelona, Tangier, Casablanca, and London on the way. A near crisis was barely averted when Joan came down with appendicitis and required an operation in Casablanca. From Rotterdam, they rented a car for a grand tour of Europe—Belgium, Paris, Switzerland, Italy, Austria (visiting the home church of the Reischauer ancestors), and Germany—and finally ended up in New York and a new life in Belmont, Massachusetts.

It was obvious to both Edwin and Haru Reischauer that their marriage was based on a shared mission to bring greater understanding and friendship between their two nations. Just how they could fulfill that mission was not at all clear. Neither had the slightest inkling that within four years John F. Kennedy would be elected president of the United States and that they would be sent to Tokyo to carry out their mission.

7

A Time to "Put Up or Shut Up!"

Looking back at Edwin Reischauer's improbable jump from the Harvard faculty to President Kennedy's ambassador to Japan, one is impressed with the extraordinary combination of talent, luck, skill, and connections that made it possible. The atmosphere in Washington, for one brief moment, was welcoming to intellectuals with large ideas. President Kennedy, after eight years of Republican control of the White House, seemed to offer the nation refreshing change, contempt for the hidebound bureaucrats, and a summons to duty. "We can do better," Kennedy repeated again and again in his campaign. The call was compelling for Reischauer, but the odds were against him.

Until 1961, elite members of the career Foreign Service had occupied the post of ambassador to Japan. Joseph Grew, a member of America's establishment, served in the post from 1932 to 1942, and one of America's most illustrious career diplomats, Robert D. Murphy, was ambassador from 1952 to 1953. Two other prominent career men followed him: John M. Allison (1953–57) and Douglas MacArthur II (1957–61), nephew of General Douglas MacArthur, the Supreme Commander of Allied Powers in Tokyo from 1945 to 1951. The Foreign Service in 1960 considered the post to be its own—a career summit and a reward for its most successful and well-connected officers. There was neither a requirement nor an expectation that the American ambassador should be a Japan expert or speak the Japanese language.

The idea of an "intellectual" serving in such an important post also worked against Reischauer. Although the McCarthy era formally ended with the Senate censure of Senator Joseph McCarthy in 1954 and his death in 1957, it left a residue of suspicion among some American voters toward "liberal intellectuals"—

especially those who favored recognition of Communist China and seemed "soft on communism" in this Cold War period. "Even when 'eggheads' were not being portrayed as potential traitors, they were often dismissed as incompetents," writes Susan Jacoby in her perceptive book *The Age of American Unreason*. "In 1954," she recounts, " President Dwight D. Eisenhower, speaking at a Republican fund-raiser, described an intellectual as 'a man who takes more words than are necessary to tell more than he knows.'"[1] Governor George Wallace of Alabama would later run for president on the notion that intellectuals were "pointy-headed liberals" unfit for government service. Even if such labels were grossly unfair, any Harvard professor was sure to face critical scrutiny from conservative members of the Senate Foreign Relations Committee and from the Senate as a whole, where a two-thirds majority is needed to confirm a presidential nominee for the position of ambassador.

Two unrelated developments, however, created an extraordinary window of opportunity for Edwin O. Reischauer. First was the giant protest movement in Japan in May and June 1960 against Diet approval of the revised U.S.–Japan Treaty of Mutual Cooperation and Security (Security Treaty), the cancellation of President Eisenhower's planned visit to Tokyo in June of that year, the forced resignation of Prime Minister Kishi Nobusuke, and the subsequent shock in Washington's foreign-policy community that America's friendly ally in the Pacific would behave in such a rude manner. A number of media accounts of that period suggested that the protest movement had been organized by Communists and that Japan was in danger of teetering over into the Communist bloc, which would have been a devastating blow to America following upon the heels of the Communist victory in the Chinese civil war. Proper attention to Japan became a pressing requirement for any incoming administration.

The second surprising development, as noted earlier, was that the new president, John F. Kennedy, a Harvard graduate, actually enjoyed the company of the Cambridge intellectuals and attracted a number of them into his administration, including McGeorge Bundy, Arthur Schlesinger Jr., John Kenneth Galbraith, Richard Goodwin (Harvard Law School graduate, 1958), Richard Neustadt (Harvard Ph.D., 1951), and Carl Kaysen (Harvard Ph.D., 1954).

On January 1, 1961, Kennedy named McGeorge Bundy as his special assistant for national-security affairs. In early January, Kennedy met in Schlesinger's Cambridge home with Bundy, Galbraith, and Jerome B. Wiesner, the MIT professor who would become his science advisor. Bundy soon learned that his task was to dismantle the bureaucratic foreign-policy machinery that had grown up under President Eisenhower. Both Kennedy and Bundy had read Richard Neustadt's 1960 book *Presidential Power*, which argued that

Roosevelt's freewheeling disorderly style actually exposed him to more information from a wider range of sources and provided him with flexibility in decision making.[2]

Within a month, the National Security Council staff was cut from seventy-one to forty-eight. As Kai Bird describes the change in his masterly biography of the Bundy brothers, William and McGeorge, "In effect, foreign policy would no longer be made at cabinet-level meetings. In theory, the men who came to advise the president in these smaller, freewheeling NSC meetings would represent no bureaucratic constituency other than the president, and they would argue the merits of each policy course based on substance. This was how intellectuals, not bureaucrats, would make foreign policy."[3]

In the climate of Kennedy's "New Frontier," where the "best minds" were being recruited to provide new approaches to cold war issues, the appointment of a scholar such as Reischauer was not completely implausible.

Even so, there were immense obstacles to overcome: resistance from the career Foreign Service personnel, objections from conservative Japanese, and skepticism among conservative American politicians toward all intellectuals. Then, too, for Reischauer in particular, there was the undeniable fact that Haru was Japanese. The story of how Reischauer was able to overcome these obstacles and become ambassador to Japan is a unique tale of Washington intrigue.

In 1959, Reischauer had never met John F. Kennedy and had made no effort to socialize with the Cambridge intellectuals who met regularly with the senator over drinks and dinner in Boston and Cambridge. Unlike Mac Bundy, Galbraith, and Schlesinger, he did not particularly enjoy the company of politicians and made no effort to cultivate their friendship.[4] Also, unlike others in this group, he did not enjoy sitting around drinking martinis. He lacked social connections with power brokers in Washington and much preferred the more orderly sequestered academic life. Unlike Galbraith, who famously took pride in "comforting the afflicted and afflicting the comfortable," he avoided open confrontation and disliked the rough and tumble of political infighting.

In addition, Reischauer was preoccupied with his new bride and three teenage children, his responsibilities as director of the Harvard-Yenching Institute, and his teaching, writing, and research. Even if he had wanted to play the political game, he continued to be slowed down by health problems, suffering from what he called a "wandering pace-maker." He found that extra heartbeats would break up the flow of his words—"a very disconcerting experience when presiding at an important meeting."[5]

But none of these factors prevented him from trying to influence American policymakers in East Asia whenever an opportunity arose, and the issue that most concerned him was America's China policy.

There was good reason in 1959 to be concerned about the danger of war with China. The two nations had come close to war in 1955 and again in 1958, a contest that could have involved nuclear weapons and even an exchange of nuclear attacks with the Soviet Union. Though the Korean War had been fought to a standstill and truce in 1953, the two small islands of Quemoy and Matsu, about six miles off the coast of mainland China, remained a source of potential conflict. The Chinese Nationalist government of Chiang Kai-shek based in Taiwan held them, and the government of Mao Zedong saw them as a potential launching point for Chiang and his forces to invade China and overthrow the Communist regime. They were also a continuing embarrassment to the nationalistic regime in Beijing that was trying to consolidate its power. Washington and Taipei saw them as potential stepping-stones for a Communist invasion of Taiwan.

In 1958, the issue nearly set off a war between the United States and China that could easily have escalated into U.S. nuclear attacks against the mainland.[6] From August to October, the mainland Chinese launched a massive artillery bombardment of the two islands, threatened an invasion, and tried to blockade the two islands against Chinese Nationalist resupply efforts. The United States pledged to support the Nationalists, and U.S. Navy ships escorted the Nationalist resupply ships. The Joint Chiefs of Staff developed plans for nuclear strikes against Shanghai, Guangzhou, and Nanjing in the event the Communists invaded the two islands, which would have resulted in millions of noncombatant deaths. The crisis finally ended in October 1958 when Communist leaders offered to negotiate a peaceful settlement with the Nationalists and ended the bombardment and blockade.

The Quemoy-Matsu crisis would figure in three of the debates between presidential candidates Richard M. Nixon and John F. Kennedy in the fall of 1960. Vice President Nixon, the Republican, attacked Kennedy for his lack of willingness to defend Quemoy and Matsu. Kennedy hinted that if elected, he might soften his approach to mainland China. This debate led to controversy over Cuba policy. Kennedy, eager to deflect criticism of his allegedly weak stance on Quemoy and Matsu, issued a provocative statement on strengthening the "freedom fighters" who opposed the newly victorious regime of Fidel Castro in Havana. Within less than a year, he would be persuaded to launch the disastrous invasion of Cuba at the "Bay of Pigs."

Controversy over China policy hung over the American political horizon from 1958 to 1960. Reischauer could see the danger of war and lost no chance to make this point to Washington policymakers. By now recognized as one of the leading scholars in America on East Asian affairs, he lectured regularly to senior military officers at the National War College. In September 1958, he and a number of Harvard faculty members met in Cambridge with Secretary of State John Foster Dulles for an exchange of views on China. Though Reischauer remained silent at this meeting, he subsequently wrote a personal, three-page letter to Dulles suggesting that the secretary needed to pay attention to East Asian specialists outside the government, most of whom were critical of U.S. policy toward China:

> From your remarks last Saturday, I gathered that you felt that public distaste for our present policy on the offshore islands (Quemoy and Matsu) and Formosa is the result of lack of clear principles, a failure to remember the lessons of history, or sheer lack of "guts." If this were true of the expert and informed public opinion of which I am writing, I should be the first to urge you not to be influenced by it, but this is most emphatically not the case. . . . My own personal divergence from present official views, for example, arises primarily out of my feeling that we have not paid enough attention to an old and basic principle of our foreign policy, the right of self-determination, and have therefore tended to view the Formosa problem too much in terms of Chiang and the continuation of a civil war (which is a virtually hopeless civil war for "our side") and not enough in terms of the aspirations of the people of Formosa to maintain their independence of the Communists as a democracy.
>
> My real purpose is to suggest that there is need for our government to sound out and draw on informed opinion more fully that it has been doing of late. . . . My own personal experience is very limited, but I believe that since the spring of 1950 no non-official "expert" of Far Eastern affairs has been asked to participate seriously in State Department deliberations.[7]

Only those who agreed with official policy were consulted in Washington, he charged. In effect, Reischauer was issuing a direct and personal challenge to the then prevailing views of the China lobby in Washington. Dulles's one-page reply a month later was polite but terse:

> The particular problem which we discussed at Cambridge was whether it is possible to bring about a re-forming of the free world position in the Western Pacific by a fallback from Quemoy and Matsu without

> seriously impairing the defensibility of the entire position. The answer to that depends upon intimate knowledge of the thinking of the governments who now hold the insular and peninsular chain from Japan to Australia. We are able to get information on this situation from our diplomatic representatives and also through CIA, etc. I am not sure that any of those with whom I was talking at Cambridge feel that they can add to our knowledge on this score.[8]

This response was a classical State Department ploy: no one can know what we know, and therefore you are not qualified criticize our policies. But Reischauer was unabashed and simply redoubled his efforts to change the official Washington view of China.

In March 1959, he joined with twelve other scholars in calling for exchanges of reporters with Communist China. Calling the embargo on travel to China by American journalists "a violation of our fundamental right to be informed about an entire quarter of the world's population," his letter to the *New York Times* stated, "We have sufficient confidence in the American system to believe that if the Communist Chinese, through legal access, learn more about our country, this will be to our advantage rather than disadvantage."[9]

During the summer of 1959, Reischauer attended a weeklong foreign-affairs conference at Lake Couchiching, north of Toronto in Canada, where he began a serious dialogue with J. Graham ("Jeff") Parsons, assistant secretary of state for the Far East from 1959 to 1961. In a letter written after the conference, Reischauer politely but firmly spelled out in some detail his basic criticism of U.S. policy regarding Asia. The letter was probably the most insightful policy statement of his whole career.[10]

The United States, he advised in this eight-page, carefully argued brief, should take a long-term view in Asian affairs, focusing more on economic and ideological matters and less on military intervention. "In the long run," he wrote, "nothing is more important to us than the confidence and good will of Asians if we are to be effective in our efforts to help them find a non-Communist path to the modernization they seek." Arguing that the "soft sell" is more likely than the "hard sell" to win Asians over to our side in the Cold War, he proposed that "we should show a sympathetic attitude toward neutralism, because this is after all a strong expression of nationalism (which is the best defense against Communism in Asia)."

The U.S. policy of not recognizing Communist China and restricting trade with the mainland was wrongheaded and ineffective, he argued. It did not hamper China's growth and in fact helped the Chinese government justify its harsh rule and bolstered nationalistic enthusiasm for the regime. The policy also forced on Taiwan the heavy burden of pretending to represent all of China. The resulting military burden had slowed the growth of real democracy on Taiwan. "In the long run, Taiwan can remain free from Communist China only if it develops a viable economy and a democratic answer to the Communist way."

Communist China should be allowed to take its rightful place in the United Nations, he wrote. "There is a vast resentment of the 'blackballing' of an Asian nation by a white nation, especially when couched in moralistic, 'holier-than-thou' terms." The United States should try to pull China away from its alliance with the Soviet Union, and there is a good chance that such a policy would succeed. This point, in retrospect, was particularly perceptive: although Reischauer may not have known it at the time, subsequent accounts agree that the Sino–Soviet split had its origins in September 1957, when the Soviet Union launched *Sputnik* into orbit and then refused to share its new technology with two Chinese delegations that had rushed to Moscow, only to be rebuffed.

Getting to the nub of the issue, Reischauer told Parsons: "The ideal of self-determination means the acceptance of the results of the civil war in China.... It also means that we must champion the rights of the people on Taiwan to self-determination.... We would be in a position to reassert our rightful position as the chief Western champion of Asian nationalism (taking away from the Russians their bogus but very valuable claim to this position)."

In sum, Reischauer urged that the United States should sponsor a package deal under which Beijing and Taipei would recognize each other, with Beijing recognized as China and Taipei as the new state of Taiwan. The offshore islands Quemoy and Matsu would go to China. Beijing would get China's permanent seat on the United Nations Security Council, "but the package might also contain other permanent Asian seats for India and Japan."

Reischauer's sensible letter is interesting today for several reasons. Most of his points have proven correct over time. U.S. recognition of the Beijing government, trade with the mainland, the Sino–Soviet split, and democracy in Taiwan have improved prospects for prosperity and stability in the region. But the pro–Chiang Kai-shek China lobby controlled the State Department at the time, and it was determined to stand by the Chiang Kai-shek government to the very end. This lobby was led by the powerful Senator William Knowland of California and Congressman Walter Judd, a former missionary to China from Wisconsin, and it received funding from the Chinese Nationalist government in Taipei, along with media support from Henry Luce and *Time* magazine.

The China lobby was entrenched in the State Department in the person of Walter S. Robertson, assistant secretary of state for the Far East from 1953 to

1959. Robertson was close to Admiral Arthur W. Radford, chairman of the Joint Chiefs of Staff, who had advocated using nuclear weapons against China in the first Quemoy-Matsu crisis of 1955. He was also close to Allen Dulles, director of Central Intelligence, and brother of Secretary of State John Foster Dulles. Robertson was a banker from Richmond, Virginia, who had been to China with General George C. Marshall's mission in 1947–48 and had developed strong sympathy for the cause of Chiang Kai-shek. As Marshall Green, an East Asian expert in the State Department would later recall, "Robertson had this extraordinary capacity of charm, real southern charm . . . together with shrewdness and a position of considerable authority beyond what would normally obtain in a situation like that, largely because the people above him were European-oriented and didn't know much about the Far East."[11]

There were no countervailing views in the State Department. Most of the China experts who would have agreed with Reischauer, such as John Service and John Emmerson, had been hounded out of the department by the McCarthy purges or exiled to posts outside of Asia. Those who remained were silent.

Parsons, to his credit, took Reischauer's letter seriously. Given Robertson's overwhelming influence within the State Department, however, it is no surprise that Parson's eventual response to Reischauer almost exactly reflected the position of the pro–Nationalist China Lobby. In an eleven-page rebuttal dated November 23, 1959, he contended that U.S. China policy "has demonstrated its worth in serving the national interest. Recognizing Peiping [*sic*] would probably be impossible without abandoning Taiwan to the Communists." The "free Chinese Government" in Taipei, he stated, represents a source of hope to anti-Communist Chinese on the mainland. It is wrong to think that we can help open up a rift between the Soviets and Chinese Communists, who have been Soviet-oriented since the birth of their party in 1921. And finally, "the will to resist Communism in Taiwan is intimately related to the conviction, held by a large and very important portion of the population, that their mission is not merely to defend Taiwan, but to work for the liberation of all China from Communism. Their morale is sustained by our recognition of the Republic of China as the government of all China; it would be torpedoed by a decision on our part to recognize it only as a small country independent of China."[12]

It is also interesting to note that Parsons, as a senior "Asian expert" in the State Department, had every right to expect that he would be the next ambassador to Tokyo, following Douglas MacArthur II. Like Joseph Grew, Robert Fearey, and Marshall Green, he had attended Groton, the elite boarding school, and Yale, and had served as Grew's assistant in Tokyo in the 1930s. Therefore, when Reischauer was nominated to the post, it is not surprising that Parsons bitterly opposed that nomination. Under President Kennedy, he was sent off as ambassador to Sweden.

Reischauer sent Parsons a polite but firm two-page reply. "Your long and full letter makes me feel guilty to have taken up so much of the time of a very busy man and his busy assistants. Needless to say, I appreciate the thoroughness with which you have replied to my letter of August 27," he wrote. But he went on to challenge Parson's "irritating" implication that critics of U.S. China policy were naive and unrealistic. "Critics of the State Department should not be quickly dismissed as being 'soft' or 'flabby' in their thinking about Chinese Communism," he declared. "I did want to call to your attention these misinterpretations of the views of some of your critics," he concluded.[13]

U.S. China policy in 1959–60 was naturally a major topic of conversation and debate among Reischauer and Fairbank's students at Harvard. Every Friday afternoon the two professors would hold court in a gathering open to several dozen of their graduate students at the Harvard-Yenching Institute at Two Divinity Avenue. Arcane aspects of T'ang Dynasty history would be discussed, but current issues in East Asia would also find their way into the conversation. The pronouncements of the two great men were received as if they were messages handed down from Mount Olympus. In this forum, Reischauer made no secret of his support for recognition of Communist China.

One of the students who attended these discussions regularly was James C. Thomson Jr., who was at the time completing his doctoral dissertation under Fairbank. Thomson had served as the head tutor in the Rice Paddies course and was a favorite of both Fairbank and Reischauer. He was intimately familiar with Reischauer's views on China and strongly agreed with them. In his youthful idealism, he saw the possibility of translating them into U.S. policy. Another young man who sat in on these discussions was Ernest Young, a student of Chinese history who shared Thomson's dream of closer relations with mainland China.

Jim Thomson was one of the brightest of a new generation of China experts in America. Like Reischauer, he was the son of Presbyterian educational missionary parents and had spent his childhood in Nanjing, China. Needless to say, the Chinese Revolution dominated the talk around the family dining-room table. He sailed from Shanghai in 1939 at the age of eight, having developed what would be a lifelong interest in U.S.–China relations.

A brilliant student, he was class valedictorian at the Lawrenceville School. In 1948, he returned to China with classmate Winthrop Knowlton to study at

Nanjing University. They found themselves caught in the final stages of Mao Zedong's Communist Revolution from July 1948 to May 1949. Nevertheless, they were able to travel to Beijing, Suchow, Shanghai, Chengdu, Chungking, Kweiyang, and Kwangchou, observing a drama that few Americans could know or understand.

Knowlton remembers Thomson at Lawrenceville as "precocious and quick-witted and scornful of the accumulation of material goods. Academically, he ranked at the top of our class; he sang in the choir and wrote and starred in musicals put on by the school drama society; he headed the debating team and ran the school newspaper and wrote for the literary magazine. In those various endeavors he captivated the faculty and most of his fellow students."[14]

Thomson's feel for the Chinese language and culture distinguished him from other scholars of his generation who could study China only from afar. After his mainland adventures, he enrolled at Yale, where he majored in history and graduated Phi Beta Kappa in 1953. After a year at Clare College, Cambridge University, he entered Harvard in 1955, earning a Ph.D. under Professor Fairbank in 1961.

Unlike many scholars, Thomson was also a skilled political operator and a man with an enormous capacity for making and keeping friends. His sense of humor was contagious. One friend said of him after his death in 2002, "Jim was the one who got Asia right. . . . [He was an] utterly charming, witty, sensitive, many-faceted man—a complete human being: loyal to a fault, of absolute personal integrity, and a boon companion."[15] At Yale, Thomson had won the coveted job of editor of the *Yale Daily News*, and he quickly displayed a knack for making himself useful to powerful men. In 1959, he became an aide to Connecticut congressman Chester B. Bowles, a fellow Yale graduate, who became his mentor in politics.

Bowles, a highly successful founder of an advertising agency and a liberal Democrat, was elected governor of Connecticut in 1948. Viewed by some as too liberal, he lost his bid for reelection in 1950 and was appointed ambassador to India, serving there from 1951 to 1953. Unsuccessful in several attempts to become a U.S. senator, he was elected to the House of Representatives in 1959 for Connecticut's Second District. It was at this point that Jim Thomson joined his staff.

Bowles was an early supporter of John F. Kennedy's presidential campaign, chief author of the Democratic Party platform in 1960, and a foreign-policy advisor to Kennedy. It is interesting that one proposal on foreign policy in this platform stipulated that there would be no American "representatives who are ignorant of the language and culture and politics of the nation" to which they are assigned. For most countries, this was an accepted and obvious policy; for the United States in 1961, it was a radical and far-fetched notion.

Kennedy appointed Bowles undersecretary of state, deputy to the aloof and hawkish secretary of state Dean Rusk. The appointment was a disaster. Bowles was accustomed to speaking out on issues, and he leaked to the press his opposition to the April 1961 Bay of Pigs invasion of Cuba. Rusk, deeply committed to the support of the Chinese Nationalists on Taiwan, had an innate suspicion of anyone who played down the aggressive intentions of Communist China. Considered a "loose cannon" by Kennedy loyalists, Bowles was removed from his post as undersecretary of state in November 1961 and named the president's special representative on African, Asian, and Latin American affairs, and ambassador at large. In July 1963, he returned to India as ambassador, a post he held until the end of the Johnson administration in 1969.

But before Dean Rusk could take firm hold of the State Department, Chester Bowles eagerly set about finding talented candidates for ambassadorships around the world. He was perfectly suited to the task. Irreverent and mistrustful of bureaucrats, he sought out and welcomed innovative thinkers. Kennedy "did not pretend or attempt to achieve an average cross-section of the country—he wanted the best," recalled Theodore Sorenson.[16] And according to Geoffrey Kabaservice, "[These men] came from the nation's finest universities, its major corporations and foundations, the boards and executive suites of the most prestigious law firms and financial institutions. Kennedy's appointments included Republicans as well as Democrats, more Jews in the cabinet than ever before, more Ivy League graduates, professors and administrators, and even fifteen Rhodes Scholars."[17]

In his ten months in office, Bowles assembled an extraordinary array of new talent. Arthur M. Schlesinger Jr. recalled:

> Bowles also wanted to bring people from outside "unhampered by past loyalties" and committed to the New Frontier into the conduct of foreign relations. He canvassed the universities, the foundations, the press and politics and was more responsible than anyone else for the high quality of Kennedy's first wave of appointments in foreign affairs. As a result, Abram Chayes became Legal Adviser, Roger Hilsman Director of Intelligence and Research, Lucius Battle Chief of the Secretariat, Harlan Cleveland Assistant Secretary for International Organization Affairs, Philip Coombs Assistant Secretary for Cultural Affairs, Wayne Fredericks Deputy Assistant Secretary for African Affairs, Arturo Morales Carrion Deputy Assistant Secretary for Inter-American Affairs, Phillips Talbot Assistant Secretary for Near Eastern Affairs. As a result, too, J. Kenneth Galbraith became

ambassador to India, Edwin Reischauer to Japan, George Kennan to Yugoslavia, Teodoro Moscoso to Venezuela, William Attwood to Guinea, William McCormick Blair, Jr. to Denmark, Kenneth Young to Thailand, Philip Kaiser to Senegal and, in due course, Lincoln Gordon to Brazil, James Loeb to Peru and John Bartlow Martin to the Dominican Republic. Bowles was also the strong advocate of the appointment of Edward R. Murrow as head of the United States Information Agency.[18]

Rusk was an unusual choice for secretary of state. Born to a poor farming family in rural Cherokee County, Georgia, and educated at Davidson College, he won a Rhodes Scholarship to attend Oxford University. A brilliant, self-made man, he lacked the elite credentials of McGeorge Bundy and had almost no connections with the Kennedys. He became a professor of government and dean of the faculty at Mills College in California, and studied law at the University of California in 1940. Serving in the army as a captain and staff officer in the China-Burma-India theater during World War Two, he came back to Washington in 1945, serving in the War Department and then the State Department. He and Colonel Charles Bonesteel were involved in drawing the fateful line across the map of Korea at the thirty-eighth parallel, separating the Communist North from the South in 1945.[19] Rusk became a strong supporter of the Chinese Nationalist government in Taiwan and cultivated something of a reputation as an expert on East Asia as a result of his time as assistant secretary of state for the Far East in 1950–51. A lifelong Democrat, he left government when Eisenhower was elected in 1952 and became head of the Rockefeller Foundation.

Bowles appointed Jim Thomson, then thirty-one, his special assistant in January 1961. Thomson lost no time in promoting the candidacy of Reischauer for a key job in the new administration. He had at first thought of the job of assistant secretary of state for Far Eastern affairs. Knowing that Reischauer favored recognition of Communist China, Thomson hoped that Reischauer would be able to use his influence and stature in the field of East Asian studies to ease the way toward such an outcome. But John Fairbank, his Harvard mentor, told Thomson that Reischauer wasn't "tough enough" for that job; instead, he should be ambassador to Japan.[20] Thomson finally agreed. He still hoped that Reischauer could help engineer a change in China policy from Tokyo. It was an inspired though perhaps naive gamble that flew in the face of overwhelming odds, but in the exciting atmosphere of the New Frontier almost any good idea seemed worth a try, or so Thomson believed.[21]

In October 1960, Reischauer had caught the attention of the foreign-policy community during the Kennedy-Nixon battle for the White House with his article in *Foreign Affairs*, "The Broken Dialogue with Japan."[22] He had gone to Japan in the summer of 1960, just after the climax of the May–June protest movement against Prime Minister Kishi and the ratification of the U.S.–Japan Security Treaty and had spent most of July 1960 interviewing the main actors. His article was a straightforward explanation of the thinking of the various left-wing opponents of the revised U.S.–Japan Security Treaty, of the conservatives who supported the treaty, and of the U.S. government. His conclusion: "Never since the end of the war has the gap in understanding between Americans and Japanese been wider than over this incident.... After 15 years of massive contact, Americans and Japanese seem to have less real communication than ever."

Rejecting the fears expressed in the American media that Japan was turning hostile to the United States, he found that the Japan was on a "surprisingly even keel" and that "there is every prospect that the governing party, which is solidly committed to the present defense relationship with the United States, will stay in power for the foreseeable future." But he noted that the protest demonstrations were a "sign of a huge current of discontent within Japanese society—a frustration with present trends and a strong sense of alienation from the existing order." Noting that the protesters included the bulk of Japan's intellectuals and college students—that is, the would-be ideological pathfinders and the generation to which the future of Japan belongs—he declared that "the growing gap between their thinking and that of Americans is a truly frightening phenomenon."

Then, in his most provocative assertion, he charged, "The shocking misestimate of the situation in May and June on the part of the American Government and Embassy in Tokyo reveals how small is our contact with the Japanese opposition." This statement enraged Ambassador Douglas MacArthur II and Assistant Secretary of State J. Graham Parsons. MacArthur summoned Reischauer to the embassy and showed him dozens of embassy telegrams that appeared to contradict his statement. Parsons wrote a long and detailed letter attempting to refute Reischauer's assertions. Reischauer later admitted in his autobiography that MacArthur "had some justification for his objections,"[23] and he agreed to tone down his remarks in a Japanese translation for *Sekai* magazine.[24] But the fat was now in the fire: Reischauer had consciously or unconsciously put himself into the political arena. Rumors began to circulate that if Kennedy (the Harvard graduate) were elected president in November, Reischauer would be high on the list of potential ambassadors to Japan. As noted earlier, the two men had never met.

Was Reischauer's article in fact an application for the job of ambassador to Tokyo? Probably not—he was too shrewd an observer of Washington politics to imagine that such an outcome would be possible. But he doubtless understood that the publication of such an article would give him a voice in any discussion of East Asian policy in the event that Kennedy won the presidency, and he relished that possibility.

Jim Thomson, however, saw an unprecedented opportunity to change U.S. China policy. Ever the loyal disciple of Fairbank and to a lesser extent of Reischauer, he would spend the next five years in the State Department and White House trying to change China policy from within. He had high hopes that Reischauer could effectively educate the foreign-policy establishment in Washington to accept his views. As he would eventually learn to his great regret, however, the legacy of the 1950s—the "loss of China," the Korean War, and the Far East policy of Secretary of State Dulles—were too powerful to overcome. In a perceptive essay, Thomson would write in 1968:

> In 1961, the U.S. Government's East Asian establishment was undoubtedly the most rigid and doctrinaire of Washington's regional divisions in foreign affairs. This was especially true at the Department of State, where the incoming administration found the Bureau of Far Eastern Affairs the hardest nut to crack. It was a bureau that had been purged of its best China expertise, and of farsighted, dispassionate men, as a result of McCarthyism. Its members were generally committed to one policy line: the close containment and isolation of mainland China, the harassment of "neutralist nations" which sought to avoid alignment with either Washington or Peking, and the maintenance of a network of alliances with anti-Communist client states on China's periphery.[25]

In January 1961, working just outside of the office of Undersecretary of State Chester Bowles, Thomson placed a file containing biographical information on Reischauer in the pile of folders on individuals that Bowles was considering for key ambassadorships. For several days, Bowles appeared not to notice Reischauer's name. Thomson would enter Bowles's office in the evening after Bowles had gone home and would find that Reischauer's file had moved into the middle of the pile. Carefully placing it on top of the pile for several evenings in a row, he finally got a reaction from Bowles. Summoning Thomson into the his office, Bowles roared, "Who is this fellow 'Rickshawer' that keeps popping up on my desk?" Bowles was of course playing on the word *rickshaw*, a Chinese pedicab. Bowles and Reischauer had met in 1957 when both received honorary degrees from Oberlin, but Bowles had forgotten about it. Thomson several times explained patiently why Reischauer would be best qualified to deal with Japan, citing his deep knowledge of the language and history, and his recent article in *Foreign Affairs*. Bowles, after some hesitation, came around to Thomson's repeated arguments and forwarded Reischauer's name to McGeorge Bundy, who was by now President Kennedy's special assistant for national security. Bundy jumped at the idea and recommended it to Kennedy, who quickly approved.[26]

Reischauer had enjoyed a long and warm relationship with Bundy at Harvard. He had known him as the "brilliant young Dean of the Faculty of Arts and Sciences" and as a trustee of the Harvard-Yenching Institute. "As hard as he was brilliant—a sort of diamond of a man—Mac simply quoted President Truman's famous statement, 'If you can't stand the heat, get out of the kitchen.' I admired Mac greatly and marveled at his capacity to keep a meeting of his blasé faculty spellbound by his virtuoso presentation of as dull a subject as the budget. It was not surprising that as the special assistant to President Kennedy for National Security Affairs he was to shine as brightly on the national stage as on the restricted one at Harvard."[27]

Mac Bundy, with his impeccable establishment and academic credentials, had been a Republican for much of his life. By all accounts, he was brilliant. In 1953, at age thirty-four, he was appointed chairman of Harvard's government department, though he had never bothered to get a Ph.D. in the field. When Harvard's president, James B. Conant, retired that year, Bundy was immediately placed on a short list of candidates to succeed him. He did not win the job, but the man who did, Nathan M. Pusey, immediately appointed him dean of the Faculty of Arts and Sciences. Leslie Gelb, a graduate student at Harvard in the late 1950s who would later become a primary author of the *Pentagon Papers*, a columnist for the *New York Times*, and president of the Council on Foreign Relations, remembered Bundy as "a man of utter self-confidence and precision of expression," with "a personality to intimidate."[28] Bundy exercised considerable clout in the early days of the Kennedy administration, both inside the bureaucracy and on the social scene that grew up around the new administration. One onlooker commented on Bundy's "fine taste for malice and a somewhat forced, giddy gaiety, most noticeable in uproarious tete-a-tetes [*sic*] with Washington's most elegant hostesses."[29]

Bundy thought his policy credentials as a budding young statesman were impressive. He had helped Henry Stimson, the legendary secretary of state (1929–33) and secretary of war (1940–45), in editing and publishing his diaries.[30] By his late twenties, he was a close friend of such luminaries as the poet Archibald McLeish, the legendary book editor Cass Canfield, Justice Felix Frankfurter of the Supreme Court, and columnist Walter Lippmann. And, as noted earlier, he met each month over dinner with other policy intellectuals including Carl Kaysen, John Kenneth Galbraith, physicist

Jerome Wiesner, economist James Tobin, and Arthur Schlesinger, to discuss foreign-policy issues.

Bundy's first brush with Japanese affairs came when he was helping Stimson justify the decision to drop atomic bombs on Hiroshima and Nagasaki. A wave of criticism over this decision arose in 1946 from respected thinkers and writers such as Reinhold Niebuhr, Admiral William F. Halsey, and Norman Cousins. Among their arguments were that Japan was already defeated and would have surrendered by November 1945 even without use of the bombs; that acceptance of Japan's condition that the emperor be kept on the throne could have hastened the surrender; and that the bombs were dropped mainly as a way to intimidate the Soviet Union. Stimson asked Bundy to write an article countering these arguments, and the article was published as the cover story in *Harper's* in February 1947 under Stimson's name. It repeated the standard U.S. government position: Japan was not nearly ready to surrender in August 1945; the atomic bomb was a legitimate weapon of war; a display of the bomb's power would not have been feasible; the Potsdam ultimatum had been rejected; the bomb was intended to shock Japan into surrender; and it prevented an invasion that would have cost millions of lives on both sides. The article was widely attacked, and later in his life Bundy seemed at least in part to recant:

> I am not disposed to criticize the use of the existence of the bomb to help to end the war, but it does seem to me, looking back on it, that there were opportunities for communication and warning available to the United States Government which were not completely thought through by our government at that time. In July and early August 1945, the United States government knew three things that the Japanese government did not. One was that the bomb was coming into existence, had been successfully tested. One was that the United Sates government was prepared to allow the emperor to remain on his throne in Japan, and the third was that the Russians were coming into the war. And the question, it seems to me, that was not fully studied, not fully presented to President Truman, was whether warning of the bomb and assurance on the emperor could not have been combined in a fashion which would have produced Japanese surrender without the use of the bomb on a large city, with all the human consequences that followed.[31]

On another occasion, however, when one of his colleagues was criticizing the internment of one hundred twenty thousand Japanese Americans during World War Two, Bundy called the surprised younger man "a bleeding-heart liberal."[32]

The question that begs to be answered is, How could Bundy—the man universally described as a brilliant scholar steeped in the history and conduct of U.S. foreign policy, a colleague who had enjoyed a close relationship with Reischauer at Harvard, and who must have known that Reischauer was America's leading scholar on East Asian affairs—have failed to seek out Reischauer's advice when the war in Vietnam lurked as a smoldering problem in 1961 and escalated dramatically in 1964? Even if Bundy had not read Reischauer's *Wanted: An Asian Policy*, he must have been at least dimly aware of Reischauer's dissenting views on China, Vietnam, and Asian nationalism. Jim Thomson, who later served on Bundy's staff (1964–66), briefed him on these views.

Several explanations seem possible. Area specialists, especially in East Asian affairs, were still suspect as a result of the McCarthy hearings. Bundy's National Security Council was devoid of experts who had spent serious time in Asia. American establishment figures such as Bundy tended to look down on Asia as a benighted, backward area that required no study or deep understanding. His main staff member dealing with Asia was Michael V. Forrestal, a New York lawyer who had specialized in international finance and the oil and gas business. Bundy may have categorized Reischauer as no more than a "Japan hand" who was not qualified to advise on other Asian issues. Yet the two men served together on the board of the Harvard-Yenching Institute, where many parts of East Asia were discussed.

Another explanation relates to Dean Rusk, Kennedy's surprise choice for secretary of state. Rusk and Reischauer detested each other, as we shall see again in chapter 9. Rusk, who claimed to be something of an Asian expert himself, clearly felt threatened by a genuine Asian expert who rejected his hard-line views on Communist China. He was also resentful of Reischauer's Harvard credentials. Formerly an impoverished student who had worked his way through Davidson College ("the Princeton of the South") by waiting on tables, he probably mistook Reischauer for a privileged and elitist intellectual.

Though Rusk was a professor and dean before World War Two, he mistrusted academics and missed no opportunity to disparage their enterprise. In his autobiography, he deplored the "publish or perish" syndrome and felt that most academic writing did not deserve to be published. When as secretary of state he sought their advice, he recalled that "by the time professors work out all their footnotes and have taken anywhere from nine months to two years to produce their studies, the issues have often changed and slipped out from under them."[33] In short, Rusk viewed Reischauer as an impractical, ivory-tower scholar who was unqualified to advise on Asian affairs.

One story, possibly apocryphal, would later become famous within the State Department about the Rusk-Reischauer relationship. Ambassador Reischauer, when asked at a press conference in Tokyo what the Japanese position should be on Communist China, responded that it was up to the Japanese government and people. When Rusk read an account of this statement, he scribbled in the margin next to it, "No it isn't."

Reischauer viewed Rusk as something of a charlatan who could not speak an Asian language and had no genuine understanding of the region. Rusk would appoint as his assistant secretaries of state for the Far East W. Averell Harriman, Roger Hilsman, and William P. Bundy, Mac's older brother—none of whom knew much about East Asia in general or about China and Japan in particular. All of them, to varying degrees, saw South Vietnam as a domino. If it fell to communism, then all of Southeast Asia would follow suit, and Chinese power would overshadow the entire region. Dissenting views were not welcomed in this bureaucracy, and genuine specialists on Asia were not appreciated.

We can see in the Rusk-Reischauer relationship a common fault line in the foreign-policy community. The generalists climb up the bureaucratic ladder through management and analytical skills and by forging useful political connections; they tend to put down the specialists by accusing them of "clientitis" or being too friendly to the country of their special knowledge. The specialists often mock the generalists as hopelessly ignorant, often unable to pronounce the names of their areas of responsibility, and unqualified to advise on policy issues. The generalists usually win. This is more true in the East Asian field than in others: the drudgery of learning three to four thousand Chinese characters exacts a toll and creates specialists whose language skills are impressive but who often lack the stomach for bureaucratic infighting.

A third explanation may be that the "Young Turks" in the Kennedy administration desperately feared looking weak in the face of Communist power. Kennedy had accused the Eisenhower administration of ignoring an alleged "missile gap" with the Soviet Union—a gap that turned out to be nonexistent. Kennedy was persuaded to launch the disastrous Bay of Pigs invasion of Cuba in April 1961 and seemed overmatched when he met Nikita Khrushchev in Vienna in June of that year. Vietnam was seen in Washington as a kind of testing ground, where American resolve and strength to resist communism could be demonstrated. Dissenters such as Reischauer, who thought that the Communist movement in Vietnam was a nationalist reaction to years of French colonial rule and that China was not the force behind the Vietcong rebellion, could not get a hearing.

A fourth explanation would seem to be hubris. Bundy did not respect scholarly expertise when it came to the hard, cold world of international politics. At the same time, however, he did not respect Dean Rusk. According to Kai Bird, "Mac quickly decided that Rusk's bland demeanor masked neither wit nor intelligence. Very early in the new administration it became clear that Bundy's shop was running circles around Rusk's State Department. Bundy had daily access to the president. Rusk did not."[34] When Bundy left Harvard for the White House, Harvard sociologist David Riesman felt uneasy: "He was so good that when he left I grieved for Harvard and grieved for the nation; for Harvard because he was the perfect dean, for the nation because I thought that very same arrogance and hubris might be very dangerous."[35]

Yet another appraisal of Bundy came from the novelist Louis Auchincloss, also a Groton and Yale graduate, in 2008: "The trouble with Groton was that, through its potent combination of religion and sport, the school trained its boys to associate nobility with domination, duty with victory, dedication with ruthlessness."[36]

Reischauer would later note, "Even McGeorge Bundy, in his crucial post as security advisor to the president saw no necessity of learning more about Japan. I constantly urged him to come for a visit to educate himself, but he never got around to it until the spring of 1966, by which time he had resigned from his White House position."[37]

However unconcerned Bundy was with Japan, he would serve to protect Reischauer from critics in the Kennedy and Johnson administrations. In fact, his ignorance of and disinterest in Japan and East Asia would work in Reischauer's favor. The Kennedy administration, preoccupied in its early days with the Berlin Wall crisis of August 1961, the Communist insurgency in Laos, and Castro's Cuba, would leave much of the day-to-day U.S. policy on Japan in Reischauer's hands. In November 1964, however, when the critical decision on whether to escalate the war dramatically or negotiate peace with North Vietnam hung in the balance, he did not bother to summon Reischauer for consultation. No one thought to seek advice from the man who had publicly warned against involvement in a war against Vietnamese nationalism, who had urged recognition of Communist China, and who scorned the prevailing "domino theory" in Southeast Asia. Only when the redoubtable Jim Thomson suggested that Reischauer should be brought back to Washington as a kind of roving ambassador for East Asia did the idea seem worth pursuing, as discussed in chapter 9. By then, it was too late.

Back in 1961, however, Jim Thomson orchestrated a meeting for Reischauer with Bowles on January 26 in Bowles's office. Reischauer came to the meeting thinking that Bowles wanted to pick his brains about Korea, where Reischauer had been a recent visitor. Bowles asked him immediately to accept the nomination to be ambassador to Japan and, more, to be a sort of "supervisory Ambassador at Large for all of East Asia." This latter thought was clearly the brainchild of Jim Thomson. Reischauer was surprised and asked for a few days to think it over. He then went to the Senate for a meeting, he thought, with John Newhouse to talk about Korea, He was instead ushered into the office of Newhouse's boss, Senator J. William Fulbright, who asked him about the possibility of going to Japan as ambassador and was delighted to learn that Bowles had made the offer just that morning. Once again, Thomson had scripted this scenario perfectly.

Reischauer's third meeting of the day was with the newly appointed secretary of state, Dean Rusk. Reischauer would recall that Rusk was "calm, non-committal and cagey—a description that I found would fit all my dealings with him."[38] Reischauer suspected that Rusk had another candidate in mind for Tokyo, but learned that Bowles was specifically charged with finding new ambassadors. Rusk clearly felt that he could not stand in the way of an appointment that Mac Bundy and President Kennedy had approved. As noted, Rusk strongly opposed Reischauer's idea of recognizing Communist China and would lose no opportunity to say so.

It is not clear that Reischauer fully understood Thomson's intention to use him as a battering ram on China policy, but he was far more realistic than his younger student. He knew that an American ambassador in Tokyo would have little power to sway East Asian policy as a whole. He thought that being ambassador to Japan and improving U.S.–Japan relations was to be his mission, a sufficiently ambitious one at that. "No animal has a stronger sense of territorial prerogatives than an Ambassador," he would later write, "and I would have been torn to bits by my colleagues if I had tried to act in a supervisory capacity outside of Japan."[39] But Thomson would continue to plot tirelessly inside the administration to bring about a change in China policy, to avert a disastrous war, and eventually to place Reischauer in a position from which he could influence China policy, as discussed in the upcoming chapters.

For five days, Edwin and Haru Reischauer debated whether to accept the nomination. Edwin was clearly thrilled by it: "I realized from the start that I had no choice but to accept. For years I had criticized America's Asian policy in my books, articles and speeches, and I could scarcely turn my back now on an opportunity to try to improve it. It was for me a case of 'put up or shut up.'"[40]

Reischauer felt he had regained enough physical strength to take on the job, but wondered whether his "deep affection for Japan might make me an unsuitable representative of the United States in Tokyo." He decided that "the fundamental interests and goals of the two countries were now so similar that my love for Japan need not clash with my loyalty to America." He also worried that he might be setting himself up for a humiliating failure, and whether Washington might keep him on such a short leash that he would be little more than an errand boy. "The only way to find out was to take the plunge and give it a try," he concluded.[41]

Haru, in contrast, made a brief pretense of resisting. She claimed to hate the stuffy social life of diplomats and worried that she would never be accepted by Americans in Japan—the business community as well as military and embassy personnel. She wondered if prominent Japanese would look down on her for being married to an American. "I was a Japanese by race and had been an American citizen for only a year. I just couldn't see the American community in Japan, especially the large military establishment, accepting me as a bonafide [*sic*] American or the Japanese seeing me as anything but a renegade Japanese."[42] In the end, however, this reluctance proved to be a "front" (or *tatemae*). As a lonely journalist five years earlier, she had felt rejected by both Americans and Japanese. Now she was being catapulted into one of the most prominent positions in Tokyo. She loved it, at least for the first several years. On January 31, five days after Bowles offered him the job, Reischauer accepted and entered a new and exciting chapter of his life.

News of his acceptance leaked immediately to the *New York Times* and to the media in Japan, causing a furor of excitement in Tokyo. Reischauer had to wait for a security clearance from the FBI and confirmation by the Senate before he could speak in public about the job. Nevertheless, he was besieged by letters, phone calls, and requests for interviews. The pause gave his critics an opportunity to shoot down the nomination.

In Washington, several prominent U.S. Foreign Service officers, among them J. Graham Parsons, were highly critical of Reischauer's nomination. A professor who opposed America's China policy was being offered a key diplomatic post in Asia. In addition to the policy dispute was a feeling of bitter resentment that an outsider might occupy a juicy diplomatic position that until then had been a preserve of the career Foreign Service . Parsons arranged for a letter to come into Bowles's hands saying that Reischauer's Japanese wife would be deeply resented by the Japanese people.[43] As noted, however, the Kennedys looked down on the traditional Foreign Service. The traditionalists' opposition probably even enhanced Reischauer's image in the eyes of the new administration.

In Japan, too, there was opposition. Reischauer understood that former prime minister Yoshida Shigeru and ambassador to Washington Asakai Koichiro, among other conservatives, objected to a professor who might be a "left-leaning dreamer."[44] *Time* magazine reported: "In Tokyo, conservative opposition mounted against the choice of brainy but blunt Edwin O. Reischauer, a Japanese-born Harvard Professor with a Japanese wife. Japan's Ambassador to the U.S., Koichiro Asakai, summoned Japanese correspondents in Washington and asked them such leading questions as 'Do you believe we should accept an ambassador who is not a full and true American?' "[45]

A number of Japanese conservatives objected on the grounds that "Reischauer knows us too well." The thought of an American ambassador getting up in the morning and reading Japanese-language newspapers with their latent nationalist biases sent fear into the hearts of the old guard. Reischauer thought the opposition came from conservative politicians and top businessmen "who didn't feel that any professor, particularly one from Harvard, would be representative of the real United States. They were a little nervous about it because their own intellectuals tend to be somewhat unrealistic men and so they don't have a good picture of a university intellectual."[46]

The Japan Communist Party organ, *Zenei*, was predictably critical of the appointment. Kennedy's diplomacy is the changed face of U.S. imperialism, it warned, and Reischauer, the pro-Japanese scholar, has been chosen to manipulate the Japanese people from inside. Reischauer's pro-Japanese background may attract many people, it stated, but the "Kennedy Line" is basically a plan to revitalize American power throughout the world.[47]

Chuo Koron, a more centrist intellectual magazine, admitted that many Japanese supported Reischauer's appointment, but warned that they shouldn't forget that he was not on their side. They needed to show great respect for him, though, and try not to disturb his efforts at improving U.S.–Japan relations. The Reischauer couple's mission was to work for America's benefit, but it should not be forgotten that even though Haru was born Japanese, she would not be working for the Japanese.[48]

But popular acceptance of the appointment in Japan was immediate and overwhelming. News stories, cartoons, and editorial commentary were so favorable that it would have been hard to withdraw the nomination. *Asahi Shimbun* commented: "To a casual observer's eyes, the ambassadorial changeover from Douglas MacArthur II to Reischauer may seem to be a mere personnel change accompanying the recent U.S. Administration change. But on close observation one notices a significant change in the U.S. Government policy. President Kennedy picked the Tokyo-born Harvard professor not merely because he is well informed with affairs in the Far East and Japan, but also because the U.S. Government is anxious to open up new avenues in diplomatic problems."[49]

Reischauer's favorite cartoon was of Prime Minister Ikeda Hayato boning up on classical Japanese with the caption, "Reischauer-san Is Coming."[50]

The official announcement of his nomination came on March 14, and hearings before the Senate Foreign Relations Committee were scheduled for March 23. On the appointed day, Reischauer was one of four nominees to be examined by the committee. Only three senators showed up for the hearings: two liberal Democrats and one conservative southern Democrat. Two conservative Republicans, Senators Frank Carlson of Kansas and Homer Capehart of Indiana, who were expected to challenge the nomination, chose to absent themselves. Democrats J. William Fulbright, committee chairman, and Senator Mike Mansfield, Democrat of Montana, carried the day.

Fulbright, a former Rhodes Scholar, a lawyer, and president of the University of Arkansas from 1939 to 1941, could have been expected to look favorably on the appointment of a Harvard professor. He led off with friendly remarks, drawing Reischauer out on his long experience in Japan, his understanding of the Japanese language, and his views about the protest demonstrations of May and June 1960 against the revised U.S.-Japan Security Treaty:

> Mr. REISCHAUER. I think there has been a great misunderstanding of the American position, American ideals and what we stand for in the Far East, on the part of certain elements of Japanese society, and I think it is important to correct some of these misunderstandings.
>
> THE CHAIRMAN. Do you see any reason why these misunderstandings cannot be corrected?
>
> Mr. REISCHAUER. No, I do not. I think our basic interests are the same. I think the Japanese and we both want to see peace in that part of the world, stability, prosperity. We are hoping for the same things.

Fulbright continued with innocuous questions about Japan's relations with Southeast Asia, its participation in the Organization for Economic Cooperation and Development, and its relations with Korea. Then, in a preemptive strike, he dropped a bombshell: "Another question which the Committee has usually shown a great deal of interest in would be your views with regard to Communist China, with regard to recognition and so on. Have you made any statements about this?"

Fulbright was being disingenuous: Reischauer's advocacy of recognition of Communist China was well known to anyone interested in the subject, and his long letter on the subject in 1959 to Assistant Secretary of State Jeff Parsons was almost surely in the hands of the Republicans on the Foreign Relations

Committee. It was clear, however, that Jim Thomson had briefed Reischauer on how to respond:

> MR. REISCHAUER. Well, I have made many statements. I have written quite a bit about it over a number of years, because this is, of course, a very serious problem that the public must think about and discuss, as well as the Government.
>
> I have been a member of the public that was interested. I looked at the hearings of Mr. Rusk and Mr. Bowles and their statements on this subject.[51]
>
> I found myself fully in agreement with the statements they made: That under present conditions recognition is completely impossible and an academic problem.
>
> THE CHAIRMAN. In general, you would agree with the views that have already been given to us by the people in the Department of State?
>
> MR. REISCHAUER. I most certainly would.
>
> THE CHAIRMAN. Does the Senator from Alabama have any questions?"[52]

Reischauer's response was clever, evasive, and deeply disappointing to his Harvard students, who had hoped he would ride into Washington on a white horse and fix what they viewed as a broken China policy. But he and Jim Thomson, with Bowles's agreement, calculated that he needed to duck the issue if he wanted to win Senate confirmation for the ambassadorship to Japan. Rusk had testified before the committee out of his own deep conviction that Communist China should not be recognized. Bowles, who personally favored recognition, felt obliged to defer to Rusk. Reischauer clearly wanted the job of ambassador to Japan, knew that in any case he could do nothing at that point to change China policy, and so went along with the game. Thomson saw Reischauer as a kind of Trojan horse: get him cleared and into the State Department and then work with him from the inside to influence China policy.

Senator John Sparkman of Alabama might well have opposed the nomination. A conservative southern Democrat, lawyer, and a racist, he had been one of nineteen southern senators to sign the Southern Manifesto opposing the 1954 U.S. Supreme Court decision *Brown v. Board of Education* and racial integration of America's schools. He could have hounded Reischauer for his stance on China, and he might have raised racially loaded questions about his Japanese wife, Haru. But he chose instead to focus on the antitreaty demonstrations in Tokyo, the Communists' role in those days, Japan–China relations. and trade between Japan and the United States, noting that Japan bought more raw cotton—an Alabama product—than any other nation in the world. This last point may have eased any doubts he might have had about the nomination. Sparkman ended his questioning with a gracious touch: "Mr. Reischauer, from what I have heard of you, I think you are well prepared for this job."

At this point, Senator Mike Mansfield, vice chairman of the committee, who had served in the U.S. Marines in China in 1922, had a master's in East Asian history, and had taught East Asian history from 1933 to 1943 at the University of Montana, took over:

> Dr. Reischauer, I think we are extremely fortunate to have a man of your ability and background designated by the President of the United States to represent our country in Japan.
>
> I personally am delighted that you have an American wife of Japanese ancestry. I am very happy that you speak Japanese and have some experience with that country and the Far East area in general.[53]

Once again, a potentially explosive issue was defused. Americans married to foreign nationals were customarily not sent to the country of the spouse's origin, but Mansfield was underlining the fact that Haru was an American citizen and laying to rest in advance any doubts about her or Edwin's loyalty to America. Both Mansfield and Fulbright made a point of meeting Haru after the hearings. "We have both been very grateful ever since for this kind gesture, which greatly boosted Haru's morale," Reischauer would later recall.[54] Many years later Mansfield commented to me that Reischauer was the greatest ambassador ever sent by the United States to any country. Neither man could have known in 1961 that Mansfield himself would subsequently serve with distinction as ambassador to Japan for eleven years (1977–88). Reischauer came to hold the same view of Mansfield.

But the China question and Reischauer's possible connections with the left-leaning Institute of Pacific Relations would not go away.[55] In the nomination hearing, Fulbright introduced an article by well-known right-wing columnist Holmes Alexander, an admirer of Senator Joseph McCarthy, who urged the Foreign Relations Committee to explore Reischauer's possible pro-Communist leanings. Alexander wrote: "The professor was born in Tokyo, 1910, of American parents, is married to a Japanese, has 38 references in the published volumes of the Senate investigation of the Red-run Institute of Pacific Relations, has worked and traveled with the very discredited group of intellectuals who clustered about Owen Lattimore and Philip Jessup, seems from the record to have been an early advocate of recognizing Red China and of encouraging amity between the mainland Chinese and a 'democratic' but apparently disarmed and isolate Japan."[56]

Once again, Fulbright was taking the initiative to give Reischauer a chance to respond before an opponent of the nomination could capitalize on this attack. Holmes Alexander was echoing the charges of Senator Joseph McCarthy and Senator Pat McCarran, who in 1952 had attacked the Institute of Pacific Relations for its alleged pro-Communist sympathies toward China.

Reischauer denied that he had ever been a member of the institute, but under questioning by Fulbright admitted that he might have subscribed to their publications for about a year. Fulbright then led Reischauer to pinpoint that Alexander's charges arose from the meeting at the State Department held in the fall of 1949 (described in chapter 4) and noted that Reischauer's advocacy of recognition of Communist China came before the outbreak of the Korean War in June 1950. Fulbright went on to bring out the fact that other countries did recognize the new regime in China and that the United States had recognized the Soviet Union.

Again citing Holmes Alexander's charge that two reputable witnesses, Harold Stassen and Kenneth Colegrove, placed Reischauer in a group of orientalists who "were not thinking so much of America as they were of other things, and that group tended to be very sympathetic to Communist China and very, very considerate of the Kremlin." He then asked Reischauer if he knew Kenneth Colegrove. Reischauer replied, "I know Mr. Colegrove slightly. We were both in Government service together at some time, and I saw that statement that he made and I thought it was a very unfair and unpleasant statement." Fulbright asked, "And have you never had any discussion of this matter with Colegrove?" Reischauer responded, "No, I have not. I do not like fights."

Senator Mansfield then intervened again to ask Reischauer to reconfirm that he fully agreed with Dean Rusk's statement to the Committee on China, and Reischauer did so. He then brought out Reischauer's record of wartime service in military intelligence, the fact that he was awarded the Legion of Merit, and that he had trained intelligence officers in the Japanese language. As for Reischauer's receiving Institute of Pacific Relations publications, Mansfield said, "It was quite natural that anyone interested in the Far East would be interested in such a magazine at that time."

Fulbright concluded with a glowing tribute:

> THE CHAIRMAN. Mr. Reischauer, so far as I am concerned, I think you are extremely well qualified to represent us in Japan.
>
> I realize that politics is a little more complex and difficult than the academic life, having been in both of them.

> I hope you do not find it so, and I wish you the best of luck.
>
> I was very gratified to notice that the press in Japan has almost uniformly endorsed this appointment and praised you very highly. . . . I wish you the best of luck.

On March 28, the committee and then the full Senate voted unanimously to confirm Reischauer, and on March 29 his appointment became official. He was one of four extraordinary scholars chosen for ambassadorships. George F. Kennan, the former diplomat turned historian of Russia, was summoned from his desk at the Institute for Advanced Study at Princeton to become ambassador to Yugoslavia. John Kenneth Galbraith, the economist and early Kennedy supporter with confident views on almost every issue, was sent to India (his friends jokingly suggested that Kennedy wanted to get him as far from Washington as possible). Kenneth T. Young, a former student of Reischauer, was sent to Thailand. Although both Reischauer and Young were Asian specialists, neither one was ever consulted on Vietnam policy.

On March 25, Reischauer met briefly with President Kennedy for the first time in the Oval Office of the White House. It was a pro forma meeting at which Kennedy gave each new nominee a signed photograph of himself with them that could be displayed prominently in the new ambassador's office—as a sign of how close he was to the president. In fact, Kennedy and Reischauer had no substantive conversation, and it would not be until Robert Kennedy, the new attorney general, visited Tokyo the following year that the Kennedys would come to understand the value of having Reischauer in Tokyo.

One amusing result of Reischauer's appointment was that several of his books that had been blacklisted for U.S. Information Agency libraries around the world under the previous Republican administration were quickly removed from the list. They presumably had been blacklisted because of Reischauer's outspoken support for recognition of Communist China.

In between the flurry of meetings and briefings, Reischauer took an unusual step that would characterize his approach to his new job. He contacted Ernest Young, the graduate student in modern Chinese history at Harvard, and invited him to come to Tokyo as his special assistant. Young had taught English at Kumamoto University and spoke Japanese. His job would be to open up lines of communication between the embassy and Japanese students and young people, in particular those who were usually anti-American. With Reischauer's strong support, he would range outside of traditional diplomatic channels to establish lines of contact with such people. No other American ambassador had created such an unorthodox position. Reischauer found it invaluable. When Young returned to Harvard to complete his doctoral dissertation, Reischauer insisted that he find a successor for this job. Young recommended me, and I succeeded him in Tokyo from 1963 to 1965.

Reischauer owned one shabby suit at the time of his appointment. He quickly bought four more suits, rushed to Baltimore to a cut-rate store that catered to less-affluent diplomats, and bought the top hat, frock coat, striped pants, white tie, and "the other plumage required in diplomatic life."[57] Reischauer's Harvard annual salary in 1959–60 was $12,000, and, with a modest stipend from the Harvard-Yenching Institute, his annual income was probably no more than $15,000. As an ambassador with the rank of Foreign Service Reserve 1, his basic pay would have been between $17,250 and $19,650. By his last year as ambassador, 1966, that figure had risen to about $27,500. The State Department would provide a modest "representation allowance" of $8,300 and an "Official Residence Allotment" of $10,000 per year, but these allowances were not nearly enough to cover the entertaining that an American ambassador in Tokyo was expected to provide. Reischauer had only modest savings, and his five and a half years in Tokyo would leave him seriously strapped. After seven months on the job, he was $7,500 in debt.[58]

There followed a round of briefings, press interviews, and farewell parties hosted by Japan-America Societies in Washington, New York, and Los Angeles. Reischauer held an unprecedented press conference for Japanese journalists, who were competing for stories to feed the public demand for news about the two Reischauers. In Hawaii, he was briefed by Admiral Harry Felt, the commander in chief of the Pacific, and then Edwin, Haru, and their youngest child, Joan, took off from Hawaii for Tokyo on April 17, 1961, for the adventure of their lives.

8

One Shining Moment

Japan and America shared an extraordinary moment of exuberant friendship from 1961 to 1963. Japan, after the protest demonstrations of 1960 against the alliance with the United States, turned its energy to its booming economy. Its population grew rapidly. For the first time in history, a confident new middle class, free of government harassment and at peace with the world, reveled in the luxury of refrigerators, washing machines, color television sets, cars, and leisure time. A compact car made by Toyota, the Corona, first appeared in the U.S. market in 1964. In 1961, for the first time, American visitors to Japan topped 100,000; by 1970, that number was 315,211.[1]

Preparing for the Olympic Games, scheduled for Tokyo in 1964, gave the nation a shared purpose and national pride. The games would come to symbolize Japan's recovery from the war. To drive home the point, the torchbearer chosen to carry the flame into the Olympic Stadium in October 1964 would be a nineteen-year-old youth named Sakai Yoshinori, who had been born on August 6, 1945, in Hiroshima, the day the first atomic bomb was dropped. Japan was at last accepted as an equal by the world's major powers. Prime Minister Ikeda Hayato, who succeeded the unpopular Kishi Nobusuke in 1960, now spoke of his nation as one of the "three pillars of the free world."[2]

Many Japanese who can remember those days, known as "Showa 30s and 40s" (1955–75 in a Western calendar), look back on them with nostalgia. "I think [we could] finally look back on the past without feeling the pain of World War Two," said one Tokyo native. "For me, it was a time of freedom and fun." Another older citizen said, "People were warm. There were human bonds. Everything was slow. We met and communicated, not like today, when everything is done on mobile phones and computers." A third citizen added, "Everyone was poor but we all got along. Now you have a huge gap between the rich and the poor."[3]

For America, it was the promise of the "New Frontier." The handsome young President Kennedy, only forty-four years old, and his glamorous family, the challenge of "we can do better," and the sense that a new generation of leaders would reinvigorate government and bring the best and brightest minds to wrestle with problems that had been ignored by the aging Eisenhower administration—all of this released an extraordinary spirit of optimism and energy. "Ask not what your country can do for you," Kennedy proclaimed in his Inaugural Address, "ask what you can do for your country." Thousands, maybe millions, of Americans were thrilled by the challenge.

In this bright and perhaps unique moment, Edwin and Haru Reischauer stood as exciting symbols of the new mood in both nations. In Japanese eyes, President Kennedy was showing deep respect: by sending a learned, Japanese-speaking historian as ambassador, along with his distinguished Japanese wife, to represent America, the President seemed to be acknowledging Japan's miraculous comeback from war and occupation full acceptance of it by its former enemy. For Americans interested in foreign policy, Reischauer's appointment seemed to prove that competence and knowledge could now be brought to bear on important policy matters. For those interested in East Asia, it signaled an end to the disgraceful McCarthyite purges in the State Department. "Who lost China?" now seemed a ridiculous question. Area and language specialists could again be respected. For educators who believed in the value of cultural diplomacy, Kennedy's creation of the new Bureau of Educational and Cultural Affairs in the State Department seemed to signal welcome relief from Cold War posturing.[4]

Reischauer's arrival in Tokyo on April 19, 1961, had all the trimmings of a state visit. All the runways at Haneda Airport had been cleared so that his plane could touch down at exactly 6:40 A.M.—just in time to broadcast his arrival statement live to the nation on 7:00 A.M. news programs. More than one hundred reporters and photographers swarmed into the airport, along with Japanese government greeters, U.S. Embassy officials, and friends and former Harvard students.

The new ambassador had worked hard on his statement over the previous weekend, drafting it first in English and then consulting two Japanese interpreters on the Japanese version. Reading it in Japanese on national TV, with Haru at his side, he said, "My wife and I are very happy to be back in Japan. As you know, we were both born in Tokyo, and therefore, to us it is like coming home. . . . I see every reason for great hope. Japan's progress and development of the past century is perhaps the greatest success story of modern times, and the growing friendship of the Japanese and American peoples are the most heartening aspects of the relations between the Orient and the Occident."[5] This spirit of optimism would set the tone for his entire tour of duty. The Japanese media eagerly snapped up this statement and repeated it endlessly.

All the streets leading from the airport to his residence had been blocked off, so he and Haru were whisked—in the U.S. Embassy Cadillac, the American flag flying from its front bumper—through what normally would have been the morning traffic jam, arriving at their palatial residence in minutes. They were celebrities overnight, at once losing any semblance of the privacy they had enjoyed in earlier years.

A memorable moment came eight days later when he was driven in the emperor's maroon Rolls Royce to present his credentials, wearing his morning coat, matching vest, stiff collar, four-in-hand tie, striped trousers, silk hat, and gloves: "The Emperor was flanked by his Grand Chamberlain, Mitani Takanobu, the brother of the Miss Mitani I had called 'aunty' in my childhood, and by an interpreter. The latter translated what I said, but after the Emperor spoke, I replied immediately. This was a serious *faux pas*. When I had finished, the translator, with a pained expression, translated carefully into English the Emperor's remark to which I had already replied and followed this with a Japanese translation of my reply. I dutifully waited thereafter for his two-way translation."[6]

On this occasion, the emperor gave no special signal of recognition to Reischauer, but at subsequent diplomatic gatherings, he would break from his normal habit of murmuring "Yo koso" (Welcome) to diplomats to utter an enthusiastic "Honto ni yo koso" (You really are very welcome) to Reischauer. Because Haru and Edwin were often the only guests at diplomatic receptions who could speak Japanese, they found themselves in frequent conversations with the emperor and empress. "The Emperor is indeed a very straightforward, genuine person without an iota of guile in him," he later recalled.[7]

Edwin and Haru developed warm relations with the crown prince and princess as well, and were touched when Princess Michiko sent Haru a bouquet of wildflowers that she had picked herself in Karuizawa during the summer of 1962. In an unprecedented move years later (1987), the prince and princess would stay in the Reischauers' home in Belmont, Massachusetts.

Reischauer would serve as ambassador for five and a half years. The first half of his tour would be triumphal, but the second half would fall under darkening shadows. The turning point would be the assassination of John F. Kennedy in November 1963.

The goals that Reischauer set for himself at this time were clear and typically outsized: he intended to purge the Japan–U.S. relationship of racial prejudice and wartime hatred, close the cultural gap, and end the feelings of inequality between the two nations. He believed that U.S.-Japan alliance was good for both parties: it allowed the United States to keep its commitments in East Asia, and it gave Japan breathing space to rebuild its economy and strengthen its new democratic institutions. But his vision went far beyond the Security Treaty: he held out a vision of an "equal partnership" in which the two nations would work together to build strong cultural bonds, maintain peace in East Asia, and assure the spread of democracy and prosperity in the region. No small dreams for this man.

Though Reischauer never said so publicly, he knew from his own experience in Japan of the 1930s how powerful were the siren songs of nationalism and militarism there. He felt that the Security Treaty could serve to curb these tendencies and buy time for the delicate greenhouse plant of democracy to sink deep and permanent roots. He did not accept the notion held by some Americans that U.S. troops and bases in Japan were designed primarily to hold back Japan's militaristic tendencies; he had faith in the people of Japan to manage democratic government, but believed that they needed time and experience to make it work well. The treaty was the cheapest and best way for Japan to assure its own security while rebuilding its economy.

Another goal was to convince the Japanese people that America was not foolishly adventurous, not militaristic, and not about to embroil Japan in new wars. He wanted Japan to feel confident that it could depend on America. At the same time, he was determined to convince American leaders not to take Japan for granted. He would work tirelessly to bring top U.S. officials to Japan to meet their counterparts, and he began making plans for a visit to Japan by President Kennedy. No American president had ever been to Japan while in office; President Eisenhower's planned visit had been thwarted by leftist demonstrations, and Reischauer believed that a visit by the popular new president could do much to bolster Japan's faith in American leadership. From the moment of his arrival he hammered on these themes in press conferences, lectures, speeches in distant prefectures, articles in the Japanese press, and of course within his own embassy.

Finally, he was determined to reach out to Japan's intellectual community, the *interi*, and to offer an alternative to the prevailing Marxist ideas that had permeated the universities, intellectual journals, and to some extent the mass media in the postwar period. In what left-wing critics would come to call the "Kennedy-Reischauer Line," he articulated the "modernization theory" that had emerged from the Hakone Conference of 1960.

Animating his mission was his supreme confidence that there were no irreconcilable differences between the two countries, that underlying their very different cultures and history were shared fundamental values—a belief in human rights, the dignity and equality of individuals, the rule of law, democratic government, and peaceful foreign relations. The better they understood each other, the closer they would become, he believed.

Reischauer wanted to end what he viewed as the "occupation mentality" of Americans in Japan—not just among military and diplomatic officials but within the business and journalism community as well. In 1961, the occupation had been officially over for nine years, but Americans persisted in acting as conquerors and the Japanese as conquered. There were 47,182 U.S. troops in Japan in 1961, many of them stationed conspicuously in urban areas. [8] Senior U.S. officers still lived in some of the best private homes, enjoyed exclusive access to luxury hotels, ran facilities such as the Sanno Hotel in central Tokyo, and kept control of golf courses and mountain resorts. Americans traveled in large left-hand steering-wheel cars on the left side of the narrow streets of Tokyo. The army operated the Far Eastern Network, FEN, a radio station devoted to American news, music, and entertainment.[9] The military issued its own currency for use in post exchanges and navy commissaries, and published its own newspaper, *Stars and Stripes*. Military wives could shop for luxury goods at nearby bases.

Many senior officers and businessmen employed one or more Japanese servants—often a housemaid and driver, who were in most cases their only Japanese "acquaintances." With the yen pegged at 360 to the dollar, local services and products were a bargain. On the whole, these Americans lived at a higher standard in Japan than they had known in America, and they took it all as a natural perquisite of victory in war. They had no sense that they were guests in a sovereign foreign nation and no reason to mingle with the "natives." The center of social life for the American business community in Tokyo was the American Club, where the only Japanese present were waiters and bartenders.

Reischauer saw the long-term danger in this situation. The Japanese would sooner or later tire of being treated as inferiors and would ask the Americans to go home. Their history of importing foreign ideas over the centuries had often ended with a reverse swing of the pendulum—a closing of the doors—and a reversion to nativism of the sort that his missionary father had encountered in 1905. He understood that the stationing of foreign troops and bases in a proud nation that had never before been occupied could lead to friction and an end to the alliance if the Japanese were not treated with respect and fairness.

For the next five and a half years, his major preoccupation was to convince both Americans and Japanese that they were no longer victors and vanquished, but rather equal partners. Reischauer personally stressed this fact to almost every important American visitor to Tokyo, believing that he had an invaluable opportunity to educate the United States about Japan. He and Haru embarked on a series of lectures and talks in coffee klatches, luncheons, and dinners with fellow Americans: businessmen, their families, officers, military wives, journalists, and academics—all aimed at portraying the Japan of the Rice Paddies course at Harvard: a nation with a history and culture worthy of respect and study. It is impossible to know exactly how effective they were, but they got many more speaking invitations than they could accept. Reischauer's books became "must reading" for American newcomers to Japan. The Reischauers went out of their way to court members of the American Chamber of Commerce in Tokyo, inviting them to briefings in the embassy and hosting receptions at the residence. He told his family: "This is said to be a unique program anywhere in the world, . . . but obviously it is the sort of thing the State Department should have done over the years to build up understanding and support. Businessmen overseas (just like the military) are traditionally hostile to our embassies. That we have very strong support from both groups here in Japan is said to be a very unusual situation, though of course it should be the rule."[10]

Reischauer's second overarching goal was to sensitize the U.S. military commanders to Japanese political realities, particularly on the issue of Okinawa. During the occupation, the U.S. Army and General MacArthur had reigned supreme. After Japan achieved independence in 1952, the U.S. military continued to maintain the upper hand in framing Japan policy. The latter could argue that Japan was for them an "unsinkable aircraft carrier," vital to the defense of South Korea and critical for the containment of Soviet or Communist Chinese offensive moves anywhere in the entire region. In their view, Okinawa was the anchor. Reischauer understood this point, but he strongly believed that U.S. troops and bases in Japan would become useless in any breakout of fighting if the civilian Japanese population opposed being dragged into war. If, for example, U.S. Air Force bases were to be used to launch bombing attacks against a North Korean invasion of South Korea, Japanese protesters, lying on the runways, could easily prevent their use. The effectiveness of the U.S.–Japan Security Treaty ultimately depended on winning and keeping the support of the vast majority of Japanese people. As the events of May and June 1960 proved, this support could not be taken for granted; it had to be earned.

It might seem quixotic today for an American ambassador to think he could prevail in a dispute with the Pentagon, but in 1961 events conspired to give Reischauer some unusual opportunities. As noted, the new Kennedy administration found itself trapped in the foolish Bay of Pigs invasion of Cuba in April 1961. Then President Kennedy met Nikita Khrushchev in Vienna in June 1961. The Soviet leader took Kennedy's measure and found him weak, leading to the construction of the Berlin Wall in November 1961 and to the shipping of Soviet missiles to Cuba in the fall of 1962, setting up the most dangerous moment of the entire Cold War. In addition, the civil war in Laos, where the pro-Communist Pathet Lao forces threatened to take over the country, consumed nearly all the time and energy of the U.S. State Department's Far Eastern Affairs Division. In addition, there were tense confrontations at home over the civil rights movement's efforts to enroll African American students in previous all-white universities in Mississippi and Alabama. As a result, high officials in Washington, happily aware of the warm public reception of the Reischauers in Japan, paid little attention to Japan policy and left the ambassador largely to his own devices.

Reischauer's basic view was, as he explained later in a 1969 interview: "In the long run, I think the bases should all be Japanese bases that they are letting us use. In the long run, they have to be responsible for any actions we take, responsible in advance. We cannot be utilizing their bases for things that seem good to us but which they have not committed themselves on. This puts the Japanese Government and the Japanese people in a very strange relationship with each other, the government seeming to bow to America, which it doesn't do. I mean, we're doing what they want us to do, but they don't take the responsibility for it. . . . This is unsound."[11]

When one added civilians and dependents to the forty-seven thousand men in uniform in Japan, the U.S. military added up to about one hundred thousand people—essentially the "direct inheritors of the American Occupation and, therefore, [they] loomed larger in the Japanese mind as being very important and probably vastly more important than the American Embassy in representing America in a way."[12]

Reischauer challenged the U.S. military dominance on a variety of fronts, small and large. "To many Japanese, an American General or admiral seemed much more of a genuine American than a Harvard professor. To make my point clear and show that even an off-beat scholar-Ambassador was the unchallenged representative of Washington in Japan, I made a point from the start of asserting my precedence over the American military in Japan. . . . I even carried the matter to trivial though visible details, such as insisting on walking first through doorways whenever I was with high American military officers in the presence of Japanese."[13]

He steadfastly opposed Defense and Treasury Department efforts to push Japan into assuming a larger share of the costs of maintaining U.S. troops and bases in Japan or into beefing up its own defense spending on U.S. weaponry. In February 1963, Deputy Defense Secretary Roswell Gilpatrick arrived in Tokyo with the intention of pressing the Japanese government to purchase U.S. weapons to offset the three-hundred-million-dollar deficit in the U.S. balance of payments caused by military spending in Japan. Reischauer, backed by the commander of U.S. Forces, Japan, General Jacob E. Smart, was able to persuade Gilpatrick to tone down his demands on the grounds that overt pressure on the Japanese government would be counterproductive. Prime Minister Ikeda and the ruling Liberal Democratic Party were at that time under constant attack from the opposition Socialists and Communists for knuckling under to the Americans. Reischauer patiently explained that a general-election victory by the left wing would spell the end of the alliance.

Reischauer also convinced General Smart of the need to give proper advance notice to the Japanese government before sudden movements of U.S. troops or equipment. The unannounced dispatch of aircraft to Thailand in the spring of 1962 was embarrassing to both governments and set off protest demonstrations. After that incident, Reischauer made a point of personally briefing the Japanese foreign minister about upcoming movements.

In another dispute, that U.S. Air Force decided to place on standby its northern base in rural Misawa, Aomori Prefecture, and move operations from there to Itazuke, near the major city of Fukuoka in Kyushu. Reischauer viewed this move as a major mistake. Itazuke was a "terrible political liability and Misawa, located in an economically depressed area, [was] a definite asset." When he protested this decision, he was told that it was too late to do anything about it because the president had already approved the decision, but eventually he got it reversed. "A few years later Itazuke was reactivated because of the pressures of the Vietnam War, but with disastrous results. An American plane crashed into a building at Kyushu University and the base had to be closed again on account of the resulting public reaction."[14]

Reischauer saw in 1961 that a Japanese demand for the return of the Ryukyu Islands, including Okinawa, with its population of a little more than a million, could easily become an explosive rallying cry for Japanese nationalists. The island had been Japanese territory since 1879.[15] In a joint communiqué on June 21, 1957, the United States reaffirmed that Japan had "residual sovereignty" over the Ryukyus, but added, "so long as the conditions of threat and tension exist in the Far East, the United States will find it necessary to continue the present status."[16] Reischauer, without any authorization from Washington, launched his own campaign to convince top U.S. military commanders of the wisdom of returning Okinawa to Japan before it became a major irritant in U.S.-Japan relations.

The U.S. Army ran the Ryukyus, including Okinawa, like a fiefdom (*han*) in Tokugawa days. The U.S. high commissioner, Lieutenant General Paul W. Caraway, behaved like a Tokugawa Era daimyo (feudal baron). U.S. forces had lost 12,500 American lives, and 37,000 were wounded in the eighty-two-day battle for Okinawa starting in April 1945, so the U.S. Army was not about to give up its control over this conquered territory. The American military men argued that "there was nothing to be feared from Okinawans, whom they felt to be 'gentle' people," but that "Okinawa must be maintained by the U.S. as a fallback position in case the close and friendly relationship with Japan were ever lost."[17]

Reischauer had a different view. Though the Okinawans were slightly different from mainland Japanese in dialect and culture, they "felt themselves to be fully Japanese. Virtually all of them wished ultimate reversion to Japan, and I saw the die had already been cast when Okinawa had adopted the Japanese school textbooks in which 'our country' (*waga kuni*) clearly meant Japan. Perhaps the American military could keep the Okinawans under control, but it was clear to me that sooner or later the other Japanese would get excited over Okinawa as an irridenta and this might ruin the whole Japanese-American relationship."[18]

Caraway saw the Japanese government as the U.S. Army's chief challenger for control of the island "and suspected our Embassy of conspiring with the Japanese" to increase their influence through economic aid. Reischauer later commented, "I would find myself in the absurd position at the annual conferences held in Tokyo of insisting on keeping Japanese aid down so that it would not exceed aid from America and thus supposedly cause the United States to lose face."[19]

Reischauer quickly sized up Caraway as running a "military dictatorship: "He was a rather unenlightened type who, while a very humorous and clever man, was politically as unschooled and unsophisticated as they come and was doing everything to infuriate the local population and therefore exacerbate the situation without realizing the terrible mistakes he was making."[20]

Caraway resisted Reischauer's attempts to visit his domain until August 1961. "He was a rigid, bull-headed man and demonstrated his autocratic ways by keeping the brigadier general who was the Civil Administrator of the Ryukyus cooling his heels for a couple of hours in an adjoining room while Caraway and I discussed conditions in Okinawa and its future," Reischauer recalled.[21] "[The] most worrisome problem of the moment is [the] danger [that] the Ryukyu problem might suddenly blow up into worldwide issue (as I have feared it might for 10 years)," he wrote his family in February 1962. By July 1964, Reischauer had almost given up on Caraway: "He and his petty dictatorial habits in Okinawa have been the biggest thorn in my side over the years."[22]

Once again, Reischauer was lucky. The commanding general of the U.S. Forces, Japan, in the summer of 1961 was Air Force lieutenant general Jacob Edward Smart, fifty-two. A genuine hero of World War Two, Smart had helped plan the famous bombing raid on Ploesti in August 1943 and was the pilot of a bomber that was shot down over Austria in May 1944.[23] Of the seven-man crew, only he and the bombardier survived. Covered with shrapnel wounds, he became a prisoner of war. Wounded again in the Korea War, he received the Distinguished Service Medal and the Distinguished Flying Cross.

Reischauer approached Smart cautiously, knowing that "Embassy relations with the American military in Japan and the Western Pacific were often as delicate and complex as with the Japanese Government." But he need not have worried; the two men hit it off immediately. "Haru and I liked Jake immensely, and he made a special effort to get to know us well, taking us on trips to visit the outlying American bases in Japan."[24] He met with Smart at the embassy almost weekly in a kind of tutorial in which he explained the origins of Japan's postwar pacifism and warned against prodding Japan to rearm more rapidly. And he made a strong argument for the early return of Okinawa to Japan. "The country team for Japan was really Jake Smart and myself," he told me later.[25]

What the Reischauers did not know at the time was that Smart, a divorced man, had fallen in love with a beautiful Japanese woman who worked as the housekeeper of his Western-style private mansion in Fuchu at the western edge of Tokyo. Saito Setsuko, who grew up in Akasaka, Tokyo, was thirty when Smart moved into the house in 1960. Smart was lonely and curious about Japanese customs and history. A friendship blossomed into a love affair. Marriage to a Japanese woman was out of the question for the commander of the U.S. forces in Japan, but the two would reunite after Smart retired in 1966 and would stay together for the next forty-one years, until Smart's death at ninety-seven in 2006. Smart's obituary mentioned his "companion," Setsuko Saito, as a survivor, along with his son and daughter, ten grandchildren, and ten great grandchildren.[26] Reischauer made only one fleeting reference to Saito: in a letter to his family on December 10, 1961, he wrote, "Lt. General Smart, top Commander here, and his 'girl friend—?' [*sic*] came to lunch."

Saito said in an interview in 2008 that although Smart spoke no Japanese, he had a genuine affection for the Japanese people; he was a "bookworm" who loved to read about Japanese history and treasured his friendship with Haru and Ed Reischauer. In retirement, he wrote two books and was a member of his county's historical society. As of this writing (2009), Saito continued to live in the home she shared with him in Ridgeland, South Carolina. She said that Smart had left the home to her in his will for the remainder of her life.[27] It is clear that Reischauer could not have found a U.S. commander who would have been more receptive to his ideas.

Jake Smart was promoted in the summer of 1963 to the position of commander in chief of Pacific Air Forces (CINCPAC) based in Hawaii. He retired in 1966 as a four-star general. His successor, Lieutenant General Maurice ("Mo") Preston, proved to be equally friendly and receptive to Reischauer's gentle "tutoring" on Japan. Another hero in World War Two, Preston had flown forty-five combat missions in the B-17 Flying Fortress. He and his charming wife, Dorothy, a talented artist, became close friends of Ed and Haru. The four of them often dined and laughed together and remained in close touch for the rest of their lives. When the Prestons' son, Tom, age twenty-four and a student in Japan, married a young Japanese woman, Ed played a key role as mediator in reconciling her outraged parents to the inevitable. Ed took advantage of this close friendship to share with Mo Preston his views on the return of Okinawa and on the alliance.

It was not self-evident that a Harvard professor and career military officers would hit it off the way Reischauer did with Generals Smart and Preston. When I asked him how he managed to do this, his immediate response was: "I've always been able to get along with anybody, businessmen, military men, whatever. It's because of my insecurity. No show of arrogance. Possibly my beginning in Japan and having to come back and adjust to America and be like the other boys. . . . I wanted to blend in. It's the natural way to be. It didn't seem to me a very unusual thing to do."[28]

Less successful was his relationship with Admiral Harry D. Felt, a feisty and aggressive former naval aviator who had seen action against Japanese fighters in the Pacific War, fought in the battle for Okinawa and was CINCPAC from 1958 to 1964. Reischauer wrote that Felt was "definitely hostile to Japan because of lingering feelings about World War Two."[29] Nevertheless, he stopped often at Felt's headquarters in Hawaii and argued that Japan's defense build-up should come at its own pace and not appear to be the result of American pressure. Reischauer thought that Felt needed "a lot of education and cajoling to be ready to really accept the Japanese as allies."[30] By October 1963, he thought that Felt was "much more relaxed and flexible than he used to be—we are first name friends now—and obviously the U.S.-Japan defense relationship has become more relaxed and much smoother in the last two years."[31]His cordial relations with top U.S. military leaders in the end helped pave the way for the return of Okinawa to Japan in 1972.

Reischauer's third aim was to convince Japanese and American political leaders that the two nations had "an equal partnership." This was a startling notion for both sides in 1961. Clearly, there was no equality in military power. The United States, one of the world's two superpowers armed with nuclear weapons, had no equal in the world. But the concept of equality was not as far-fetched as it might have been a decade earlier. Japan's economy, devastated in World War Two, began its miraculous comeback with U.S. military purchases during the Korea War (1950–53). From 1960 to 1970, its gross domestic product was growing at the unprecedented rate of 10.9 percent a year. Prime Minister Ikeda Hayato had pledged in 1960 to double national income in ten years, and the nation reached that goal by 1967. In 1965, for the first time, Japan ran a current account surplus in merchandise trade with the United States.

In his early speeches, articles, press conferences, and other forums, Reischauer tried to frame a vision of partnership far above the narrow notion of a mere military alliance. He defined "partnership" as an all-embracing combination of mutually beneficial trade, cultural and intellectual exchange, cooperation in aid to the less-developed countries, the effort to build a democratic world order, respect for the rule of law, and the presence of the United Nations—in short, a merging of the ideals, interests, and objectives we share.[32]

By 1961, the vast majority of the Japanese people had come to accept Japan's democratic constitution, imposed on the nation by U.S. occupation authorities. The demonstrations of May–June 1960 against the revised Security Treaty had gotten violent. On May 19, the aged Speaker of the Lower House, Kiyose Ichiro, had to be carried to the rostrum in a rugbylike scrum to call for a vote. On June 15, 1960, a female student, Kamba Michiko, was crushed to death in a melee outside the Diet gates. Many police were injured. The rioting brought down the Kishi government and blocked a visit by President Eisenhower. But the protest movement, far from signaling a left-wing takeover, was coming to be seen as a flowering of free speech and national pride. As soon as the demonstrations subsided, the nation reverted to its orderly, democratic rule. There was a lingering sense of exhilaration that ordinary citizens had stood up to their own government and to the Americans.[33]

By 1964, Japan was accepted into the Organization for Economic Cooperation and Development and the International Bank for Reconstruction and Development. In 1964, the "Bullet Train" (Shinkansen) between Tokyo and

Osaka began to set world standards for railroad engineering, speeding passengers on new tracks at 168 miles per hour in state-of-the-art comfort. The October 1964 Olympic Games in Tokyo were a triumph. In that same month, large headlines in all the newspapers announced that Japan had overtaken England in its gross national product. Japan, if not exactly equal, was a rising power worthy of respect. And Reischauer took every opportunity to drive the point home in Washington.

His first opportunity came when Prime Minister Ikeda visited Washington in June 1961. Reischauer arrived in Washington a few days beforehand and met privately with President Kennedy. He found the president very interested in visiting Japan and eager to learn more about the relationship. During the Ikeda-Kennedy talks and in the final communiqué, the two leaders regularly used Reischauer's term *equal partnership*, and even if it were only a goal, not a reality, it took on a life of its own.

As a result of this summit, Reischauer took the lead in organizing three new high-level groups: a cabinet-level group, the U.S.–Japan Committee on Trade and Economic Affairs; the Joint U.S.–Japan Science Group; and the U.S.–Japan Conference on Cultural and Educational Interchange (later known as "CULCON"). The cabinet-level group—headed by Secretary of State Dean Rusk and including Secretary of Interior Stewart L. Udall, Secretary of Agriculture Orville L. Freeman, Secretary of Commerce Luther H. Hodges, and Secretary of Labor Arthur J. Goldberg—met at Hakone November 2–4, 1961. It was the largest number of cabinet members to go on a single trip in U.S. history. No important decisions were reached, but Reischauer felt that it went far to symbolize the "equal partnership." It also gave top leaders on both sides a unique opportunity to know each other and put Japan on the map for Washington policymakers. It shifted the focus from military to economic affairs. The third meeting of this group was scheduled to be held in Japan in November 1963, but the plane carrying the U.S. delegation turned back in midair on hearing the devastating news of President Kennedy's assassination.

Reischauer understood that the meetings were important mainly for the images they created of two nations drawn together by shared trade and economic interests. "But beyond that," he said, "they had the value of getting a large part of the American Cabinet every year to think for three days about Japan, which, not being a crisis area, they'd usually not think about for 365 days of the year."[34]

CULCON met first in January 1962 and exists to this day. It has been useful in identifying ways to expand cultural, educational, intellectual, and grassroots exchanges between the two nations. The science group spawned a number of useful specialized study groups.

The Reischauers were lucky to have succeeded Douglas MacArthur II and his wife, Laura (nicknamed "Wahwee"), the daughter of former vice president Alben Barkley. The two were widely viewed as "holy terrors" by the junior officers and their wives. "I served under eight Ambassadors, and MacArthur was the most difficult of them all," recalled Roy Mlynarchik, chief of the Office of Translation Services. "His wife drove the other Embassy wives insane."[35] She held weekly meetings to lay down edicts on protocol and dress code. Embassy wives were compelled to show up for receptions in white gloves and were forbidden to sit down or to leave before the last guest had left. She assigned each wife a place to stand and watched them carefully. One wife was required to attend receptions while pregnant into her eighth month.[36] When at a Christmas party for some 120 embassy children eight and older Reischauer merrily led them through the entire residence, including the basement and attic, their amazed parents told him that Mrs. MacArthur had roped off most of the house to keep them out.

Wahwee's drinking was legendary, according to a former ambassador who preferred not to be identified. She carried a flask of martinis strapped to her leg and often engaged in loud public arguments with her husband on how the receiving line was to be set up. At one formal luncheon, a servant brought to the table a gift Wahwee had received. She read the card: "It's from a Mr. F-U-K . . . I wouldn't dream of trying to pronounce that!"

MacArthur once flew into a rage in 1959 at the chief of his translation section for distributing translations of a top-secret draft of the Status of Forces Agreement that was being negotiated with the Japanese government. The document had been leaked and appeared on page two of the *Yomiuri Shimbun* (with a circulation of eight to nine million at that time). "Why should we give this to the Russians?" he shouted, not remembering that the Russians also had translators. In the months leading up to President Eisenhower's visit planned for June 1960, he ordered the embassy translators to ignore articles critical of the Security Treaty and translate only those that were favorable. He was enraged when told that there were no favorable articles at that time.[37] The MacArthurs, in anticipation of the president's visit, painted most of the second floor of the embassy residence pink, allegedly because it was Mamie Eisenhower's favorite color. The Reischauers got rid of the ghastly pink as soon as they could.

After Asanuma Inejiro, head of the Japanese Socialist Party, visited China in 1959 and signed a communiqué charging that U.S. imperialism was the common enemy of Japan and China, he requested a meeting with MacArthur. MacArthur hesitatingly agreed to the meeting, but kept his visitor waiting and then refused to shake hands. Each time Asanuma began to speak, MacArthur cut him off with a demand to know if he had really been quoted correctly. "This was MacArthur at his very worst," recalled Albert Seligmann, a political officer who was present at the meeting.[38]

The Reischauers adopted a much more easy-going and informal style. Embassy receptions became fun for junior officers, many of whom could circulate among the guests, chatting in Japanese. The MacArthurs had reserved the large swimming pool between the Chancery Building and residence for themselves and special guests. The Reischauers opened up the pool to all members of the embassy who resided or worked in the embassy compound. Haru was shocked to discover that U.S. Embassy wives had been prohibited from taking Japanese lessons, and she promptly encouraged them to learn the language. She also invited about 650 women—Japanese and American—from the embassy staff to morning coffee. Many of the lower-level workers had never seen the face of an ambassador's wife.

Reischauer sat at the top of a huge bureaucracy consisting of about three hundred Americans and more than six hundred Japanese employees. Every cable or dispatch that went out from the embassy was now signed "Reischauer." He was in charge of what President Kennedy would call the "country team," presiding over four main divisions: political, economic, consular, and administrative. In addition, there were a large U.S. Information Agency contingent, a Military Assistance Advisory Group, the three military attachés, the CIA, representatives from the Labor and Treasury departments and assorted other government agencies, U.S. Marine guards, motor pool drivers, maintenance workers, cleaning crews, and so forth. It was a daunting organizational chart, and Reischauer tried valiantly to understand what all the obscure government agencies were doing in his name. He never quite succeeded, but he did maintain tight control over the political section and drove its junior officers crazy, repeatedly editing their bureaucratic prose to sharpen a point or shade a nuance.

He had no previous experience as a manager, and it showed. What he needed most was a chief of staff at the embassy to sort through and prioritize diplomatic negotiations, events required by protocol, other invitations, and requests for interviews, speeches, articles, and appearances. Chester Bowles had also advised him to take "his own man to cover his back" against jealous career bureaucrats who might want to undermine him.

Reischauer ignored this advice and relied on his deputy chief of mission William Leonhart, a skilled professional who could have been resentful about having to report to a political appointee and, with his superior knowledge of diplomatic protocol, could have sabotaged Reischauer at every turn. But Leonhart turned out to be a broad-gauged and generous man who came to like and support Reischauer and patiently walked him through the niceties of State Department customs and usages. The two developed genuine respect for each other. When Leonhart left in 1962 and was succeeded by the kindly but deferential diplomat John K. Emmerson, there was no one to help organize Reischauer's time efficiently, so they spent far too much time rushing from one trivial event to the next.

Reischauer's typical day began at 6:45 A.M., when he arose, scanned three Japanese daily newspapers and two English-language papers over breakfast, and then spent thirty minutes studying Japanese with an embassy teacher. He would then walk down the short hill to his office in the Chancery Building, check the incoming cables from Washington, and then meet with ten top staff members, usually at 10:30 A.M. Reischauer never spoke first and welcomed dissent and argument. A favorite game of officers at the morning staff meeting was to see if they could tell him some news that he didn't already know. They seldom won. He liked to wander about the embassy in and out of Chancery offices—to the dismay of Alice Seckel, his secretary, who "lost" him for long periods. He preferred getting information firsthand from the officer on top of any issue, and he enjoyed quizzing them for further details.

The career Foreign Service officers in the embassy were at first skeptical about this untested newcomer in their midst. Minister-Counselor for Political Affairs John Goodyear, for example, was a traditional career man who, in a description of his own job in Tokyo, wrote that knowledge of French and German was a firm requirement. He explained that one could pick up a great deal of useful intelligence by chatting with French and German diplomats at embassy receptions. Reischauer quickly rejected this description and instead wrote in that the Japanese language was desirable for anyone is this position.[39]

Japanese-language officers trained during World War Two or afterward became Reischauer's strongest supporters. He naturally paid more attention to their views and was skeptical of the views of the "generalists" who understood no Japanese, ducked tough issues, and worried only about avoiding flaps on their watch. For a brief moment, the Japan specialists' arduous quest to master the language was appreciated, and they enjoyed a rare upper hand against the generalists. "I find Embassy people are fine on reporting," Reischauer confided to his family, "but don't tend to think in terms of what should be done. Bureaucrats don't have the habit of sticking their necks out."[40]

Reischauer was not good at distinguishing between friends and jealous enemies or rivals on his staff. He made a big effort to bring his old friend and fellow graduate student Charles Burton Fahs to the embassy as a minister for cultural

Reischauer, as ambassador, kept a tidy desk but loved editing drafts of cables to the U.S. State Department by officers in the political section. Photograph by U.S. Embassy Tokyo photographer, 1963. Courtesy of the author.

affairs—the only post in the U.S. Information Agency at the ministerial level in the world—in an effort to upgrade this aspect of the American cultural presence and to decrease the prominence of the military. Unfortunately, Fahs, a dreary presence who had worked at the Rockefeller Foundation, was carried away with his own self-importance and jealous of the headlines Reischauer was getting. He set about undermining or upstaging Reischauer whenever he could. When Fahs left the embassy in 1966, the ministerial rank disappeared with him.

A number of serious and complex bilateral issues had to be confronted and resolved. Most time-consuming were the myriad issues, small and large, that arose from the massive presence of U.S. troops and bases on Japanese soil. Crimes committed by U.S. servicemen and accidents involving the loss of Japanese lives demanded constant attention and utmost delicacy. He saw to it that apologies were properly carried out with proper attention to Japanese sensitivities. Prior notification to the Japanese government on troop and aircraft movements and ship visits was also a constant problem because the U.S. military had grown accustomed to operating with a free hand. Reischauer worked hard to earn the trust of U.S. military commanders.

A special headache was the Treasury Department's pet project, the interest equalization tax (IET). The United States ran chronic balance of payments deficits in the early 1960s, and President Kennedy proposed the IET in July 1963 to raises the prices Americans would have to pay for foreign assets in western Europe and Japan. Needless to say, the measure was highly unpopular in the target countries, and it took all of Reischauer's missionary skill to persuade the Japanese to go along. The measure failed to stem the outflow of U.S. capital and had the unintended consequence of fostering the growth of foreign financial markets.

The Pentagon also urged Reischauer to push Japan into buying more U.S. weapons in order to reduce the current account deficit. He told Washington privately that the price in irritation of forcing Japan to buy U.S. weapons and limit textile exports was far higher than any benefits that could be achieved. Throughout his time as ambassador, he recommended firm Executive Branch resistance to U.S. industry demands for protection against Japanese imports.[41]

Perhaps the most persistent issue involved the unhappiness of U.S. textile makers in the South with the flood of imported Japanese cotton textiles. Another was the question of halibut fishing rights in the eastern Bering Sea. He usually took his cues from the various bureaucracies in Washington, but on occasion he would soften or temper American demands if he thought they were excessive. The issues would become explosive later; in 1968, Richard Nixon would win southern votes and the presidency by promising to curb these imports. At this point, however, America was running a current account surplus with Japan; not until 1965 did the tide turn and Japan begin to run up huge bilateral trade surpluses.

In all these matters, Reischauer had to deal with visiting members of Congress who came to Tokyo in what he called "the annual salmon run."[42] These were people with a real stake in the issues. Reischauer developed a good-humored and effective way of dealing with them, listening carefully, educating them about Japanese realities when he could, but avoiding confrontation. He had little interest in "the exact yardage of cloth of various types, with or without zippers, that the Japanese would be allowed to export"—the minutiae of these talks—but he did learn enough to make the American case when he thought he had one.

His most successful effort was with Congressman John Rooney, chairman of the Appropriations Subcommittee that controlled the State Department's budget. Rooney terrified the State Department, regularly ranting and raving against the "striped-pants cookie-pushing diplomats" who were wasting American taxpayers' dollars with fancy dinner parties abroad. When he headed for Tokyo in the fall of 1961, he sent word ahead that he wanted meat and potatoes for dinner and "no natives." Reischauer would wryly note later, "Haru obviously didn't count. [Rooney] had a marvelous time and was very garrulous. At one point, quivering with remembered rage, he thundered, 'At some embassies they serve me little birds standing up in jelly.'"[43] Reischauer believed that his successful hosting of Rooney resulted in a higher representation allowance for Tokyo and in the end kept him from going further into debt.

Reischauer insisted that important U.S. Congressman and other businessmen stay in the residence—often at his own expense because his entertainment allowance could be spent only on Japanese guests. He used these occasions to educate his visitors, many of whom were making their first visit to Japan. "At Harvard," he recalled, "I only lectured several times a week. In Tokyo, sometimes I tutored as many as ten people per day."[44]

And he did for the first time develop a keen interest in economics: noting the rapidly growing size of Japan's gross domestic product in comparison with its neighbors in East Asia, he had large maps mounted on cardboard made for his lectures. The maps were drawn to show the size of each nation's economy rather than its geographical dimensions. Japan on these maps towered over China and its other neighbors. The point, of course, was to persuade his listeners that Japan's new economic strength gave it the power and the obligation to play a larger role in the region.

His relations with the CIA were cordial but distant. He had the good fortune to work successively with two wise and seasoned station chiefs: William V. Broe, a former FBI agent who would go on to become inspector general of the CIA, and William E. Nelson, a former graduate student in Chinese studies at Harvard. He asked them to keep him informed of any operations that might explode into the news, and they did. But most of the CIA's covert work at that time involved collecting intelligence on China; he did not ask them for details.

On at least one occasion, he discussed with U.S. military and intelligence officers the most effective way to ensure the victory of pro-American Liberal Democratic Party candidates in a 1965 local election in the Ryukyus. He argued that it would be "much safer" to let this party's national officials handle the money than to channel it directly to local candidates. "Okinawa is a small place, like a small town in the U.S.," he said. "Okinawa is also like a small country prefecture in Japan, where political maneuvers—particularly involving money—are well known. The Japanese conservatives are going to be involved with funds and other activities in the Ryukyuan elections anyway, and it would be a perfect cover to simply add to their resources rather than trying to carry it out directly in the Ryukyus." He added, "If the U.S. is caught with its hand in the cookie jar there will be a serious blow-up in Japan."[45]

Other recently declassified documents indicate that the CIA was involved in supporting certain conservative politicians, thus helping to keeping the conservative Liberal Democratic Party in power. A book published in 2007 by Tim Weiner claims that the CIA funded the rise of Kishi Nobusuke to the position of prime minister in the years 1954–57 and other right-wing members of the Liberal Democratic Party up until the 1970s.[46] It is not clear whether Reischauer knew of these alleged operations, if they in fact took place. But he would not have been shocked. "There was intelligence showing that the Communist Chinese and Soviets were funding the anti-treaty organizations, and some estimates predicted that the left wing Socialists would come to power by 1970, when the treaty could be renounced," commented Albert Seligmann, an embassy political officer, in a recent interview.[47] Reischauer, if he knew of these payments, would probably have considered them a necessary but temporary by-product of the Cold War. The CIA took care to give an ambassador the ability to issue a "plausible denial" in matters of this sort.

Reischauer spent an inordinate amount of time on the so-called Government and Relief in Occupied Areas (GARIOA) negotiations. After long and complex discussions, Foreign Minister Kosaka Zentaro and Reischauer announced in June 1961 that Japan would fork over $490 million in partial payment for the goods and services it had received during the occupation. Reischauer felt this agreement was reasonably generous, not unlike the one with Germany, where about one dollar was repaid for every three dollars spent. A part of this sum was later combined with another $25 million received from Japan in connection with the return of Okinawa in 1972 to establish the Japan–U.S. Friendship Commission. This commission exists today and funds important new cultural exchanges.

Another purely personal initiative was Reischauer's success in persuading the U.S. Army to give up its base in central Tokyo, known as Washington Heights, the former Yoyogi Parade Ground, for use as the Olympic Village in 1964. Washington Heights was an enormously valuable piece of real estate next to the Meiji Shrine in Harajuku, close to the main Olympic stadium. The army had offered Camp Drake, in the northern suburbs of Tokyo, for this purpose, but Reischauer, seeking to lower the U.S. military profile, persuaded the army to give up Washington Heights. One result was the stunning Aquatic Sports Arena designed for the Olympics by the great architect Tange Kenzo, which still stands today on the former U.S. Army base.

Both Reischauers loved their new lives, at least for the first two years. Haru, who grew up in the wealthy Matsukata family surrounded by servants, quickly adapted to managing a staff of fourteen household employees. Ed (as he now preferred to be called by his friends), thoroughly enjoyed the perks of office: several secretaries and assistants, a car and driver, the use of military aircraft, and glamorous receptions where he could meet literary giants such as Kawabata Yasunari, Mishima Yukio, and Osaragi Jiro; the great architects Yoshimura Junzo and Tange Kenzo; the political scientist Maruyama Masao; the historian Hayashi Kentaro, who would become president of Tokyo University; the Zen expert Suzuki Daisetsu; and the great Kabuki actor Utaemon. It was equally exhilarating for this academic couple to dine with Golda Meir, Duke Ellington, Leonard Bernstein, Aaron Copland, Arthur Rubinstein, Seiji Ozawa, Van Cliburn, Danny Kaye, Frank Sinatra, Robert Penn Warren, Shirley McLaine, and Astronaut (later Senator) John Glenn. (Glenn was a memorable houseguest who slid side-saddle down the banister of the long stairway from the second floor of the residence.)

If anyone expected the fifty-year-old Harvard professor to be an aloof intellectual, they were soon disabused. Reischauer plunged into the job as if he had been born for it, which in a sense he had. Calling on his experience in the army and State Department, he delighted in the challenge of learning the intricate games of the bureaucracy. With the flair and self-confidence that he had gained as a popular lecturer, he reveled in his new public role as perhaps the most important American figure in Tokyo since General MacArthur.

Several of his former students noticed that he seemed to grow taller in the job. At five feet ten and one-half inches and 165 pounds, Reischauer was not a physically imposing man, but he seemed to dominate every room with his erect carriage—chest puffed out, hands gesticulating, voice nearly shouting, then chuckling to make a point, his long, lean, angular face in animated, earnest conversation. Years later people would greet his son, Robert, who at six feet five inches is a truly tall man, with the remark, "Oh, you're tall, just like your father."

"What was really fun," Reischauer later recalled, "was the fact that you had a chance to educate on a scale and in a different way than what I'd ever had before, or would have again. Cabinet members and Senators would come through, and you'd give them a new view of things, and give them a concept of what Japan was and was becoming and could be—a worthwhile activity, and I never tired of doing that."[48]

The Reischauers fell easily into the diplomatic routine of luncheons, teas, receptions, and dinners, and although they both hated cocktail and dinner parties, they learned to move swiftly through these gatherings, making a brief appearance (*kao o dasu*) and talking with the most interesting people.[49]

Ambassador Reischauer calls on Mrs. Hatoyama Ichiro, president of Kyoritsu Joshi Gakuen, a college in Tokyo where he delivered a lecture in October 1963. She was the widow of Hatoyama Ichiro, prime minister of Japan from 1954 to 1956, and grandmother of Hatoyama Yukio, who became prime minister of Japan in 2009. The author (*left*) served as special assistant to Reischauer from 1963 to 1965. Photograph by an unknown person at Tsuda College. Courtesy of the author.

Reischauer's single greatest aversion was to geisha parties, with their endless drinking and childish games. "Silly women for dinner parties may be a trial, but when they are paid to be silly I really can't stand it," he wrote to his family.[50] Also burdensome was the need to pay a formal call on each of his sixty-five fellow ambassadors in Tokyo. He viewed this custom as an idiotic hangover from the nineteenth century.

Reischauer had several different modes of dealing with the variety of people in his new life. Among fellow diplomats, he developed a genial, comradely style, smiling blandly and making small talk. He learned to do it well, although he never really enjoyed it. In official meetings with bureaucrats, both American and Japanese, he often appeared bored, and his thoughts seemed to be elsewhere. When meeting professors, scholars, intellectuals, graduate students, or former students, however, his demeanor changed; he assumed an authoritative, even commanding presence, which I learned to take as a high compliment. This was Reischauer Sensei indicating that maybe you knew something about Japan that he didn't know! He honored his students by treating them as intellectual equals,

Ambassador Reischauer was a good listener to the many Japanese visitors who asked to meet with him. Here, in 1963, he is pictured meeting with one of those visitors. Undated photo by U.S. Embassy photographer. Courtesy of the author.

asking tough questions, expecting them to know the answers, and devouring new information like a hungry tiger receiving scraps of red meat.

A typical "Dear Family" letter of Sunday, May 28, 1961, provides a glimpse of his frantic schedule:

> We have as usual been incredible busy. I have met repeatedly with the Foreign Minister over the schedule of Ikeda's Washington visit but mostly over the GARIOA debt which we hope to get cleared up very soon now. As the papers say the figure is in the $500,000,000 neighborhood. One night we met secretly after a dinner party at 11:00 P.M. and then we had a final meeting suddenly yesterday afternoon. Also had long talk with the Vice Foreign Minister over Korea problem which is a real headache. All this has necessitated a heavy flow of telegrams to Washington.... Wednesday we took largely off to go with part of diplomatic corps out to Imperial stock farm in Chiba—a nice rail ride to pretty country and pleasant relaxed day. Haru rode in carriage but I tried horse, getting myself somewhat shaken up when it trotted, but with no serious ill effects.... Yesterday A.M. early I took helicopter to Grant Heights (on outskirts of Tokyo) where I officially opened Little League season, made talk, threw out balls for four simultaneous games, then flew to Washington Heights (old Yoyogi Parade Grounds) where did same there though I hit the first ball as well as throwing it there. It was fun and I signed several hundred balls, gloves, bats, notebooks, programs, and whatnot for the American kids who really mobbed me.[51]

One top priority was to get to know Japan's top leaders. As a college professor, Reischauer had had few opportunities to meet politicians in either country. But he and Haru soon found themselves dining in the private residence of Prime Minister and Mrs. Ikeda Hayato. To his surprise, he enjoyed an "entirely informal, pleasant Japanese meal, and we had a very pleasant cozy time. In [the] Japanese [language] he relaxes and is quite outgoing, not stiff, as he appears in most relationships. He spoke very frankly about his career and his colleagues."[52] Reischauer viewed Ikeda as a man of "great integrity." "Ikeda turned out to be an extraordinarily fine man—I think a very sensible person who was following what he called the low posture, a process of educating his public and not pushing them. It was a concept of communications between leadership and public that was a little bit new in Japan."[53]

Reischauer also liked and admired Miki Takeo, Miyazawa Kiichi, and Nakasone Yasuhiro, all future prime ministers. He met a number of times with Yoshida Shigeru and Kishi Nobusuke, but found he had little in common with them.

His favorite Japanese politician was Ohira Masayoshi, who became foreign minister in 1962. He felt a special bond with Ohira, both having been born in 1910. They joked about Ohira being six months older. Reischauer learned to trust Ohira, to respect his blunt honesty and common sense. He was "always straight forward and reliable. The fact that he was a Christian—a member of the group of intellectuals known as the 'No Church' Movement—may have contributed to these traits."[54] In a letter to Harvard's president Derek Bok in 1978, after Ohira became prime minister, Reischauer wrote that he had previously discouraged awarding honorary degrees to Japanese prime ministers due to the "nonintellectual qualities of the incumbents, . . . but Ohira is a different case. He is a real intellectual as well as statesman and a man of character and principle. He is also a very good politician. I think we can expect great things of him."[55] Ohira died suddenly in June 1980 before Harvard could award the degree.

In an effort to repair the "broken dialogue," he also met with Socialist Party labor leaders Sohyo (General Council of Trade Unions) and Zenro (Japan Trade Union Congress), usually without publicity (their request) in his private residence. He found them personally more open-minded than he had expected. After a lunch with the new secretary general of the Japan Socialist Party, he wrote, "[Narita] was distressingly doctrinaire and bound by Marxist terminology, though he is personally a likeable sort."[56] But some left-wing leaders such as Yasui Kaoru left him fuming: "Yasui, head of the Anti-Nuclear Bomb Society, which is virtually [a] Commie-front organization[,] called to present series of questions for [Bobby] Kennedy. . . . But list of questions when examined proved pure propaganda and he immediately gave to press inaccurate account of our interview. So I replied with a letter which politely implied his 'insincerity' and propagandistic Communist bias."[57]

Reischauer believed that Japan's left-wing intellectuals, with their "pervasive Marxist assumptions," were some of the "harshest critics of American democracy" and that they "sometimes helped to undermine democracy in Japan." In a classified memo for the State Department and representatives of private U.S. foundations in June 1961, written shortly after his arrival as ambassador in Tokyo, he warned that "their influence is among the factors which could within the next several years push the Japanese into a course of action that would be highly detrimental to the cause of democracy within Japan and the prospects of peace and freedom in Asia."[58]

He went on to offer an approach to the problem. Noting that "many Japanese intellectuals lacked solid knowledge about conditions in other countries" and "knowledge of the best in recent Western thought," he suggested that Americans should foster intellectual contacts between Japanese and Americans in a "broad, free and undirected dialogue. In such a dialogue, the facts that are most relevant and the ideas that are most sound will emerge of themselves more effectively than if we attempt consciously to single them out and 'sell them.'" He called for improving the quality of exchange programs. "We should probably improve the experience of Japanese students and scholars in the United States, [and] increase meaningful Japanese participation in American and international scholarly conferences." He thought that labor leaders and university students should get special attention in this regard. And he added that "European intellectual leaders can do more in this field than Americans (because of Japanese intellectual 'snobbism,' greater similarities of Japanese intellectual problems with those of Europe, and the relative paucity of contacts in recent years with Europeans as compared with Americans)."[59]

Reischauer's greatest disappointment was that he was never invited to give a lecture at Tokyo University, Japan's most prestigious institution of higher learning and the campus where he had studied in the 1930s. Todai, as it was known, was a hotbed of Marxism and antitreaty activists, and when, as special assistant, I approached several professors to inquire about a lecture, the answer was always that the university feared massive protests and did not want to embarrass Reischauer.

In reaching out to Japanese intellectuals, he drew a distinction between those he considered hopelessly Marxist and therefore unreachable, on the one hand, and those whom he considered thoughtful, open-minded, and educable, on the other. He found many leftist intellectuals theoretical to the point of irrelevancy. In August 1962, he gave a major speech in Kyoto entitled "The Role of the American Intellectual," which, he explained in a letter to his father, "allowed me to compare (and thus really criticize) Japanese intellectuals, and explain why an American intellectual like me is asked to take and accept job like this. It was a scholar's rather than an ambassador's speech, but seems to have been well received, and as my staff says, I can get away with this sort of thing where another Ambassador couldn't."[60] In a November 1964 speech in Japanese at Nihon University, he went further: "Anyone who believes in democracy has to be against Communism." He wrote his family, "This may seem obvious enough, but in Japan 'anti-Communism' is still not a respectable point of view."[61]

Whenever he could, he would offer up his own interpretation of Japanese history, pointing out the connection between Japan's feudalism and its subsequent rapid modernization. This connection was a direct assault on the Marxist version, "which I feel is our most basic enemy," he argued in January 1963. "I have come to the conclusion," he wrote his family in October 1962, "that talk of diplomats being honest men paid to lie for their country, is a serious misconception of how diplomacy should work. I am becoming increasingly convinced that the only effective way to play an Ambassador's role is to be scrupulously honest about everything one says. Just as in personal life, anything else can lead to serious troubles."[62]

Reischauer tried to visit all forty-six of Japan's prefectures and municipalities (*todofuken*) and succeeded in getting to thirty-nine of them. Here, in a typical visit, he calls on the Reverend Kiyohara (*on Haru Reischauer's left*), the priest of the Yamadera Buddhist Temple outside Yamagata City in northeastern Japan, March 7, 1965. The author is third from the right. Photograph by the Yamagata prefectural government photographer. Courtesy of the author.

After Christmas 1964, he wrote his friends that his "running fight in the journals with the Marxist interpretation of history has stirred up a storm of anguished cries from the Communists, so it is apparently having some good effects."[63] Starting in 1962, Communists tried and often succeeded in blocking his planned lecture at a number of universities. Nakayama Ichiro, whom Reischauer considered to be Japan's leading economist, told him in September 1963 "that nothing has shaken Japan 'philosophically' from the outside in recent years so much as my [Reischauer's] various articles on Japanese history."[64]

There were disappointments, of course. Reischauer made a special effort to have lunch with Japanese intellectuals whom he had known in the past. In the summer of 1962, he invited popular young author Oda Makoto for lunch. Oda had studied at Harvard and came to write a highly critical book on America titled *Nan Demo Mite Yaro* (Let's Look at Everything). Later, when Oda wanted to return to the United States, Reischauer made a special effort to help him get a visa. "He repaid me with another nasty book on America."[65]

Reischauer, speaking in English to the Japan–U.S. Society in Akita City, Akita Prefecture, in northeastern Japan, on March 8, 1965. Although he could speak fairly good Japanese, he preferred to rely on the talents of Sen Nishiyama (*right*), an extraordinarily gifted Japanese American at the U.S. Embassy who became a close friend. Reischauer sometimes corrected Nishiyama's interpretation to the delight of their audiences. The author is on the far left. Photograph by unknown person hired by Akita City. Courtesy of the author.

Reischauer believed that the appeal of Marxism in Japan to intellectuals and students lay in its rejection of the pragmatic society about them. They were attracted to the rigidly theoretical German thinkers such as Karl Marx, he thought. "In the 1930's only the Marxists, armed with their rigid dogmas, stood up firmly against the wave of hyper-nationalist mysticism that inundated Japan. The idea became firmly implanted, therefore, that Marxism, rather than liberal democracy, was the chief enemy of militarism and authoritarianism."[66] Reischauer sought to undermine this idea and to prove that the Western industrialized democracies were in fact the best hope for preserving peace. This debate might seem to be a trivial academic squabble in other countries, but in Japan it lay at the heart of the postwar political conversation about power and policy.

Reischauer had no patience with American bureaucrats who blindly barred any Japanese who had been involved in left-wing activities from getting visas to travel to the United States. One of Japan's best-known economists today, Professor Aoki Masahiko, was a young graduate student in the summer of 1963 seeking a visa to study at the University of Minnesota. He came to the U.S. Embassy and applied for a visa. He admitted on the application form that he had once been active in a Communist organization called the "Bund" (Bundo) and was instantly turned down. Through an introduction of a mutual friend, he came to my office and explained that he was no longer a Marxist and wanted to study modern economics. I was convinced that he was telling the truth and took his story to Reischauer, who instantly overturned the earlier rejection and authorized a visa for Aoki. Aoki went on to a brilliant career as a professor at Stanford and Kyoto universities and became president of the International Economics Association.[67]

Reischauer's most original act was to appoint a special assistant whose job it was to carve out time for activities that interested Reischauer most, such as travel to the prefectures—his aim was to visit all forty-six *todofuken* (he wound up visiting thirty-nine of them)—and talks with students and intellectuals. As noted, from 1961 to 1963 Ernest Young did the job, and from 1963 to 1965 I was that assistant.[68] Before traveling, Reischauer would sift through various invitations, look at his calendar, and pick the dates when he could get away. It was my job then to visit the host prefecture; set up meetings for Reischauer with the governor, mayor of the major city, several schools, regional press, security people, leaders of local industry, an occasional Buddhist temple, local points of historical interest; and arrange for the hotel or *ryokan* where the Reischauers would stay. The arrangements were elaborate and painstaking—even more so than a visit from the emperor, one governor told me. Meanwhile, back at the embassy, official diplomatic duties would pile up and exasperated senior officers would try to persuade Reischauer to cancel or postpone the trip. Aware of the planning and trouble that his visit was causing, Reischauer invariably stuck to his travel plan.

In fact, Reischauer reveled in this aspect of his job. On the night before he left on a trip outside Tokyo, he would review piles of information on the history, economy, and politics of the prefecture to be visited. Much of this information was already familiar to him. While en route, for example, he would immerse himself in its history, noting the number of bushels (or *koku)* of rice each *han* contributed to the shogun in the Tokugawa Era. On one occasion, Sen Nishiyama, his extraordinarily gifted interpreter, and I did our homework in advance. Then, seated across from him on the train, we pretended to have an argument about whether it was the fourth or fifth daimyo who had started a war against a neighboring *han*. Without looking up from his reading, Reischauer said calmly,

"It was the fourth." He was right. When he met local officials and media, he would drop these facts into the conversation, causing amazement and embarrassed laughter that this foreigner (*gaijin*) would know more than they did about their own history.

Did Japanese officials resent his knowledge of Japan and his ability both to penetrate their thinking and to read their unadulterated opinions in the Japanese-language media? He thought that some officials probably did: "There were some professionals in the Japanese Government who thought it would be best not to have an Ambassador all that knowledgeable, and had some anxiety on that score. But certainly in terms of the Japanese public, a great deal of my popularity had to do with the fact that they felt I understood them and knew them."[69]

He seized on every opportunity to interact with students. On one occasion, he was asked to speak at Seikei University in northwestern Tokyo at 3:00 P.M. on January 25, 1964. After accepting, he learned that Dean Rusk, his boss, would be arriving at 6:45 P.M. on the same day. Protocol dictated that he meet Rusk at Haneda Airport, but there was no way he could get there by embassy limousine through the pre-Olympic jumble of torn-up roads. He asked me to look into the possibility of going to Haneda by ordinary commuter train, and I figured he could just make it if he left Seikei at 5:00 P.M. Reischauer agreed. Senior embassy officials were horrified at the thought of the ambassador riding on an ordinary train; none of them had ever done so.

On the appointed day, Reischauer gave the lecture and was answering questions when 5:00 P.M. rolled around. He showed no signs of slowing down, so I handed him a note: "Rusk is arriving at 6:45 P.M." He put the note in his pocket and kept on talking with the students. Finally, at 5:15, we escaped and boarded a train on the Inokashira Line, then the Yamate Line, changing at Shinagawa for Haneda. When we paused briefly at Shinagawa to look for the platform for Haneda, a kindly plainclothes policeman directed us to the right platform. We had not noticed until then that we were being followed. Reischauer got to the airport with only five minutes to spare. "It's more important to talk with students than to be on time for the Secretary of State," he explained, and I think he meant it. The Tokyo police, for their part, were not about to let Reischauer embarrass himself by being late if they could help it.

The media could not get enough of the Reischauers. He eagerly sought out serious journals such as *Sekai*, *Bungei Shunju*, *Chuo Koron*, and *Asahi Journal*, as well as the three leading daily papers, *Nikkei Shimbun*, and the Japanese television and radio broadcasting network NHK for on-the-record interviews or off-the-record backgrounders.[70] The monthlies begged him for articles, giving him a free platform for his message. He also gave interviews to less well-known publications, such as the youth magazine of the Tenri Buddhist Sect. The weeklies played up scenes of the couple in familiar Japanese settings, attacking bowls of noodles with chopsticks or strolling around the Imperial Palace outer gardens.

If Reischauer was making a mark as a diplomat and historian, "Haru Fujin" (as she became known) was even more adored by the media. Ed wrote his family that Haru got more media attention than anyone in Japan except Taiho, the sumo idol.[71] In endless newspaper, magazine, and television portrayals, she emerged as the granddaughter of Prince Matsukata Masayoshi, wife of an exceptional American, and adoptive mother of three children. They explored every detail of the Reischauer family history in Japan and interviewed the family maid mentioned earlier, Kuwabara Motoko, who told *Shufu no Tomo* (similar to the *Ladies' Home Journal*) that Haru and Ed's marriage was great because it joined a man who understood and appreciated the Orient with a woman who had benefited from a Western education.[72] *Fujin Koron* asked how she managed to become intimate with the children, especially the boy. She explained that she had learned to ask their opinions when she wanted to change something in the house rather than simply making the change.[73]

Haru gave lunches and receptions for a broad variety of Japanese who had never been to the embassy. One luncheon honored a Socialist Diet member, Mrs. Chiba Chiyose, who remarked at the time, "In 1960 I was demonstrating outside the Embassy gates; now I'm having lunch inside."[74]

Reischauer also cultivated the twenty-eight resident American journalists in Tokyo and became a close friend of A. M. (Abe) Rosenthal of the *New York Times*, Keyes Beech of the *Chicago Daily News*, and Don Connery of *Time-Life*. His off-the-record meetings were "more like a history seminar at Harvard than anything else."[75] He found these sessions informative and useful for gauging Americans' views of Japan and the U.S.–Japan relationship. In turn, the journalists wrote glowing articles about his accomplishments and helped bolster his influence in Washington.

Richard Halloran, then of the *Washington Post*, remembered an interview he conducted with Reischauer in April 1966. He prepared for the interview by reading everything written by or about Reischauer during his first five years as ambassador. "Mr. Ambassador," he said, "I have come to the conclusion that you are the biggest 'con man' to come down the pike in years." "What do you mean?" asked a startled Reischauer. Halloran went on, "You have wrapped yourself in the mantle of the great *sensei* (teacher), stood on a pedestal, and have faithfully laid down the official U.S. policy line for five years." Reischauer thought about that for a moment, and then said, "Well, I hope you won't write it that way."[76]

Reischauer detested far-right conservatives, whether American or Japanese. Of a party of right-wing American Congressman visiting Tokyo, he wrote to his children, "[They are] real Neanderthals, against any sort of aid to anybody (fortunately we are pretty free of aid here but they lit into my idea for using Peace Corps people for English-language teaching with real fury) and are down on imports from anybody, which is a touchy subject here."[77]

He was equally contemptuous of Japanese right-wingers. The arrival of John K. Emmerson as deputy chief of mission set off a flurry of attacks by old-line ultraconservatives. Hashimoto Tetsuma, seventy-three, head of the Purple Cloud Society (Shiunso) embarked on a letter-writing campaign charging that Emmerson was a "proven ultra-leftist."[78] Emmerson was an old friend of Reischauer's since their days together as students in Kyoto in 1936. He was a "Japan hand" who had been stationed in China during World War Two as a liaison officer to Mao Zedong and the Chinese Communist Party. Senator Joseph McCarthy later attacked him and ten other American China hands for alleged sympathy for the Communists. Emmerson was also in Tokyo during the first six months of the occupation when Communists were released from jail. Japanese conservatives blamed him for the subsequent purge of pro-war leaders.

Reischauer never wavered in defending his old friend. He believed "the charges are absurd that he was responsible for American policy, right or wrong, but the intensity of feeling shows how strong are continuing resentments among right wing conservatives over the purge and other Occupation policies. On top of that, these groups reflect the criticism in the U.S. of the Kennedy Administration and are worried about me as being an intellectual (since they consider most Japanese intellectuals to be idiots.)."[79]

He embarked on a series of meetings with conservative leaders in an effort to put out this fire. "It's a sort of Japanese McCarthyism," he wrote his family, "and if it stirs up a McCarthyist response in the U.S., we could be in for real trouble. I am furious about it, and when I saw the Vice Foreign Minister on Friday, I gave him a piece of my mind to be passed on to these types. I said that as Ambassador, I felt most indignant that *any* Japanese, so long as Japan was so feeble in its stand against Communism, would have the gall to criticize or doubt the U.S.'s anti-Communist stand etc. etc."[80]

He worried that the Foreign Ministry might bypass the embassy and go straight to Washington with its concerns, so he also quietly asked William Broe, the CIA station chief, to vouch for Emmerson as a trustworthy and loyal American among his Japanese contacts.

A month later, over dinner with former foreign minister Kosaka Zentaro and his brother Tokusaburo, Reischauer was disturbed to hear further criticism of the Emmerson appointment. "I was much distressed to find that even level-headed people like that were somewhat worked up about the Emmerson appointment. I have come to the conclusion that one should never underestimate the depth of Japanese ignorance about the United States," he wrote to his family.[81] He also believed that some of the attacks against Emmerson were in reality attacks by Kishi and other conservatives against Prime Minister Ikeda, who advised Reischauer to take no notice of the whole affair.

Holding the family together was a challenge. By 1961, Ann, his oldest daughter, had married Stephen Heineman, a student at California Institute of Technology who would become a molecular biologist (geneticist). Bob, twenty, was finishing his sophomore year at Harvard. Only Joan, seventeen, just out of high school, came to Japan with her parents and worked briefly for television and radio before finding the glare of publicity too much to handle. Both his father, now eighty-two, and his sister, Felicia, forty-seven, back in Belmont, needed help. A. K. Reischauer's mind was slowly failing, and he was turning into a curmudgeon. Haru's sister, Miye, who lived nearby, did her best to look after them, but there were constant financial and other problems to take care of. The old man blamed Haru for keeping Ed in Tokyo. In a note to Ann Reischauer, Haru wrote: "Sorry to hear about father being anti-me. I hope he is off it by the time I arrive. He is sadly mistaken about my being responsible for keeping D. [Dad] here—if I had my way I would have D. out of here very soon, but he is enjoying his work and he is needed out here and so as a good wife I am enduring it, making myself enjoy it because I know its for a good cause."[82]

Reischauer had instilled in his children his lifelong scorn for pretense or pomposity of any sort, and now it was their turn to strike back, making fun of his new social life. Just two months after their arrival in Tokyo, Haru felt compelled to write Ann and Steve, defending herself and her husband:

> After receiving your letter of admonishment, I was most discouraged and very unhappy, because you were right in saying that you were getting bored with all the recounting of our week's schedule. . . . It's difficult for Joan and Bobby and even you or any outsider to realize what both Daddy and I have gone through in adjusting to this new life. You see it purely from

> the outside, such as my wearing hats and criticizing me and buying lot of clothes etc., But actually, for us our necessity to change our clothes, habits etc. are the least of our adjustment. It's something very hard to explain, and I am not asking for any sympathy, but I can assure you, we've gone through a lot of mental struggle and gear shifting, and disregard of our own personal wishes and wants.[83]

Bob Reischauer at twenty was feeling his oats: the long-haired, motorcycle-riding rebel took pleasure in making life hell for his father when he visited in the summer of 1961. He made his disdain for the diplomatic life quite obvious with the torn blue jeans and casual zoris that he wore around Tokyo. Two weeks after his arrival in Tokyo, Ed wrote his family, "Bob has been no ray of sunshine. He seems to feel that it is a matter of principle that he should oppose all concessions in dress or conduct to our position in Japan. (Logically he should have refused as a matter of principle the free trip out here that my position gave him—but he is happy to take advantage of the position while opposing it in principle.)" In a further fit of pique, he wrote,

> This is a sort of sign-off letter—that is the last general [mailing]. We shall continue our weekly account to Father, in Belmont (and so as to keep some record for ourselves of our lives here) but unless we receive special requests from the rest of you for copies, we shall send no more. The reasons for this are twofold: Ann and Bob have been emphatic in saying that everyone is bored to death with our letters (which is easy enough to believe) and now that the first whirl is over there is progressively less of general interest to record. . . . [N]ow we find our job here unduly burdensome, dull and frustrating. If it weren't for the danger of destroying the new tone we have set and undoing the demonstration of having Haru in this job, we would be inclined to throw up the whole thing and go home right now.[84]

It seems clear that the tumultuous events of the past six years had taken a toll on the family: Adrienne's suffering and death, Ed's hasty marriage to Haru, his intense preoccupation with his work and career, and his sudden burst into public life—all had left scars. Bob had been captain of his high school soccer team, and Ed had gone to only one of his games in three years. Ed had been surprised when Bob told him of his admission to Harvard in 1959; he had thought his son was applying to Swarthmore. When Bob married Charlotte on October 26, 1962, in Belmont, Massachusetts, Ed was too busy to attend the wedding and had not even met Charlotte at the time. "He was pretty caught up in his own life," Bob recalled. "I got over it. Then we had kids, and he got along very well with them."[85]

Reischauer would be extravagantly proud of his son in later years: Robert would go on to get a Ph.D. in economics, serve as president of the Urban Institute in Washington and as a much admired director of the U.S. Congressional Budget Office (1989–95), and join the seven-member Harvard Corporation, which governs the university. In September 1961, however, after Bob and Joan had returned to Belmont, their father was still annoyed: "I wish I could wring Bob's neck and give Joan's a twist," he wrote to Haru's sister. "They seem to grow up only very slowly. They won't ever really grow up until they are really on their own. We all do too much for them."[86]

Yet four months later he wrote his old friend Arthur Billings, "Bob is a junior at Harvard in Government; six feet four, a charming, humorous personality (when not concentrating on destroying the ego of parents and siblings), brilliant in some ways, with an extraordinary memory and gift for gab (though his penmanship and spelling are those of an 8-year-old)." Of Joan, he wrote,

> Joan is a Freshman at Oberlin; is well organized, neat, balanced and hard-working (virtues all notably lacking in the other two), beset and browbeaten by her two domineering older siblings, but apparently emotionally unscarred by it all, and developing now into a self-reliant and attractive adult. All three seem to be turning out much better than I once feared. Adrienne's terrible long illness was an awful strain on all of them, as well as me, and after she finally died I was afraid the whole family was really cracking up; but with Haru's great aid, we are now all well past that crisis and the children are becoming the delight of our gradual coast into senility.[87]

Joan was clearly not unscarred. She would drop out of Oberlin, go through periods of anxiety and depression, and for a time be a source of great concern to the family. She would eventually recover, though, and graduate from Tufts University, work at the Harvard Center for International Affairs and in book publishing, and become a wife, mother, and well-rounded adult. But in those embassy years she needed her parents more than they realized and wanted more than they could give her.

Reischauer deeply loved his family, but his single-minded focus on his work, his walling off the tragedies in his life, and his reluctance or inability to communicate on a personal level left emotional scars on both sides. He never thought to give Haru Christmas or birthday gifts, and Haru took to buying and wrapping her own presents at Christmastime. On her fifty-fourth birthday, she wrote to Ann and Steve, "Today being my birthday, I got reminders of this day from Daddy's office staff, and the Embassy Women's Club. While in Kyoto, I bought myself a lovely blue bowl for Daddy to give me, so I don't feel neglected." On the same day, she wrote her friend Kitty (Mrs. John Kenneth) Galbraith, "Ed and I are so busy, we found we weren't talking to each other too much, as at night in bed when we should be talking, we have been so tired, we went off to sleep right away."[88] Reischauer was as curiously insensitive to the deepest emotional needs of those he loved most as he was to his own needs.

A group of five Japanese-speaking junior embassy officers formed a group they humorously called the Furyo Gaijin Kai, or Unwholesome Foreigners Group.[89] The Japanese media used this name for the shady characters who appeared in Tokyo during and after the occupation: black marketeers, gamblers, pimps, prostitutes, and petty criminals. The group met monthly for dinner with five younger Japanese officers from the Foreign Ministry and sometimes from other ministries. The latter quickly named themselves the Furyo Gaijin Taisaku Iinkai (Unwholesome Foreigners Countermeasures Group).[90] We consumed large amounts of sake as we debated in a free and uninhibited manner the serious problems affecting both governments. On one occasion, John Fairbank, visiting from Harvard, joined the group for a dinner meeting. He could scarcely believe the camaraderie of the evening. Reischauer delighted in hearing reports about the conversations and felt that they offered a useful glimpse into the thinking of Japan's younger generation.

Reischauer was eager to meet student radicals who had opposed the alliance with the United States. At his request in 1963, I invited half a dozen leaders of Zengakuren to my home for an informal supper. These individuals were the same students who had led the snake-dancing protests outside the U.S. Embassy and the Diet in 1960. Ed and Haru, arriving in the huge embassy Cadillac, startled my neighbors in the small community Yoshikubo-cho, Meguro-ku. They sat on the living-room floor of our small Japanese house and talked with the students in Japanese for three hours. Koyama Kenichi, who would become a conservative professor of economics at Gakushuin, told me afterward that he couldn't believe an American ambassador would take time to talk with people of his age and radical views.

Reischauer's own spoken Japanese, learned mainly as an adult, was only fair. He could conduct lengthy conversations on familiar topics, such as Ennin (Jikaku Daishi) and Buddhism or other historical issues, but he insisted on using an interpreter for formal speeches and official business. "It's hard enough to give a good speech in your own language," he often said. His reading ability was excellent, and he probably knew as many Chinese characters as any well-educated Japanese college graduate: perhaps three to four thousand). On one occasion, an aide drafted for his signature a typewritten letter of thanks in English to a Buddhist priest for a book that the priest had given Reischauer during a visit to his temple. One character in the Japanese title of the book had several possible readings. The embassy translation section did its best to find the correct romanization for the character, but they got it wrong. Reischauer took one look at the book itself and sent the letter back unsigned, but with the correct reading and a scribbled note: "Please do not involve me in illiteracies of this sort." The translators, hoping to prove him wrong, quickly called a scholar at Toyo Bunko (Oriental Library) and found out that Reischauer's reading of the character had been correct.[91]

Japanese reporters loved to test his verbal comprehension. At one press conference, a reporter used the expression *shusse barai*, and Reischauer, to the reporter's surprise, immediately made it clear that it meant "to pay back someone who helps you along the way if and when you succeed."[92] Another used the word *rakkasei*, and Reischauer shot back, "I love peanuts." On many occasions, Reischauer explained that America's "containment policy" toward the Soviet Union was not the aggressive posture suggested by the Ministry of Foreign Affairs' normal rendering of the phrase *fujikome seisaku.* He would comment that *fujikome* implied a proactive stuffing of something back into a container, whereas the U.S. policy was a peaceful, rather passive policy of reacting only to aggression from the other side: a line in the sand. The Ministry of Foreign Affairs finally changed its official translation to the less aggressive *sekitome seisaku* (to check or to dam).[93]

Sen Nishiyama, Reischauer's interpreter, was a gifted linguist who had grown up in Utah but returned to Japan in the 1930s and became a Japanese citizen. His accent in both languages was pitch perfect, and beyond that, he could convey the humor, approval, surprise, or doubt that Reischauer intended with subtle nuance. The two men became close friends. "Sen made mistakes at times, but these were usually because of his lesser knowledge of Japanese history and his resulting misinterpretation of my meaning. I would listen carefully to everything he said and would pick up even the slightest slip or a modest omission of a laudatory remark about him. To hear me correct his statements in Japanese, we discovered, delighted the audience, no matter what its composition, so we always made the most of these corrections."[94] Some Japanese suspected that Sen made mistakes on purpose in order to give his boss a chance to correct him and look smart, but Sen steadfastly denied it.

The Reischauers made a point of greeting Japanese Embassy employees with handshakes and often personal conversations. Handshaking presented a special problem for Haru. A Japanese wife would be expected to bow, but never to shake hands with fellow Japanese, but they decided that as the American ambassador's wife, she should be fully American in this respect, so they both shook hands in all circumstances. Treatment of Japanese employees was a special concern. Up until this time, such employees were almost invisible. They were vital to the functioning of the embassy as translators, interpreters, secretaries, teachers, motor pool drivers, guards, cleaning crew, and so forth, but were somehow looked down upon by Americans as second-class citizens. One suspects they were also looked down upon by fellow Japanese citizens outside the embassy who probably saw them as having "sold out" to the Americans. Reischauer, however, made a point of stressing their value to the U.S. government and met with them once a year to explain U.S. policy and hear their concerns. They responded with enthusiasm, and subsequent ambassadors took their cue from Reischauer's example.

He summed up his first fifty days on the job in a letter to his family in June 1961: "Japanese welcome overwhelming, American welcome extremely warm, both welcomes much greater than anticipated." But he added, "The one big problem is the question of time and energy (we still have to learn to lick this, because up to now we have found our strength gradually being drained by this heavy schedule."[95]

Given the frenzied demands on his time, Ed and Haru Reischauer constantly overextended themselves and often reached the point of exhaustion. Ed started to suffer from migraine headaches again and saw his cholesterol count shoot up to dangerous levels. At one point in 1962, he was secretly hospitalized at the Yokosuka Naval Base and put on a diet of rice and water for five days.

Their one escape was the small Japanese-style home owned by Haru's family in Aburatsubo, Misaki, at the tip of the Miura Peninsula, a little more than two hours' drive from the Tokyo embassy. Here they could, swim, fish, lie on the beach, row in a small boat, and enjoy spectacular views from one hundred feet above the sea. They managed to get there seven times in their first five months and treasured the privacy and freedom. A caretaker with children ages nine and three lived in the back and made it seem more of a home than the stately embassy residence. It was here that Reischauer often banged out his weekly letters to his family, wrote speeches, and reviewed proofs of manuscripts and articles. A nearby helicopter pad allowed the U.S. Navy to whisk him back to Tokyo if necessary. "The police surveillance was inconspicuous," he remembered. "In fact, we were completely unaware of their presence except occasionally when I returned from rowing my rowboat and a man would emerge from the bushes to help me haul it in above high tide."[96]

Edwin and Haru Reischauer loved to escape from their official duties by going to Aburatsubo, Misaki, about two hours' drive from Tokyo on the Miura Peninsula. Here, in November 1964, he rows the author to the Reischauers' small Japanese-style home down the bay on the point to the right. A bystander took this photograph and sent it to the embassy. Courtesy of the author.

The real key to Reischauer's early success in challenging the military was the very close relationship he formed with Robert F. Kennedy, then the attorney general in his brother's cabinet. Reischauer met with Bobby in June 1961 during Prime Minister Ikeda's visit to Washington and laid plans for him to visit Tokyo in February 1962. Kennedy's trip was billed ostensibly as an opportunity to negotiate with President Sukarno of Indonesia, but the real motivation was to scout out the possibility of a Japan visit for President Kennedy. The Kennedys were keenly aware of the fact that Eisenhower's planned visit in 1960 had been blocked by popular protest. A successful visit by his successor, Jack Kennedy, could reap enormous rewards in the 1964 elections.

It is hard to imagine two more different personalities: Bobby, at the age of thirty-seven, was a hardened political professional, suspicious of bureaucrats, always watching his brother's back, with a reputation for ruthlessness. At Washington dinner parties, he was famous for challenging guests to push-up contests, which he invariably won. Reischauer, the intellectual historian who had no real political experience, had little in common with this tough Irish American Catholic operator. Yet they formed a lasting friendship based on vast mutual respect. Reischauer would later recall, "I had been a little dubious about Bobby's past record and reputation, but I was completely won over by his sincerity. He talked and listened well, always remaining calm, cool and reasonable."[97]

Bobby and Ethel Kennedy created a whirlwind of activity in Tokyo, filling every hour as if it were an election campaign. The climax of their visit was Bobby's speech at Waseda University on February 6, 1962, where he was mobbed and shouted down by pro-Communist students. Bobby invited one of the Communist students onto the stage for a debate, but the sound system went dead, and pandemonium broke out. "The whole thing was turning into a fiasco," Reischauer wrote, "and I knew the responsibility for the Attorney General's safety rested with me. I could see my diplomatic career ending suddenly and dramatically. I decided that I had better go into action to try to salvage what I could. I got up and chased the Japanese and foreign news photographers off the stage. Then I turned to the crowd and with my sternest look raised both my arms. To my amazement, the big hall fell silent, and Bobby and the student could continue with their debate."[98]

The Waseda visit was a media triumph for Bobby Kennedy, both in Japan and in America, and it led to an extraordinary bond of friendship and trust with Reischauer, who reported that Kennedy's "youthful energy was appealing and the clear, steady flame of his idealism won me over completely."[99] On February 10, four days after the Waseda incident, Reischauer briefed Kennedy on the need to push the military toward greater autonomy for Okinawa and its eventual reversion to Japan. Kennedy took notes and conveyed these ideas directly to the president. This was the start of Reischauer's real influence in Washington. He now had a reliable back channel to President Kennedy and began using it to plan for a visit by the president to Japan. In fact, a high-level team was on its way from Washington to Tokyo to plan such a visit when Kennedy was shot in Dallas on November 22, 1963. The visit would have taken place in January 1964.

In January 1964, Bobby Kennedy made another visit to Tokyo, less than two months after his brother's death. He ostensibly came to meet again with President Sukarno, but the visit was clearly a first step in his campaign to be president of the United States. Even before he arrived on January 16, he declared that he wanted to visit Waseda again, undoubtedly hoping for another spectacular media triumph. Reischauer asked me (his special assistant) to approach

President Ohama Nobumoto of Waseda cautiously because he suspected that Ohama felt that the earlier incident was unforgivably rude to Kennedy. He was right. Ohama, a distinguished Okinawan, declared that he could under no circumstance risk another shameful incident. I carried this news to Reischauer and Kennedy around midnight on January 16. When I relayed Ohama's polite refusal, Kennedy flew into a rage, calling me names that cannot be printed here. "I have arranged hundreds of meetings with students for my brother. If you can't do it, I'll get someone who can," he fumed. After we got back to the embassy and Kennedy had retired, Reischauer looked worried. "Go back tomorrow and reason with President Ohama," he said. By now, we both realized that Kennedy's visit to Japan was precisely for the purpose of revisiting Waseda University.

I spent thirty minutes with President Ohama on January 17, explaining how much a visit to his campus meant to Kennedy and to Reischauer. With great misgivings, he reluctantly yielded, and a visit was set for Saturday, January 18. I then contacted a group of students who had helped organize the memorial service for President Kennedy the previous December. Some of them were members of a weight-lifting group. All were athletes, and all were fans of Bobby Kennedy. Together we came up with a plan to keep Communists who were not Waseda students from entering Okuma Hall, where Kennedy would speak. The athletes proved to be up to the task. On the day of Kennedy's speech, they stationed themselves at all the entrances to Okuma Hall and made sure that all students entering were actually enrolled at Waseda. Communist agitators were kept out.

Kennedy spoke to the crowd of more than two thousand students, with five thousand more standing outside in the rain. The only protests came from a small group of students who held up a sign saying "Return Okinawa" and from two others outside holding placards saying "Kennedy Go Home." Other students quickly ripped down the signs. The crowd loved the speech and roared its approval when Bobby and Ethel joined in singing the Waseda song. The whole event was covered on national television. American reporters headlined the speech as a triumph for Kennedy. Reischauer wrote to his family, "One can't help but feel that he may be destined in time to succeed his brother."[100] My own view was that he might have preferred a rowdy confrontation with Communist protesters where he could appear to be standing up for America in a foreign land—always a vote winner in American politics.

In March 1962, a month after Reischauer first briefed Bobby Kennedy on the desirability of returning Okinawa to Japan, President Kennedy took the first step by making clear that the Ryukyus would someday be returned to Japan. The statement promised cooperation with the Japanese government in developing the Ryukyus and a continuous effort to transfer authority and responsibility to the Ryukyuans. An American civilian would replace the military as civil administrator. General Caraway, however, flouted Kennedy's policy.

When the Japanese government offered to increase its aid to Okinawa, Caraway, in an effort to limit Tokyo's influence over his domain (*han*), tried to divert it to harbor construction rather than to improving social conditions. But Reischauer fought back, with support from the State Department, and won several rounds. Nevertheless, he felt that Caraway remained "a serious irritant in Japanese-American contacts, threatening a vastly important overall relationship by his high-handed rule in his little bailiwick."[101]

Reischauer continued for the next year and a half to use his special access to Bobby Kennedy to push for the return of Okinawa to Japanese sovereignty. Had President Kennedy not been assassinated in 1963, it is quite possible that reversion would have come sooner.[102] Then, when President Johnson became bogged down in the Vietnam War, and Okinawa was viewed as a vital base for supporting the U.S. troops in Vietnam, the idea was shelved. Reischauer had clearly planted the seeds in Generals Smart and Preston, however. It seems fair to say that Reischauer had a decisive hand in placing the return of Okinawa on the table for consideration and turned the subject from "unthinkable" to "thinkable" within senior U.S. military circles.

In his last cable to Washington on the subject in 1966, Reischauer argued that instead of resisting most government of Japan efforts to play a larger role in the Ryukyus, the United States should avail itself of the Japanese government's assistance in dealing with Ryukyuan problems, realizing that it is fundamentally an ally motivated by the same basic objectives as the United States. The United States, he insisted, should continue to accept as much Japanese economic aid for the Ryukyus as can be effectively used there.[103] The fact that Reischauer still needed to make this argument to Washington indicates that U.S. military resistance to the reversion was still strong.

In November 1968, lame-duck president Lyndon Johnson, who had renounced running for another term due to antiwar protests, announced that the United States intended to return the Ryukyu Islands, including Okinawa, to Japan. In January 1969, at a conference organized by the Japanese government, Reischauer played a key role behind the scenes. By now, there was an upsurge of popular demand for the return of Okinawa. Japan wanted Okinawa back on condition that the United States would abide by the same terms that it accepted in 1960 for bases on the main islands: no introduction of nuclear weapons on bases there ("*kaku nuki hondo nami*"). Reischauer quietly sounded out two other key Americans at the conference, Admiral Arleigh Burke, former chief of naval operations, and General Maxwell Taylor. When he learned that they could accept the reversion of Okinawa with these conditions, he relayed this information to Japanese government officials, who were then emboldened to formally request reversion without fear of an official and embarrassing rebuff.

President Richard Nixon, in his famous meeting with Prime Minister Sato Eisaku in November 1969, agreed to the reversion in return for what he understood was Sato's promise to limit Japan's textile exports to the United States.[104] On May 15, 1972, the Ryukyus were reunited with Japan, thus ending what could have become a serious threat to the alliance.[105]

After the Sato-Nixon communiqué in November 1969, Reischauer wrote in an article for *Asahi Shimbun* that "the solution of the Okinawa problem . . . is to my mind the best solution. In fact, it is the only solution, because anything else would have been no solution at all and would have instead been the source of future troubles. For the U.S. to have administrative control over close to one million Japanese is a most unnatural situation that has long needed correction."[106] Reischauer's efforts to have Okinawa returned to Japanese rule contributed substantially to the fact that there were no new massive protest demonstrations against the Security Treaty in 1970, the first year in which Japan could have given formal notice of its intention to abrogate the treaty after one year's advance notice.

Reischauer well understood Japan's "nuclear allergy," born of the devastation of Hiroshima and Nagasaki in 1945. He sympathized with the "three nonnuclear principles" declared by Prime Minister Sato in 1967: no possession, no production, and no introduction of nuclear weapons into Japan. The U.S. government, in a note attached to the revised Security Treaty of 1960, agreed that it would not make major changes in the equipment of its troops in Japan without prior consultation with the government of Japan. This note was clearly intended to refer to nuclear weapons, but what about nuclear-powered navy ships? And what about nuclear weapons carried on U.S. vessels visiting these ports? Japan at first resisted the idea of allowing U.S. nuclear-powered submarines to enter U.S. naval bases in Japan, but in 1962 Reischauer felt the time was ripe to test Japanese public opinion on this question, and Foreign Minister Ohira agreed. In January 1963, Reischauer announced that the United States had asked for permission to bring nuclear-powered submarines into Japanese ports. This announcement led to large protests, heated debate, and much study. In November 1964, however, the first nuclear-power submarine, USS *Seadragon*, entered Sasebo with very little furor.

The matter of "introduction" (*mochikomi*) of nuclear weapons was more complicated. On one hand, it was U.S. policy never to confirm or deny the presence of nuclear weapons on board its ships. On the other hand, it was only a matter of common sense to assume that some U.S. Navy ships were armed with nuclear weapons and that these weapons could hardly be offloaded before a port call in Japan. The question was: Did the visit of an American naval vessel armed with nuclear weapons to a Japanese port constitute "introduction" (*mochikomi*) of nuclear weapons into Japan requiring prior consultation with the Japanese government? In the negotiations leading up to the signing of the 1960 treaty, the matter was not clarified, and memories differed: Reischauer later wrote, "I had understood that . . . there had been an oral agreement that nuclear weapons on board naval vessels which came and went did not constitute 'introduction,' (*mochikomi*) because it would have been entirely impractical to remove such armaments before entering Japanese ports. Some of the participants in these negotiations have recently stated that the matter was too delicate even to discuss, but that the negotiators on both sides had taken for granted that nuclear weapons would be allowed to be retained on board."[107]

Reischauer became disturbed in 1963 when spokesmen for the Japanese government, in Diet interpellations, implied that there were definitely no nuclear weapons on U.S. Navy ships entering Japanese ports, and if there were, it would be an infringement of the exchange of notes that were signed in conjunction with the treaty. That exchange provided that any major change in the equipment (read nuclear weapons) of U.S. forces in Japan would be the subject of prior consultations between the two governments. The government of Japan maintained that, if consulted, it would reject any move to equip U.S. troops with nuclear weapons. Because the United States had not asked for such consultations, Japan trusted the Americans not to bring in nuclear weapons.[108] Reischauer, the historian and the diplomat, was concerned. He could see that this stance was placing at risk the Japanese public's confidence in the U.S. government's integrity and that he personally risked being seen in later years as a liar should the truth leak out.

At first, he asked Washington for permission to air fully the contents of the 1960 negotiations with the Japanese government with a view to reaching an agreed interpretation. He was turned down, so on April 4, 1963, he invited Foreign Minister Ohira to the embassy residence for breakfast (which would attract less press attention) and explained the U.S. discomfort with the Japanese government's posture. As he would later recall, "Ohira immediately understood the problem and asked me to leave matters to him and speak to no one else about it. I do not know what he did, but the undesirable exchanges in the Diet on this matter stopped almost at once; they never were repeated during my stay in Tokyo."[109]

He wrote his family two days later: "It was a red-letter day in Japanese–US relations though it will never be noted in even the most detailed history book."[110] In this assumption, he was quite wrong. The matter would arouse controversy that continues to this day. It arose again in 1981, as we shall see in chapter 10, and it continues to be the subject of intense press interest and speculation.

Reischauer became involved in one other highly sensitive matter involving nuclear weapons in the 1960s. In 2005, the newspaper *Asahi Shimbun*, using newly declassified State Department documents, reported that Prime Minister Ikeda had told Rusk in November 1961 that there were advocates of nuclear armament by Japan in his cabinet. According to these documents, Ikeda's successor, Sato Eisaku, told Reischauer in December 1964 that "it is common sense that we should possess nuclear arms if everyone else does."[111] This statement, of course, followed the surprising announcement by Communist China of its first testing of nuclear weapons two months earlier. Reischauer was convinced that Japan's development of nuclear weapons would be a terrible mistake, not because he feared the return of Japanese militarism, but rather because such a move could set off a nuclear arms race in Asia and because possessing nuclear weapons would not lead to greater security for Japan. If anything, given Japan's narrow island base, it would add to Japan's insecurity: a single nuclear weapon dropped on Japan between Tokyo and Osaka could wipe out nearly half of its industrial capacity. It was a no-win situation for Japan. Reischauer cabled the State Department: "As reported, Sato is more indiscreet than Ikeda. His frankness and enthusiasm are new to me, but I see a serious risk there as well. We need to educate him more than we did Ikeda so that he will not go down a dangerous path."[112]

Rusk agreed with Reischauer on this point, and the result was that President Johnson, in his summit meeting with Prime Minister Sato in January 1965, offered to provide Japan with a U.S. "nuclear umbrella," meaning that any external threat to Japan's security would be met with the full power of U.S. military force, up to and including the use of nuclear weapons, obviating the need for Japan to have its own nuclear capacity. This arrangement continues in force to this day.[113]

Reischauer felt strongly that Japan and the Republic of Korea (South Korea) should normalize their diplomatic relations, but he had no clear mandate to become involved. The matter was exquisitely delicate. Most Koreans hated the nation that had occupied and dominated them from 1910 to 1945 and felt they deserved significant reparations and apologies from Japan. They insisted that all treaties and agreements entered into from 1910 to 1945 be considered null and void and that the South Korean government be recognized as the only lawful government in Korea. The government of Japan was prepared to restore diplomatic relations, but could not, for domestic political reasons, appear to be caving in to excessive Korean demands. The whole issue was complicated by the existence of the Democratic People's Republic of Korea (North Korea), which would surely demand comparable reparations someday. The existence of some six hundred thousand Koreans in Japan, most of them brought in as slave laborers during the occupation and war and still treated as second-class citizens, and most of them sympathetic to North Korea, was a further complication. There were other thorny issues: fishery rights and the ownership of Takeshima (Dokdo) Island that lay between them. Both nations claimed the island; South Korea occupied it.

Reischauer, without explicit instructions from Washington, decided to serve quietly as honest broker or mediator between the two nations. He believed deeply that both nations would benefit from restored diplomatic relations in terms of trade, investment, and cultural exchange. He also thought that it was in the U.S. national interest to see that these two allies patched up their differences. U.S. troops and bases were in Japan in large measure to defend South Korea against further attacks from North Korea.

Reischauer began to meet regularly with Samuel Berger, U.S. ambassador to Seoul, with the Japanese Foreign Ministry negotiators on this issue, and secretly with the Korean negotiators. Both sides apparently saw him as a friend. He listened to Korean demands and tried them out on the Japanese Foreign Ministry. Berger pushed for concessions by Japan, but Reischauer felt that Japan would never meet all of their demands and looked for compromise, believing that normalization would stimulate trade and thus help South Korea more than a higher indemnity would. Reischauer considered going to South Korea, but rejected the idea; he was somewhat well known there, and if his involvement became public, it could have backfired, with both sides resenting pressure from the United States.

There will probably never be a complete record of Reischauer's involvement in what turned out to be a four-year tug of war, but we can get glimpses of the long and difficult negotiations from his confidential letters to his family. In May 1961, just a month after his arrival, he met secretly with a Foreign Ministry official over the Korea problem and told his family it was "a real headache." In September, the special envoy from South Korea called on Reischauer one morning with Berger present. He then gave a special lunch for Japanese officials dealing with the Korean issue. That afternoon "Berger and I had a long talk with the Vice

Foreign Minister about Korea. There is probably no more important problem in [the] whole Far East right now than normalization of Japanese–Korea relations, but the Js and Ks seem to have great trouble getting together, and Berger and I are doing our best from both ends to push it along. This was one reason why I had a long conference with the Foreign Minister the next day, and at his suggestion, another conference with the Prime Minister [Ikeda]." The next month, October 1961, Reischauer confided to his family that the talks seemed to be off. "Koreans were unhappy about choice of Japanese negotiator, but on Tuesday I had long talk with Korean representative and I believe convinced him of suitability of choice and 'sincerity' of Japanese—possibly contributing to the decision yesterday to start the talks at last next Friday [October 20]."[114]

The talks dragged on sporadically for four more years, with Reischauer leaning in whenever he thought he could make a difference. "I talked often, however, with both sides, though I was careful to do so in secret and to say the same thing to both. . . . Berger felt we should apply strong pressure on Japan to get Tokyo to give in to Korean demands, but I knew that the Japanese would never do this. I suggested that in the long run a small American contribution to sweeten the pot for both sides and thus hasten a solution would be a worthwhile investment, but this met with flat rejection in Washington."[115] In April 1962, he confided to his family, "I am afraid the normalization of relations with Korea is entirely off for the foreseeable future (confidential). At Xmas I suddenly realized that we might be missing the bus and urged strenuous action but was slapped down (confidential). Now I am afraid the bus has pulled out completely, leaving us with our would-be Korean bride standing forlornly in the road. This has been a major disappointment."[116]

After many stops and starts, the talks finally came to a successful conclusion in 1965, with Japan agreeing to provide eight hundred million dollars in grants and government and commercial credits, and to leave several issues (fishery rights, commercial relations, and Takeshima Island [Dokdo]) for later settlement. The full extent of Reischauer's involvement in this final settlement may never be known, but in his final press conference in Washington in 1966, as he was stepping down as ambassador, when asked what he considered his greatest achievement on the job, he without hesitation pointed to the restoration of relations between Japan and South Korea. This was a surprising revelation from the man in charge of U.S.–Japan relations.

For the rest of his life, Reischauer remained loyal to the Korean people, who in his view had been dealt a harsh hand by history and geography, caught between two great powers. He had deep sympathy for Kim Dae Jung, who was kidnapped in Japan by South Korean intelligence thugs. Invited by Korea University around that time to be keynote speaker at a conference in Seoul in November 1973, Reischauer sent an angry reply: "I trust that the deplorable Kim Dae Jung kidnapping will have been set straight soon by his unconditional release and return to Japan. Until that has been cleared up, my conscience would not permit me to go to Korea."[117]

Reischauer's new and strong relations with the Kennedys promised even greater rewards and possibly greater influence over U.S. policy within the administration regarding Japan. In December 1962, the second cabinet-level conference on economics and trade took place in Williamsburg, Virginia, further advancing the "growing sense of partnership between our two countries."[118]

After the conference, he and Haru were guests of honor at a dinner hosted at Hickory Hill, home of Bobby and Ethel Kennedy. Other guests included Secretary of Defense Robert McNamara, National Security Advisor McGeorge Bundy, Supreme Court Justice Potter Stewart, and other top figures in the Kennedy crowd. Edwin Reischauer was on a path toward becoming an "insider." That week, President Kennedy, along with Rusk, Harriman, and Bundy, asked him to stay on in Tokyo, so he gave up his tenured position at Harvard and made plans to sell his home in Belmont. In the fall of 1963, he could look forward to an historic visit to Tokyo by the president of the United States in February 1964—the first ever by an incumbent U.S. president– and could take credit for making it happen. Ed and Haru Reischauer were at that moment arguably the most successful diplomatic team the United States had ever sent to any major nation.

Then, on the morning of Saturday, November 23, 1963 (Tokyo time), all their plans came crashing down. Kennedy was dead, the war in Vietnam was heating up, and a deranged youth was preparing to attack the American Embassy compound with a rusty kitchen knife.

9

A Darkening Sky

The call came at 4:30 A.M., Saturday, November 23, 1963, Tokyo time. President Kennedy was dead. Reischauer was at his desk before 6:00. Foreign Minister Ohira called on him before 8:00, expressing his condolences. The plane carrying Rusk and five other cabinet members heading for Tokyo was an hour west of Hawaii when the news came; it turned around and headed back to Washington. They were headed for the third of the cabinet-level economic conferences that Reischauer had launched in 1961. Ironically, Rusk's secret mission was also to plan for President Kennedy's visit to Japan the following February.

What happened next was truly extraordinary: instantly, as if planned, an orderly line of Japanese citizens started to form outside the embassy, growing to as long as four hundred yards. The embassy, normally closed on Saturdays, was in a state of chaos. There were no protocol guidelines for an event of this sort. We hastily placed a photo of the president, draped in a black cloth, on a table at the front door of the Chancery and residence, along with a book to sign. Japanese-speaking officers stood by the table to accept murmured expressions of sympathy and to return bows.

The line outside continued to grow, and deeply grieving Japanese of every age and description filed past our small shrine for the next thirty-six hours, until late on Sunday night. The last visitor was Yoshida Shigeru, eighty-five, who had driven up from his home in Oiso. Meanwhile, thousands of telegrams, letters, and flowers poured in. Kennedy had truly touched a chord among the Japanese people. Prime Minister Ikeda and Foreign Minister Ohira flew off to attend the funeral in Washington. A memorial mass was held in Tokyo on Tuesday, November 26; the crown prince and princess and every other cabinet minister attended.

Reischauer went on national television the next day to thank the public for its outpouring of sympathy. On December 12, in the same Okuma Hall at Waseda University where Bobby Kennedy had spoken, Reischauer expressed his appreciation to a large gathering of respectful students and faculty who gave him an eight-minute ovation.

Television and radio reporters clamored for a statement, and Reischauer obliged, speaking in English and then Japanese, emphasizing that despite this tragedy, U.S. policy would not change. The truth was, however—and he knew it—that everything had changed. The generation of leaders that came to power with Kennedy would never again feel the youthful idealism and optimism of the Kennedy years. President Johnson, unprepared for the foreign-policy decisions that would face him, would lead the nation into the disastrous war in Vietnam. Bobby Kennedy would leave Washington to run for the Senate from New York and eventually to form a "government in exile." Reischauer would thus lose his main link to power in Washington. Rusk would gain influence in the State Department and advise against any change in U.S.–China policy. And Reischauer would be surrounded by such tight security that never again could he stroll around the Imperial Palace on Sunday mornings or sneak out with Haru for a bowl of soba.

Four months later, a deranged youth would stab Reischauer in the leg at the front door of the embassy, damaging his health and sapping his energy for the rest of his life. All of the gains in U.S.–Japan relations of the past two and a half years were at risk. The remainder of Reischauer's term as ambassador, until August 1966, was a time of darkening shadows.

Reischauer considered resigning. Haru wanted to leave right away. Neither of them knew Lyndon Johnson personally, nor did they feel any particular loyalty to him. In fact, Ed thought Johnson might be prejudiced against him because he was a Harvard professor from New England—"another one of the damn intellectuals who can't come down to earth."[1] Cambridge intellectuals did indeed scorn and ridicule Johnson for his Texas accent and crude manners—a stark contrast to the witty, sophisticated, and Harvard-trained Kennedy. It is normal for a new president to ask for the resignation of all incumbent ambassadors. Instead, President Johnson asked all ambassadors to remain at their posts. Reischauer told himself that he might be needed even more by the Texas politician who was inexperienced in foreign policy. He was by now deeply invested in improving U.S.–Japan relations and felt that all his good work and reputation might go down the drain if he packed up and went home.

Reischauer had met at least four times alone with John F. Kennedy during his visits to Washington. Johnson never called him until July 1966, by which time he had decided to retire. Neither Rusk nor Reischauer's former Harvard colleague McGeorge Bundy, who agreed to remain on as national-security advisor, asked for his advice on Japan or Vietnam or China. Unlike Kenneth Galbraith, who freely volunteered advice from his embassy in India and vigorously opposed the war in Vietnam, Reischauer took the position that U.S. policy toward Japan was paramount, and he would weaken his position there if he stepped forward on other issues. He had opposed President Truman's policy of helping the French keep control of Indochina, as Vietnam was then called, and he was on the record as far back as 1949 in support of recognizing Communist China. In *Wanted: An Asian Policy*, he had warned against support for the French in 1955. And he was firmly opposed to sending U.S. troops into combat in Vietnam. But it would have been out of character for him to volunteer his views, even in classified cables or secret meetings.

Reischauer had three choices as the United States escalated the war in Vietnam:

1. He could follow Galbraith's lead and work vigorously from within the administration to prevent escalation of the war.
2. He could resign on principle with maximum publicity for his antiwar views. (Given his prominence as an Asian expert, there was no way he could have quietly resigned and remained silent on Vietnam.)
3. Or he could stay on and loyally support whatever policies were decided on in Washington.

To his lasting regret, he chose the third course.

Tuesday, March 24, 1964, started out as a routine day. Reischauer was comfortable with his decision to stay on as ambassador for at least another year, even though much of his enthusiasm for the job had been snuffed out with Kennedy's death. On this day, he was scheduled to have lunch at 12:30 with Kim Chong P'il, the ousted South Korean military leader.

As Reischauer approached the front door of the Chancery Building, his aides as always deferred to him, allowing him to go through the door first. When he stepped through the doorway heading for the waiting Cadillac, its engine running, a young man wearing a raincoat and thick glasses darted toward him and, before anyone could react, stabbed him in the right thigh with a six-inch kitchen knife, slicing open his femoral artery and breaking off the tip of the knife against his thigh bone. The wound was four inches deep and twelve inches long.

Reischauer, bleeding profusely, lurched backward into the embassy and was helped to a bench. John Ferchak, an embassy officer who had been trained in hand-to-hand combat in World War Two, wrestled the assailant to the ground with the help of the marine guard, Sergeant Carl Macek, who happened to be talking on the telephone about fifteen feet from the door when the attack occurred. Macek would normally have snapped to attention and given a salute to the exiting ambassador.

The femoral artery, about the width of an index finger, is the main route from the heart to each leg. When punctured, it is possible to lose all the blood in the body in about five minutes. Blood pressure drops drastically, oxygen cannot be delivered to vital organs, and body temperature falls. Understanding this danger, Ferchak ripped off his necktie and fashioned a tourniquet around Reischauer's upper thigh. A secretary who happened to come by at that moment took off her flimsy scarf and added it to the necktie. These measures probably saved his life. Four aides then carried the bleeding Reischauer into the limousine.

As Reischauer reconstructed the event later that night, he thought first of his brother, Robert, who had died in Shanghai from loss of blood in 1937 when a Chinese bomb, intended for Japanese troops, exploded in the lobby of the hotel where he was registering and sheared off his heel. What an irony, Reischauer thought, if he too should bleed to death this day.

The driver of his limousine, Aiko Yoshie, rose to meet the emergency. After several horrified aides helped load Reischauer into the back seat, he gunned the car down the hill and raced two blocks to the emergency entrance of Toranomon Hospital, where a medical team was ready to receive him. After a four-hour operation in which he received massive blood transfusions, he woke up just after 5:00 P.M. with a twenty-inch scar curving from close to his knee up almost to his waist. The surgeon had repaired the nerves and artery, but never found the tip of the knife.

Three U.S. Navy doctors arrived by helicopter a few hours after the attack and praised the quick work of the Japanese surgeons, Dr. Okinaka Shigeo and Dr. Matsushita Ryoji. The Americans discussed whether Reischauer should be transferred immediately to the navy hospital at Yokosuka Naval Base. When Reischauer got wind of the issue, he absolutely refused to go, arguing that it would be insulting to the Japanese doctors and unnecessary. Because of his weakened condition, the navy doctors agreed to leave him at Toranomon.

From his hospital bed that evening, Reischauer dictated the following statement for the press:

I want to express my deep appreciation to the many Japanese who have indicated their friendship at this time. I have been much impressed again by the great efficiency and kindness of the Japanese doctors and nurses.

It is a sad fact that there are unfortunate, unbalanced persons in all the world. We have had a particularly tragic example of this recently in the United States.

My only concern about this small incident is that it might seem to some people to mar the deep friendship and cordial relations that exist between our two countries.

However, I have every confidence that our partnership will continue to grow closer and stronger.[2]

Later that evening Reischauer asked his press attaché to draft another statement reassuring the public that he was alright. Reischauer looked at the draft and tossed it out. He then asked me to try my hand, but he tossed out my draft as well and asked for a pad and pencil. He then scribbled the words that became headlines and legend all over Japan on March 25: "I was born and grew up in Japan, and now that I have received Japanese blood, I finally feel I have become half Japanese."[3] He continued to heap praise on the quality of the care he received and was grateful that the Japanese government paid all his medical expenses over this period.

This statement set the tone for officials in Washington and Tokyo: the incident would be downplayed in order to minimize any hostile reactions in America and any embarrassment in Tokyo. It was, of course, just six months before the Tokyo Olympics, and the Japanese government was only too happy to go along with Reischauer's studiously casual attitude toward the event that nearly cost him his life. In its first story about the incident, the *New York Times* placed the article on page 4. The next day, the embassy released a picture of a smiling ambassador lying in his hospital bed with Haru at his side. The *Times* reported that he was in "good condition."[4]

In truth, the Japanese government was horrified. No foreign dignitary had been attacked in Japan since May 1891, when a policeman had tried to cut down the Russian czarevich with his sword. The Russian survived and became Czar Nicholas II, who would die in 1917 at the hands of a Bolshevik firing squad.[5] Japan took justifiable pride in its reputation for courtesy and hospitality to foreigners. The idea that Japan's best American friend should be wounded in this manner was almost unbearable. Reischauer learned later that if it had not been for his gracious and forgiving statement that evening, the whole Ikeda cabinet would have been compelled to resign in disgrace. As it was, Chairman

Hayakawa Takashi of the National Public Safety Commission took responsibility for the incident and resigned.

Foreign Minister Ohira arrived at the hospital within an hour of the stabbing to express his deepest apologies. Prime Minister Ikeda visited the embassy that day and then, on the day after the incident, in the first ever trans-Pacific live telecast by satellite from Japan to America, told the American people, "Yesterday Ambassador Reischauer was wounded by a misguided ruffian [*bokan*]. It was a very regretful and unfortunate incident." Before the telecast, he sent a cable to President Johnson that said:

> It is an unfortunate coincidence that on this occasion I have to express my heartfelt regrets on behalf of the people and government of Japan for the incident in which Ambassador Reischauer was assaulted and injured by a mentally deranged young man. On behalf of the people of Japan, I express my deepest regrets for the stabbing.
>
> The entire nation is indignant over the dastardly act of violence committed against the representative of a nation with which we have especially close and friendly relations. We all pray for the Ambassador's earliest recovery.

President Johnson responded:

> On behalf of the people, and government of the United States let me thank you most warmly for your message of sympathy and regret for the act of one individual against Ambassador Reischauer.
>
> We have been happy here to learn that he is expected to make a full recovery and you can be assured that all Americans will understand that such an act has nothing to do with the deep friendship and understanding which exists between our two countries, and to which Ambassador Reischauer himself has made so important a contribution.[6]

The emperor and empress sent a box of fruit. Strings of a thousand folded paper cranes (*senba-zuru*) arrived from school children all over Japan. Thousands of messages, flowers, and gifts arrived from ordinary citizens from all parts of the nation.

The Japanese press was quick to report that the assailant was not a member of a right-wing organization, as was first suspected. There had been several politically motivated stabbing incidents by right-wing fanatics in 1960. Chairman Asanuma Inejiro of the Social Party had been run through and killed by a seventeen-year-old youth wielding a samurai sword as he sat on the stage in Tokyo's Hibiya Hall in October 1960. Prime Minister Kishi had been stabbed in the leg at a garden party in July of the same year, again by a prewar right-wing zealot. The first reaction to the assault on Reischauer was that it might be another attack by an ultranationalist.

The police soon learned that the assailant was Shiotani Norikazu, a nineteen-year-old high school dropout with a history of mental illness. His parents ran a shoe (*geta*) shop in Numazu, Shizuoka Prefecture, about seventy-five miles southwest of Tokyo. Diagnosed with Meniere's disease, a disorder of the inner ear, Shiotani dropped out of high school in his second year, shut himself in his room all day, and became eccentric and violent at home. Later diagnosed as schizophrenic, he was committed to a mental hospital for three months, but left after ten days. He began to think of himself as the reincarnation of General Tojo Hideki and became interested in militarism. He took up the cause of near-sighted people, blamed Western-style education for their problems, and blamed the U.S. occupation for promoting coeducation. He was angry that boys and girls were made to sit at the same desk in schools. Before his attack on Reischauer, he had made an abortive attempt to kill Miki Takeo, a rising political figure, as a way to publicize his views.

In January 1964, he turned his attention to the American Embassy, pouring gasoline in the lobby of a nearby apartment and setting it on fire. Arrested and later released by the police for lack of evidence, he began loitering around the Chancery Building where Reischauer worked. On February 24, 1964, he approached the gate and asked for a meeting with Ambassador Reischauer. After presenting a petition to improve the condition of near-sighted people and education policy, he was sent away.

Returning to the embassy in the late morning of March 24, he was able to climb over the east side of the six-foot wall that surrounded the compound. Taking advantage of an appalling lack of security, he lurked unnoticed near the entrance of the Chancery Building until eight minutes past noon, when he saw a group of men coming out the front door. The odds that the first man out the door that day would be Reischauer, his intended victim, were astronomically against him, but it happened, and he moved quickly.

Diagnosed as insane by the Public Prosecutors office, he was never indicted, but was placed in an isolation cell in Matsuzawa City Hospital in August 1964. Several times in the next few years he left the hospital without permission and was returned to an isolation cell. His mental condition deteriorated, and on January 8, 1971, he committed suicide by hanging himself in the men's bathroom of the hospital.[7]

In the aftermath of the stabbing incident, the Japanese government and press engaged in much soul searching about the lack of adequate care for the mentally ill in Japan. The Health and Welfare Ministry reported that about two-thirds of an estimated 1,240,000 mentally ill persons in Japan were free to roam the streets and called measures to guard against crimes by these persons insufficient.[8] Most of the mentally ill persons who did get help entered private mental hospitals set up with government subsidies, where their care was uneven and often inadequate. Many families tried to take care of their own mentally ill children, keeping them hidden away at home. In part as a result of this event, and at the urging of the National Police Agency, the government amended the Mental Health Law to establish mental health centers in every prefecture, provide subsidies for half of the cost of outpatient care, and strengthen the emergency compulsory hospitalization system.[9]

Another result was a sharp tightening of security around the embassy grounds and around Reischauer himself. The six-foot wall that Shiotani had scaled so easily was built up to a height of twelve feet. The police assigned at least two plainclothes bodyguards to Reischauer every time he stepped out of the compound. His last shred of anonymity was gone. Embarrassed by this incident, the police were determined that nothing like it should ever happen again.

The assailant's parents and eldest brother delivered an apology to John Emmerson, the deputy chief of mission, on March 27, three days after the stabbing. Prostrating themselves on the floor of his office, they begged forgiveness. In a written message, they said, "We have no way to convey our deepest sympathy to Ambassador Reischauer and the United States for this grave offense our third son committed and for our own failure to provide him with adequate supervision. We pray from the bottom of our hearts for the speedy recovery of Ambassador Reischauer."[10]

Meanwhile, Japan's press, radio, and television reported for several days that Reischauer was steadily recovering and even showed pictures of him propped up in bed and smiling. Every major newspaper ran editorials of apology and sympathy. A mountain of flowers, gifts, and strings of folded paper cranes continued to pour into the hospital and the embassy. The nation seemed to breathe a collective sigh of relief. The American press, for its part, found a silver lining. The *New York Times* editorialized on March 26, two days after the event, that "[Ambassador Reischauer] has worked hard and successfully to build a good relationship and to help ease the tensions inevitable when two nations are so closely linked in so many ways as are Japan and the United States. The attack on him was a tragic and mad deed; but its aftermath provides eloquent evidence of how effective his efforts have been."[11]

Haru in this period was again the subject of adulation and sympathy in the press. The media used the words *devoted* (*kenshinteki ni*) as well as *hard-working*, *capable*, *strong*, and *confident* to describe her daily routine of cooking and caring for her husband. She was described as calm, confident, and composed in the crisis.

But things were not so simple. The hallways around Reischauer's hospital room were chaotic. It seemed that Shiotani's behavior had aroused other mentally ill persons; they flocked to the hospital and scuffled with police, who were hard put to keep them away from his room. One unemployed twenty-eight-year-old man was dragged from the building shouting that he wanted to see Dr. Reischauer because he wanted to go to the United States.

Despite his cheerful countenance in photographs, Reischauer was in agony for the first several nights. I sat next to his bed all of both nights, and he talked almost the whole time, sometimes rationally and sometimes almost deliriously due to his high fever and the antibiotics and painkillers he was receiving. It was an extraordinary experience to hear his views on life and death. Of course, I did not take notes, nor will I cite from memory anything he said, except to make this observation: every word he spoke in this feverish state was consistent with what he said within the embassy and in public: improving the U.S.–Japan relationship meant more to him than life itself. Never once did he show any sign of anger or reproach toward his assailant or his fate or the irony of being attacked by a citizen of the country he loved and often defended. Every effort, he felt, had to be made to minimize the importance of this incident. He talked repeatedly about his family, his love and concern for them. He regretted the various tensions that had arisen since Adrienne's death and his absence from their lives once he became ambassador. He knew how close he had come to dying, and he resolved that if he survived, he would work even harder at his job. The relationship required constant attention. To quit now would be to surrender to the forces of irrationalism.

In a letter dictated to his family three days after the incident, he praised the doctors and nurses: "Since the self-esteem of the whole Japanese nation is at stake, I am getting incredibly careful attention," he wrote. Seven doctors appeared each day to examine his wound, led by the chief surgeon and including the head of the hospital, the retired head of the hospital, and four nurses. Also the top doctor from Yokosuka Naval Hospital or a colleague flew in each day by helicopter to check on his condition. "The doctors from Yokosuka also turned up with a nerve pain-killer, which I am sure is opium. For 4 hours I feel no pain, but I have a great sense of euphoria, feeling like the luckiest guy in the world from every point of view, and then it begins to wear off. . . . The nurses, or course, are simply wonderful. I can see why rich old men always marry their nurses. People are around to minister to my every want all the time, so I am really having a grand time."[12]

On Saturday, March 28, the embassy released a report that his fever was down, he had eaten a large breakfast, and the wound appeared to be healing well. But the typical bravado and ironic humor expressed in his letter to his family did not last long. Just four days after the stabbing, his temperature shot up, and it was discovered that he was bleeding profusely from an ulcer caused by stress to his gastrointestinal tract. Surgeons considered another operation but worried that he would not survive because of his weakened condition. Instead, they gave him new blood transfusions. The ulcer was fortunately self-healing. By Sunday afternoon, the hemorrhaging had stopped.

The ironies continued to pile up, though. The blood he so gratefully received contained the hepatitis C virus, for which there is no cure. It would lead to a gradual deterioration of his liver, bouts of internal bleeding, several strokes, and a painful death in 1990 at the age of seventy-nine, far younger than his father was when he died at age ninety-one. Blood for Japanese hospitals was at that time routinely purchased from poor day laborers, unemployed people, or hungry students, many of them anemic, and was not properly tested. This incident led to an end of blood purchasing and a law that all future blood had to be donated.

His doctors ordered him to keep work and visitors to a minimum, but he did agree to see one unusual visitor, former vice president Richard M. Nixon, who appeared in Tokyo ostensibly as a lawyer for Pepsi Cola, but mainly to keep up his foreign-policy credentials. Reischauer, the lifelong liberal Democrat, wrote, "I had always looked on Nixon with abhorrence, but in the flesh he was much larger, better looking and more pleasantly spoken than one would gather from television. In calls he later made on me at my office, he would speak forcefully of the desirability of recognizing Peking [*sic*] sounding for all the world like John Fairbank. I felt that the American public had been ready for this for some years, and, when as President he finally did this, I was in no way surprised."[13]

In still another irony, among the thousands of personal notes Reischauer received at this time, one was missing: he received no personal communication of any kind from Secretary of State Dean Rusk. In his later years, when the hepatitis C disease caused constant pain and then numbness in his leg, a permanently damaged digestive system, bouts of internal bleeding, strokes, and a coma, his family approached the State Department to see if he qualified for disability payments. The answer was no: he had not been injured in the line of duty! The family never pressed his case, even though he was severely wounded on embassy property while heading out for lunch on State Department business.

During his recuperation from a stabbing incident, Reischauer worked from a temporary office at the Toranomon Hospital, where doctors saved his life on March 24, 1964. The author is on the right. Photograph by U.S. Embassy photographer, April 1964. Courtesy of the author.

On April 15, after twenty-two days in Toranomon Hospital, Reischauer left the hospital doing his best to appear healthy and cheerful. One hundred policemen, five hundred spectators, and a large contingent of radio, television, and newspaper reporters watched as he rose from his wheelchair to read statements in English and Japanese expressing appreciation for his care at the hospital. He told the waiting press, "My doctors decided it would be best for me to stay far away from my duties for a while and exercise my leg by swimming."[14] Haru, Ed, his doctor, navy captain Ralph E. Faucett, and I flew in General Preston's plane to Hawaii, where Ed and Haru stayed with General Jake Smart at Hickam Field.

As far as the public in Japan knew, this sojourn was the beginning of his smooth recovery. In fact, however, he soon again faced a life-threatening and mysterious illness. On April 21, he started to run a high fever and was moved to Tripler Army Hospital for the next two months. The doctors never did figure out what was wrong. The incubation period for hepatitis was longer than the time that had elapsed since the blood transfusions. There was speculation later that it was mononucleosis. He suffered a serious deterioration of his liver. "I believe I was near death's door a good bit of this time," he remembered later.[15] By the end of May, he seemed to be recovering, but then on June 4 he suffered another serious setback, which turned out to be the feared onset of hepatitis C. It left him weak and depressed, and further damaged his liver. His right leg was partly paralyzed and constantly painful, and he thereafter required a spring in his shoe so that he could walk somewhat normally.

By June 20, nearly three months after he was stabbed, his spirits seemed to lift, his energy was flowing back, and he longed to get back to work. He was allowed to spend four hours each day on Waikiki Beach. He told his family, "I could give you a report on Bikinis on Waikiki, which have to be seen (if you can find them) to be believed. Last summer I was startled when we went through here but it seems much more startling this year."[16] As always, even when recuperating, Reischauer had an eye for pretty women.

He typically used his time in the hospital to read deeply in the history of India and to revise his book *The United States and Japan.* He also worked on the last chapter of *East Asia: The Modern Transformation* with John Fairbank, who happened to be passing through Honolulu at that time. From this point on, his lectures and writing took on an even more positive and decisive tone. Intimations of mortality seemed to drive him toward the "last lecture" syndrome: make your points now or never.

By early July, he felt well enough to fly back to Tokyo and resume work on a half-time basis. He walked with a pronounced limp and was twenty-three pounds lighter, but he did his best to appear robust and cheerful. On his first morning back, he held a press conference attended by eighty newsmen and photographers. Sporting a Waikiki tan, he again made headlines: he dismissed the stabbing incident as meaningless—nothing more significant than an auto accident—and assured people that he was healthy and happy. "The Japanese were tremendously impressed at the way that Americans accepted the incident," he declared. "The net result was to strengthen relations."[17]His smiling picture appeared the next day on page one of the major papers. He wrote later that he never considered resigning. "To have done so would have made the Japanese public feel all the more remorseful, so we decided we would have to stay on for at least another year."[18]

He felt that the worst fallout from the whole incident was the tightening of security around him and Haru. Threats from cranks and mentally ill people continued to arrive at the embassy, so marine guards took to walking with him the one hundred yards from the residence to the embassy and back. When the Reischauers escaped to their sanctuary in Misaki, a policeman checked into their home every hour, and at least eight others guarded the property. "I have probably been more secure in the last few days than ever before in my life—but frankly all this attention makes me nervous," he wrote his family.[19]

The Reischauers decided to skip all social events for the next several months, but they did host one buffet supper reception for the thirty-three doctors and nurses who had cared for them at the Toranomon Hospital: "It was a very warm, pleasant occasion," he reported to the family, "and one I had been looking forward to ever since I was in the hospital. The nurses all looked so cute in their pretty dresses."[20] In this gesture, he and Haru clearly showed an understanding of the Japanese system of reciprocal kindness.

From this point onward, Reischauer redoubled his speaking and writing for the Japanese public, driven as if by a new sense of his own mortality. From September 1964 through the following January, he was at the center of a whirlwind of activity, giving lectures, meeting with students and intellectuals, and developing his ideas about Japanese history. In January 1965, two leading monthly magazines, *Bungei Shunju* and *Chuo Koron*, devoted large sections to the Meiji Period. The managing editor of *Bungei Shunju* confided to Reischauer that he could not have dealt with this topic until Reischauer stirred up new interest in the period.

Still another dark cloud loomed on the horizon. When Reischauer first arrived in Japan in 1961, there were only about 700 U.S. military "advisors" in Vietnam. He felt confident that President Kennedy would stay out of what he viewed as a civil war fomented by Vietnamese nationalistic reactions to French colonial rule. But Kennedy gradually increased this number to a total of 16,000 by the time of his death in 1963. President Johnson, along with Kennedy's top advisors, saw the choice as either escalating U.S. involvement in the civil war in Vietnam or withdrawing and allowing the Communist North to take over the South.

America's ignorance about the facts on the ground in Vietnam was appalling. Paul Kattenburg, a young Foreign Service officer who had served in Vietnam, recalled that at a meeting of the National Security Council on August 31, 1963, "there was not a single person there that knew what he was talking about. . . . They didn't know Vietnam. They didn't know the past. They had forgotten the history. They simply didn't understand the identification of nationalism and Communism." Kattenburg was dismissed from the Vietnam Task Force in January 1964, largely at the insistence of Bill Bundy, who charged that his pessimism was a "disservice."[21]

For an insecure president whose strength lay in domestic politics, the moment was agonizing. Johnson's priorities were to pass a strong civil rights bill and a voting rights bill that would assure African Americans of the right to vote and to provide generous aid to secondary education (he had been a high school teacher early in his career). On March 15, 1965, he gave one of the most memorable speeches in U.S. history in support of the Voting Rights Act. He declared, "We shall overcome," the words of Dr. Martin Luther King and his African American supporters. The bill quickly became the law of the land.

But Johnson worried about appearing weak in the face of a foreign enemy. Senator Joseph McCarthy's legacy was that one should never be associated with a loss to the Communists, never appear weak in foreign affairs. Vietnam was a mystery to Johnson, but he knew that he must appear to stand strongly against any new Communist victory in Asia. He had to run for election in November 1964, and the candidacy of the bellicose Barry Goldwater loomed before him. Air Force general Curtis Lemay was growling that America should " bomb North Vietnam back to the Stone Age."

A fateful debate over Vietnam was raging. The anti-Communist South Vietnamese prime minister Ngo Dinh Diem had been assassinated in coup d'état in November 1963 with U.S. complicity, and his successor, General Duong Van Minh, was in turn quickly ousted by General Nguyen Kanh on January 30, 1964. It was clear to most observers that the government of South Vietnam was losing the battle for the people's hearts and minds. Johnson's hawkish advisors, all inherited from the Kennedy regime, began to believe that only massive U.S. intervention could prop up the regime and prevent a takeover by the Communist forces.

Top Pentagon leaders had drawn the wrong lessons from the Cuban missile crisis of 1962. They had come to believe that "controlled escalation" would bring an end to North Vietnam's aggression in the South. They were convinced that U.S. military power could not be successfully challenged anywhere in the world.

Other leaders argued against intervention. Senator Mike Mansfield warned Johnson against becoming involved as early as January 6, 1964, stating that Americans had a tendency to "bite off more than we were prepared in the end to chew." When Johnson replied that he did not want to see another "Who lost China?" debate in Vietnam, Mansfield replied that neither did we want another Korea—a war that ended in stalemate. U.S. interests in Vietnam were not worth the "blood and treasure" that would accompany armed intervention. Mansfield urged that the United States should seek a peaceful solution, perhaps through neutralization.[22]

Other liberals such as Walter Lippmann, the influential columnist, and John Kenneth Galbraith, Kennedy's outspoken ambassador to India, agreed. As early as November 1961, Galbraith cabled Bundy from Saigon, "We must not forever be guided by those who misunderstand the dynamics of revolution and imagine that because the communists do not appeal to us they are abhorrent to everyone." He added, "It is those of us who have worked in the political vineyard and who have committed our hearts most strongly to the political fortunes of the New Frontier who worry most about its bright promise being sunk under the rice fields."[23] Within the government, Undersecretary of State George W. Ball was quietly opposing the idea of escalating U.S. military involvement, as was Michael V. Forrestal, a key aide to Mac Bundy as deputy for intelligence and Far Eastern affairs. [24] Jim Thomson, another member of Bundy's staff and a serious China scholar, made similar arguments.[25]

It was Johnson's misfortune to inherit two of Kennedy's most arrogant advisors, Mac Bundy as national-security advisor, and his brother, Bill Bundy, as assistant secretary of state for the Far East. As noted earlier, neither had any background or training in Asia. Mac had never been to Vietnam. A major review of the Vietnam situation took place in Honolulu on June 2, 1964, while Reischauer was recuperating there. Bill Bundy, who had taken over as assistant secretary of state for the Far East in March, was the prime mover at this meeting, which included Secretary of Defense Robert McNamara, Ambassador to Saigon Henry Cabot Lodge, Chairman of the Joint Chiefs of Staff General William Westmoreland, CIA director John McCone, Assistant Secretary of Defense for National Security Affairs John McNaughton, and veteran diplomat William Sullivan. The group accepted Bill Bundy's "action plan," which called for a congressional resolution authorizing U.S. military action to be followed up with U.S. air attacks on North Vietnam.[26] The congressional resolution was shelved for a time, but preparations for military intervention went forward. In July 1964, Johnson announced that 22,000 noncombat troops would go to Vietnam in a "pacification program." At this time, only 168 Americans had so far lost their lives in combat in Vietnam.

While in Honolulu, Bill Bundy managed to find time to have lunch with Ed and Haru. Reischauer liked him. "I find him virtually as brilliant as Mac [Bundy] and a lot more human—that is, less like a computer."[27] But it was now clear that Reischauer did not know Bill Bundy well and certainly had no influence over either Bill or Mac Bundy. Neither brother ever bothered to ask Reischauer for advice on Vietnam—a subject that Reischauer had thought and written about ever since his book *Wanted: An Asian Policy* appeared in 1955. Had Bundy asked, Reischauer would have told him that the "domino theory" was nonsense, that the civil war in Vietnam was not caused by China; that Vietnam, even if the Communists won, would be a Tito-like obstacle to Chinese expansion into Southeast Asia, and that the Vietnamese would see U.S. troops simply as new colonial oppressors. The United States could not bring about the kind of social revolution that was needed in Vietnam. It would suffer heavy casualties and eventually lose.

It is easy enough to look back and see that Reischauer was right, but the Bundy brothers were not interested in listening to scholars or specialists who understood the situation. They were intent on preserving their power and elite status in Washington, which meant staying in Johnson's good graces and helping to win the election against Barry Goldwater in November. Mac had lunch with President Johnson each Tuesday, along with Rusk and McNamara, and was seen as their equal. Bill was married to the daughter of Dean Acheson, an iconic figure in U.S. foreign-policy circles. Nor was Bill the congenial man Reischauer imagined him to be. In fact, he was a kind of terror in the State Department. Marshall Green, Bill Bundy's Groton and Yale classmate, and now his deputy in the State Department, often heard him screaming at people. "He wasn't an easy person to work with. He was extremely tense. He always took upon himself more than he should have, and this alone set many people against him. People felt uneasy in his presence, precisely because he was so exacting. Bill could do the dirty work. He wouldn't hesitate to knife you in the chest."[28]

Given this background, it is not surprising that neither of the Bundy brothers thought to ask Reischauer, whom they knew well, for his views on Vietnam or its relation to China or how an escalation might affect U.S.-Japan relations—then or ever. Mac Bundy tellingly put himself forward on June 6 as a possible successor to Lodge as ambassador to Saigon, listing among his qualifications the fact that he could speak French! Once again, high Washington officials' hubris and their scorn for specialists who understood Asian nationalism and the region's culture were evident. It should have been clear to Reischauer that his value in

Washington was simply to keep Japan as a safe base for U.S. military operations through the considerable prestige and the good will he had generated since arriving as ambassador in 1961.

In 1969, in an oral history interview of Reischauer concerning the Vietnam War for the Lyndon Baines Johnson Memorial Library, the following interchange took place:

> [QUESTION]: What about you individually as an Asia scholar of note, was there consultation, not with what you thought the Japanese Government would do, but with you on—
>
> REISCHAUER: No, no. And there had not been any under the Kennedy Administration either. . . . They never did come to me and say, do you think in view of your having written about Southeast Asia . . . that we should do this or that? It would have been a difficult thing because I was not following the intelligence reports that closely, nor were they normally coming to me in that kind of detail.
>
> QUESTION: You didn't offer unsolicited advice?
>
> REISCHAUER: No I did not. I didn't because I thought it would weaken my position on Japanese advice.[29]

The U.S. Congress finally did enact Bill Bundy's resolution after the Tonkin Gulf Incident of August 4, 1964. We now know that President Johnson and his top military advisors knowingly gave false information to Congress and the public. No second attack by North Vietnamese ships had taken place. In a deception eerily similar to President George W. Bush's move in 2003 authorizing an invasion of Iraq, Johnson used the false report of an attack by the North Vietnamese to start escalating U.S. combat operations on the ground and bombing of the North.[30] By 1966, there were 240,000 U.S. troops on the ground, and this number would rise to well more than 535,000 in 1968. Incredibly, even at this point it was still true that no one in the decision-making group knew anything about Vietnam.

Reischauer returned to Washington for the first summit meeting between President Johnson and Prime Minister Sato in January 1965.

This visit reinforced his determination to bring Japan's importance and interests to the attention of top policymakers, but he somehow missed the signs that a major war in Southeast Asia was being hatched. The lure and the glamour of being one of America's most admired ambassadors continued to captivate him. Lionized by powerful Washington figures, he received an unusual round of honors: a speech at the National War College; a luncheon in his honor by the American Federation of Labor; a dinner in his honor at the home of Averell Harriman, where he met Alice Roosevelt Longworth, eighty-one, daughter of President Theodore Roosevelt and the grand dame of Washington's social circuit; and a meeting with Vice President Hubert Humphrey. He told his family, "I am lucky that so much of the top attention is concentrated on Vietnam etc.... This together with my distance from Washington leaves me an extraordinarily free hand to try to shape U.S.-Japan relations according to my own ideas. And this seems to me infinitely more important in the long run than things like Vietnam."[31]

But he was either naive or disingenuous in this judgment. He did not get to meet President Johnson, nor did Rusk, Bundy, and McNamara bring him into the intense policy debate then raging over Vietnam policy. Clearly, his role was to keep the Japanese happy and the Security Treaty viable. His views on policy were irrelevant to the decision makers in Washington.

When he was back in Tokyo, the reality began to set in. In his weakened physical condition, routine diplomatic chores were growing ever more burdensome. "The trouble with this sort of diplomatic job," he complained to his family, "is that one never reaches a smooth stretch of water. If one gets through one difficult problem successfully (let's say the Interest Equalization Tax problem of two weeks ago), then one runs smack into fish, and when they calm down, Okinawa, textiles, dumping charges, a military base incident, excitement over nuclear bombs or something is sure to flare up. It's like walking on hot coals. You have to move fast not to burn your feet, but the next place you put your foot down is another hot coal."[32]

It was becoming clearer each day that the escalation of the war in Vietnam would overshadow all other issues and that he could not duck it. In March 1965, a month after the United States started to bomb North Vietnam, he told his family, "Vietnam is giving me lots of worries. The Japanese have been fairly subdued about it—at least as compared to many places in the world, and what it would have been like if it had happened four or more years ago—but emotional reactions are building up.... Unless our policies succeed pretty fast in Vietnam, we are sure to lose a great deal in our relationship with Japan."[33]

In April 1965, President Johnson authorized U.S. troops to engage in ground combat. Reischauer could sense the danger that all his efforts to generate good will were at risk in Japan. He confided to his family, "Vietnam will go on making quite a storm for us and all we can do is ride it out—blunting the violence of the attack where we can but inevitably losing a little ground rather than gaining steadily as we have over the four last years. It is not a desirable situation."[34]

He well understood that photographs of death and destruction from bombs dropped on Vietnamese reminded many Japanese of the destruction caused by B-29 raids in 1945. A Western power was once again killing helpless Asians.

Reischauer chose not to weigh in with his misgivings about the whole misguided effort, nor did he have a feel for the fierce opposition to the war that was building among intellectuals whom he respected at Harvard. At this point, with the benefit of hindsight, he probably should have resigned and publicly denounced the war. Whether such a move could have tipped the balance in Washington seems doubtful, given Johnson and Rusk's hardened positions. But it is clear now that Secretary of Defense Robert McNamara and Undersecretary of State George W. Ball were increasingly opposed to the war. McNamara admitted in his blockbuster book in 1995 that in 1967, while still in office, he concluded that the war could not be won, but nonetheless remained silent, refusing to disclose his doubts.[35] It is conceivable that outspoken opposition by a scholar and public official of Reischauer's reputation might have emboldened others in the government to declare their opposition to the war openly. The media would certainly have loved to broadcast his views, which might have helped fuel the growing protest movement.[36]

It appears that Reischauer had succumbed to what Jim Thomson, in his perceptive analysis of how Vietnam happened, would later label "the *effectiveness trap* that keeps men from speaking out, as clearly or as often as they might, within the government. And it is the trap that keeps men from resigning in protest and airing their dissent outside the government. . . . The inclination to remain silent or acquiesce in the presence of the great men—to live to fight another day, to give on this issue so that you can be 'effective' on later issues—is overwhelming."[37] It is clear that Thomson wanted his mentor either to fight hard within the government or to get out and lead the opposition.

Another, simpler explanation for Reischauer's silence might be that he hated confrontation, did not like to rock the boat, and wanted to "fit in." Like so many in the third generation of immigrant families, he felt insecure and wanted to be fully accepted in the land adopted by his grandfather. He was by no means conservative, but rather believed in the liberal version of the American dream—where truth can be trusted to win out if left free to compete in the marketplace of ideas. The dirty work of political action and persuasion had no charm for him. Having decided to stay on in Japan as ambassador, he felt he had no choice but to defend the war. "I was very different from Ken Galbraith," he later recalled, "who liked to shock the bourgeoisie and to show that he didn't give a damn for the State Department or Foreign Service."[38]

Japan was involved in the war mainly through Kadena Air Force Base on Okinawa, which served as the take-off point for U.S. B-52 bombers to attack North Vietnam, Laos, and Cambodia. At one point in 1965, the U.S. government informed Japan that due to a typhoon, several B-52s would be moved from Guam to an airfield in Kyushu. Soon afterward, it informed Japan that thirty B-52s had taken off from Okinawa to bomb Viet Cong positions outside Saigon. Prior consultation, as stipulated by the Security Treaty, never happened. [39]

At the height of the war in 1969, some 50,000 American troops were posted in the Ryukyus, occupying as much as 10 percent of the total land area of the islands. Because Okinawa was not part of Japanese territory under the terms of the revised 1960 Security Treaty, the United States could use it for any military purpose it wanted, including storage and delivery of nuclear weapons. Okinawa served as a jungle warfare training ground for U.S. Special Forces headed for Vietnam and was a major storage area for poison chemicals, a port for nuclear submarines, and the site of thirty-two nuclear-tipped Mace B missiles in underground launch shelters. The *Pentagon Papers* would later reveal that Japan was not briefed about the first U.S. bombing of North Vietnam on February 7, 1965, although the governments of Australia, New Zealand, Canada, and Britain were.[40] The Japanese Left argued compellingly that Japan faced the danger of being dragged into a wider war with China or even the Soviet Union against its will and better judgment, and these fears led to the creation of a powerful antiwar movement spearheaded by the group Beiheiren, which organized rallies almost every weekend from the spring of 1965 to October 1973 in parks in central Tokyo.

Like it or not, Japan was deeply involved in the war. The secret and top-secret cables that came across Reischauer's desk gave no real sense of how badly the war was going. Lyndon Johnson and his top advisors, with cooperation of the Joint Chiefs of Staff, were engaged in a massive deception to fool Congress, the public, his allies, and his own envoys, including Reischauer. The war escalated by stealth. As H. R. McMaster sees the disaster in Vietnam, it came as a result of "arrogance, weakness, lying in the pursuit of self-interest, and, above all, the abdication of responsibility to the American people."[41] Ignorant of the facts on the ground in Vietnam, unable to influence Washington policymakers, out of touch with younger Americans' views, and serving as a heat shield in Tokyo against a rising storm of protests, Reischauer now found himself isolated on the issues within his own family. He made the worst decision of his life: to defend the U.S. war effort in Vietnam. His last two years as ambassador were as painful as the earlier years had been triumphal.

Adding to his discomfort was the fact that a former Harvard student, novelist Oda Makoto, and Nobel Prize–winning writer Oe Kenzaburo were among the leaders of Beiheiren. They were precisely that kind of intellectuals whom Reischauer had hoped to engage in a new and useful dialogue.

In 1966, Reischauer told his family that he wished he had resigned in 1965, "but this was impossible. My stabbing . . . made it necessary for us to stay on for a while to show that it had not driven us out; meanwhile the Vietnam situation had gone sour and we had to stay on to show we were not running out on that or expressing disapproval of policies by resigning; and so it went on until now."[42] He had come to see his personal popularity in Japan as a kind of immunity from attacks against U.S. policy in Southeast Asia, and he enjoyed the power and importance of his position too much at this point to walk away. He would regret this decision.

For Haru, Kennedy's death and her husband's stabbing were especially painful, sending her "on a downward spiral of depression."[43] Seeing, perhaps even more clearly than Ed, how unpopular the war in Vietnam was becoming to ordinary Japanese, she pleaded with him in the summer of 1964 to resign and go back to Harvard. "The constant pressure of people to see us because of our position, not ourselves," Reischauer wrote in a letter, "the constant flattery of the insincere, the apple-polishing of our subordinates (it is part of their jobs)—all these are very wearing, but harder on her than on me."[44]

There followed a series of highly personal attacks from his own children. All three were unsparingly critical of their father. Joan criticized his stance on Vietnam and urged him to resign. In response, he referred to his 1955 position of opposing U.S. involvement in Vietnam, as outlined in *Wanted: An Asian Policy*; admitted he had questions about Johnson's sending of troops into the Dominican Republic and about Kennedy's support for the Bay of Pigs attempt to overthrow Castro in Cuba, and then fell back on a rather weak defense: "If every government official resigned whenever there was a policy he did not approve of somewhere in the government, there would never be any officials." He then added, "I do approve basically of our Vietnam policy—at least I see no other really feasible that would obviously be better. As for resigning," he added, "to resign just now would be a particularly unfortunate time for me to do so because it would be interpreted here as a sign that I disapproved of our Vietnam policies." When Joan warned that he was ruining his image in Japan, he admitted that his effectiveness had been reduced. "This all is reason for us to think about closing up shop here, but this does not seem to be the time. We are too much under fire right now for the field commander to quit. A good time to think of might be a year from now—if we can stick it out that long."[45] That he saw himself as a "field commander" suggests that the taste of power had gone to the head of this formerly modest professor.

Ann, the older daughter, always a free spirit and his bluntest critic, accused him of "slinging bull [about Vietnam,] trying to fool your Japanese friends." In his angry and defensive handwritten response, he remonstrated, "Now it is permissible to say to another person that he is all wrong, or even that he is stupid, but it is not permissible to say that he is dishonest, which is what your statement adds up to. Even a father has a right to be irritated at that sort of thing."

Ann persisted in sending him articles about the protest movement among students and intellectuals that was gathering steam in America, but Reischauer fought back: "Anti-establishment criticisms of intellectuals do more harm than good when based on ignorance. That's what worries me about so much of the recent anti-Vietnam agitation in university groups. While some of it is informed, so much of it seems to be purely emotional (sometimes psychiatric) in origin, rather than intellectual. That's been the bane of Japanese so-called intellectual life in recent years, and I hate to see it growing in the U.S. We get enough stupid emotionalism of all sorts from the non-intellectual classes or at least elements in them that I hate to see this spread to the supposedly intellectual classes."

When Ann sent him an antiwar piece by Walter Lippmann, he reacted with cold fury: "Lippmann is just an old fool—impossibly ignorant and unconcerned about Asia and distressingly sentimental about the French and many other European matters. He has been terribly wrong in the past on major matters—and he is again on this. My once considerable admiration for him has drained away completely—because I believe he is too fundamentally a man of an earlier age in his thinking to be of much help today. A pundit who has never seen Asia and doesn't really give a damn about Asia one way or the other is no pundit for the 1960's."[46]

This posture was surprising because Reischauer had been picking up hints that the war was going badly. On November 4, 1965, Henry Kissinger spent a day in Tokyo and gave him "a rather gloomy report on Vietnam, where he had been for three weeks and where he found many things not nearly as optimistic as they are being reported."[47] Nevertheless, when Ann sent him news reports of violent protests in America, Reischauer expressed a warning about

> extremists of the left and their anti-democratic tactics (because flouting "authority" of duly elected government is highly anti-democratic—and by flouting authority I don't mean protesting or demonstrating opinions, but clearly illegal actions such as draft card burning, trying to stop troop trains, sit downs that obstruct people doing their normal work or performing duties). Such things naturally stir up equally anti-democratic

> responses from the corresponding lunatic fringe of the right, which happens to be bigger than the lunatic fringe of the left. Unless the really democratic center is overwhelmingly big, it can be ground to pieces between these actions of anti-democratic extremes. This we see in Japan and have learned time after time from history—but self-righteous, elitist young intellectual prigs are so ignorant and inexperienced that they don't see this. They talk about defending democracy when doing things most likely to endanger democracy.[48]

There was more than a grain of truth in this argument: when the anti–Vietnam War protests reached a climax at the Democratic National Convention in Chicago in the summer of 1968, Mayor Richard Daley's policy unleashed a violent counterattack, causing many injuries. Richard Nixon, in a speech on November 3, 1969, made popular the term *silent majority* for citizens who were opposed to the protesters and the burgeoning counterculture. At Kent State University on May 4, 1970, Ohio National Guardsmen fired on student protesters, killing four and wounding nine. Nixon was elected president in 1968 at least in part because he represented a right-wing reaction to the excesses of the Left. But all this was in the future. The Reischauer children were unimpressed in 1965.

When Ann pointed out that "we should never have been in Vietnam in the first place" (ironically just as her father had argued in 1955 in *Wanted: An Asian Policy*), he replied that this attitude was "just the new isolationism. . . . If I were a Japanese, I'd be terrified if [isolationism] would win out in the U.S., because the Japanese have most to lose if South Asia disintegrates into chaos, as I believe it would if we decided to avoid any commitments in difficult areas."[49]

In June, Professor Howard Zinn, who had known Reischauer at Harvard, visited him and argued passionately against the Vietnam War. Reischauer reported to his family, "He is badly misinformed on the situation there, as are most activists of this sort, and has the typical arrogance of self-righteous, pacifistic types of person who usually seem to assume that the only reason other people do not agree with them is because others are somehow dishonest or have sold out to something or other."[50]

Torn between his conviction that the United States should never have intervened in Vietnam and his sense of duty as an ambassador, Reischauer did his best behind the scenes to get the Japanese government to launch peace feelers with the Soviet Union, and in February 1966 persuaded Foreign Minister Etsusaburo Shiina to initiate peace talks, but this effort produced no results. It was clear, however, that he had lost his perspective on the war. Realizing that he was wrong, he came to lash out even more strongly against its critics.

In publicly defending the war, Reischauer made what he later called the "worst blunder" of his diplomatic career. After U.S. air attacks against Hanoi in the fall of 1965, Omori Minoru, foreign editor of the *Mainichi Shimbun*, reported from Hanoi that the bombs had landed on a hospital for lepers and had killed a number of innocent civilians, including children. Reischauer went out of his way to criticize Omori by name, charging that his reports were unbalanced and reflective of Communist propaganda. He charged that Japanese reporters in Hanoi were swallowing whole the "propaganda handouts of a police state." He later wrote in his memoirs, "For an Ambassador to criticize by name a newspaper and reporter is inexcusable, and the moment I made the remark I realized what a gaffe I had committed. In retrospect I can see that I had become too relaxed and self-confident in my ambassadorial role."[51]

This unprecedented criticism caused a brief uproar in Japanese media circles. Omori subsequently resigned, probably as a result of pressure from his superiors. There followed a few weeks of "self-reflection" in media circles, and then the incident faded away. *Asahi Shimbun* decided to treat the whole affair as a "warning from a close friend."[52] Reischauer wrote: "On the whole, I've been much satisfied with the reaction to my Osaka blast. The shock waves naturally blew back on me personally to some extent, as I had assumed they would, but we really seemed to have started a lot of very healthy 'self-reflection.' Of course the Osaka statements were only the more visible part of a fairly extensive campaign I have been conducting to get Japanese to start looking a little more rationally at some problems they face."[53]

But he was placing his own credibility on the line to defend a war he did not believe in and was drawing down heavily on the fund of good will he had built up.

Omori got the last word. Writing in the monthly *Bungei Shunju*, he argued that Reischauer was better than Douglas MacArthur II, but that he didn't really understand Asians and the complicated Vietnam problem. Originally a modest scholar, he had been spoiled by servile Japanese during the past five years, making him the Lord (Tonosama) of Akasaka (the part of Tokyo in which the American Embassy was located).[54]

In his weak defense of U.S. policy in Vietnam, Reischauer tried to argue that the Japanese needed to understand how much their national interest depended on a non-Communist Southeast Asia for trade and investment. He urged Japanese critics to think about how Japan could provide aid to the less-developed countries as a means of securing peace and stability. But his argument was not convincing. Japan could perfectly well have traded with a Communist Vietnam. Defending the war clearly bothered his conscience. In May 1965, Reischauer told his family, "I eased my conscience by writing a long and hard-hitting telegram about what adverse results the North Vietnam bombing has had in Japan to be sure that Washington really understands this and how it affects all our other relations with Japan."[55]

In his last year on the job, he continued to make speeches on intellectual and historical topics, made triumphal tours through a number of outlying prefectures, and negotiated disputes over fisheries in the North Pacific, air routes for Japan to New York and beyond, and the proposed interest equalization tax. The celebrity couple continued to receive an outpouring of affection from the Japanese people. The Japanese media generally tended to separate Reischauer the scholar-ambassador from America's Vietnam policy, but this period was still a painful time of anguish for the Reischauers. Many of their old friends came by to talk of their sorrow over the U.S. bombing of Asians and urged him to do what he could to end the war. These people were not wild-eyed student radicals, but rather thoughtful liberals for whom the Reischauers had great respect with whom they shared many concerns, but could not say so publicly.

Reischauer nonetheless could not bring himself to denounce the president and the war. I recall a revealing conversation with him on the subject. I had told him in January 1965 that I planned to resign from the Foreign Service the following summer because I could no longer defend the U.S. war effort in Vietnam. I wanted to give him ample time to find my replacement. In June 1965, he called me in and asked me to reconsider and to stay for one more year. I told him that although I respected his achievements as ambassador, I could not continue to try to persuade Japanese students, intellectuals, and journalists that Japan should support the U.S. government in this war. He was silent for a moment and then said, "I envy you." He clearly wanted to resign, but out of a sense of duty and a desire to preserve and solidify the gains he had made in U.S.–Japan relations, he could not do it.

The U.S. military decided that Reischauer should have a VIP tour of Vietnam, and he agreed to fly there in December 1965. He dined with General William C. Westmoreland, commander of U.S. forces there, and Ambassador Lodge. He was flown to Cam Ranh Bay, Da Nang, and Vung Tao, where he was briefed on "pacification" efforts. His account of the trip mentions how precarious was the American position there—when landing, his aircraft spiraled down in tight circles to avoid enemy gunfire—but he didn't seem to grasp at this point that the Communists were winning. He told his family only that "progress in any direction is at a snail's pace and the dangers of some sort of collapse are not inconsiderable. . . . I'm basically confirmed in my very pessimistic view of the future of the less developed half of the world."[56]

One of his main tasks from 1964 to 1966 was to ease the way for the U.S. Navy to bring nuclear-powered submarines into Yokosuka and Sasebo naval bases. He understood and was sympathetic to Japan's aversion to any nuclear devices, but also knew that the U.S. Navy was coming to rely more and more on nuclear-powered subs that could remain under water for long periods of time, hidden from Soviet radar, and that the U.S.–Japan Security Treaty would come under real strain if the navy were prevented from using the two ports. He therefore worked closely with the Foreign Ministry and the U.S. Navy to make clear to the media and the public the difference between nuclear power and nuclear weapons and to put to rest any doubts about the safety of nuclear-powered submarines. The first nuclear-powered submarine came to Sasebo in November 1964 and resulted in some minor protests, but the subs' use of these bases continued and became routine in a few months.[57]

Meanwhile, pressures for the reversion of Okinawa to Japanese government rule were growing. Reischauer continued to press General Albert Watson, the new U.S. high commissioner for the Ryukyus in 1965, to allow the Japanese government to increase its aid and involvement on the islands, but Watson resisted. Okinawa, with its strategic Kadena Air Force Base, had become a critical piece of the U.S. long-range strategy, and the Pentagon was in no mood to give it up, so he could only tug at the fringes of the issue.

Reischauer had one final battle with the U.S. military and won it in the spring of 1966 as his term was nearing its end. Despite all his efforts to cultivate the friendship and understanding of Generals Smart and Preston, he learned in April 1966 to his great surprise that the U.S. Marine Corps was storing nuclear warheads on an LST (landing ship tank) named the *San Joachin County*, anchored along the shore at the main base of the U.S. Marine Air Base at Iwakuni on the Inland Sea near Hiroshima. The weapons were to be ready for instant use in any outbreak of war with North Korea or China. Such storage was a flagrant violation of the Security Treaty arrangements of 1960. It was a tightly held secret, known only to a handful of senior officials at the State Department, including Robert Fearey, Marshall Green, and William Bundy.

It happened that William L. Givens, the political-military affairs officer on the Japan Desk of the State Department was present at a meeting where the nuclear weapons were discussed. Givens, who had served under Reischauer in Tokyo, suspected—correctly, as it turned out—that no one had informed the ambassador of this potentially explosive issue. A graduate of West Point and a Korean War combat veteran, he felt that Reischauer needed to know about the weapons and on a visit to Tokyo six weeks later made a point of informing Owen Zurhellen, the deputy chief of mission, who in turn informed Reischauer.

Reischauer's reaction was swift and furious. He called in the chief of U.S. Forces, Japan, and confronted him with the allegation, which the general confirmed. He then sent a personal message to U. Alexis Johnson, deputy undersecretary of state, advising that if the nuclear weapons were not removed from Japan within ninety days, he would resign as ambassador and take the issue public. Rusk, hearing of Reischauer's fury, said he thought Reischauer had known about the situation and promised to have the weapons removed. In July, the ship was moved to Guam and then to Okinawa. When Robert Fearey learned of Reischauer's outburst, his reaction was, "What we can't figure out is: who told Ed?" Givens said, "I told him."[58]

Reischauer made one cryptic reference to this incident in a postscript to a letter home: "Actually something has come up this past week (don't even try to guess what it could be because you never could) which might induce me to quit quite suddenly and almost at once regardless of what Washington says—but I doubt that this will happen."[59] There can be no doubt that he was serious in his threat to resign and go public.[60]

As Givens later recalled,

> I was surprised to learn that the military had decided to violate the US–Japan Security Treaty, and was really ticked off that they had done so, because there was no possible military justification for such a move. I didn't *know* whether Reischauer knew or not, but assumed he didn't, for the following reasons.
>
> The people in [the] State [Department] most likely to know were Robert Fearey, Marshall Green, William Bundy, Averell Harriman, U. Alexis Johnson, and Secretary Dean Rusk. These were the people in my clearance chain for all of the nuclear stuff (ships and weapons—I was principal drafting officer for all correspondence on both). The President, also, regularly reviewed these cables and sometimes signed off on them. None of these people (except Rusk) had had military experience, and they had the inordinate respect for the uniformed services that goes with that. It seemed very probable to me that they would have agreed to the barge idea.
>
> It also seemed virtually certain to me that they wouldn't have told Reischauer, because they knew (as I did) from his previous conduct of these negotiations that he would never agree to a deliberate, covert violation of the Treaty. His reaction when he did find out amply demonstrates that.
>
> My quick take, then, was that the Pentagon, with the complicity of a group of sympathizers in State, were engaging in a wholly gratuitous violation of the Security Treaty (almost certainly with the knowledge and

> approval of the President) and were leaving poor Ed out there, twisting in the wind, in case the barge was discovered. I thought (still think) what they were doing was outrageous and decided I would do something about it.[61]

In the final months of his time in Tokyo, Jim Thomson made a desperate last-ditch effort to bring Reischauer back to Washington to take charge of China policy. Thomson, as noted in chapter 7, had stage-managed the original appointment of Reischauer in 1961 and was a member of the National Security Council staff in the White House in 1966. In a secret memo to Mac Bundy in January 1966, Thomson wrote: "I have a rather simple proposal that would serve our national interests in the Far East and also, parenthetically, preserve a rare talent within government service: that Ed Reischauer be designated this spring as Special Assistant to the Secretary of State (or Ambassador-at-Large) with responsibility for China operations coordination and China policy planning."

Thomson was well aware that this idea was far from simple. Rusk would fight against it, just for starters. But Thomson, undaunted, went on to point out that there was a precedent for this sort of move. Chip Bohlen, Tommy Thompson, and Foy Kohler had played similar roles vis-à-vis the Soviet Union with great success. Reischauer could review "the full sweep of our China activities from Tibet through Southeast Asia."

Would Reischauer agree to take the job? Here Thomson may have exaggerated a bit to make his case: "I have talked with Ed about his future, and I gather that the only government job he craves beyond his present post would be that of Ambassador to Peking [*sic*]. (I suspect that he might also accept the FE [Far East] Assistant Secretaryship if that position were vacant and his arm were twisted, but I don't think that this move would be particularly healthy for him or for the country as long as Vietnam is at full boil). What I am suggesting is that Ed be asked to serve, in effect, as Ambassador to Peking in exile."[62]

Thomson knew that if Reischauer accepted any of these jobs, he would work toward recognition of Communist China, which in turn might have led to an end to the fighting in Vietnam. Thomson, who had kept open a "back-channel" line of communication with Reischauer, was prepared to stay on as his top assistant.

This proposal was breath-taking. There was no American ambassador to Beijing (as we now call it) because there were no diplomatic relations with China, and the United States recognized Taiwan as the government of all of China. The assistant secretary of state whom Reischauer would have displaced was none other than Mac Bundy's brother, Bill Bundy. There had never been "an ambassador in exile." Nevertheless, Thomson knew exactly what he was doing, and Mac Bundy encouraged his iconoclastic thinking. There is no record of a response from Bundy to this memo.

Thomson traveled to Vietnam with his boss, Mac Bundy, later in January 1966, and after spending a day and a night in the Mekong Delta with Ward Just, a *Washington Post* reporter, and Richard Holbrooke, a Foreign Service officer, he met with Bundy. "I told him that the war was unwinnable, that we were losing it, that it would take a million or even two million American troops, and that we should get out." Bundy ignored the advice and gave a rather optimistic report to the president.[63] But Bundy had decided to retire, and in the next month, at his farewell party in the White House mess, he shook Thomson's hand and said patronizingly, "Well, bye-bye Mao Tse-Thomson, my favorite dove." Bundy left office on February 28, 1966.[64] He was replaced by another Cambridge intellectual, Walt W. Rostow, who turned out to be even more hawkish on the war.

Thomson, Fairbank and Reischauer's former Harvard student, had served as an in-house critic of U.S. Asian policy for five years under two presidents. That he was tolerated, even encouraged, to argue for recognition of China and for staying out of Vietnam seems quite extraordinary and probably could not happen today. As he explained it later, in-house dissenters had been "warmly institutionalized" and thus neutralized. His views, having been heard and considered, could now be safely ignored.[65]

As U.S. prospects in Vietnam worsened, Thomson explored every possible avenue to get a hearing for his views. At one point in the spring of 1966, he leaked to *Newsweek* a story that the State Department was considering a major change in China policy, hoping to stimulate a broad policy review. His effort failed. Undaunted, he soldiered on and turned to Reischauer as his last best hope.[66]

He managed to float his scheme for Reischauer to Senators Mansfield and Fulbright, who signed on with enthusiasm and encouraged President Johnson to pursue the plan. Rusk, knowing that Reischauer disagreed with him on China and on almost every other policy in Asia, was horrified. And Johnson probably did not relish the idea of having a renowned expert on Asia in a position to expose the weakness of his policies, but he most likely felt that he had to pretend that he was exploring all alternatives to the disastrous war.

Reischauer got wind of the plan to keep him on in some capacity as early as March 1966, but he wanted no part of it. Harvard had invited him to join its faculty as University Professor (the most revered and coveted title in all of higher education) starting July 1, 1966—a huge honor that would permit him to teach anything he liked, or nothing, upon his return. He wrote his family that "[Bill] Bundy and others have been trying to persuade me to take on a very important but I feel absolutely hopelessly frustrating job—which I intend to resist vigorously."[67] In a confidential letter to Jim Thomson, he wrote "Regarding your nefarious scheme, I can see only futility and frustration in it, because I am not enough on the same wave length with the Secretary on this specific subject [China] and not enough of the type to ever develop a close relationship with the President to be at all effective."[68]

He was intrigued by the thought of influencing Washington policymakers to shift China policy, but he was bone-tired, still weakened from the stabbing and hepatitis, and from the debilitating migraine headaches that had returned with a vengeance. He mainly despaired of changing the minds of President Johnson, Dean Rusk, and Bill Bundy. "I have no empathy with the President and do find myself even less in accord with Rusk on such basic matters, and feel Bundy is too much a day to day operator to be much in tune with the basic reshaping of thinking that is needed," he wrote to his children.[69]

Three years later Reischauer would reveal more about his feelings toward Rusk: "I think Dean Rusk's fixation with the China problem that he got during his earlier service in the government . . . also was part of the skewing of the decision. He just could not get rid of the idea that this [war in Vietnam] was somehow, basically, you know, a fight with China."[70]

Could Reischauer's arm have been twisted?

"You know, if he [President Johnson] had really said, 'look, we are thin on our knowledge of Asia. We've got Averell Harriman here, and he does the Russian things, and he is awfully useful at that kind of level, won't you stay by us as a sort of ambassador-at-large to see if we can't have more of that.' Well, he probably could have twisted my arm and my wife would have objected greatly, but maybe we would have gone to Washington. Conceivable, you see. But you know that wasn't—he didn't really want me at all. . . . He didn't want to be criticized for letting me go, but he didn't want me. And Rusk is a difficult man to know too. . . . Nobody feels very close to him."[71]

If he had been in robust health, he might have been able to put up a good fight for change within the Johnson administration. Jim Thomson was a skilled operator who could have guided him through the Washington policy jungle and helped him forge a consensus for change. But Reischauer never learned to love bureaucratic politics—the deal making, backstabbing, and influence seeking; the conspiratorial partnerships; the leaks, flattery, and favor exchanging that are the life blood of Washington politics. He preferred to speak and write and let the logic of his arguments carry the day. He never grasped the need to build and support a network of disciples (*deshi*) who could watch his back and do the dirty work for him as a leader (*dai-senpai*). Unfortunately, his was a losing strategy.

Surprisingly, Reischauer never lost his admiration for Mac Bundy, one of the chief architects of the Vietnam debacle. Mac, who had by now become president of the Ford Foundation, and his wife, Mary, visited Tokyo in May 1966. The Reischauers pulled out all the stops to expose them to Japanese leaders and a variety of cultural events. He wrote Ann before the visit, "I don't know why Bundy's public image is so bad—probably the result of the position he was in as behind the scenes operator for a president with a poor public image. Mac is perhaps the most able man I have ever known." In a letter the following month, he told his family that Mac Bundy would return to Washington someday as secretary of state.[72]

This is an odd judgment for a scholar whose life had been dedicated to the study of foreign languages and cultures. Bundy's glaring weakness was his complete disinterest in foreign cultures and his single-minded concern with military power. Richard Holbrooke, as a young Foreign Service officer, had dinner with Bundy during his visit to Vietnam in February 1965. "There was no question he was brilliant, but his detachment from the realities of Vietnam disturbed me. In Ambassador Porter's dining room that night were people far less intelligent than Bundy, but they lived in Vietnam, and they knew things he did not. Yet if they could not present their views in quick and clever ways, Bundy either cut them off or ignored them."[73]

Reischauer seemed to have no sense of the calamity that Bundy had helped to create and no reservations about his intellectual prowess. He was not alone in this judgment. When Bundy resigned in February 1966, Walter Lippmann, an antiwar critic, praised Bundy's "incomparable ability to reduce complex problems to the choices which the President must make." Columnists Joseph Kraft and Stewart Alsop joined in heaping praise on Bundy. Arthur Schlesinger described Mac Bundy as a "professional intellectual with the instinct for hard judgment. . . . He knew everybody, feared nobody, respected the President's power of decision, stated each side of an argument better than the protagonists and was always cool, swift, lucid, precise and funny—a great public servant."[74] Once again America's ignorance of Asia was on display. Reischauer should have been pointing out this ignorance instead of serving as a cheerleader for Bundy.

Bundy, after leaving office, continued until late in his life to defend the war and his role in advising two presidents to become involved in Vietnam. It was not until his friend and colleague Robert McNamara in 1995 published *In Retrospect: The Tragedy and Lessons of Vietnam*, admitting "we were wrong, terribly wrong" about Vietnam, that Bundy decided to revisit the issue. In 1996, in the last year of his life, he came to believe that President Kennedy would not have escalated the war in 1965 had he lived to win a second term, and Bundy questioned his own culpability. He died before he could complete this review.[75]

Arthur Schlesinger, who remained a friend and admirer of Ed Reischauer, came to believe in 1974, ironically, that it was America's missionary zeal—the very motivation that took Ed's father to Tokyo in 1905—that was to blame for the Vietnam disaster: "Missionaries wanted to change souls and societies. Their evangelical spirit helped to infuse the American role in the world with the impulses of a crusade. Many things contributed to the disaster in Indochina, but one element was surely the notion that Americans had a special capacity and duty to 'build' nations—an illusion strengthened by the experience of occupied Japan. . . . In a double sense, Vietnam can be seen as a missionary legacy, not only because the French went in to protect the missionary enterprise, but also because the Americans went in to achieve the missionary goal."[76] There is no evidence that Reischauer ever thought about this irony.

President Johnson summoned Reischauer back to Washington in July 1966. After keeping him waiting for three days, he invited him to the White House on July 22 and pretended to offer him a high policy role on East Asia, knowing that he was unlikely to accept. "I tried to use my time with the President to talk about China policy," he wrote, "but he conducted a monologue most of the time, complaining of Senatorial criticism of his policies."[77] Johnson urged Reischauer to stay on as ambassador or to consider taking on the job of assistant secretary of state for the Far East or deputy undersecretary. When Reischauer politely turned him down, as expected, Johnson called Senators Fulbright and Mansfield and announced to them that he had made the offer and that Reischauer, who was sitting right there, had turned him down. "Here, Ed, you tell Mansfield I have tried to get you to stay," Johnson urged. Reischauer's resignation was announced on July 26.

Senator Mike Mansfield called on Reischauer to testify before his Foreign Relations Subcommittee on July 22, and he was asked to air his views on recognizing China. Present were Senators William Fulbright, George Aiken, Edmund Muskie, Daniel Inoue, Wayne Morse, and Claiborne Pell. All of them urged him to stay on as ambassador.[78] Mansfield said, "I speak not only for myself, I know, when I say that today's meeting emphasizes the great need that the nation has for Ambassador Reischauer in what is, presently, the most important and difficult diplomatic job in Asia—that of Ambassador to Japan."[79]

By this time, Ed and Haru had come to view Johnson's behavior toward the Japanese as ludicrous. His popping Texas-size Stetson hats on visiting Japanese cabinet members at a White House luncheon in the summer of 1965 was the turning point. He resolved at this time "to lay my head on the block if necessary to prevent him from visiting Japan."[80]

Jim Thomson, frustrated in his last attempt to use Reischauer's clout to change China policy and end the war in Vietnam, returned to Harvard in 1966 and began work on the seminal article on the Vietnam War from which I quoted earlier, "How Could Vietnam Happen?" published in the *Atlantic Monthly* in April 1968. He went on to teach at Harvard and Boston University and was curator of the Nieman Foundation, which awarded yearlong fellowships to midcareer journalists from 1972 to 1984. He wrote two superb books: *While China Faced West* and, with Peter W. Stanley and John Curtis Perry, *Sentimental Imperialists*.[81] His friends and admirers felt that he never fully lived up to his full potential or brilliant promise as a policymaker. Yet he was fully vindicated five years after he left government: Henry Kissinger showed up in China in 1971 to negotiate a restoration of diplomatic relations. President Nixon visited Shanghai the next year. The United States and China reached a rapprochement that helped end the war in Vietnam—all of which Thomson had foretold ten years earlier.

The Japanese government, media, and public showered affection on the departing Reischauers. During their formal farewell call at the Imperial Palace, the emperor said with a smile that now that Reischauer was resigning as ambassador of the United States to Japan, he hoped Reischauer would serve as cultural ambassador of Japan in America. Reischauer later mentioned how at a televised discussion with the eighty-eight-year-old Yoshida Shigeru, Yoshida called the Japanese people "fools" (*baka*), and "I of course had to rush to their defense."[82]

After a round of adulatory news articles, photos, features and editorials, interviews, farewell luncheons, dinners, and ceremonial toasts, Ed and Haru embarked for America on August 19, 1966, exhausted but satisfied that they had made a difference in the attitudes of both Americans and Japanese toward each other. The *Japan Times* gushed, "It is no exaggeration to say that he is generally considered to be one of the most popular foreign envoys ever to have served in Japan."[83] His welcome home was triumphal. Harvard, Princeton, and Yale offered him honorary degrees, which he turned down. Writing in the *Boston Sunday Globe* on June 12, 1966, Richard Halloran said that the four most famous Americans in U.S.-Japan relations were Commodore Matthew Perry, Consul General Townsend Harris, Ambassador Joseph Grew, and General Douglas MacArthur. Now a fifth had to be added: Edwin O. Reischauer. Noting that Reischauer had established contacts with Japan's moderate Left, Halloran reported, "He has been so successful that *Akahata*, the Communist Party paper, once complained that since the advent of Reischauer, 'more and more progressive people visit America and come back with pro-American ideas.'"[84]

In his final press conference at the State Department, Reischauer was asked to name his greatest success and greatest disappointment as ambassador. Without hesitation, he said that his greatest achievement was to play a role in bringing about the normalization of relations between Japan and South Korea in 1965, as noted in chapter 8. His greatest failure was his inability to persuade the Japanese government to accept one hundred Peace Corps volunteers to teach English in Japanese schools. With a wry smile, he added later that he had given the conservative Education Ministry and the radical Teachers' Union (Nikkyoso) an issue to agree on. The former feared that native English speakers would show up incompetent Japanese English-language teachers, and the latter feared that the young Americans would show up the fallacies of Marxism.[85] In a letter to his family, he wrote, "I think that without doubt [Haru's] impact on Japanese women has been the biggest single aspect of our combined impact on the Japanese nation."[86]

On Vietnam, he waffled. Shortly after resigning, he was interviewed on the Sunday morning talk show *Face the Nation* and asked: "Since you have been back here with the State Department, in talking with newsmen and so forth, you have said that you support policy in Vietnam as long as it is conducted with restraint.... It seems to me this is less than a ringing endorsement. What are your reservations?" He replied: "Oh, my reservations would be that we shouldn't have gotten into the position that we are in; anyone can say this historically.... If we were wiser twenty years ago we might have made some turns in history that would have led us to a better position. What I was saying was not a criticism of our stand there or a suggestion that there is anything we can do there now that would be different. I think at this point in history we probably have been making the right decisions and doing the best thing in a very difficult situation."[87]

So ended Edwin O. Reischauer's five and a half years as ambassador. The final two and a half years were deeply disappointing to him. The assassination of President Kennedy, the attempt on his own life, Haru's depression, the need to defend a disastrous Vietnam policy, and his physical weakness and exhaustion caused by hepatitis cast a dark shadow over this period. Heading back to Harvard, he looked forward to teaching some of America's brightest students about Japan and East Asia, but more troubles awaited him in Cambridge. An antiwar movement among students and scholars of East Asia, some of whom had originally studied under him, was gaining momentum, and Reischauer would become their symbol of wrong-headed U.S. imperialism in Asia—a Cold Warrior and anti-Communist who was responsible for the misguided U.S. policy. The irony of being blamed for a war he had always opposed was just one stem in another bouquet of ironies that he and Haru now faced at home.

As his departure loomed, Reischauer's innate modesty returned. He wrote Ann: "I look to the future with great apprehension. There will be so many demands for me to do so many things—there are already—and I don't know what I should do or what I will be able to do. I am sure I will be a big flop in many ways since I am so over-built in reputation now. It's all very frightening and distressing."[88]

In his final letter to his family from Tokyo, Reischauer offered a very different picture from the one portrayed in the media. Worried about the uncertainties that lay ahead, he wrote: "There's not just the matter of finding a house and getting settled back into life in America—hard though that may be. I don't know what I am, except that I am not the ancient historian who came to this job five and a half years ago. I don't know what sort of thing I can or should try to do around Harvard or where and how I will fit in. . . . In any case what I am saying is that you should expect the arrival in Cambridge of two very confused, bone-weary, gloomy characters on the edge of total collapse. And so, as the lights on the stage gradually dim, we see the old couple trudge wearily and a little sadly down the path toward oblivion. Love, Dad."[89]

A Hard Landing

The Reischauers' homecoming in the summer of 1966 was markedly different from the warm send-off in Tokyo. Cambridge—and America—had changed dramatically since Ed and Haru had embarked on their great adventure in April 1961. The Harvard campus now was a hornets' nest of angry students protesting the war in Vietnam. Many were young men subject to the draft and facing the prospect of being sent off to die in the jungles of Southeast Asia. A new generation of scholars of East Asian affairs—including many of Reischauer's former students—was accusing him of complicity in the war effort.

It was not just the war in Vietnam that accounted for the upheavals. The "baby boomers," born soon after World War Two, were rebelling against what they viewed as their parents' staid culture. They rocked to Elvis Presley and then the Beatles, who had burst on the scene in 1964. They reveled in sexual freedom undreamed of by their parents. Young women burned their brassieres and demanded equal opportunities. Dr. Martin Luther King was leading an heroic movement to win greater freedom and equality for African Americans. Urban riots were taking place in major American cities. Authority everywhere was being challenged. "Don't trust anyone over thirty" was the new battle cry.

Reischauer found the abrupt transition back to the academic world bewildering at first, switching "from a day in which every minute is scheduled and supported and planned and organized by a supporting staff running into the hundreds, to one in which I do it all myself, including standing in line. It makes you feel, at best, about one-tenth as productive as you were before. This makes you feel frustrated—sort of premature old age."[1] Though he had read about the student protests, he now understood their full fury.

He could not escape from Vietnam. His views, those of a leading scholar of Asian affairs, were eagerly sought by the Congress, the media, students, and scholars. As ambassador, he had loyally supported the Johnson administration even while pointing out that we never should have been engaged there in the first place. As a Harvard professor, he was now free to change his position or remain silent. Instead, in a doomed effort to be consistent and loyal to the president, he chose to continue his support for the war, but this position was hard to sustain back in Cambridge. The first polite but firm challenge came from a surprising source: his former student and former champion within the government, Jim Thomson. In an extended dialogue on October 15, 1966 (Reischauer's fifty-sixth birthday), Thomson rolled out a hand grenade:

> THOMSON: You surprised some of your friends in recent months by sounding like a stronger supporter of our actions in Vietnam over these past several years than many of us had thought. I recall, for instance, that you shared my strong doubts, in the early part of 1965, about the wisdom of bombing North Vietnam. Have your views changed?
>
> REISCHAUER: No. I felt that the situation we're in in Vietnam is obviously the kind of thing we should have avoided if we'd had enough perspicacity soon enough. We made a lot of bad judgments. To be involved in major fighting on the Asiatic continent is wrong. . . .
>
> I had doubts about the bombing of the North. . . . You can perhaps gradually cut it off. My own feeling would be, probably that would be the wise course.
>
> THOMSON: What's your solution for Vietnam?
>
> REISCHAUER: I think we just have to stick it through. I'm worried about the fact all we can think of is a further escalation. I think the time has come to find ways to de-escalate the war.

At this point, Reischauer suggested that the protest movement against the war was giving hope to the North Vietnamese and was therefore prolonging the war. Thomson was not about to let him up on this one.

> THOMSON: But the problem of dissent is built into our society, and I would argue that it is perhaps dubious, and certainly dangerous, to cite dissenters as factors in prolonging the war. . . . You certainly don't mean to imply by what you say that dissenters border on treason and should be shut up.

REISCHAUER: No, that would be much worse. I just wish that dissenters—this of course is wishing more than human nature is capable of—would be responsible in their dissent.

THOMSON: Who is to determine the criteria of responsibility? The Secretary of State? The Chairman of the History Department at Harvard?

REISCHAUER: According to basic democratic philosophy, no one can decide it. All you can hope for is a more educated public, so that both support and dissent will be better argued.[2]

Thomson clearly had the better of this argument, and Reischauer knew it. Thomson was merely articulating Reischauer's own liberal views formed in his Oberlin days. Self-determination was one of his guiding principles. If U.S. involvement in the war was a tragic mistake in the first place, why should young Americans continue to die in this lost cause? His entire career spoke to the need for language and area competence among policymakers, yet he lacked those qualifications when it came to Vietnam. This was not Reischauer's finest hour.

He seemed to move to a more dovish stance in his testimony before the Senate Foreign Relations Committee on January 31, 1967: "I am myself a supporter of the Administration's objective in Vietnam, which as I understand it, is to bring the war to as speedy an end as possible, without resorting to either of the dangerous alternatives of withdrawal or major escalation. I might add that, in my view, this objective can best be attained by prudent de-escalation of the conflict's purely military aspects—for instance the bombing of the North."[3]

As reported by the *New York Times*, Reischauer argued for a policy of reconciliation—or containment without isolation—toward Communist China. Of China's leaders, he said, "They're not supermen. Their feet of clay extend almost up to their brains." But then he reverted to his earlier position on Vietnam: a "helter-skelter" U.S. withdrawal might "pump back enthusiasm." Instead, we should consider a "simmering down" of the war by setting up a massive border blockade at the seventeenth parallel, extending it into Laos, and by halting the bombing of the North. He saw no hope for negotiations while bombing continued. There would be "more hope of valid negotiations if we were not bombing the North."[4]

In April, before the Joint Economic Committee of Congress, he called for an end to the total trade embargo on China, suggesting that a "rich and strong" China might serve U.S. interests and the cause of world peace better than an unstable and sick China.[5] He was finding his voice again.

In July 1967, he completed a new book, *Beyond Vietnam: The United States and Asia*, in which he repeated many of the sound ideas that he first outlined in

1955 in *Wanted: An Asian Policy.* He again explained why U.S. involvement in Vietnam was wrong, that we should side with Asian nationalism and reconsider our policy of rigid hostility toward China. He wrote of the war's huge cost and the "unbearable strain" it placed on U.S.-Japan relations. He asked how long we could stand the "disunity and spiritual confusion" it was causing. He said that the bombing of the North was not working, but that we could not count on a negotiated settlement. Nevertheless, he advocated staying the course, while working toward a "slow simmering down" of the conflict. In effect, he was arguing that although negotiations wouldn't work, we had to try to negotiate. If he had been one of his own students, he would have flunked himself.[6]

Reischauer was out of touch with the sea change that was taking place in top policy circles in 1967. President Johnson was finding it impossible to appear in public because of the vehement and sometimes violent antiwar protesters who shouted him down. Robert McNamara, one of the war's chief architects, had come to believe it could not be won. He resigned in February 1968 to become head of the World Bank and was succeeded by Clark Clifford, a lawyer, a longtime Washington insider, and friend of LBJ. Clifford's assignment was to find a way out of the quagmire. Even so, on November 1, 1967, Johnson met with a group of "wise men"—the most respected foreign-policy experts he could assemble—and all of them supported continuation of the war with the exception of George W. Ball, who had resigned from his position as undersecretary of state in 1966.

In January 1968, Reischauer joined with ten other distinguished Harvard faculty members, including John Fairbank, Paul Doty, Franklin Ford, Talcott Parsons, and Stanley Hoffman, in sending a telegram to President Johnson calling for a negotiated settlement and deescalation of the war, allowing the National Liberation Front (Vietcong), along with others, to participate in the political life of South Vietnam. Jim Thomson, another of the signers, was the prime mover of this effort.[7]

The decisive change in Reischauer's view—and in President Johnson's view—came in early 1968. I happened to be watching the evening news with Reischauer in his Belmont home on the night of January 31, 1968, as Vietcong troops were shown racing through the U.S. Embassy compound in Saigon. It was the beginning of the Tet Offensive. Whether this incident was a true defeat for the United States—historians still argue about it—it was a public-relations disaster for the Johnson administration. Reischauer recognized immediately that it was the beginning of the end of whatever was left of public support for the war.

Yet he continued to equivocate in public. At a congressional hearing on February 29, 1968, when Representative Clement J. Zablocki asked him if he now disagreed with Vietnam policy, Reischauer responded: "I have not really changed my mind on that." Pulling out of commitments in Vietnam, even if they should never have been made, "would be a serious mistake for us. . . . While I feel it is in the American interest to get ourselves out of Vietnam as fast as possible, I think we could get into even worse troubles and create greater disasters if we should get out of Vietnam simply by washing our hands of the problems there."

In response to a question by Congressman Lee Hamilton, he said, "I am very much against any major escalation of the war in the sense of utilizing nuclear weapons, entering Cambodia, going into North Vietnam, or bombing civilian populations in the North, because any of these acts would run grave new risks while holding out very little promise of ending the war in South Vietnam."[8]

Events moved rapidly after the Tet Offensive. In February, Senator Eugene McCarthy of Minnesota won 42 percent of the vote in the New Hampshire Democratic primary election on a platform opposing the war, coming surprisingly close to the 49.9 percent won by Johnson. Senator Robert Kennedy let it be known that he was "reassessing" his earlier decision not to challenge the president and began to denounce the war. General William Westmoreland, commander of the U.S. forces in Vietnam, asked for 200,000 more troops on top of the 550,000 already in Vietnam and was turned down. He was soon relieved of his command. Senator J. William Fulbright, in a note to the psychoanalyst Erich Fromm, wrote, "There is literally a miasma of madness in the city, enveloping everyone in the administration and most of those in Congress. I am at a loss for words to describe the idiocy of what we are doing." [9] Lyndon Johnson now understood that his chances for reelection in November were bleak and announced on March 31, 1968, that he would not seek another term and that the bombing of the North would cease.[10]

Four days before Johnson's dramatic announcement, Reischauer finally rediscovered his conscience and called for the resignation of Dean Rusk. In a televised discussion program in San Francisco, he said that Rusk "has been associated with an approach to the war which now seems to be the wrong approach."[11] In a speech six weeks later, he called U.S. intervention in Vietnam "a disastrous mistake" that had resulted largely from ignorance about Asia among American political leaders.[12] Finally free from the shackles of bureaucracy, he spoke his mind.

The rest of 1968 was one of the most turbulent periods in U.S. history. On April 4, Dr. Martin Luther King was murdered in Memphis, Tennessee. The next day, large sections of Washington, D.C., and other big cities were ablaze. A month later, on June 5, Bobby Kennedy was murdered in Los Angeles. In August, as antiwar protesters clashed with Chicago police outside the convention hall, Vice President Hubert Humphrey won the Democratic nomination for president. In November, he was soundly defeated by the Republican candidate, Richard Nixon. Nixon continued and expanded the war for four more years. College campuses, including Harvard, were wracked by storms of protest. Reischauer supported Hubert Humphrey in 1968 and lowered his profile on Vietnam. By 1969, he was publicly calling for the withdrawal of all combat troops within a year and all other troops within a second year.

Relations with Japan suffered during Nixon's first term. Campaigning in 1968, Nixon had used a "southern strategy" to win votes in the traditionally Democratic states. The strategy involved promises to textile makers in the South that he would curb the inflow of Japanese textiles to protect the South's less-efficient plants and workers. In 1969, after he and Prime Minister Sato Eisaku cut a deal, as described in chapter 8: the United States would return Okinawa to Japanese sovereignty, and Sato would (so Nixon thought) voluntarily limit textile exports to the United States. When Sato, according to Nixon, failed to live up to his end of the bargain, Nixon was livid. There followed three "Nixon shocks," as the Japanese press described them.

The first shock came in the summer of 1971 when Henry Kissinger made a secret trip to China aimed at opening up diplomatic relations. Tokyo was informed only a few minutes before the public announcement and felt betrayed. So did Reischauer. "I myself had promised [the Japanese] at the highest levels that they would be informed before the U.S. opened diplomatic talks. . . . It would have been good for U.S.-Japan relations, and it certainly would have been good for the Japanese psychology if they had been allowed to help in reconciling our differences with China."[13] The second Nixon shock came on August 15, 1971, with his sudden move to cut the dollar loose from the gold standard and from its fixed rate of 360 yen, allowing the yen to appreciate and thus making Japanese exports more expensive. A 10 percent surcharge on most imports from Japan was accompanied by a threat to take further harsh measures under the 1917 Trading with the Enemy Act if Japan failed to cut back its exports of textiles. Nixon called the economic threat "far more serious than the challenge we confronted even in the dark days of Pearl Harbor."[14]

Though Reischauer had been out of office for five years, he took all of these shocks personally. He had tried as ambassador to build Japanese confidence in America's good faith and reliability as an ally and had put his own integrity and trustworthiness on the line. He could see the fruit of his labors slipping away. He made no secret of his contempt for the Nixon-Kissinger policy toward Japan. In a letter to Graham Allison, a strategic thinker on the Harvard faculty, he declared, "Your analysis of the [Nixon] Administration's conscious ignoring of Japan and Kissinger's attempt to recreate Metternich's nineteenth century world are both frightening, but all too correct, I am afraid."[15] He was referring, of course, to Kissinger's reliance on balance-of-power politics and his flirtation with Beijing.

His personal integrity regarding these matters once again came into the spotlight around ten years later. In early May 1981, a reporter for *Mainichi Shimbun*, Komori Yoshihisa, interviewed him at Harvard for a series of reports on the U.S.–Japan alliance. The nature of this alliance had been called into question when Prime Minister Suzuki Zenko had visited Washington earlier that month. Suzuki's foreign minister, Ito Masayoshi, used the term *military alliance* (*gunji domei*), but Suzuki, most likely thinking that it would arouse public fear of Japan's becoming further entangled in U.S. strategic plans, balked at using the term. Ito was fired or resigned and was quickly replaced by Sonoda Sunao.

When Komori asked Reischauer to clarify his understanding of the Security Treaty as it related to the word *introduction* (*mochikomi*) in reference to the bringing of nuclear weapons into Japan, Reischauer made it perfectly clear that the word did not apply to U.S. Navy ships making calls at Japanese ports or passing through Japanese waters. He further indicated that there had been an understanding on this point with the Japanese government in 1960 and that he had reaffirmed this understanding with Foreign Minister Ohira Masayoshi in April 1963 (as reported in chapter 8). (Ohira had died suddenly in 1980.) The U.S. position was, as it always had been, that Washington would neither confirm nor deny the existence of nuclear weapons on any ship, but Reischauer explained that it was just a matter of common sense to assume that some vessels would carry nuclear weapons when they docked in Japanese ports. "It is obviously impossible for American ships, which constitute a large part of the defense of Japan, to change their armaments each time they enter Japanese waters," he later explained.[16] He had already published this position in the 1981 edition of *Japan: The Story of a Nation*,[17] and Admiral Gene La Rocque had mentioned it as far back as 1974. For Reischauer, it was no big deal.[18]

As noted in chapter 8, the Japanese government in 1967 had announced its "three nonnuclear principles": no possession, no manufacturing, and no introduction of nuclear weapons into Japan. It based its interpretation on a literal reading of the First Exchange of Notes to the U.S.–Japan Treaty of Mutual Cooperation and Security, which said in part: "Major changes in the deployment into Japan of United States Armed Forces, major changes in their equipment, and the use of facilities and areas in Japan as bases for military combat operations to be undertaken from Japan other than those conducted under Article V of the said treaty, shall be the subjects of prior consultation with the Government of Japan."[19]

According to this interpretation, the U.S. government was obligated to consult with Japan before introducing or bringing nuclear weapons into Japan, even for port calls. Because the U.S. government had not consulted Japan, and because the Japanese government trusted the Americans, the latter took the position that no nuclear weapons were on U.S. Navy ships making port calls in Japan. If the United States had consulted with Japan when such occasions occurred, Japan would have refused entry.

Komori published his account of Reischauer's words on May 18, 1981, in *Mainichi Shimbun*, setting off a sensation in Tokyo. Foreign Minister Ito Masayoshi had resigned on the previous day over his interpretation of the joint communiqué that Prime Minister Suzuki and President Ronald Reagan had issued at their summit conference in Washington on May 7–8. The issue was whether the U.S.–Japan Security Treaty was a military alliance (*gunji domei*). Ito had denied that it was a military alliance, but was contradicted by Prime Minister Suzuki, who barely escaped a nonconfidence vote in the Diet. High officials in Tokyo accused Reischauer of senility and bad manners. The new foreign minister, Sonoda Sunao, charged that Reischauer was an uncalled-for meddler who "pokes his nose into matters that are absolutely none of his business." Sonoda added "This, indeed, is [a manifestation of] American people bloated with great-power egotism." He even said that Reischauer was the worst-mannered person (*reigi shirazu*) that he had ever heard of.[20] Even Reischauer's old friend Miyazawa Kiichi, who was then chief cabinet secretary, piled on, saying, "Although Mr. Reischauer is a truly respected and distinguished scholar, he has now retired from his government post so his remarks should not be construed as an official view of the U.S. Government."[21]

The conservatives in Japan clearly feared a strong public reaction to the revelation that nuclear weapons were onboard incoming U.S. Navy ships. In this case, however, Reischauer knew better. I happened to be staying with him at this time and helped him set up a press conference to deal with this issue for a throng of Japanese reporters on May 18 at the Harvard-Yenching Institute. As we drove from Belmont to Harvard, he told me he trusted the Japanese public to understand the U.S. position: the same ships that carried nuclear weapons into Yokosuka also carried them into Norfolk, Virginia. The American people understood the need for their presence, and so would the Japanese people, he said. He turned out to be right. After a few mild protests, the issue went away.

Top State Department officials, dismayed that Reischauer's statement might set back their efforts to push Japan into greater defense spending, checked with the Justice Department to see if he could be prosecuted for violating his oath of office as ambassador and leaking state secrets. Justice saw no basis for this action.[22]

Reischauer was pleased with the whole incident: "After the affair calmed down, I came to the conclusion that I had inadvertently gotten rid of a bothersome gray spot in Japanese-American relations, but I had taken a lot of flak in the process."[23] As an historian, he had also satisfied himself that there would be no embarrassing revelations after his death.

Despite the Vietnam controversy, Reischauer was clearly at the top of his game after returning to Harvard. Invitations to speak came from schools and universities, business groups, bankers, lawyers, think tanks, foreign-affairs councils, and Harvard alumni groups. Japan was a hot topic, and Reischauer was the acknowledged expert. Not only was it proving to be a friendly and peace-loving ally in the Cold War, but its color television sets, motorcycles, cameras, and watches were being gobbled up by American consumers. It began to run an export surplus in bilateral trade with the United States in 1967. In 1970, Herman Kahn, the military strategist at the RAND Corporation, predicted that Japan would be a giant economic, technological, and financial superstate and was likely to be a military superpower as well. In 1979, Reischauer's Harvard colleague Ezra Vogel declared in *Japan as Number One* that Americans had much to learn from Japan.[24]

Reischauer took immense satisfaction from Japan's rise to prominence and strove with his usual missionary zeal to educate the broadest possible American public about this rise. He never failed to emphasize Japan's success as a democracy and its importance as an ally. He appeared twice on *Meet the Press*, and a 1969 CBS documentary, *The Japanese*, in which he appeared won an Emmy Award in 1970. He became a member of the National Committee on U.S. China Relations and of the Institute of Politics at the John F. Kennedy School of Government at Harvard. He worked on a twenty-six-hour video-cassette series on Japanese history and culture for use in universities. He served as chairman for the American Advisory Committee of Kodansha Ltd. on the *Encyclopedia of Japan*—a bible for any student of that nation.

In 1970, he spoke to the American Society of Newspaper Editors, an annual gathering of the most prestigious and influential journalists in the nation. The next week he received a letter of thanks from Norman Isaacs, the president of the association:

> Your talk will go down as one of the top presentations in ASNE history. This is not burbling flattery. Every once in a while we get these breaks. One was when Dean Acheson was Secretary of State and went after Senator Joe McCarthy. Another was the afternoon we had a "loyal opposition

Following his return to Harvard, Reischauer spoke frequently to audiences around the United States. Here, at a press conference at the *Philadelphia Bulletin* newspaper on May 14, 1970, he discusses the importance of the U.S.–Japan partnership. Photograph by an unknown *Bulletin* photographer. Courtesy of the author.

> panel featuring Adlai Stevenson, [British opposition leader] Hugh Gaitskill and [former Canadian prime minister] Mike [Lester] Pearson, and they went at it freehand. Your talk rang just that kind of bell and we were deluged with requests for texts all through the week. What you did was to give America's editors the most thorough up-to-date educational briefing they have ever had—and you could tell how much they appreciated it from their explosive applause.[25]

His position as University Professor allowed him great freedom. He could have opted to teach an advanced seminar on arcane subjects that would contribute to a new specialized book. Instead, he chose to resume teaching the Rice Paddies course on the grounds that he could reach more of the brightest students in this way than in any other way`. For many of these students, he reasoned, it would be their only brush with Japan, and he wanted to be sure they got the right picture. He worked with John Fairbank and Albert Craig to consolidate his and Fairbank's original two volumes into a single volume: *East Asia: Tradition and Transformation.*[26] This book would become standard reading for university courses throughout the nation. Three new chapters dealt with Vietnam; Reischauer wisely let Fairbank and Craig deal with that subject. The three authors later divided the book into two books, one on Japan and the other on China.

He also began to revise and add chapters to his earlier book *The United States and Japan*, which had first come out in 1950, with revised editions published in 1957 and 1965. He also embarked on an entirely new book, *The Japanese*, which came out in 1977 and was probably the best of all his writings. By 1980, it had gone through nineteen printings. Revised in 1988 and again in 1994 after his death by Marius Jansen as *The Japanese Today*, it was in its fifth printing in 2003.[27] The book combined his earlier historical insights with what he had learned as ambassador. He was now able to take advantage of the burgeoning field of Japan studies, drawing on recent monographs, some of them by his own former students. Writing with characteristically bold generalizations and with extraordinary grace and style, he created the most popular introduction in English to Japan up to that time.[28] It remains remarkably relevant today.

Frank Gibney, a journalist and longtime resident of Japan, wrote in his review of the book for the *New York Times*, "Of all the books that have recently set out to demolish our still ghastly stereotypes of Japan (including Reischauer's earlier ones) *The Japanese* is probably the most successful, for a very good reason. Reischauer, a distinguished historian, combines great academic learning with a clear, attractive and often witty writing style. This time he is writing not only as a scholar, but as a friend and longtime observer of the Japanese, who wants to explain and relate as well as instruct. The book reads beautifully, like a long, quiet and informal chat in your favorite professor's study." When his former student Jim Thomson asked him what had pushed him to write yet another book on Japan, he replied, "I presume it's the missionary instinct. I do want to spread the word."[29]

When Reischauer turned sixty on October 15, 1970, his Harvard colleagues gave him a merry *kanreki* celebration. Albert Craig and Donald Shively assembled sixty-six close friends at the Harvard Faculty Club for a black tie dinner. John Fairbank, wearing a Tokyo University undergraduate's cap, spoke and sang about Ed's life. Benjamin Schwartz, wearing his old barracks cap, told of Ed in wartime. John Hall, Otis Cary, and Jim Thomson spoke of other parts of his career. Henry Rosovsky, Richard Neustadt, Hugh Borton, Jackson Bailey, and Ezra Vogel joined in the fun. The climax of the evening came when Craig presented him with the book *Personality in Japanese History*, which had been surreptitiously assembled. Craig and Shively, wishing to salute Ed's interest in biography (Ennin) and personality, had gathered essays by fourteen of Ed's former students.[30] The gathering that evening can be forgiven for assuming that their understanding of Japanese history would be the standard account in the field for the next one hundred years.

It so happened, though, that a new and feisty generation of scholars was coming along at a moment when icons were toppling all over America. John Fairbank used to joke that each new generation of scholars stands on the faces of the previous generation. It was an ironic twist on the old adage about younger scholars standing on the shoulders of the giants that preceded them. He was more prescient than even he could have known.

Despite Reischauer's fame, or perhaps in part because of it, his status as a dominant figure in East Asian studies and his defense of Johnson's Vietnam War made him a perfect villain for the younger generation of scholars who opposed the war.

The first published assault came from a group calling itself the Committee of Concerned Asian Scholars—a subgroup of the larger Association for Asian Studies that Reischauer had helped to found. They published a book in 1969 called *America's Asia: Dissenting Essays on Asian American Relations*.[31] The book grew out of discussions at a seminar in the summer of 1968 and turned out to include a sustained attack on the writings of Reischauer and Fairbank. Two of the participants were John Dower and Herbert Bix, both of whom would later win Pulitzer Prizes for their work on Japan. Here was the beginning of a fault line that would fracture the field of Japan studies for years to come.

"More than two decades ago," the editors announced, "the Occupation of Japan set the course for the militarist and anti-popular character of American intervention in Asia. . . . American economic and military power swept in to fill the void left by the departing colonial powers—achieving for America many of the dreams of empire it had denied a vanquished Japan, its rationale then as now the necessity to crush Communist aggression."

Taking direct aim at Reischauer, the best-known advocate of "modernization theory," the editors declared: "An ideology of modernization has carefully been constructed to play down to a null point American aggression and exploitation and play up as a dominant motif American benevolence in assisting Asians to traverse the treacherous evolutionary course to the modern world. In this worldview, revolution emerges as a menace to be crushed, not a solution and a natural response to overwhelming evolutionary horrors."

It is important at this stage to look briefly at the modernization theory that was being attacked to see what the fuss was all about. Its critics saw it as an insidious attack against their Marxist ideology, a kind of "anti–Communist Manifesto"—an imperialists' trick to distract Japan's intellectuals from their ideology of class struggle and social revolution and to lay a theoretical foundation to advance the goal of American power in East Asia and elsewhere. A "modernized" country can be defined by the following criteria:

1. A comparatively high concentration of population in cities and the increasing urban-centeredness of the total society.
2. A relatively high degree of use of inanimate energy, the widespread circulation of commodities, and the growth of service facilities.
3. Extensive spatial interaction of members of a society and the widespread participation of such members in economic and political affairs.
4. Widespread literacy accompanied by the spread of a secular, and increasingly scientific, orientation of the individual to his environment.
5. An extensive and penetrative network of mass communication.
6. The existence of large-scale social institutions such as government, business, industry, and the increasingly bureaucratic organization of such institutions.
7. Increased unification of large bodies of population under one control (nations) and the growing interaction of such units (international relations).[32]

Reischauer's own definition was simpler: modernization involved mechanization, the factory system, urbanization, development of the scientific method, the concept of progress, centralization of economic and political power, the breakdown of the family unit, and the spread of education.[33] Modernization, he insisted, was not the same as westernization.

Reischauer's critics charged that he and his colleagues had concocted this theory as a means of advancing the imperial ambitions of Presidents Kennedy and Johnson. They argued that the theory was simply a tool by which the aggressive U.S. government could crush any resistance from Marxist scholars in Japan. They were partly correct: Reischauer was unapologetically opposed to communism, both in theory and in practice, as noted in chapter 3 and elsewhere. As a liberal anti-Communist, he believed that a Socialist takeover of Japan in the 1960s would be disastrous for the nation. It would bring Japan into the Sino-Soviet bloc and turn it into another Poland.[34]

But he never saw modernization theory primarily as a Cold War doctrine or tool. He believed it was a better description of what had happened in the West and of how Japan had gone through a similar process. In fact, he played down its importance as a "vague term covering all the tremendous changes that had been occurring in Japan since the mid-19th Century."[35] He resented the implication that he was a Cold War agent and that his views were designed solely as a weapon to defeat communism rather than a product of his genuine convictions, and he was startled by the ad hominem nature of the attacks. He was a consistent opponent of ideological rigidity of right or left. He never felt compelled to respond to the charges against him, however.

In these concerned scholars' view, the Vietnam War was no aberration: it was a link in the chain of creating and maintaining an Asian Pax Americana. Revolutionary communism was the only solution for Asian nations to move forward and to avoid aggressive American imperialism. Mao Zedong was heroic. The United States was the aggressor in the Korean War, provoked combat with China, and supported anti-Communist elites in Asia so long as they accepted U.S. military and economic domination. Thus, the effort to sell modernization theory to Japanese historians was simply another weapon in the American Cold War arsenal.

John Dower intensified his assault on Reischauer in 1975 with his fiery introduction to selected writings of his hero, E. H. Norman.[36] In a sustained polemic of ninety-eight pages, Dower lavished praise on Norman and defended his interpretation of Japanese history against Reischauer's. It is a brilliant defense of Norman's Marxist interpretation of Japanese history, and it became a watershed in the field of East Asian and Japan studies in both America and Japan.

I introduced E. Herbert Norman in chapter 1 as Reischauer's boyhood friend—the two had played tennis together in Karuizawa—and they had met again as fellow graduate students under Professor Serge Elisseeff at Harvard in 1938. Norman was born of Canadian missionary parents in rural Karuizawa, Nagano Prefecture, in 1909, and Reischauer a year later in Tokyo. Their careers form a fascinating counterpoint. Both reached maturity in the depths of the worldwide depression of the 1930s. Growing up, Norman saw abject rural poverty in Nagano, whereas Reischauer experienced the rapid development of modern urban life in Tokyo. Norman studied at Cambridge University's Trinity College from 1933 to 1935, while Reischauer was studying in Paris. At Trinity College, according to Norman's biographer Roger Bowen, Norman's interest in Marxism grew, and he joined the Communist Party.

Returning to the United States from England, he continued his study of East Asian history at Harvard and Columbia. In 1938, he joined the research staff of the Institute of Pacific Relations and wrote his first book, *Japan's Emergence as a Modern State*, published in 1940.[37] In 1939, he entered the Canadian diplomatic service and was sent to Japan as a language officer until the outbreak of war forced him to come home. For the next fifteen years, he continued his historical studies, examining the roots of Japan's militarism. He discovered in the works of Ando Shoeki, an eighteenth-century intellectual, the roots of an indigenous democratic tradition.[38]

Norman served in Washington during World War Two and in Tokyo during the occupation. He, along with John K. Emmerson, visited the imprisoned Communist leaders Tokuda Kyuichi and Shiga Yoshio in October 1945 to tell them that they would be released and later drove them from the prison to downtown Tokyo. For this and because of his Institute of Pacific Relations contacts with known Communists, Norman would be investigated in 1950 as a suspected Soviet agent. Over the next seven years, both the Canadian and U.S. governments investigated him, but he was exonerated in Canada. When he was Canadian ambassador to Egypt in 1957, he heard that a third U.S. congressional investigation was preparing to call him to testify once again. At the age of forty-eight, he committed suicide by jumping off the roof of his apartment building.[39] Both in Japan and in America, admirers of Norman have tried to build a case that Reischauer was his implacable enemy and was even responsible somehow for his death. In this view, they are utterly mistaken.

John Dower and others who admired Norman undertook to revive his reputation and to use his interpretations of history to combat what they believed were Reischauer's erroneous views of history and current policy. A cottage industry of Japanese scholars and critics also took up the hue and cry. Eto Jun, a popular literary critic, wrote in 1974 that modernization had forced the Japanese people to destroy their lives.[40] Ouchi Hyoe, a venerable Marxist intellectual, argued that the United States could not truly favor independence for Japan unless and until it withdrew all its armed forces from the nation.[41]

This battle continues even today in academic circles, and it is worth a brief examination. Contrary to the views of the then dominant Marxist scholars in Japan, Reischauer believed that the late Tokugawa Era marked the beginning of modernization, a period of slow but positive change in which the economic, social, and intellectual foundations were laid for modern Japan under conditions of tranquility and order. In this period, Japan acquired a highly developed legal system and concept of legal rights; a complex integrated society; a relatively independent business community that was somewhat protected from exploitation by the government; an entrepreneurial spirit; and an encouragement of long-term investment.[42]

Japan was ready in 1868, he contended, to shed its feudal past because of its growing economic productivity, the spread of technology, the growth of cities, marked advances in education and literacy, the growth of a merchant class, and the spread of trade in a national market. New prosperity in rural areas and the rise of peasant entrepreneurs would form the backbone of a future middle class. Villages learned to govern themselves with some degree of autonomy. All this prepared Japan to move rapidly toward modernization. The arrival of Commodore Perry in 1853 and the threat posed by Western imperialism merely accelerated internal changes that were already well under way in the mid-nineteenth century.

For Norman, in contrast, the Tokugawa Era had no redeeming features: it was a crushing and oppressive nightmare for the Japanese people. "In any feudal society," he wrote in 1944, "we find a narrow privileged ruling class deriving its power from control over the land, and the people who work for it; an oppressed peasantry living on the threshold of starvation; agricultural productivity at so low a level that famine is endemic; decentralization of power and consequent obstruction of trade; political life marked by plots, intrigues and coups d'état rather than by organized movements; and finally the destiny of individuals governed by concepts of social status. All this is exemplified by Japanese feudalism, particularly of the Tokugawa era." Where Reischauer saw order and tranquility, Norman saw regimentation, the use of secret police, rigid thought control, torture, drabness of life, and the stultification of intellectual ambition that at the end of the Tokugawa Era left Japan "spiritually and intellectually exhausted to such an extent that that effect was felt long into the succeeding era."[43]

It is not surprising, then, that these two scholars saw the Meiji Era in very different terms. Reischauer saw the period from 1868 to 1912 as a successful and promising stage in Japan's progress toward modernization and democracy. He argued that the abolition of feudal rule and institutions; the centralization of political power; the promulgation of a constitution; the rise of political parties, elections, and a parliamentary system borrowed from England; the conversion of samurai into civil servants; the spread of universal compulsory education; and rapid industrialization laid the groundwork for a modern nation-state. "Japan stands alone," he wrote of the Meiji Restoration, "as the one great non-Western nation to have made the transition to a modernized society and economy with relatively little turmoil and extraordinary success."[44]

For Norman, the Meiji Era represented an incomplete revolution, or at most a revolution from above: it involved the seizure of power by lower-level samurai and their rich merchant allies. The government remained in the hands of the former feudal elite, who were quick to suppress any popular or mass movements that might threaten their power. None of the Meiji reforms that Reischauer praised could change the fact that "the continuity of class rule from feudal to modern times was not broken."[45]

Planners for the U.S. occupation of Japan had to decide in essence between the two theories. If one believed Reischauer and like-minded specialists, one accepted the thesis that he prewar experience of elections, party cabinets, Diet influence over budgets and foreign policy—prepared the Japanese people for independence and lasting democratic rule in the post–World War Two era. In this view, militarism and expansion were aberrations caused by the coincidence of a worldwide depression, the rise of fascism in Germany and Italy, turmoil in China, the perceived threat of the Soviet Union, and the rise of a new political elite in Japan who took advantage of fundamental flaws in the Meiji Constitution. In short, Reischauer believed that the ordinary Japanese citizen, given an adequate standard of living and a liberal education, would be fully able to choose his own leaders and policies—that is, to make democracy work.

In Norman's view, however, the 1930s were a natural consequence of Japan's history: class structure was unchanged from feudal times, the samurai and zaibatsu (powerful financial and industrial conglomerates) were still in charge, and it was foreordained that they would crush any liberal movements that might limit their power. A social revolution was still needed.

As I have reported, Reischauer and fellow liberals such as Hugh Borton, along with State Department officials such as Joseph Grew, Robert Fearey, George Blakeslee, Joseph Ballantine, Eugene Dooman, and ultimately, of course, General MacArthur himself, prevailed: the occupation would be short and benign. With

Reischauer's strong backing, the emperor would be retained as a symbol of the unity of the state, and the occupation authorities would administer the nation through the Japanese bureaucracy. The liberal constitution that took effect in 1947 rested on the assumption that the Japanese people were peace loving and ready for democracy. In short, it rested on faith in what Reischauer called Japan's "common man" (or what we might today call "ordinary citizens").

Given the strength of democracy in Japan today, the survival intact of the 1947 Constitution, and the strength of antiwar sentiment in Japan today, along with the collapse of world communism, one might say that the argument is over: Reischauer got it right, and Norman got it wrong. But Norman's views continue to carry weight in academic circles both in Japan and in the United States. John Dower has gone on to a brilliant career as a history professor at MIT.[46] Herbert Bix won a Pulitzer Prize for his biography *Hirohito*, in which he contends that the emperor was far more involved in leading Japan's aggressive war effort than is commonly believed and thus should have been treated as a war criminal.[47] The younger critics of Reischauer have gone on to occupy many of the tenured positions in the Japan field in American universities today and probably outnumber those who agree with Reischauer's interpretation of history.[48]

Some of the more recent treatment of Reischauer, however, has turned vicious. In *Japan: A Reinterpretation*, published in 1997, Patrick Smith states:

> The Chrysanthemum Club [meaning Reischauer and all who agreed with him] was high among the Cold War establishment's intellectual appendages, a major producer of the victory culture that animated the American century. In the age of witch-hunts, its perspective prevailed without serious challenge, so eclipsing the work of entire generations. After a time it became dangerous to question the new orthodoxy. Scholars were prohibited from pursuing any analysis that conflicted with the paradigm, for to dwell upon Japan's complexities, or the paradigm's inconsistencies, was to face that dreadful condemnation of the Cold War years: it was to be "political." The intellectual chicanery of the era has thus discolored an entire country's understanding of Japan, for many were those who, braving the prevailing wind, found themselves forced from jobs, institutions and communities.

He continues:

> The most tragic case concerned the Canadian writer and diplomat E. H. Norman, surely the seminal Japan scholar of his generation. Norman,

> more than anyone else, was responsible for the understanding of Japan the Chrysanthemum Club was dedicated to erasing—a complex, altogether human Japan with no stock characters or easy notions of a "tradition," a Japan with many serious problems, in need of the drastic change of course the Japanese wanted after the defeat. Norman's analysis rested on history; indeed it was in Norman's work before the war that much of Japan's authentic modern history was recovered. Norman was respected on both sides of the Pacific. Then his work was labeled, summarily and unfairly, "Marxist." In 1951 he was denounced in Senate hearings as a communist. And as Reischauer and other scholars stood silently by, Norman was driven to suicide six years later.[49]

The truth is much different. Reischauer and Norman had genuine respect for each other, despite their different understanding of Japanese history. Far from being bitter rivals, they admired each other. Norman wrote a favorable review of Reischauer's first book: "I have known Dr. Reischauer for many years as a scholar with a rich and varied background of training both in Japanese and Chinese studies; thus in any work of his I would expect to see both an impeccable care for detail and a well-balanced objectivity. I was not disappointed in these expectations when I read his *Japan: Past and Present.*" Although Norman gave a hint of their differing historical views when he suggested that it might be "an over-simplification to limit the aggressive element in Japanese politics to the army only . . . and to place businessmen and bureaucrats without discrimination in the peaceful camp," the overall thrust of his review was positive.[50]

After Norman's death, Reischauer offered a moving tribute to Norman at a symposium in Toronto on Norman's life and scholarship. He spoke of their long friendship and recalled that when he and Haru became engaged in Tokyo in 1956, they asked Herb Norman's older brother, Howard, a missionary, to conduct the ceremony. They stayed in Howard's home in Kobe on the night before they embarked on their voyage home in 1956. And Reischauer remembered visiting Herb Norman in 1935 at Cambridge and then reading his thesis in 1939 at Harvard, when both men received their Ph.D. degrees. They met again briefly over lunch and for the last time in the fall of 1948 in Tokyo.

Reischauer had high praise for Norman's *Japan's Emergence as a Modern State*, calling it the most important influence on U.S. policy thinking in the early stages of the occupation and on his own thinking as well: "Norman's gloomy views of the prospects for democracy and social justice in Japan undoubtedly contributed greatly to the strongly reformist and often radical nature of occupation policy. Without this influence, the occupation, in the hands of a military force dominated by such an essentially conservative and often reactionary figure as MacArthur, might very well have never opened the doors in Japan very wide to healthy democratic growth and sweeping social change."

He placed a high value on Norman's success in renewing contacts with Japanese historians in the postwar period, and he deplored the witch-hunting McCarthyite attacks against Norman, concluding: "As a lifelong friend and admirer, I seriously hope that Herb Norman in death will not be made the controversial figure he was forced to be in life. He was a great and talented writer and scholar. He was a deeply learned, sensible, thoughtful and kind man. As a man and scholar, he greatly influenced his time, and he deserves to be remembered as a significant figure, both as a historian and as a shaper of history."[51]

Norman's biographer, Roger Bowen, perhaps summed up the relationship between Norman and Reischauer best: "Both men were fundamentally liberal in outlook, i.e., they both were thoroughly decent human beings who cared deeply about the common man's lot in the midst of chaotic change."[52]

Reischauer, in his remarks in Toronto, took note of the attack on modernization theory launched by John Dower. On one hand, he welcomed the controversy: "Such an ebb and flow of scholarly interpretation is the heartbeat of healthy scholarship." But he added that in this controversy "some of the participants unfortunately made intemperate accusations against the intellectual honesty of those they were criticizing and extravagant claims were put forward about the originality of Norman's views. . . . Accusations against the honesty of scholars with whom one disagrees are an unfair and thoroughly despicable form of intellectual debate."[53]

Dower's attack on Reischauer did not go unchallenged. George Akita, a former student of Reischauer and later a professor at the University of Hawaii, wrote a detailed rebuttal in 1977.[54] In the course of preparing his article, he asked Reischauer about his relationship with Dower. Reischauer replied, "Dower was our student here, and a very good one indeed. It is a pity to see him so absorbed in such a fruitless type of endeavor." He added, "One problem with the revisionists' tendency to look for sinister plots in everything is that it takes their attention away from the real subject matter and problems of history and also wastes the time of those, who like you, bother to reply."[55]

Akita pressed for more information on Dower. Reischauer recalled that he had written three letters recommending Dower for tenured positions. In one of them, to the University of Wisconsin, he had written that "Dower is a very able, diligent and also broad scholar," but also that his introduction to Norman's writings is "a seriously flawed work. He might have consulted with some of those he was attacking in it to learn what their attitudes in fact were, because he is grossly inaccurate in much of the thrust of his argument. . . . Now having said all this, let me state quite clearly that I think Dower is basically one of the outstanding scholars in modern Japanese history of his age group. His scholarship and publishing record are both excellent and would seem to me ample justification for the promotion you have in mind. I have no hesitation in recommending it."[56]

Reischauer was surprised and annoyed that his former student had not talked with him before launching his attack, but he was not inclined to "waste his time" (as he saw it) forging a scholarly response. He knew that this new era was different from the one in which he had grown up, when historians disagreed politely in scholarly journals. The gloves were off: the new generation would take no prisoners, and this was just the beginning.

The years in which Reischauer returned to academia should have indeed been golden for him. Lecturing to hundreds of eager students every week, working with supportive colleagues to build up the field of East Asian studies at Harvard and elsewhere, and reaching out to a vast public thirsty for knowledge about the "new Japan" should have made wonderful life for him, but personal difficulties once again intervened. The main cause this time was Haru's problem in adjusting to the role of a Harvard professor's wife. After the luxury of directing a household staff in a mansion on a hill, adulation by the Japanese press and public, and meeting famous personalities from around the world, cooking three meals a day in their small home in Belmont, Massachusetts, came as something of a shock.

Haru was exhausted from the arduous task of playing many roles for over five years—Japanese lady of aristocratic upbringing and American ambassador's wife being only two of them. She had carried it off beautifully while on the stage, dealing brilliantly with the highest echelons of the Japanese government, ordinary Japanese citizens, U.S. military officers and their wives, and visiting congressmen, but playing multiple roles had taken its toll, and her emotional reserves were depleted.

Haru went into a deep depression that would stay with her intermittently for the rest of her life. As a Christian Scientist, she would not see a doctor and would not even consider taking the kind of antidepressant medicine that is so commonly used today. She withdrew into a shell and began to avoid all social engagements. Her friends at Harvard tried to get her engaged in some sort of useful enterprise. At one point, they persuaded her to take care of visiting Harvard-Yenching scholars as a kind of therapy. She found herself scrubbing the grease off stoves used by Chinese visitors to deep fry their dinners in woks. These efforts did no good.

"Ed was a romantic: he loved to dance, he loved sports and games," recalled Selma Janow, one of Haru's oldest American friends. "But Haru was distant. They had an amiable but not a romantic relationship. When they returned to Cambridge, she would pull away if Ed got within four inches of her. She couldn't go shopping by herself."[57] Haru's only pleasure seemed to be gardening around the beautiful home they built in 1967 at 863 Belmont Avenue, near a bird sanctuary and lovely woods on a sloping hillside in Belmont, Massachusetts—about twenty minutes' drive from Harvard. Sadly, their strongest bond—based on their shared project of bringing Japan and America to a better understanding of each other—had been weakened by success. Their marriage had been built upon this undertaking, and once the challenge was removed, one of its major underpinnings slipped away. Both Ed and Haru were desperately lonely, yet they could not communicate with each other.

For a brief period after their return, they were besieged with invitations to dinner parties, but both Ed and Haru found such parties tiresome, especially the long cocktail hour that usually preceded dinner. Neither of them drank liquor of any kind, and Ed found that standing around on his numb right leg making inane chit-chat with strangers was a kind of torture to be avoided. They stopped going out and almost never invited people to their home. Neither of them had close friends in whom they could confide. Ed, always a private person, had no close male friends. His children were busy with their own lives: Ann and her husband, Steve Heinemann, had moved to California with their five children and visited only in the summer. Robert and his wife, Charlotte, were forging their own lives at Columbia University, where he got his Ph.D. in economics. After conducting research in Latin America, they settled in Washington, D.C. with their two children. Joan, Reischauer's youngest child, had her own life as a student at Tufts and then in the publishing business. She would marry William Simon and start a family of her own.

The only other relatives nearby were Ed's aging father, A. K. Reischauer, who was eighty-seven in 1966 and whose mind was gradually fading, and his sister, Felicia, who lived with her father in her isolated, silent, and lonely world. This arrangement could not work for long. One day in 1967, suffering from a nervous breakdown, she attacked her father with a kitchen knife. He was able to defend himself, but Ed then had to find a separate apartment for his sister in Belmont, not far from his own home. In 1983, he moved her to a home for the elderly deaf in Los Angeles, where she died in 1987. A. K. Reischauer eventually also moved to a home for retired missionaries near Los Angeles, where he died in 1971 at the age of ninety-one.

Ed's closest friend and confidant at this time was Nancy Monteith Deptula, executive director of what in 1985 came to be called the Reischauer Institute of Japanese Studies at Harvard. She had worked as his personal assistant for many years, and her husband, George, had taught Russian to Bob Reischauer at the Browne and Nichols School.[58] Nancy and George were the only regular visitors in Belmont in the 1970s and 1980s. Only with them did Ed relax and reveal his rigidly concealed emotional distress. They would visit on Sunday afternoons for long conversations. Ed would have a football game on television and a newspaper in his lap, and he would talk sports with George. He had also studied Russian, could read it quite well, and asked George questions about various Russian authors. But his loneliness and his difficulties in reaching out to Haru came up often. When Nancy suggested consulting a psychiatrist or a clergyman, Ed dismissed the idea out of hand. His health was deteriorating rapidly in those days, and he would often talk about his own death— not in a lugubrious way, but always with regret that he would not live to find out how world events would evolve. He remained an optimist and continued to see the United Nations as an embryonic system for curbing aggression and keeping the peace.[59]

As in his unhappy earlier days when Adrienne was dying, Reischauer was able to shut himself off from the world and write a book that in many ways remains his most relevant today. During his years as ambassador and after returning home, he had often lectured about education. Now he collected and refined his thoughts and in 1973 distilled his ideas into a slim volume called *Toward the Twenty-first Century: Education for a Changing World*.[60]

The book is today, in the wake of September 11, 2001, startlingly prophetic. He warned Americans that weapons of mass destruction would be available to the poor and backward nations in the twenty-first century—not just nuclear weapons, but also biological weapons. He wrote that an observer from outer space, seeing America's huge military budgets and tiny State Department budget, might well conclude that the State Department is only a minor service organ for the military. His major point was that the advanced industrialized democracies would face disaster if they did not reform their education systems to make elementary school children understand that they were citizens of a world community, not just of a nation-state. "Education . . . is not moving rapidly enough in the right direction to produce the knowledge about the outside world and the attitudes toward other peoples that may be essential for human survival within a generation or two."

Here was the classic liberal view: more knowledge leads to better understanding and provides the groundwork for rational policies and peaceful relationships. But it was also a shrewd look into the future: weapons of mass destruction would surely spread to the poorest people on the earth, with drastic consequences for the rich nations. As in the case of his 1955 book, *Wanted: An Asian Policy*, this one quietly disappeared. "The book caused no sensation, receiving only a few tepid reviews," he noted later.[61] Nevertheless, he was invited during the 1980s to join a Harvard committee to design a new core curriculum, and he played a leading role in making sure that foreign-area and language study was a requirement for undergraduates at Harvard.

Reischauer knew that hepatitis C was incurable, and he felt his energy draining away in the 1970s. His least favorite activity was fund-raising, but Harvard was relentless in pressing him to use his famous name in Japan to gather corporate donations for its Japan Institute. He gamely made several trips to Tokyo for Harvard, calling on Keidanren (Federation of Economic Organizations) leaders and others, and eventually raised almost seven million dollars for the Harvard-Yenching Institute. But he disliked the work and was embarrassed that American corporations and foundations were unwilling to match the Japanese gifts.

In February 1975, he suffered a mild stroke that affected the frontal lobe of his brain where language and memory are stored. From this point on, he lost his ability to converse in Japanese; his speaking skill in English also suffered, but his writing ability was unimpaired, and his memory came back after a few months. Some of his finest work was still to come.

There followed a succession of brushes with death, each more serious than the previous one. In August 1980, after playing tennis in the hot sun, he again suffered massive internal bleeding and was rushed to a hospital. At this point, his diseased liver was working at only about 40 percent of capacity, unable to throw off poisons from the body. These poisons in turn caused varices—something like varicose veins—to form in the esophagus. The varices would sometimes open up, leaving a pool of blood in his stomach, and he would throw up blood in clots.[62] Though the doctors saved his life in 1980, he was left with diminished energy and weakened vocal chords that made lecturing difficult. When word of his illness leaked out, his hospital room was flooded with flowers from friends in Japan and around Harvard. He decided then that he would never have a funeral ceremony and so directed in his will. This was enough.

Reischauer turned seventy on October 15, 1980, and, following Harvard rules, headed for retirement at the end of the spring semester of 1981. His last lecture on April 22 was packed with a standing-room-only crowd of students, faculty colleagues, and television cameras from the Japanese broadcaster NHK, which showed the lecture in prime time the following month. NHK later that year resumed its filming of a five-hour biographical portrait of the Reischauers, showing them in Belmont, tracing his childhood in Japan, his student days in Europe and China, his wartime service in Washington, and his years as ambassador. His stroke had left him unable to converse in Japanese, so he was interviewed in English with subtitles added. The program was aired during the spring of 1982 and shown again that summer.

Reischauer continued to drive himself, traveling frequently to Japan. He nearly died on a visit to Tokyo in 1983. After following a brutal schedule, with 4 one-hour question-and-answer sessions with the Young Presidents Organization, he was rushed to Tokyo University Hospital when the internal bleeding started again, where he went into a coma for about ten days. After regaining consciousness, he was unable to speak for several more days. At this point, he experienced a life-changing "semi-trance," as he later called it: "I remained in a state of semi-trance, not really aware of my surroundings, and envisioning myself as sleeping on a marble couch in a Chinese palace surrounded by rivulets of clear flowing water and looking out over a broad valley lush with green rice plants. I even had a vision of floating in a stone boat down a stream a few inches deep and passing below the towers of Angkor Wat. During this vision, I actually held forth semi-consciously in an oracular sermon on world brotherhood, delivered in reasonably fluent Japanese to my bewildered nurse."[63]

This was a remarkable account from a scholar who had prided himself on his rational approach to life and to history, and who often made fun of beliefs that were based on spiritualism, faith, or superstition. From this time on, Reischauer believed that he had been "born again" with a special mission to redouble his efforts to cement the ties between the United States and Japan. He thought the end was near and told me in July 1983, "I'm seventy-two, almost seventy-three. I can't ask for a much longer life than that."[64]

The news of this brush with death was kept from the Japanese press and public. Reischauer was checked into the hospital under the name "Edo Rai." Only as he was leaving Japan did he have a brief encounter with news reporters at Narita Airport. He was touched that Ambassador Mike Mansfield and his wife, Maureen, came to see him off. Reischauer called Mansfield "incomparably prestigious and competent."[65]

For four years, I had been urging him to allow me to place his name on the new Center for East Asian Studies at the Johns Hopkins School of Advanced International Studies, arguing that his life and scholarship would inspire the next generation of students to pursue careers combining scholarship and policy-making.[66] He had steadfastly refused. "Why would I want my name on anything?" he grumbled. But soon after this mystical experience in Japan, he called me and, with a bit of embarrassment, said that if I still wanted to use his name in that way, he could approve. He told me that in his coma, he had a premonition of serious conflicts arising between the two nations and that he would do anything possible to head off this confrontation. Accordingly, in 1984, with Ed and Haru present, we launched the Edwin O. Reischauer Center for East Asian Studies. The center has attracted a stream of bright graduate students and has produced leading scholars, Japan specialists, and policymakers. One of them, Michael Green, served as top advisor on East Asia on the National Security Council from 2001 to 2004 and now holds a prestigious chair at Georgetown University.[67] Another, Timothy Geithner, now serves (2009) as secretary of the Treasury under President Barack Obama. Others are following.

In 1982, Haru persuaded Ed to buy a small home in La Jolla, California, about a mile from where Ann and Steve and their five children were living. They began to spend the cold winter months of January through March in that warm and sunny climate. Both he and Haru turned to writing their autobiographies. Ed's first draft was about nine hundred double-spaced typewritten pages. Under pressure from Robert and a harsh editor, he cut it back by about one-third. He submitted it to the Harvard University Press, which turned it down. Haru then submitted her account of her life and that of her two grandfathers, entitled *Samurai and Silk,* a manuscript on which Ed had kibitzed mercilessly on the historical sections, and Harvard's prestigious Belknap Press promptly accepted it.[68] Ed and Haru traded much good-natured bantering about this competition, but Ed was in truth stung and embarrassed. A slimmed-down version of his book, *My Life Between Japan and America*, was eventually published by Harper and Row in 1986.

I have already noted that U.S.–Japan relations entered a stormy period in the early 1970s after the "Nixon shocks." For the next two decades, Japan continued its meteoric economic growth and challenged American industry across a broad spectrum of products. In autos, electronics, semiconductors, and machine tools, Japanese products seized a growing share of the American market. In color television sets, for example, Japanese exporters virtually wiped out their American competitors. Using mercantilist tactics, Japan built up huge current account surpluses, and America ran up huge deficits, mostly attributable to its trade deficit with Japan. American exporters charged that Japanese markets were closed to their products and that they used unfair tactics to "target" U.S. industries. Trade negotiations became acrimonious. The U.S. Defense Department demanded greater contributions from Japan, which steadfastly held its defense spending to less that 1 percent, compared with about 6 percent in the United States. Japan was accused of enjoying a "free ride" at the expense of American taxpayers.

These trade frictions and alliance squabbles gradually came to a boil. Japan's image as a peaceful ally and warm friend was being transformed into that of an unfair, even sinister competitor. American auto workers destroyed a Toyota Corolla with sledge hammers in Chicago Heights, Illinois, in 1981. Reischauer watched in dismay as tensions reached a climax in 1985. This was the year of the perfect storm. It ushered in a decade in which millions of Americans came to believe that the greatest threat to their security came not from communism or terrorism, but from a Japan that sought to win by economic means what it could not win by military means in World War Two.

The U.S. global trade deficit surged from $67 billion in 1983 to $160 billion in 1987, setting off alarms in Congress and among American industries clamoring for protection. The largest trade surplus belonged to Japan. President Ronald Reagan and Prime Minister Nakasone Yasuhiro tried to ease tensions with their famous "Ron-Yasu" friendship, but it was impossible. A critical moment came when Japan, after a late start in the field, captured the leading share of the world semiconductor market from America. Vice President Walter Mondale warned in his 1984 presidential campaign that American children might be destined to grow up and find that the only jobs available were sweeping up around Japanese computers.

Treasury Secretary James Baker, in an effort to head off a clash, negotiated the Plaza Agreement in September 1985, which resulted in a dramatic appreciation of the yen and a weakening of the dollar. A tidal wave of Japanese capital swept across the world, with the Japanese buying up "trophy properties" such as Rockefeller Center in New York and the Pebble Beach Golf Course in California. Matsushita acquired MCA, and Sony acquired Columbia Pictures. In their inflammatory book *Selling Our Security,* Martin and Susan Tolchin warned that Americans were selling their "national security" to the Japanese.[69]

Several other factors contributed to the perfect storm in 1985. This was the year in which Mikhail Gorbachev began to push glasnost and perestroika, the first steps in ending the Cold War four years later. The Soviet Union no longer seemed the "evil empire" that President Reagan had branded it. America's military-industrial complex needed a new enemy; Japan made a perfect target. The idea of America's decline also began to permeate the academic world: Professor Paul Kennedy of Yale set the tone in *The Rise and Fall of the Great*

After his retirement from Harvard, Edwin and Haru lived in their home in Belmont, Massachusetts, surrounded by the garden they loved and a bird sanctuary. Here, in August 1984, they are photographed for the publication that would announce the establishment of the Edwin O. Reischauer Center for East Asian Studies at Johns Hopkins University. Photograph by the author.

Powers in which he praised the "Japanese miracle" and suggested that "the American Century" touted by Henry Luce in *Life* magazine in 1941 might have ended prematurely.[70]

The American media, in its most shameful period since William Randolph Hearst's yellow journalism fanned the flames of nationalism leading up to the Spanish-American War, now piled on. On July 28, 1985, the *New York Times Sunday Magazine* proclaimed in large print on its cover, with a rising sun in the background: "Today, forty years after the end of World War II, the Japanese are on the move again in one of history's most brilliant commercial offensives, as they go about dismantling American industry. Whether they are still only smart, or have finally learned to be wiser than we, will be tested in the next ten years. Only then will we know who finally won the war."[71]

The article's author, Theodore "Teddy" White, at seventy, was a kind of role model and guru for American journalists. His highly successful "up-close and personal" coverage of U.S. presidential elections since John F. Kennedy's victory in 1960 had made him a hero to many younger reporters. White had studied Chinese history and language at Harvard under John Fairbank before traveling to China as *Time* magazine's correspondent. He witnessed some of the appalling atrocities committed by the Japanese army at Nanjing and covered the Sino–Japanese fighting right up to Japan's surrender on the battleship *Missouri* on September 2, 1945. Of that event, he wrote in 1985, "I bristled at the sight of [the Japanese leaders]. I had seen the Japanese blast and flame Chungqing, the city I had lived in years before, then bring their planes down to machine-gun people in the streets. Japanese had shot at me, I had fired at them, and so the luxury of this moment was one I enjoyed."

Evoking wartime imagery, White painted a picture of a Japan that had not changed since Pearl Harbor. He described Japanese history in lurid terms: "infanticide, savage civil wars, coiled aggressions, superb adapters, government-industry partnership, tangled bureaucracy, unfair trading, and aggressive." He planted the seeds that would sprout in hundreds of books and articles over the next decade. He ended with a dire threat: "The superlative execution of their trade tactics may provoke an incalculable reaction—as the Japanese might well remember of the course that ran from Pearl Harbor to the deck of the U.S.S. Missouri in Tokyo Bay just 40 years ago."

White died the following year, but his ideas resonated in Congress as well as in the bureaucracy, media, and academic worlds. The point was not that these ideas were original—many had surfaced earlier—but that they were written by so prestigious a journalist and featured so prominently in America's most authoritative newspaper and that they evoked the deeply embedded prejudices against the Japanese from the 1930s and World War Two. Old embers of racism were being fanned into flames.

White was not all wrong: Japan had indeed used protectionist and aggressive trade practices, had kept its markets mostly closed, and had used nontariff barriers to block imports of American products. But the portrait he painted was a caricature: his Japan was a one-dimensional, sinister, vengeful, and aggressive threat to America. Nowhere did he mention successful occupation reforms: parliamentary democracy, the rule of law, the peace constitution, political parties, freedom of speech, elections, a constitutional monarchy with a humanized emperor, labor unions, women's rights, social welfare, land reform, and the other profound changes after 1945. In effect, White signaled that Japan had not changed since the 1930s, was still the implacable enemy seeking revenge, and was now fair game. And he brought back the idea of "the Japanese" to denote a people marching in lockstep—a single undifferentiated horde of Orientals—reminiscent of the "Yellow Peril" threats of the early 1900s.

With the floodgates open, a host of critics calling themselves "revisionists" surged out. In 1982, Chalmers Johnson, in a useful new study of Japan's commercial policies and practices, had described how the bureaucrats of the Ministry of International Trade and Industry (MITI) were directly descended from and operating in the same manner as the prewar Ministry of Commerce and Industry (later, in 1943, the Ministry of Munitions). He argued that Japan was not like other Western democracies; it was a "capitalist development state," a latecomer that used central planning to catch up with Western rivals.

Johnson's analysis stood Reischauer's approach on its head. Reischauer argued that the better one knew Japan, the more one could appreciate its society and civilization and its commonalities with the West. Johnson argued that to truly know Japan was to understand how differently it behaved and why the United States needed to defend itself against this threat. The Japanese were not "like us." At one point, Johnson even suggested that the United States needed to establish a "DITI"—department of international trade and industry—to take on MITI. He famously declared that the Cold War was over and that the Japanese had won. And he endorsed the view that "Japan is the only communist nation that works."[72]

In the late 1980s, a frenzy of critics of Japan now took up this theme. Clyde Prestowitz, a former Commerce Department official, argued in his book *Trading Places* that Japan was an industrial giant that was using trickery to grab the lead in the semiconductor market.[73] Japan was different, threatening, and undemocratic. His Economic Policy Institute was funded in part by labor unions and in part by Roger Milliken, a conservative southern textile manufacturer.[74] Prestowitz singlehandedly caused the renegotiation of a 1988 agreement on the division of labor in producing the FSX model of Japan's new fighter plane, arguing in January 1989 that the United States was giving away vital military technology to a potential enemy.

Tension mounted in Washington. In 1986, Japan agreed to limit its sales of semiconductors in the United States, but the United States claimed in 1987 that Japan had violated the agreement and slapped sanctions on its imports. In 1987, Congresswoman Helen Delich Bentley, Republican of Maryland, and several others pounded on a Toshiba radio with sledgehammers before a battery of TV cameras to protest the Toshiba Corporation's violation of a ban on exports of high-tech machinery to the Soviet Union.

In 1989, Morita Akio, one of the founders of Sony Corporation, and Ishihara Shintaro, the current governor of Tokyo, published *The Japan That Can Say No: Why Japan Will Be First Among Equals*, an inflammatory book in Japanese that, among other things, called for Japan to withhold its semiconductors from the Pentagon and sell them instead to the Russians. An English-language version soon hit the market.[75] Military and intelligence officials began to speak ominously of Japan as the next threat to the United States. Douglas Paal, a respected Republican Asian expert on the National Security Council famously remarked in 1986, "In order for a young man to get ahead in government today, he must first show utter contempt for the Japanese."

Newspapers and weekly magazines rushed into print with portrayals of Japan as an ominous threat. Even the respected *New York Times* joined in the scare mongering. Under the headline "Big Japanese Gain in Computers Seen," a page 1 story in February 1984 warned grimly that "the Japanese have forged ahead in a heated international race for sophisticated supercomputers by creating machines that are more flexible, easier to use and aimed at a wider market than the specialized computers manufactured in the United States."[76]

The covers of *Time*, *Newsweek*, *Business Week*, and *U.S. News* featured drawings of huge samurai wrestlers towering over a tiny Uncle Sam. A *Wall Street Journal* reporter in Tokyo, Jacob Schlesinger, told me that his editors tended to turn down any story that did not reinforce the image of Japan as a threat to U.S. security.

Popular novelists such as Tom Clancy quickly jumped on the bandwagon with racist themes.[77] Michael Crichton, acknowledging his debt to the "revisionists," wrote *Rising Sun* in 1992. A lurid and xenophobic novel that became a popular movie, it depicted an abject America where blonde women are forced to cater to the sexual perversions of Japanese males, American politicians sell themselves to Japanese corporations, and American workers lose their jobs because of high technology introduced by Japanese bent on economic enslavement of Americans. In an afterword, he wrote: "And the Japanese have invented a new kind of trade—adversarial trade, trade like war, trade intended to wipe out the competition—which America has failed to understand for several decades. The United States keeps insisting the Japanese do things our way. But increasingly, their response is to ask, why should *we* change? We're doing better than you are. And indeed they are."[78]

In this climate, Japan was fair game everywhere. Prime Minister Edith Cresson of France described the Japanese as ants imbued with a single-minded devotion to vanquish the Western world. "They sit up all night thinking of ways to screw the Americans and the Europeans. They are our common enemy."[79]

Even writers for allegedly "thoughtful" monthly magazines joined the fray. One of the most superficial among them was James Fallows, a Harvard graduate who had spent several years in Asia, including Japan. Passing himself off as an expert, though he could neither speak nor read Japanese, Fallows argued that there was a basic and irreconcilable conflict between Japanese and American interests, that Japan was not likely to change, and that the United States needed to "contain Japan" as it had contained the Soviet Union during the Cold War. Indulging in the worst kind of racism, he quoted approvingly from the work of an obscure German expatriate, Kurt Singer, who lived in Japan during the 1930s: "'The Japanese . . . are peculiarly sensitive to the smell of decay, however well screened, and they will strike at any enemy whose core appears to betray a lack of firmness.'" He concluded, "Unless Japan is contained, therefore, several things that matter to America will be jeopardized: America's own authority to carry out its foreign policy and advance its ideals, American citizens' future prospects within the world's most powerful business firms, and also the very system of free trade that America has helped sustain since the Second World War. But we do have the right to defend our interests and our values, and they are not identical to Japan's."[80]

It was a measure of American ignorance of Japan and the hysteria about Japan in Washington that a monthly magazine of this quality and reputation, the *Atlantic Monthly*, could allow a journalist of such limited qualifications to be its authority on Japan. It is unimaginable that a writer who could not speak or read French or German would be allowed to pontificate on French or German affairs.

But Fallows was not finished. With breathtaking arrogance, he trashed the entire field of American Japan specialists—the field that Reischauer had worked so hard to build up—as belonging to one of four categories:

- Political-military types whose only motive was "Don't rock the boat" and who tried to stifle complaints about the Japanese trade surplus in order to preserve a strong military alliance
- Pure free traders who failed to recognize that Japan played by different rules
- Lobbyists in Washington on the Japanese payroll
- "Japan handlers," for whom Fallows reserved special contempt: "As a general rule, people who have invested years in learning the language and living in Japan quite understandably begin to see things Japan's way."[81]

Here, in a nutshell, was a new, repackaged version of McCarthyism. The idea was that a loyal American who applied himself or herself to learning a foreign language and culture must be somehow tainted by that experience, guilty of divided loyalty, and somehow less American than those innocent souls who remained free of the taint of any foreign-language skills. Senator Joseph McCarthy in the early 1950s destroyed a generation of patriotic American Foreign Service officers who had studied Chinese. Fallows was drawing on one of the most deep-seated prejudices of isolationist America that continues to this day (as could be seen when Senator John F. Kerry was accused during the 2004 presidential elections of knowing how to speak French, as if this were a disqualification for the presidency). He charged that the Japan specialists in the U.S. Foreign Service "have particularly compelling reasons to feel protective of Japan."[82] Nowhere did he recognize the good work of dozens of loyal Americans (some of whom were trained by Reischauer) who made the effort to learn Japanese but remained totally loyal to their country. Oddly enough, few voices rose to challenge Fallows publicly.[83]

That the mainstream media rushed like lemmings to attack Japan is not surprising, given the heated trade battles that were being waged in Congress, the powerful U.S. trade groups, and lobbyists in whose interest it was to demonize Japan, and given Japanese leaders' failure to understand the pain they were inflicting on many American industries. What is surprising, from a perspective two decades later, is the persistence in America of its historic sense of moral superiority over Asians. If Americans were buying Toyotas instead of Fords, the wicked and devious Japanese must be cheating. If Japan continued to prosper, it would become a threat to U.S. security. It seemed that all of the work of Reischauer and other scholars and writers to educate the American public about Japan had been a waste of time. The Japan specialists understood that Japan had no strategic planning, no wicked scheme to threaten U.S. security and to dominate the Asia-Pacific region. In fact, thoughtful Japanese leaders understood that their security depended on a strong alliance with America.

The most absurd of the "revisionists" was a previously obscure Dutch journalist in Japan named Karel von Wolferen, who published *The Enigma of Japanese Power* in 1989.[84] In it, he projected a Japan that was an export machine that was dangerously out of control. No one stood at the helm. There was no center of political accountability; the juggernaut had no brakes. Only he understood how this enigmatic system worked. And it was dangerous. If left to its current course, it would overwhelm the United States. When Van Wolferen did a book tour of the United States in 1990, he won respectful, even awed, silence from such audiences as the Council on Foreign Relations.

Also in 1990, Pat Choate, a well-known trade protectionist who would become Ross Perot's running mate in the presidential election of 1992, came out with *Agents of Influence*, in which he charged that Japanese influence had penetrated and corrupted all aspects of American political life—that Japanese money was buying influence and determining the outcome of the decision-making process in Washington.[85] Perot and Choate won 19 percent of the popular vote in 1992, thus helping Bill Clinton (43 percent) to defeat George H. W. Bush (38 percent). Clinton came into office in 1993 surrounded by advisors who were strongly influenced by the revisionists.

The reductio ad absurdum of this feeding frenzy came in 1991 with the publication of *The Coming War with Japan* by George Friedman, a political scientist from Dickinson College, PA, and Meredith Lebard, a poet from Australia with no knowledge of Japan. Neither author had been to Japan before they went there to sell the book. In a perfect irony, the frontispiece has a 1953 quote from Reischauer. James Fallows praised the book for demonstrating "with surprising thoroughness" why the interests of the United States and Japan would diverge more and more, leading to open rivalry.[86]

So feverish was the anti-Japanese feeling in Washington in 1990 that many feared that a new wave of McCarthyism would sweep across the political landscape, with Japan experts being hounded out of government as China experts had been harassed in the 1950s. In 1991, John Creighton Campbell, a respected professor at Michigan University, wrote the article "Japan Bashing: A New McCarthyism?" in which he noted the similarities between American attitudes toward Japan with those toward the Soviet Union three or four decades earlier.[87] Alan Murray, the *Wall Street Journal*'s Washington Bureau chief at the time, was convinced that a new wave of McCarthyism was sweeping the capital and that it was halted only by the bursting of Japan's economic bubble in 1990–91 and by Saddam Hussein's invasion of Kuwait in the summer of 1990.[88]

Ed Reischauer was at first amused by the revisionists. He found some merit in the scholarship of Chalmers Johnson's book on MITI, but thought the others were simply opportunistic journalists taking advantage of the trade frictions. When his friends urged him to respond, he would laugh and say that they were a passing phenomenon and would soon go away. Why take them seriously? He never wavered in his confidence that Japan would continue to adapt its trade policies to meet its new international challenges. He believed that "not knowing history can be dangerous, but knowing it inaccurately can be worse."[89] He was sure that Japanese leaders would wake up to the danger of a new wave of world protectionism if they continued to flood American and other markets with their exports and that they would not risk their alliance with America over trade disputes. He took every opportunity privately to warn his Japanese friends that they were close to provoking a tsunami of nationalism in America that could come crashing down on them.

But he did on a few occasions reveal his frustration. In a letter congratulating Professor Yoshi Tsurumi at Baruch College for opposing the revisionists, he said:

> I am delighted to see you bringing the "revisionists" up short. Their primary error, I feel, is their assumption that the Japan they came to know in the 1960s is the permanent Japan and it is incapable of change. Any broader focus will show at once that Japan has been changing rapidly ever since the Bakumatsu Period at least and that no country has changed more successfully in the past century and a half.
>
> There is evidence of its rapid continuing change and adaptation almost daily in the newspapers. How can the "revisionists" be so blind? More power to you in your battle with them.[90]

In a 1986 interview with Japanese editors, he advised Japanese leaders to pay more attention to Americans' feelings in their own interest. "They should be more willing to compromise with the U.S. and give up some of their advantages. It's not wise to give up things only with great reluctance." He thought that the American people believed Japan produced better and cheaper products, and that they were generally friendly toward Japan, that it was just the special interest groups that generated the emotion. "I think Japan's most important problem, more than a lack of natural resources, is the ability to be in real communication with the outside world, to have leaders that can have that kind of understanding."[91]

As the revisionists came to dominate the American media in 1989, however, he decided to rouse himself to rebut their claims. A chance came on October 2, 1989, when Karel Van Wolferen came to Harvard to push his book on the Harvard campus radio station. Reischauer was in the last year of his life. His voice was reedy and thin, his vocabulary diminished by a stroke, and his balance poor, but his mind remained sharp. The moderator this day was a kindly clergyman, Reverend Herbert F. Vetter, who could not have known what he was getting into. The dialogue was recorded for airing later that day.[92] It is the only record of a direct face-off between Reischauer and one of his critics. It was clear early on that Reischauer was loaded for bear.

Van Wolferen began with a summary of the main points in his book *The Enigma of Japanese Power*. It was, he said, a book about how power is exercised in Japan. The book argued that there was no center of power, no check on the system. Reischauer said he thought that it was much healthier for Japan to have no clear center of power rather than the more centralized system that had previously pushed the nation into wars.

Van Wolferen countered that "there being no center of accountability is a central problem," and for this reason, "I believe that a collision between the United States and Japan is all but inevitable." Reischauer said that the Diet was in fact the center of power in Japan. Van Wolferen replied that the Diet was essentially a rubber stamp on most issues. This comment set off fireworks.

REISCHAUER: That's not true at all, because there are many things that the members of parliament would like to have voted in the last forty years that they just did not dare to vote because the people would not go along with . . .

VAN WOLFEREN: (interrupting) Of course I am aware of them, and I have mentioned them in the book . . .

BOTH TALK AT THE SAME TIME

REISCHAUER: The voter has really the final judgment as to what can be done and what cannot be done.

Van Wolferen argued that there was little political input into the administration of Japan, that a "powerful economic machine" ran the country.

The moderator then lost control as the two began to shout.

REISCHAUER: Japan changes a great deal more that you seem to realize.

VAN WOLFEREN: No, I have my nose right on top of it, and I can tell you that . . .

REISCHAUER: That's the trouble . . . your nose is right on top of it, and you don't see anything. You should move your nose a little bit further away and take a look at what you . . . (drowned out)

Van Wolferen said that the voter in Japan didn't count, that there was no public debate. Reischauer then turned to his favorite theme: "The common people of Japan have a very clear idea of what they want, what kind of society they want." Van Wolferen interrupted: "No, I don't think they are given the conceptual tools to choose differently." Reischauer replied, "Oh yes they are."

At this point, a voice from the control booth warned them not to speak at the same time. Van Wolferen then went into a long explanation of how Japan's financial administrators would gain control over the international financing system. "Already they are close to doing so."

Reischauer countered that the Japanese were not stupid, that they would realize that a clash with the West would be a catastrophe, that they were vulnerable and would have learned from past missteps.

Van Wolferen cut him off, shouting, "Look, let's cut it short because this is getting nowhere. . . . You don't understand the seriousness of this problem." Reischauer, now angry, said, "No, you keep quiet," but was drowned out. He resumed: "There are Japanese leaders who were perfectly aware of this problem and worry about it a great deal."

VAN WOLFEREN: (shouting) Can I say something about my book? Listen, I came here to talk about my book. . . . I am very upset. This is a serious problem. You are not addressing the problem.

REISCHAUER: If you don't want to talk about anything but your book, I can leave the room at this point . . .

VAN WOLFEREN: I'm sorry, I'm sorry, this is what I said to you this morning. This is a very serious problem.

REISCHAUER: You aren't being very reasonable about this sort of thing and . . .

VAN WOLFEREN: Give me two minutes to respond to you.

REISCHAUER: I gave you a very long time.

VAN WOLFEREN: You don't stop, because you are talking about how wonderful Japanese leaders are . . .

REISCHAUER: I didn't say they were wonderful . . .

VAN WOLFEREN: (shouting) We're not getting anywhere. I don't want to . . . Please, I tear this thing. . . . [Vetter later said it was the consent form permitting broadcast of the dialogue.] [Sound of ripping paper.]

I don't want this to be broadcast. . . . I cannot do this. I'm sorry, Professor Reischauer, we are not addressing the same problem. I'm sorry.

REISCHAUER: What's the matter with you?

VAN WOLFEREN: I'm sorry, I don't want this. I am talking about a very serious problem; you're talking about something else.

REISCHAUER: I'm talking about a serious problem too.

VAN WOLFEREN: No, you're not. You give me an opportunity to explain, but you go on and on. And you don't give me an opportunity to explain why you are wrong. Because that's the essence of my book. . . .

As Van Wolferen got up to leave the room, he said, "The whole point is that, of course on a private level, these officials are concerned. The point is that the system does not allow this concern to be translated into political action." When Reischauer asked, "How do you know . . . ," Van Wolferen left the room, shouting, "Because I know the system!" The tape ends here. It never aired. Reischauer was well pleased with his morning's work.

11 Nearing the River's Mouth

"Long ago the best and dearest Japanese friend said to me a little before his death: 'When you find in four or five more years that you cannot understand the Japanese at all, then you will begin to know something about them.' After having discovered that I cannot understand the Japanese at all, I feel better qualified to attempt this essay."[1]

These words from Lafcadio Hearn's 1904 book *Japan: An Attempt at Interpretation* captured the essence of popular American feelings toward Japan then and through much of the twentieth century. Lafcadio Hearn, an American journalist, lived in Japan from 1890 to 1904, became a Japanese citizen (taking the name Koizumi Yakumo), married the daughter of a samurai, and taught English literature at Tokyo University. His depiction of a mysterious, unknowable people gave many Westerners their first image of the Japanese.

Edwin Reischauer made it his life's work to correct this portrayal and to present the Japanese as real human beings sharing a common humanity with the peoples of the West. His goal was to cut through the barriers of language, culture, and history that made Japan seem inaccessible. In many ways, he succeeded.

The challenge was immense. Starting in the late nineteenth century, a few Japanese and American observers introduced singular aspects of Japanese culture to Americans: the samurai tradition, the tea ceremony, Zen Buddhism, flower arranging, and architecture.[2] But these introductions offered at best fleeting and partial portraits of a people who still seemed exotic, distant, alien, and unknowable. George Sansom, the English diplomat and historian, made a breakthrough in 1931 with his book *Japan: A Short Cultural History*,[3] treating his subject with scholarly research and respect. But Hearn's contention that no foreigner could understand the Japanese, a conceit often cultivated by the Japanese themselves, still permeated American attitudes through World War Two and has even persisted in some quarters until recently. Mike Mansfield, America's great ambassador to Tokyo (1977–88), used to tell American graduate students of Japan, "Don't even try to learn the language; it can't be done."

The images of Japan at war in the 1930s and 1940s further blocked any effort to offer a balanced account of the nation's history and culture. Most Americans saw the Japanese people through the prism of wartime propaganda: they were portrayed as emperor-worshipping, treacherous, fanatical, subhuman robots. Such portrayals were not due purely to racism. China, an Asian culture at least as different from America as Japan, became a subject for sympathetic treatment by Western scholars such as Joseph Needham, the British scientist, in the 1940s.[4] Many Americans came to admire China and to like what little they knew about the Chinese people. Japan's problem was that it had posed a threat to America's imperial ambitions in East Asia, and it had to be demonized. The ugly wartime images of the entire Japanese people die hard and too often come roaring back in times of tension, as they did in the 1980s. Even today, the Japanese attack on Pearl Harbor on December 7, 1941, is a defining image of the Japanese for many Americans old enough to remember that day.

It was not until Reischauer published his pathbreaking *Japan: Past and Present* in 1946, placing that nation in historical context and comparing it with Western nations, that Americans began to have access to "the dark side of the moon." Reischauer took dead aim at the notion that the Japanese were a race apart. His task, of course, was made easier because, in defeat, Japan was no longer seen as threatening; it was in fact available as never before to American scholars and journalists, not to mention to thousands of occupying American GIs who were surprised by the friendliness they encountered. But Reischauer had a larger vision. In the footsteps and with the zeal of his missionary parents, he felt it was his duty to educate the American people more deeply about the true nature of Japanese history, society, and culture. Other scholars and journalists would no doubt have risen to this challenge, but it is hard to imagine anyone offering the kind of masterly, sweeping, and authoritative account that Reischauer provided for students and scholars as well as general readers. One has only to imagine what the field of Japanese studies would look like today had he shrunk from the task.

He had a strategy. First, he established himself as a scholar of impeccable credentials with his work on Ennin and study of classical Chinese, with which he gained a tenured position at Harvard. Next, with John K. Fairbank, he persuaded Harvard to establish what was then the entirely new field of East Asian studies.

Their Rice Paddies course attracted and launched the training of many scholars who would go on to teach and write in the field. He seeded the field with his own graduate students. Many of today's leading Japan scholars in America were students of his students. Through his writing on Japan's history and culture, he established a core narrative that would give future scholars a sound launching pad for further study.

As ambassador, he helped end the "occupation mentality" and move the two nations toward an "equal partnership." He took steps to mitigate the military domination of the alliance and to stress the alliance's cultural, economic, and political importance. Finally, in his later years, he used his prominence to reach out to broad segments of the public both in Japan and in America through lectures across the country, articles in popular magazines, book reviews, media interviews, and especially through his own highly regarded book *The Japanese.*

He was unique in his ability to engage in serious scholarship at Harvard, but also to reach out to a larger public. Few university intellectuals in America are willing to write for the popular media, such as the *Reader's Digest*. They feel it is beneath their dignity and that it might stand in the way of career advancement. Reischauer, however, was a born communicator with a knack for speaking simply and without condescension to ordinary Americans.

He zealously tried to respond quickly to all mail from the public. An interesting question about his objectivity as an historian came in a letter from a Californian who had read his books. Quoting Isaiah Berlin, who wrote that "the individual who plays a part in historical events never understands their significance," the writer asked, "Since [as ambassador to Japan] you were involved in the actual making of history, would you say this involvement is an attribute or a detriment to the historical writer?" In his reply, Reischauer called Berlin's assertion an "obviously artistic exaggeration." He continued, "Since I have been studying U.S.-Japan relations from an academic and historical point of view for a long time, I don't think that I suddenly lost all perspective as soon as I became personally involved—though the dangers of distorted perception or myopia naturally do increase when one gets involved directly."[5]

He never lost his optimism about Japan's future, and he saw no threats to the health of its parliamentary democracy. "Japanese democracy was not made in the U.S. or in England but in Japan," he wrote in 1967. "If democracy is to succeed elsewhere in Asia, it must be homegrown too." He knew that his critics found him far too optimistic:

> I was much more optimistic about Japan's political future than were almost all the other contemporary scholars and popular writers. I based

> my optimism on Japan's spontaneous growth toward democracy in the years before 1931, and, while I viewed Japan's economic future with deep concern, I was less pessimistic than most. Almost all of the criticism of my writing singled out what was considered my excessive optimism, but each time I came to revise one of my books, I found that I had to make my predictions much more optimistic than before. One can guess how wrong my critics were, but I have discovered that pessimism somehow is regarded as being more scholarly than optimism.[6]

But he was far from being a congenital optimist and in fact worried about the rest of the world: the North–South division between rich and poor nations, the population explosion, and the control of weapons of mass destruction by poor and backward nations in the twenty-first century. The prospects were "very very grim," he told Jim Thomson.[7]

Reischauer died on September 1, 1990, just short of his eightieth birthday, without finding out how or whether the mounting frictions between the United States and Japan would be resolved. Japan's "bubble economy" was only just beginning to burst, and he could not have anticipated the "lost decade" that would result. His final months were spent in La Jolla, California, where he and Haru were surrounded by children and grandchildren, and where he was visited occasionally by his former students, journalists, and friends. Despite his failing health, these days were happy for him. He was reconciled with his children. His work as a lecturer and as a member of several boards made him financially secure for the first time in his life.[8] He never wavered in his confidence that his teaching and writing were sound and accurate and would be vindicated by events. Nor did he lose his faith in the "common man" in Japan.

In the days before his death, however, he was surprised and saddened by the apparent success of the "revisionists," who once again portrayed Japan as hostile, threatening, enigmatic, and unknowable. He knew that a Harris poll in July 1990 showed that 68 percent of Americans viewed the economic threat from Japan as a more serious threat to the future of the United States than the military threat from the Soviet Union.[9] The revisionists had for the moment gained the upper hand in the media.

My last talk with him was at his home in La Jolla in May 1990, just three months before he died. He was unsteady on his feet and suffered from fatigue, but he remained feisty and optimistic. When I asked about the revisionists' attacks on him, he said, "Why can't they understand that Japan can change?" I asked him if there were one or two books that he would still like to write, and he said without hesitation that there were two. The first would be a general history of the world based on the idea that progress results from technological advances combined with cultural receptivity to change. The second would be an account of the influence of Japanese culture on life in America.

Reischauer knew that the end was near during the summer of 1990. Taken to the hospital on August 25, he asked that no heroic measures be taken to prolong his life. The chronic viral hepatitis C had caused cirrhosis of the liver and then hepatocellular carcinoma, or primary liver cancer. There was no cure except possibly a liver transplant, but his age and weakened condition ruled out this option. At the end, he was being fed through a tube, and on August 31 he asked that the tube be removed. He died peacefully on September 1, 1990, at the Scripps Clinic in La Jolla.[10]

We can imagine his thoughts in those final days. In 1986, he had written: "My droplet of life, falling where it did, has had a long, sometimes tumultuous, sometimes placid flow, but always in the mainstream of world events. Its whole course has been interesting and rewarding. Now it slows as it nears the river's mouth and prepares, in the Buddhist metaphor, to merge in the great sea of infinity. My only regret is that of the historian. I am not satisfied with my moment in history but am consumed by a desire to see how everything turns out."[11]

The river metaphor likely arose from his study of Buddhism. We can assume he was familiar with his father's words, written in 1917: "The effort of man to make provision for his soul in a future life is of all efforts the most vain. It is as if a rain-drop sought to retain within itself the rainbow colors caused by the rays of the sun falling on it for a moment or two. The rain-drop inevitably falls to the ground and then, united with others, it flows down the stream and into the ocean, there to be lost in the eternal depths of Oneness; and what has become of the drop or the rainbow colors it hoped to treasure up for all eternity?" He added: "[Buddhism] teaches that all rivers finally flow into the ocean. However dirty, or crooked, or sluggish the stream may be, it reaches the ocean at last and in its depth all waters are purified."[12]

Reischauer, in his text for the Rice Paddies course, explained the Buddhist concept of Nirvana this way: "Although literally meaning 'emptiness,' Nirvana was felt to be not simply extinction but something more like the peaceful merging of a drop of water in the sea."[13]

Reischauer wanted no funeral, no flowers, and no religious ceremony of any sort. In accordance with his wishes, his family gathered on a hill near the Pacific Ocean and watched as a small plane circled over them, dipped its wings, and then scattered his ashes on the blue water that connected the two lands that he loved.

Did he think of his life as tragic or ill fated, given that his sister was born deaf, mute, and intellectually challenged; that his brother was killed by a stray bomb at the age of thirty; that the two countries he loved fought each other in a bloody war; that his mother, often an invalid, had to abandon him in his early years and later suffered from nervous breakdowns; that his first wife, whom he adored, died at age forty-three, leaving him to raise three teenage children; that he was stabbed and nearly killed by a Japanese youth and died a lingering and painful death from the resulting blood transfusions; and that in his final days he was savagely attacked by younger scholars in the field he had helped to create? Not in the least, his children aver. "On balance, my father had a good life, and he thought so," said his older daughter, Ann.[14] Reischauer spent very little time feeling sorry for himself.

Every major Japanese newspaper featured an affectionate obituary, often on page one. Even a small, local paper, *Shinano Mainichi*, ran a large page one feature under the headline: "Dr. Reischauer Dies with Dignity While Remembering Japan in a Hospital That Looks Out Over the Pacific Ocean; According to Haru Fujin."[15] Several papers called him an "Edokko Taishi"—a colloquial expression meaning a "Born in Tokyo Ambassador." *Yomiuri*'s headline said simply: "We Have Lost a Precious Man of Understanding." The headline in *Mainichi Shimbun* stated: "Former Ambassador Reischauer Dies; He Gave His All for Postwar U.S.–Japan Friendship."[16] *Asahi's* popular page-one column "Tensei Jingo" (Vox Populi, Vox Dei) said, "Many Japanese felt about him as if he were a personal friend, and repeated the words he spoke after nearly dying from a stab wound in 1964: 'I was born and grew up in Japan, and now that I have received Japanese blood, I finally feel I have become half Japanese.'"[17]

Back at Harvard on October 19, 1990, a memorial service was held, with Benjamin Schwartz, McGeorge Bundy, Marius Jansen, Albert Craig, Nancy Deptula, and John Fairbank offering moving tributes. Fairbank remembered first meeting Reischauer in 1938 and calling him "Eddie," not "Ed." "His openness and enthusiasm, his quickness of wit and athletic physique naturally made him an Eddie. To call him Ed would not have done justice to his youthful qualities. . . . His very American personality and lifestyle were combined with a linguistic competence that would always be envied by his colleagues. The fact was that he was a very able man even though he didn't spend much time thinking so."[18]

Schwartz, noting that the United States and Japan were "inextricably entangled with each other in ways which exacerbate hostilities," declared: "Many long for the days when we [Japanese and Americans] could ignore each other. In this atmosphere, the strident voices of the terrible simplifiers and cultural chauvinists on all sides win ever more credibility. In this cacophony, the voice of Ed Reischauer will sorely be missed."

Marius Jansen said: "To the larger public he became identified with Japan to an altogether remarkable degree. Only George Kennan, I think, comes to mind as someone so automatically the source for interviews, explanation, and counsel. Ed did this not as a surrogate for Japan, but as the independent clear-eyed critic he had always been. He helped to keep matters in perspective while radiating the same optimism, and speaking the same common sense, to both societies. We have lost him much too soon."

The Harvard Faculty of Arts and Sciences adopted a "memorial minute" for Reischauer a year later, praising his "sharpness of intellect, integrity, kindness and freedom from pretense," and recalling him as a "sparkling speaker—rapid-fire, intense, demonstrative, and humorous. Even when lecturing on basic history, he conveyed the same excitement of intellectual discovery that is found in his many books."[19]

Reischauer would be the first to say that it is too soon to judge whether he was right on the issues or not; in a century or so, perhaps, firm judgments can be made. A brief review nearly two decades after his death can indicate, however, that his achievements as a scholar, policymaker, and teacher were extraordinary. In four major respects so far, he has been vindicated by events.

First, he believed even during the darkest days of World War Two that the Japanese people, once liberated from their military oppressors, would be fully capable of managing a constitutional democracy, according to his definition: "A modern democracy is a non-limited democracy which has grown to involve the whole adult population of a nation in meaningful participation in the choice of leadership and policy decisions through elections and parliamentary government."[20]

Japan is today, by any standard, a healthy democracy. Richard Samuels, a leading American scholar on contemporary Japan, wrote in 2007: "First, Japan is a robust democracy, and democracies tend to self-correct for policy excesses. Although much maligned by analysts and participants alike, the Japanese political process has never been more transparent and has never engaged the public more fully than it does today."[21]

Democracy in Japan is arguably working better in some ways than it is in America. Political campaigns are short; voting turnouts are higher; the role of money, although substantial, is less prominent; paid political television advertising is strictly regulated.[22] Lifetime wage disparity between the rich and poor is much lower in Japan than in America. Although Japan's education system has been much criticized for failing to nourish creative and original thinking, it is worth noting that in a recent poll, 78 percent of Japanese accepted the theory of evolution compared with 40 percent of Americans.[23] There is no group or organization in Japan that has a serious chance to overthrow the system.

A cottage industry of critics, both Japanese and foreign, disagrees. They charge that Japan's democracy is dysfunctional: either weak or paralyzed. They point to the long period of single-party dominance, frequent changes of weak prime ministers that have led to paralysis in the making of foreign policy, and the heavy hand and corruption of entrenched bureaucrats. They cite the persistent efforts of hard-core nationalists to whitewash Japan's wartime atrocities. They are critical of Japan's inability to recover from the "lost decade" that followed the bursting of the economic bubble in 1990.They blame an "iron triangle" of big business, bureaucracy, and politicians that seems to make the major decisions. They point to the self-censorship in the major media outlets and forced confessions by police. They cite Japan's aging population and negative birth rate to paint a picture of a nation in trouble. All of these criticisms have some basis in fact. But it is also true that Japan, which is wide open to researchers and in which there are few or no secrets, receives harsher scrutiny from its scholarly and media critics at home and abroad than does China or many other countries. And there are always Japanese pundits who enjoy latching on to and accelerating the most dire predictions for their country.

Defenders of Japan's democracy argue that the Japanese people prefer weak government to the strong governments they had at most other times in their recent history. Were Reischauer alive today, he would ask: Do ordinary voters have the power to change policies, elect new leaders, and safeguard their own interests? He would cite the dramatic victory of the Democratic Party of Japan in August 2009 as evidence of the beginnings of a two-party system that would strengthen Japan' democracy. Reischauer would argue that the problems of Japanese democracy can and will be solved by more democracy. And he would ask, "Compared to what?" Where is this ideal democracy that Japan is being compared to?

First, Reischauer was convinced that Japan's urban population would gain strength at the expense of the agricultural sector, leading in time to a realigned two-party system. It was absurd and unsound to protect the farmers on grounds of national security in the modern world of free trade and freedom of the seas, he argued. But he defended the reluctance of Japan's corporations to fire tens of thousands of employees in times of recession, as is the practice in America. The social compact that emerged after World War Two remained more nearly intact in Japan and was a healthy phenomenon, he thought. By the same token, he supported the more modest salaries of Japan's top corporate leaders as compared with the outlandish pay and bonuses awarded to top American executives.

Second, Reischauer's belief that the Japanese are among the most peace-loving people in the world has been confirmed. They have steadfastly resisted pressure from the U.S. government and from some of their own conservative leaders to amend or abolish Article 9 of the Peace Constitution of 1947. Contrary to the views of his critics, such as Norman and Dower, Japan did not require a social revolution in order to create and preserve democratic rule and a peaceful foreign policy. Retention of the emperor was a wise and far-sighted decision. To have forced Hirohito to abdicate or to have treated him as a war criminal might have created turmoil and further suffering for the Japanese people during the occupation. The current emperor and empress, Akihito and Michiko, have been admirable influences for democracy and pacifism. Japan has foresworn the production, possession, and introduction into Japan of nuclear weapons and strictly limits the export of arms to other nations. It poses no threat to any nation.

Third, despite the tensions in U.S.–Japan relations in the 1980s and 1990s, Reischauer remained certain that these relations would continue to stand on a solid base of shared interests and ideals. "There can be no repetition of the great tragedy that once engulfed my two homelands in a war with each other," he stated in his memoirs[24] On this point, too, he was right, and the "revisionists" were wrong. The idea that Japan and America were on a collision course was "quite absurd," he said.

Far from being a potential threat to America, Japan is today among its most reliable allies. Recent polls show that more than 90 percent of America's foreign-policy community view Japan as a "trustworthy" ally. An astounding 59 percent of Americans support a free-trade agreement with Japan.[25] The ability to station troops and bases in Japan has enabled the United States to keep its commitments to South Korea and Taiwan. The U.S.–Japan Security Treaty might well have unraveled in 1970 had Reischauer not set in motion the reversion of Okinawa to Japan and dealt wisely with other sensitive issues as Kennedy's ambassador to Tokyo.

He fought against the lingering sense of superiority in the Pentagon. Many top generals and admirals could not get over the fact that Japan was a defeated enemy that could be pushed around at will. Some of them felt that U.S. troops and bases served as the "cork in the bottle"—a restraining influence against any possible resurgence of Japanese militarism and aggression.[26] Reischauer challenged these assumptions and made a convincing case that if these attitudes persisted, there would be a backlash from the Japanese people that could threaten the future of the alliance. Joseph Nye and Ezra Vogel, two Harvard professors in the Clinton administration who shared his view, took up this theme. As a result, President Clinton and Prime Minister Hashimoto Ryutaro in 1996 reaffirmed the treaty and took steps to strengthen cooperation in case of war.

Fourth, the "revisionists" and protectionists who claimed that "Japan Inc." was out of control and could never change were proven wrong. Japan has taken steps to curb its self-destructive mercantilism, is a solid member of the World Trade Organization, and, with the exception of its agricultural sector, has opened its market to many foreign imports. Even leaders of America's embattled auto industry who had demanded voluntary restraints on Japanese exports eventually admitted they had been wrong. An astonishing admission came from the president and chief executive officer of General Motors, John F. Smith Jr., in 1995: "Japan should not be a scapegoat for the U.S. trade deficit, which is due mainly to America's own practices. The U.S. trade deficit mainly reflects a severe savings-investment imbalance. In short, the United States as a nation consumes too much and saves too little." Smith added, "Americans should know that 'Japan Inc.' does not exist. 'Japan Inc.' was a convenient way for the U.S. to avoid dealing with Japan's impressive competitiveness. Has Japan been mercantilist? Yes. But I am convinced that these mercantilist practices have cost Japan far more than they have cost Japan's trading partners."

On the question of why Americans were buying Japanese cars, he added: "We in the U.S. auto industry believed for far too many years that we knew what American car buyers wanted, and we weren't about to change. The result of this arrogance was that consumers flocked to purchase Japanese cars in great numbers. Japanese manufacturers offered higher quality cars that better met the U.S. consumer's changing needs. We learned a painful lesson. But in the end, Japanese competition forced us to improve the quality of our products and the productivity of our manufacturing."[27]

In the last year of his life, just before Japan's real-estate and stock-market bubble collapsed, Reischauer spoke out forcefully against Japanese protectionism. Looking back at the whole postwar period, he stated, "You can say, well, we [Americans] were a little bit overgenerous, perhaps, in letting them go on with their self-protectionism much more than they needed to, and we should have been a little more insistent that they give up protectionism at an earlier date and gotten used to the normal practices of international trade that the rest of us have. That criticism can be made today." In the same interview, he warned that if Japan did not "begin to put on the brakes of some sort, the whole world trade is going to get so out of balance that there will be a tremendous collapse and Japan will be the country that gets most hurt." He added that the Japanese have enough wisdom to avoid such a collapse and that they should invest more heavily at home in housing, infrastructure, and better wages for workers.[28]

On Americans' fear of the Japanese buying up "trophy properties" in the United States, such as Rockefeller Center or the Pebble Beach golf courses, he noted that there would be no problem if the Canadians or Dutch owned these properties. Racism, he thought, lay at the heart of this outcry, but, he quickly added, "the Japanese are much more racist than we are."[29]

Reischauer's record on East Asian affairs is at least comparable to George F. Kennan's on the Soviet Union. As a young State Department intern in the summer of 1941, Reischauer opposed the imposition of an oil embargo against Japan, arguing that it would force Japan to go to war before the United States could get ready for it—which, in fact, is what happened.

On China, he advocated recognition and trade relations with the Communist government soon after it came to power in 1949. He predicted that the Sino-Soviet alliance of 1950 would fall apart, as it did in the mid-1960s, and argued that a stable, prosperous China would be in the best interests of the United States.

On Vietnam, he warned in 1955 that the United States had made a huge mistake in supporting the French colonial regime in 1945 and that the it should have supported Ho Chi Minh from the start of the civil war there. He never thought the Communist insurgency owed its strength to support from China, nor did he think its victory would set off a domino effect in Southeast Asia. Even in 1967, when the United States was losing the war in Vietnam, he asserted, correctly, that nationalism was a far more powerful force than communism in Southeast Asia. His decision to support the U.S. war effort in Vietnam when he served as ambassador to Japan and even afterward was the major mistake of his life.

In 1973, he warned Americans that weapons of mass destruction would become available to the poor and backward nations in the twenty-first century. Kim Jong Il of North Korea has unfortunately borne out this prediction. Reischauer also believed in a better balance between military and diplomatic efforts in U.S. foreign policy. In 1955, he wrote, "It is easy to see that the status of India forty years from now is really of vastly more importance to the U.S. than now."[30] In 1980, he made the prediction that "we may be at a turning point in history when the economic center of the world shifts back again to the Asian part of the world. I say shift back, because between the years 500 and 1500, for a thousand years, that was economically and in most other ways the center of the world, far ahead of Europe."[31]

Reischauer's outstanding service as ambassador and his role in raising consciousness in Washington regarding Japan's importance and sensitivity have had two lasting effects. First, the American ambassadors to Tokyo who followed him have been extraordinarily prominent and competent. They include former vice president Walter F. Mondale (1993–96), former Speaker of the House of Representatives Tom Foley (1997–2001), and former Senate majority leader Howard Baker (2001–2005), who was accompanied by his talented wife, former senator Nancy Kassebaum. In addition, Dr. Michael H. Armacost, an outstanding Japanese-speaking career officer, served with distinction from 1989 to 1993. And J. Thomas Schieffer, a close friend and former business associate of President George W. Bush, was a respected envoy from 2005 to 2009. No other country has received in recent years such an array of American leaders.

Reischauer was especially proud of his connection to the Mondales. Joan Mondale was his first cousin's daughter. She called him "Uncle Ed." He fervently supported Mondale's bid for the presidency in 1984. He did not live to see Mondale appointed as President Clinton's ambassador to Tokyo in 1993, but would have applauded Mondale's superb performance in dealing with the bitter trade negotiations and military base problems that arose during his time in Tokyo, and he would have loved the fact that Joan was much admired in Japan for her support of the arts.

Second, the fact that Reischauer could speak and read the language of the country to which he was accredited has had a broad ripple effect within the government and academic circles. He made the case for using language and area specialists in high positions and inspired others to immerse themselves in foreign-area studies. American diplomacy still lags far behind the other advanced industrial democracies, where this practice is taken for granted. Americans still too often mistrust specialists as somehow "un-American" if they appear too comfortable in foreign cultures, but Reischauer managed to show the value of knowing the land to which he was appointed, and others are today following in his footsteps.

His most important insight was his call for an overhaul of the entire American education system, urging that students in primary school be taught to understand that they are citizens of a world community and not just a single nation-state. He helped embed foreign studies in Harvard's core curriculum, and he was an ardent believer in what has come to be called "soft power," using America's cultural resources, values, and ideals as a basis for diplomacy rather than the military or hard power.[32] He worried that America's deep-rooted isolationism, mistrust of foreigners, arrogant confidence in its own "exceptional" virtue, contempt for other nations, parochial refusal to learn foreign languages and cultures, and supercharged nationalism might doom its foreign policy for decades to come.

Reischauer's predominance in his field, his absorbing so much of the available oxygen, has led to a curious phenomenon: he has become an almost irresistible target of criticism for the following generations of scholars in both Japan and America. Just as a sumo grand champion (*yokozuna*) stands in the training ring (*dohyo*) and wards off a succession of charging young challengers one after another, Reischauer has been attacked repeatedly by Japanese and American scholars and journalists who wish to gain fame by proving him wrong.[33] He viewed this challenge as a kind of backhanded compliment. The difference between the *yokozuna* and Reischauer was that Reischauer rarely bothered to fight back, but rather let the younger assailants bounce off him. He was mystified, however, by the hostility of some of the younger scholars who succeeded him and by the ad hominem attacks on his personal motives.

Reischauer's historical works on Japan have largely been superseded by subsequent research. In fact, in an ironic twist that would have amused him, a recent (2003) history of modern Japan written by a Harvard professor who was at the time director of the *Reischauer* Institute of Japanese Studies (my emphasis) provides a "select bibliography" of 181 works on Japan without including a single book by Reischauer (although it does list Haru Matsukata Reischauer's *Samurai and Silk).*[34]

Reischauer rejoiced when younger scholars went beyond his own research to open up new insights on Japan. He well understood that pioneering in a new field of scholarship leads to refinement, specialization, and revision. He felt, however, that specialization closed gateways to the field, leaving fewer teachers for the introductory courses. For his own part, he chose to concentrate on introductory courses that might bring new minds to the subject. Only a small handful of current scholars have even attempted the sweeping generalizations and large judgments that Reischauer attempted.[35]

In some political science departments today, a beguiling new theory called "rational choice" argues that people and political actors of all cultures universally behave in ways that maximize their interests, and it is therefore not necessary to understand the particular language and culture in which they operate. Hence, according to this theory, no foreign scholar needs to learn Japanese or experience the Japanese people's culture in order to understand, explain, and teach about their behavior. Reischauer would have found this theory absurd.

He would be pleased today by the number of universities with serious Japan study programs, the number of American students at all levels studying Japanese and Japan,[36] the number of Japan specialists who have moved into high government positions (although this number varies with each administration), and the much improved coverage of Japan by the American media.

He would be happy to see how Japanese culture has permeated popular culture in America: the novels of Murakami Haruki in bookstores; sushi in supermarkets; karaoke in bars; anime, *manga*, and Pokemon in the hands of teenagers everywhere; baseball heroes such as Ichiro, Matsui, and Matsuzaka beloved in the American cities that are homes to their teams. But he would still be critical of aspects of the popular media treatment of Japan, which too often either ignores or caricatures or lumps all Japanese together. When, for example, a British bank buys part of an American company, the headline reads: "Barclays Bank Buys Part of Lehman Brothers." When Mitsubishi Bank buys part of Morgan Stanley, the headline proclaims: "Japanese in Bid to Buy Morgan Stanley." He deplored the practice of lumping "the Japanese" into an undifferentiated hoard. He would have been amazed and pleased to see Clint Eastwood's film *Letters from Iwo Jima* (2006), in which Japanese soldiers are portrayed as real humans.

Reischauer's best book, *The Japanese*, is unequaled as an introduction for Americans who wish to discover the dark side of the moon.[37] It is punchy, literate, sophisticated, and sound. There is nothing like it in the English language. With short, deft brushstrokes, he takes the mystery out of what at first seems quaint or different to Americans. Just for starters, he speaks to the American image of Japan as a very small, crowded country, but notes that it is considerably larger than Italy and half again the size of the United Kingdom. Throughout the book, he compares Japan to familiar European countries. About Japanese homogeneity, he writes that "there is little of the ethnic divisiveness that persists in the British Isles even though geographic barriers there are much less formidable." This is basic stuff, but he wanted Americans to think about it.

Sweeping through Japanese history, he tackles the broad subjects of the role of the group in Japan, relativism, hierarchy, the individual, women, education, religion, and mass culture. He then outlines government, politics, and business. But his major new contribution in this book falls under the final heading, "Japan and the World." Here, disguised as an account of Japan's foreign policy, he delivers three of his most heartfelt and urgent messages to the Japanese people. He presented them as scholarly observations because he did not want to seem to be preaching to a proud nation.

First, he deplores Japan's weakness in learning English. "Unfortunately the Japanese have proved notably inept at learning to speak foreign languages or to comprehend them aurally. Throughout the world one hears this commented upon with surprise and contrasted to the skill Japanese show at almost everything else." He continues: "Only a handful of men and women speak for Japan to the outside world or learn directly what others may say or write about Japan. . . . This certainly is not a tolerable situation for a leading nation in the world. Most Japanese live basically behind their high linguistic walls, largely unheard by others and listening only to what they wish to hear from abroad. There is no easy give and take that would put them into real intellectual contact with the rest of the world."

Second, he deplores the continuing obsession with "Nihonjinron," or the essential characteristics of what it means to be a Japanese. He feels that the Japanese should get over the sense of being unique, that this preoccupation will doom Japan to isolation from the main currents of international life. The Japanese should gladly join the human race as equal citizens, no better and no worse than other ethnic groups. "Japan naturally is much admired, but it is not widely liked or trusted," he wrote in a harsh appraisal of the country he loved. "Lingering feelings of separateness and uniqueness are still serious problems for the Japanese themselves." Asked in 1989 by a Japanese reporter for advice to the Japanese people, Reischauer said in a rare moment of pique, "Tell them it is time to join the human race!"[38]

Reischauer was particularly critical of arrogant or racist statements by Japanese politicians. Prime Minister Nakasone said in September 1986 that Japan was far ahead of the United States as a well-educated and "intelligent" society and suggested that the reason for this difference was the large population of blacks, Puerto Ricans, and Mexicans in the United States. [39] Reischauer saw statements like this as a throwback to the era when the Japanese language was an impenetrable barrier that could shield Japan's politicians from the world's attention. Japanese leaders were slow to understand that their country's great economic power drew scrutiny and criticism from all over the world. There was no longer any way for politicians to get away with closet racism.

Will Japanese and American societies "converge" and look like each other at the end of the modernization process? Some of his critics charged that Reischauer preached such a doctrine and that he was wildly mistaken in this view. In his most thoughtful response, however, he dealt with the issue of Japanese uniqueness:

> Among the great shaping forces of Japan as she now exists are characteristics deriving from the past, some shared with the rest of East Asia, but some *uniquely Japanese*. Among these are the strong work ethic, a pervasive

> esthetic sense, an intense feeling for decorum and orderly processes, and above all a strong orientation toward group identification and group activity, albeit with a matching sense of individual endeavor, achievement, will power and personal improvement. These are but a few examples of strong survivals from the past which, when manifested in modern institutions, make Japan *different* from the countries of the West and the rest of the world as well. They are hardly to be identified as Eastern traits in general, though some could be called East Asian. But basically they are Japanese. Japan is and will remain very Japanese.[40]

In other words, the combination of traits that survive today in Japan may be considered unique, but the Japanese people as a whole should not dwell on this fact or consider themselves different or superior; this uniqueness should never be the basis for looking down on other nations.

Reischauer was particularly critical of the kind of Japanese nationalism found in the book *The Japan That Can Say No* by Ishihara Shintaro and Morita Akio. In one of his last interviews with a Japanese reporter, he declared, "Japan should be internationalist, not nationalist. Ishihara is absolutely going in the wrong direction. He is trying to take Japan into the most dangerous of all courses, because I think a return to narrow nationalism would be close to suicide for Japan. It's a terrible thing. The very fact that Ishihara and Morita published this basically only for the Japanese, and didn't want to have any English translation shows a tremendous lack of understanding that Japan is part of the world. . . . Nobody else in a democratic country would dream of trying to do a thing like that. There is no nationalist role for Japan."[41]

Reischauer would deplore right-wing groups' efforts to whitewash the atrocities committed by Japan's militarists in World War Two. He would hope that school textbooks would honestly recognize the facts about "comfort women" and other war crimes. He would hope that the Yasukuni Shrine might somehow separate itself from the issue of the convicted war criminals and that Japan might find a way for all its citizens genuinely to pray for the spirits of the war dead and put aside all the other issues that enrage its Korean and Chinese neighbors through the joint creation of a careful, objective, and agreed-upon historical account.

He was disappointed that the Japanese government was not exerting the leadership, especially in Southeast Asia, that its wealth and strength warranted. He looked forward to the day when Japan would condemn human rights violations around the world and join in United Nations peacekeeping operations (as indeed it has).[42]

If Reischauer were alive today, he would take great satisfaction in the achievements of the country of his birth. It is a peace-loving, wealthy, democratic society and a beacon for other Asian nations. But he would ask for more. His guiding philosophy might be summed up in the words of Johann Wolfgang von Goethe, who wrote, "Treat people as if they were what they ought to be, and you help them to become what they are capable of being."

Edwin Reischauer would be dismayed today by the lack of competent political leadership in Japan and the lack of a coherent set of foreign-policy goals. He would wonder why leaders like his favorite politician Ohira Masayoshi no longer seem to rise to positions of power. During his life, he was confident that Japan's postwar education system, purged of militarism and rooted in democratic ideals, would produce a new generation of independent thinkers and voters who viewed themselves as citizens not just of Japan, but of the world. He would find hope in the new leaders of the Democratic Party of Japan in 2009. He was certain that new leaders, sharing a global outlook with their American counterparts, would come to manage the alliance.

He would expect that the United States and Japan, in their own and mutual interests as the world's two largest economies and strongest democracies, would work in partnership to resolve today's pressing issues: terrorism, environmental degradation, the search for renewable and clean energy supplies, piracy, disaster relief, and the like.

He would look at the state of the U.S.–Japan alliance and ask why Japan's voice is so weak and passive. Why did Japan meekly support President George W. Bush's terrible mistake in invading Iraq in 2003 and send six hundred troops as evidence of its support? Why could Prime Minister Koizumi not have emulated President Chirac of France or Chancellor Schroeder of Germany, who refused to support the unilateral invasion, and wished instead to place the matter before the United Nations? In this matter, Reischauer would renew his call for a truly equal partnership.

He would call for major changes in force and base structure: the withdrawal of most U.S. troops from Okinawa and the sharing of land and naval bases with Japan's Self-Defense Forces. He would be embarrassed for his country that Washington is demanding that Japan help pay for the shift of U.S. troops to Saipan. He would favor closing down Futenma and shifting U.S. air power to Kadena Air Force Base. He would rely on American air and naval power to deter any possible North Korean aggression.

Reischauer would have applauded Koizumi's initiative in traveling to Pyongyang in 2002 to meet with top North Korean leaders. He would have deep sympathy for the abductees and their families, but would have suggested to Koizumi that the issue of nuclear weapons on the Korean Peninsula represents a far more serious threat to Japan and the alliance, and would have urged Japan to be more forthcoming in negotiations leading to a nuclear-free Korean Peninsula, mutual recognition, economic aid, reparations, and the opening up of travel and communication between North Korea and the outside world.

Reischauer would believe that North Koreans, like all other humans in similar situations, will eventually come to understand how much they have suffered under the cruel dictatorship of Kim Il Sung and Kim Jong Il if exposed to the freedom and much higher standard of living in South Korea, Japan, and other advanced industrial democracies. He would strongly support steps toward the peaceful reunification of the Korean Peninsula.

He would be critical of those in Washington who keep urging Japan to become a "normal nation."[43] By "normal," Americans usually mean a nation that joins in U.S. military actions under the rubric of collective self-defense. He believed that Japan does have the right of collective self-defense, but that this right should be exercised judiciously and not just as a knee-jerk reaction to Americans' demands. He would feel that the Japanese people have been right to retain Article 9. He would feel that, as a responsible ally, Japan should make its true voice heard.

Reischauer would be amazed that a leader as inexperienced in foreign affairs and as incompetent as George W. Bush could have been elected and reelected president of the United States. He would welcome the election of Barack Obama and his appointment of foreign-policy advisors who are knowledgeable, experienced, and thoroughly internationalist in outlook.

Reischauer believed that Japan, through its defeat, recovery, and commitment to peace, should stand on the high moral ground and base its foreign policy on the peaceful resolution of conflict through the United Nations and other multinational venues. He would hope for an improvement in Japan's education system, particularly in its graduate schools. He would expect a new generation of young Japanese to be as creative and independent as their Chinese and American counterparts. Japan's schools, he thought, all too often stifle initiative and bold new thinking.

Finally, he would be confident that the Japanese people have the common sense to reject the arguments of the new nationalists who urge that Japan should possess nuclear arms, which, he thought, would lead to an arms race in East Asia and ultimately to disaster for Japan, which would lose out in any struggle with China.

In short, Reischauer imagined a Japan led by statesmen of international outlook and stature, fluent in English, and influential among world leaders. He was, by his own admission, an idealist. Without ideals, without a vision of a better world, he thought, there can be no human progress.

Along with his obituary, *Shinano Mainichi Shimbun* published a handwritten note he had scribbled in English at his home in Belmont on November 27, 1984, in response to a request for a contribution to a column on education. He wrote: "Peace in this world depends on international understanding and understanding on knowledge and skills at communication. Thus, peace ultimately depends on education."[44] These words formed the guiding beacon for an unwavering lifetime of service.

Epilogue

Reischauer's legacy remains strong. The Edwin O. Reischauer Institute of Japanese Studies at Harvard, endowed with a base of seven million dollars that he helped to raise, has thirty-three Japanese studies faculty associated with it. Four professorships and one visiting professorship bear his name. His former home in Belmont, which was purchased by Kodansha Inc., is now called the Edwin O. Reischauer Memorial House. A visiting scholar stays there each year, and the Reischauer Institute sponsors a major event there every October, around the time of his birthday (October 15). The institute also runs the Noma-Reischauer Prize competition for the best essay on Japan by an undergraduate student and by a graduate student. It sent eighty-six Harvard undergraduates to Japan in 2007–2008 for internships, study, or research.

As the institute's director, Professor Susan J. Pharr, explained to me, "In the spirit of Ed's role as a public intellectual with a deep concern about U.S.–Japan relations and Japan's role in the world, Harvard has had, since 1980, a program on U.S.–Japan Relations that invites to Harvard each year some 15–16 academics and professionals from Japan . . . including [Ambassador] Hisashi Owada, UN Secretary General Ban Ki-moon, former Democratic Party of Japan president Okada Katsuya, [*Asahi Shimbun*'s] Matsuyama Yukio, and [economist] Takenaka Keizo. Last year, Takemi Heizo, former member of the Upper House, was with us."[1]

The Edwin O. Reischauer Center for East Asia Studies at the Johns Hopkins School of Advanced International Studies in Washington, D.C., has also flourished, with more emphasis on training graduate students for careers in public service. It emphasizes the study of economics, international relations, and Japanese politics, language, and foreign policy.

The center sponsors a Reischauer Memorial Lecture series; conducts U.S.–Japan Internet dialogues; organizes conferences; publishes monographs on political and economic issues; puts out an annual report on the state of U.S.–Japan relations; invites Japanese scholars, journalists, business leaders, and senior government officials as visiting fellows in residence; and sends graduate students to Japan for internships. Directed by Professor Kent Calder, who earned his Ph.D. under Reischauer, the center is a focal point in Washington for airing critical issues in the alliance between the two countries. It has enlisted two outstanding former career Japan specialists who served as deputy chief of Mission in Tokyo, William Sherman and Rust Deming, as resource contacts for graduate students at the School of Advanced International Studies.

Stanford University runs the Reischauer Scholars Program, an intensive distance learning program on Japan aimed at twenty-five exceptional high school juniors and seniors drawn competitively from throughout the United States. Using the Internet, the students receive lectures from top scholars and government officials on Japanese history, religion, art, politics, economics, and contemporary society, with special focus on the U.S.–Japan relationship. Students who complete the course successfully earn Stanford Continuing Studies Program credit. Now in its sixth year (at this writing in April 2009), it provides a gateway for students to pursue advanced study of Japan in colleges and universities.

Haru Reischauer lived in a sunny house with a view of the Pacific Ocean in La Jolla, California, until she died at the age of eighty-three of a heart attack on September 23, 1998. Her ashes, like Edwin's, were scattered over the Pacific Ocean. In her last years, she enjoyed frequent visits from her three children, nine grandchildren, and three great-grandchildren.

Ann Reischauer Heinemann, Ed and Haru's oldest daughter, and her husband, Stephen F. Heinemann, a neurophysiologist at the Salk Institute, live in La Jolla, California. They have four sons—Nathan, Danton, Thadden, and Quentin—a daughter, Eden, and eleven grandchildren who live nearby.

Robert D. Reischauer, president of the Urban Institute in Washington, D.C., and his wife, Charlotte, have a daughter, Alyssa, and a son, Peter, and three grandchildren who live on the West Coast.

Joan Reischauer Simon and her husband, William Simon, a lawyer, have a daughter, Kate, and a son, Richard, and live in San Diego, California.

Reischauer would perhaps consider his greatest legacy the fact that a growing number of Americans have discovered on the "dark side of the moon" the true nature of the nation and the people he loved. His faith in the Japanese people's common sense would remain strong. That would be enough.

Notes

PREFACE

1. Edwin O. Reischauer, *My Life Between Japan and America* (New York: Harper and Row, 1986).

2. Edwin O. Reischauer and Marius Jansen, *The Japanese Today: Change and Continuity* (Cambridge, Mass.: Harvard University Press, 1995, 2003).

3. Letter to the author from Marius Jansen, June 29, 1992.

4. Anthony Grafton, "The Origins of Scholarship," *The American Scholar* (Spring 1979): 236–61, quoted by Keith Thomas in *The New York Review*, March 13, 2003.

1. BORN IN JAPAN

1. Edwin O. Reischauer, *My Life Between Japan and America* (New York: Harper and Row, 1986), p. 103, hereafter *MLBJA*.

2. Sir George Sansom, foreword to Edwin O. Reischauer, *Japan: Past and Present* (New York: Knopf, 1946), p. viii.

3. Edwin O. Reischauer, *The Japanese* (Cambridge, Mass.: Belknap Press of Harvard University Press, 1977). Reischauer produced a new edition of this book in 1988, this time titled *The Japanese Today: Continuity and Change*; Marius Jensen updated this edition in 1995, after Reischauer's death, and a new paperback version was issued in 2003.

4. John W. Dower, *War Without Mercy* (New York: Pantheon Books, 1986), pp. 8–9.

5. Five years later (September 15, 1858), Jonesboro, three hundred miles south of Chicago, was the site of the third historic debate over slavery between Abraham Lincoln and Stephen Douglas. In a recent biography of Lincoln, Ronald C. White Jr. describes the town of eight hundred people as rural, poor, and strongly conservative, known for its hatred of blacks. Ronald C. White Jr., *A. Lincoln: A Biography* (New York: Random House, 2009), p. 273. It is

almost impossible to imagine Edwin Reischauer's parents staying for long in such a racist environment.

6. *MLBJA*, p. 14.

7. Letter to family, December 24, 1961, copies of letters to his family 1961–66 provided by Nancy Deptula, executive director of the Edwin O. Reischauer Institute of Japanese Studies, Harvard University. See also Edwin O. Reischauer, "Life with Father (and Also Mother)," an essay in *The Life of Dr. A. K. Reischauer* (Tokyo: Kyobunkan, 1961), p. 43.

8. *MLBJA*, p. 17.

9. The Reischauer family history is described in detail in *MLBJA*, chapter 3.

10. Helen Ballhatchet, "The Modern Missionary Movement in Japan: Roman Catholic, Protestant, Orthodox," in Mark R. Mullins, ed., *Handbook of Christianity in Japan* (Leiden: Brill, 2003), p. 35.

11. James A. Field Jr., "Near East Notes and Far East Quotes," in John K. Fairbank, ed., *The Missionary Enterprise in China and America* (Cambridge, Mass.: Harvard University Press, 1974), p. 35.

12. *Proceedings of the General Conference of the Protestant Missionaries of Japan, 1883* (publication information not given), p. 183.

13. Field, " Near East Notes and Far East Queries," pp. 35–37.

14. *Proceedings of the General Conference of the Protestant Missionaries of Japan, 1900* (publication information not given), pp. 994–97.

15. James Reed, *The Missionary Mind and American East Asian Policy, 1911–1915* (Cambridge, Mass.: Harvard University Press, 1983), p. 18.

16. Field, "Near East Notes and Far East Queries," p. 20.

17. John K. Fairbank, "Introduction," in Fairbank, ed., *The Missionary Enterprise*, pp. 7–8.

18. A. K. Reischauer, "Material for a Biographical Sketch of A. K. Reischauer," an English-language essay in *Hakari Nawa wa Tanoshiki Chi ni Ochitari: A. K. Raishawa Hakase Den*, a booklet published by Kyobunkan in Tokyo for Meiji Gakuin University on the occasion of A. K. Reischauer's return to Japan in 1961 as father of the American ambassador to Tokyo.

19. Quoted in Eleanor Tupper and George E. McReynolds, *Japan in American Public Opinion* (New York: MacMillan, 1937), p. 22.

20. Quoted in ibid., p. 5.

21. Sidney L. Gulick, *The American Japanese Problem* (New York: Scribner's, 1914), p. 172.

22. The "scratched image" picture is borrowed from the title of Harold R. Isaacs's 1958 classic work *Scratches on Our Minds: American Images of China and India* (New York: John Day; reprint, Armonk, N.Y.: M. E. Sharp, 1980). Sun Yat-sen's revolution of 1911 ended the Ching Dynasty and ushered in the period of modernization.

23. Quoted in Reed, *The Missionary Mind*, p. 30.

24. Quoted in Gulick, *The American Japanese Problem*, p. 199.

25. Ibid., pp. 199–200.

26. Homer Lea, *The Valor of Ignorance* (New York: Harper and Brothers, 1909).

27. Edwin O. Reischauer to George Akita, September 1, 1978, copy provided to the author by Nancy Deptula.

28. James Murdoch, *A History of Japan*, 3 vols. (Tokyo: Asiatic Society of Japan, 1910), revised and edited by Joseph H. Longford (New York: Routledge, 1996); Basil Hall Chamberlain and W. B. Mason, *A Handbook for Travellers in Japan* (London: John Murray, 1901). A. K. Reischauer cites Murdoch three times in his *Studies in Japanese Buddhism* (New York: AMS Press, 1917).

29. A. K. Reischauer, "A Catechism of the Shin Sect," from R. Nishimoto, Japanese *Shinshu Hyakuwa* (Honolulu, T.H.: Publishing Bureau of the Hongwanji Mission, August 1921).

30. The lectures were edited and published in 1917 as *Studies in Japanese Buddhism*.

31. Arthur M. Schlesinger Jr., "The Missionary Enterprise and Theories of Imperialism," in Fairbank, ed., *The Missionary Enterprise in China and America*, p. 372.

32. A. K. Reischauer, "Material for a Biographical Sketch," p. 10.

33. A. K. Reischauer, *Studies in Japanese Buddhism*, p. 296.

34. Ibid.

35. Ibid., pp. 310, 83. A. K. Reischauer was overly optimistic. Today, there are only about 600,000 Christians in a population of 127 million Japanese. About half of them are Roman Catholic.

36. Ibid., p. 177.

37. Ibid., p. 90.

38. Ibid., pp. 82, 99, 92–93, 115. The last statement echoes the thought of Lafcadio Hearn, who wrote that "the Japanese are the happiest people in the world." Quoted in Robert A. Rosenstone, *Mirror in the Shrine* (Cambridge, Mass.: Harvard University Press, 1988), p. 176.

39. A. K. Reischauer, *Studies in Japanese Buddhism*, p. 128.

40. Ibid., pp. 137, 139, 147.

41. Ibid., p. 152.

42. *MLBJA*, p. 18.

43. A. K. Reischauer, "Material for a Biographical Sketch," pp. 15–16.

44. The lectures were published in A. K. Reischauer, *The Task in Japan* (New York: Fleming H. Revell, 1926), p. 25.

45. Ibid., pp. 26, 60, 56, italics in original.

46. Edwin O. Reischauer, interviewed by the author, Belmont, Mass., May 17, 1981.

47. *MLBJA*, p. 17.

48. Edwin O. Reischauer, *Wanted: An Asian Policy* (New York: Alfred A. Knopf, 1955), pp. 206–7.

49. Reischauer interview, May 17, 1981.

50. Fred Notehelfer, e-mail exchange with the author, November 10, 2006.

51. Unpublished manuscript version of *MLBJA*, p. 42, copy provided by Nancy Deptula.

52. E. O. Reischauer, "Life with Father," p. 44.

53. Ibid., pp. 45–47.

54. *MLBJA*, p. 9.

55. Letter to Ann, December 20, 1964.

56. Joan Reischauer Simon, interviewed by the author, New York City, February 27, 2003.

57. *MLBJA*, p. 18.

58. E. O. Reischauer, "Life with Father," p. 45.

59. Edwin O. Reischauer to George Akita, September 1, 1978.

60. *MLBJA*, p. 11.

61. Edwin O. Reischauer to Mr. J. E. Aurell, August 8, 1969, Edwin O. Reischauer Correspondence, Box 2, HUGFP 73.10, Harvard University Archives.

62. Nitobe Inazo, *Bushido: The Soul of Japan* (Boston: Tuttle, 2001; orig. pub. 1899).

63. *MLBJA*, p. 19.

64. A. K. Reischauer, "Material for a Biographical Sketch," p. 27.

65. *MLBJA*, pp. 3, 4.

66. Ibid., p. 3.

67. Ibid., pp. 6–7.

68. Ibid., p. 6.

69. Ibid., pp. 9–10.

70. From the author's notes on Reischauer's speech to the Federal City Club, Washington, D.C., June 14, 1977.

71. Interview in the *Harvard Gazette*, January 12, 1990.

72. *MLBJA*, p. 10.

73. Unpublished manuscript version of *MLBJA*, p. 24.

74. Edwin O. Reischauer to George Akita, September 1, 1978.

2. JAPAN, "THE DARK SIDE OF THE MOON"

1. Edwin O. Reischauer, *My Life Between Japan and America* (New York: Harper and Row, 1986), p. 36, hereafter *MLBJA*.

2. Handwritten letter to Ann Reischauer, July 12, 1964, copies of letters to his family 1961–66 provided by Nancy Deptula, executive director of the Edwin O. Reischauer Institute of Japanese Studies, Harvard University.

3. Edwin O. Reischauer, unpublished manuscript version of *MLBJA*, p. 85, copy provided to the author by Nancy Deptula.

4. *MLBJA*, p. 33.

5. John K. Fairbank, *Chinabound: A Fifty-Year Memoir* (New York: Harper and Row, 1982), p. 145.

6. John Barnard, *From Evangelicalism to Progressivism at Oberlin College, 1866–1917* (Columbus: Ohio State University Press, 1969), p. 6.

7. Both quoted in ibid., pp. 50–51.

8. *MLBJA*, pp. 33–34.

9. *Presbyterian Life* magazine, July 15, 1964.

10. Edwin O. Reischauer, interviewed by the author, Belmont, Mass., May 17, 1981.

11. Carol Shaw, interviewed by the author, Washington, D.C., May 4, 1993.

12. Unpublished manuscript version of *MLBJA*, p. 84.

13. *MLBJA*, p. 36.

14. Unpublished manuscript version of *MLBJA*, p. 90.

15. Edwin O. Reischauer to George Akita, September 19, 1994, copy provided to the author by Nancy M. Deptula.

16. Unpublished manuscript version of *MLBJA*, p. 91.

17. Ibid., p. 92.

18. *MLBJA*, p. 39.

19. *MLBJA*, p. 40.

20. Unpublished manuscript version of *MLBJA*, p. 99.

21. *MLBJA*, p. 39.

22. Edwin O. Reischauer to George Akita, September 1, 1978, copy provided to the author by Nancy Deptula. Robert earned his Ph.D. in 1935 with a thesis titled "Alien Land Tenure in Japan," the first Ph.D. awarded in Japanese studies at Harvard. Edwin would earn the second in 1939, followed by E. H. Norman in 1940.

23. Unpublished manuscript version of *MLBJA*, p. 100.

24. *MLBJA*, p. 41.

25. Ibid., p. 42.

26. Ibid.

27. Ibid., p. 43.

28. Ibid., p. 37.

29. Ibid., p. 44.

30. Ibid., p. 45.

31. Ibid., pp. 46, 47.

32. Ibid., p. 48.

33. Ibid.

34. Ibid., p. 45.

3. ON THE TRAIL OF ENNIN

1. Marius B. Jansen, The Making of Modern Japan (Cambridge, Mass.: Harvard University Press, 2000), p. 587.

2. Andrew Gordon, *A Modern History of Japan: From Tokugawa Times to the Present* (New York: Oxford University Press, 2003), p. 199.

3. Edwin O. Reischauer, *My Life Between Japan and America* (New York: Harper and Row, 1986), p. 57, hereafter *MLBJA*.

4. Hugh Borton, *Spanning Japan's Modern Century: The Memoirs of Hugh Borton* (Lanham, Md.: Lexington Books, 2002), pp. 35–36. Borton would go on to a distinguished career as an historian of Japan at Columbia University and as president of Haverford College.

5. In Dorothy Storry, *Second Country: The Story of Richard Storry and Japan, 1913–1982* (Woodchurch, England: Paul Norbury, 1986), pp. 41, 39, 42. Richard Storry would go on to become professor of Japanese studies at Oxford University.

6. Borton, *Spanning Japan's Modern Century*, pp. 54, 57, 58, 61, 58.

7. Ibid., p. 58.

8. Norman's interpretation is eloquently presented in in E. H. Norman, *Origins of the Modern Japanese State: Selected Writings of E. H. Norman*, edited by John W. Dower (New York: Random House, 1975), pp. 3–101. See chapter 10 for a further description of this controversy.

9. Edwin O. Reischauer, *Japan Past and Present*, 3rd rev. ed. (New York: Knopf, 1954), p. 161.

10. *MLBJA*, p. 56.

11. Ibid., p. 55.

12. See Edwin O. Reischauer, *Ennin's Diary: The Record of a Pilgrimage to China in Search of the Law* and *Ennin's Travels in China,* both published by Ronald Press of New York in 1955.

13. Reischauer, *Ennin's Travels in T'ang China*, p. viii.

14. The 1963 Japanese edition was published by Jitsugyo no Nippon Sha. A second edition appeared in 1984 by Hara Shobo, and a paperback version by Kodansha appeared in 1999.

15. Nakamura Hajime, introduction to the Japanese paperback edition of Edwin O. Reischauer, *Ennin's Travels in T'ang China* (Tokyo: Kodansha, 1999) , p. 13.

16. Shiba Ryotaro, Eizan no Shodo, *Asahi Bunko, Asahi Shimbun Sha* (Tokyo: n.p., 1985), pp. 60–61.

17. The Japanese broadcasting company NHK has aired several broadcasts of these travels retracing Ennin's footsteps. Anami's book *On the Trail of Ennin* was published in Japan by Random House Kodansha in 2007.

18. Richard Dyke, e-mail message to the author, February 10, 2007.

19. Reischauer, *Ennin's Travels in T'ang China*, preface, p. vii.

20. Reischauer, *Ennin's Diary*, p. xiv.

21. Edwin O. Reischauer to Professor Harlow Shapley, April 28, 1950, Edwin O. Reischauer Correspondence, 1933–67, Box 1, HUGFP 73.8, Harvard Archives.

22. Reischauer, *Ennin's Travels in China*, p. 136.

23. Donald Keene, interviewed by the author, New York, January 19, 2005. There are actually 1,551 footnotes in *Ennin's Diary*.

24. Reischauer, *Ennin's Travels in T'ang China*, p. 38.

25. Letter to family, April 27, 1963, copies of Reischauer's letters to his family 1961–66 provided by Nancy Deptula, executive director of the Edwin O. Reischauer Institute of Japanese Studies, Harvard University, unless otherwise noted.

26. Robert Scalapino, interviewed by the author, San Francisco, April 25, 1994.

27. Quoted in Marius Jansen, " Edwin O. Reischauer Lecture," *IHJ Bulletin* 13, no. 4 (Autumn 1993), 1–3.

28. Edwin O. Reischauer, *East Asia: The Great Tradition* (Boston: Houghton Mifflin, 1958), p. 170.

29. Albert M. Craig and Donald H. Shively, eds., *Personality in Japanese History* (Berkeley: University of California Press, 1970).

30. Unpublished manuscript version of *MLBJA*, p. 146, copy provided by Nancy Deptula. The published *MLBJA* version of this comment was even stronger: "[this] discriminatory treatment, though now illegal, is still very much alive and constitutes a major blot on Japanese society" (p. 59).

31. For a fuller account, see *MLBJA*, pp. 62, 66.

32. Robert Reischauer, *Japan: Government–Politics* (Nashville, Tenn.: T. Nelson and Sons, 1939).

33. *MLBJA*, p. 66.

34. "Danton" was, of course, Adrienne's maiden name.

35. Unpublished manuscript version of *MLBJA*, p. 155.

36. *MLBJA*, p. 67.

37. Ibid., pp. 70–71.

4. THE SCHOLAR AT WAR

1. Edwin O. Reischauer, *My Life Between Japan and America* (New York: Harper and Row, 1986), p. 79, hereafter *MLBJA*.

2. Ibid., p. 81.

3. *Time* magazine, February 8, 1932.

4. Barbara W. Tuchman, *Stillwell and the American Experience in China* (New York: Grove Press, 1970), p. 174.

5. Marius B. Jansen, "The Legacy of Edwin O. Reischauer," *International House of Japan Bulletin* 13, no. 4 (Autumn 1993), pp. 1–6. Jansen noted that after Robert Reischauer's tragic death in 1937, only four Japan scholars remained in the United States. After the war, Bowles would play a large role at the International House of Japan and Tokyo University; Borton would be at Columbia; Fahs would work at the Rockefeller Foundation and in Reischauer's Tokyo embassy; and Edwin Reischauer would become U.S. ambassador to Japan.

6. Ibid. The military presumably did not survey the Japanese American population, fearing (without justification) that they might have divided loyalties in the event of war.

7. Robert Karl Reischauer, "Conflicts Inside Japan," *Harper's Monthly Magazine* 173 (July 1936), pp. 157–58.

8. Ibid., p. 162.

9. Nathaniel Peffer, "Japan Counts the Cost," *Harper's Magazine* 175 (September 1937), pp. 354, 355 (*Harper's* took *Monthly* out of its name in 1937).

10. Eliot Janeway, "Japan's Partner: Japanese Dependence upon the United States," *Harper's Magazine* 177 (June 1938), p. 1.

11. John Gunther, "The Japanese Emperor," *Harper's Magazine* 178 (February 1939), pp. 225, 235, 236.

12. Nathaniel Peffer, "Our Job in the Far East ," *Harper's Magazine* 180 (April 1940): 489–97.

13. *MLBJA*, p. 85.

14. Unpublished manuscript version of MLBJA, p. 190, copy provided to the author by Nancy Deptula, executive director of the Edwin O. Reischauer Institute of Japanese Studies, Harvard University.

15. Another theory, of course, is that President Roosevelt actually wanted Japan to start a war in the Pacific and tricked it into doing so, thus enabling America to rush to the defense of England in its war with Germany. A surprising number of allegedly well-informed Japanese and Americans actually believe some version of this theory, and the argument continues to this day.

16. Unpublished manuscript version of *MLBJA*, p. 191.

17. Quoted in *MLBJA*, pp. 87–88, italics added. Reischauer admitted later with embarrassment that in this memo he had failed to call for the independence of Korea and Taiwan, and that he thought Manchuria would become an independent nation. "This probably showed a lingering Japanese bias in my thinking," he recalled (ibid.).

18. *MLBJA*, p. 88. It is noteworthy that he was silent about the U.S. colonization of the Philippines.

19. Robert A. Fearey, "Diplomacy's Final Round," *Foreign Service Journal* 68, no. 12 (December 1991), p. 22.

20. Quoted in ibid., p. 26.

21. The best account of U.S. preparations for the occupation of Japan can be found in John Curtis Perry, *Beneath the Eagle's Wings* (New York: Dodd, Mead, 1980).

22. Joseph C. Grew, *Report from Tokyo* (New York: Simon and Schuster, 1942), pp. 42, 70.

23. Edwin O. Reischauer, "Ideal Answer Is Not War," *Washington Post*, October 28, 1941.

24. Unpublished manuscript version of *MLBJA*, pp. 194–95.

25. Edwin O. Reischauer and J. C. Goodbody, "Our Overconfidence: The Military Might of Japan," *Washington Post*, December 19, 1941.

26. Ibid.

27. *Report of the Commission on Wartime Relocation and Internment of Civilians in Personal Justice Denied* (Seattle: University of Washington Press, 1997), p. 459.

28. Reischauer and Goodbody, "Our Overconfidence."

29. *MLBJA*, p. 94.

30. Ibid.

31. Sir George Samson, title not given, Oxford Pamphlets on World Affairs, no. 70 (Oxford, U.K.: Oxford University Press, 1944), cited in Katharine Samson, *Sir George Sansom and Japan: A Memoir* (Tallahassee, Fla.: Diplomatic Press, 1972).

32. John W. Dower, *War Without Mercy* (New York: Pantheon Books, 1986), pp. 19–20.

33. Edwin O. Reischauer, "Memorandum on Policy Towards Japan," September 14, 1942, pp. 1–2, in 291.2 Army-AG Classified Decimal File 1940–42, Entry 360, Box 147, records of the Adjutant General's Office, 1917–, Record Group 407 (RG407), National Archives, College Park, Md. The memo is cited by T. Fujitani in "Former American Ambassador Reischauer's Plan for a Puppet Regime Emperor System" (in Japanese), *Sekai* (March 2000): 137–46, and in the longer article T. Fujitani, "The Reischauer Memo: Mr. Moto, Hirohito, and Japanese American Soldiers," *Critical Asian Studies* 33, no. 3 (2001): 379–402. Fujitani is highly critical of Reischauer's proposal that the emperor be retained as a "puppet regime" at a time when Americans were proclaiming the advent of democracy in postwar Japan, and he charges Reischauer with having a "racist" attitude.

34. Letter to the Reischauer family, January 1945, Edwin O. Reischauer Correspondence, Box 1, HUGFP 73.6, Harvard University Archives. For a very different view of the emperor's role, see Herbert Bix, *Hirohito and the Making of Modern Japan* (New York: HarperCollins), 2000.

35. Unpublished manuscript version of *MLBJA*, p. 200.

36. See *MLBJA*, pp. 91–101.

37. *MLBJA*, p. 89.

38. Howard Hibbett, interviewed by the author, Cambridge, Mass., January 8, 2008. Hibbett was editor, with Itasaka Gen, of *Modern Japanese: A Basic Reader* (Cambridge, Mass.: Harvard University Press, 1967), a two-volume set that would become a standard reference work in the field.

39. Sumner Redstone, *A Passion to Win* (New York: Simon and Schuster, 2001), p. 49.

40. Sumner Redstone, telephone interview by the author, April 16, 2007.

41. Henry Graff, telephone interview by the author, New York, March 26, 2007.

42. *MLBJA*, p. 94.

43. Graff interview, March 26, 2007.

44. Unpublished manuscript version of *MLBJA*, p. 217. I have not been able to find out why this paragraph did not appear in the published version.

45. *MLBJA*, pp. 100–101. This reasoning has of course been widely challenged and remains controversial in academic circles. For two competing views, see Richard B. Frank's *Downfall: The End of the Imperial Japanese Empire* (New York: Random House, 1999), an account that largely supports Reischauer's view, and Hasegawa Tsuyoshi's *Racing the Enemy: Stalin, Truman, and the Surrender of Japan* (Cambridge, Mass.: Harvard University Press, 2005), which disagrees with it.

46. *MLBJA*, p. 101.

47. Ibid., pp. 102, 103.

48. *Washington Post*, August 17, 1945. The pejorative word *Jap*, as offensive to the Japanese as the pejorative *nigger* is to African Americans, remained in the American vocabulary for many years after the war and can occasionally be heard even today.

49. *Time* magazine, August 27, 1945.

50. Willis Church Lamott, "What *Not* to Do with Japan," *Harper's Monthly Magazine* 190, no. 1141 (June 1945), p. 585.

51. Quoted in Ray A. Moore and Donald L. Robinson, *Partners for Democracy: Crafting the New Japanese State Under MacArthur* (New York: Oxford University Press, 2002), p. 36. For the account of MacArthur's decisive role in dealing with the emperor, I have relied heavily on chapter 2 of this excellent work.

52. Takemae Eiji, *The Allied Occupation of Japan* (New York: Continuum, 2002), p. 203.

53. Moore and Robinson, *op. cit.*, p. 38.

54. *MLBJA*, p. 108.

55. Giles MacDonogh provides an appalling account of the brutality that followed the defeat of Germany in 1945 in *After the Reich: The Brutal History of the Allied Occupation* (New York: Basic Books, 2007).

56. This point is well made in Moore and Robinson, *Partners for Democracy*.

5. A TIME OF LARGE IDEAS

1. Geoffrey Kabaservice, *The Guardians: Kingman Brewster, His Circle, and the Rise of the Liberal Establishment* (New York: Henry Holt, 2004), quoting from Minutes of the Faculty of Arts and Sciences, Harvard University, December 12, 2000.

2. Ibid.

3. Ibid., pp. 127–28.

4. This phrase was coined by author Tom Wolfe in his 1987 novel *Bonfire of the Vanities* (Middletown, Penn.: Franklin Library).

5. John Kenneth Galbraith, *The Affluent Society* (Boston: Houghton Mifflin, 1958).

6. John F. Harris, *Washington Post*, May 8, 2006.

7. Walt Whitman Rostow, *The Stages of Economic Growth: A Non-Communist Manifesto* (Cambridge, U.K.: Cambridge University Press, 1960), p. ix. The book went through seventeen printings by 1968, an extraordinary record for a book on economics by a university professor.

8. Albert M Craig, interviewed by the author, Cambridge, Mass., June 22, 1994. See James Murdoch, *A History of Japan*, 3 vols. (Kobe, Japan: Office of the "Chronicle," 1903), and George Sansom, *Japan: A Short Cultural History* (New York: Appleton-Century-Crofts, 1931).

9. Edwin O. Reischauer and John K. Fairbank, *East Asia: The Great Tradition* (Boston: Houghton Mifflin, 1958), p. 8.

10. Ibid., pp. 5, 6–7.

11. Unpublished manuscript version of Edwin O. Reischauer, *My Life Between Japan and America* (New York: Harper and Row, 1986), p. 269, hereafter *MLBJA*, copy provided by Nancy Deptula, executive director of the Edwin O. Reischauer Institute of Japanese Studies, Harvard University. Senator Pat McCarran (Democrat of Nevada) was chairman of the U.S. Senate's notorious Internal Security Subcommittee, which issued wild and unsubstantiated charges of pro-Communist sympathy against innocent individuals.

12. John W. Dower, *War Without Mercy* (New York: Pantheon Books, 1986), p. 300.

13. Unpublished manuscript version of *MLBJA*, pp. 182, 183.

14. Both books were published in Boston by Houghton Mifflin, the former in 1958 and 1960 and the latter in 1965. In 1973, the two volumes were merged into a single 969-page work, John K. Fairbank, Edwin O. Reischauer, and Albert Craig, *East Asia: Tradition and Transformation* (Boston: Houghton Mifflin).

15. John K. Fairbank, eulogy for Edwin O. Reischauer at Harvard, October 19, 1990, italics added, from double-spaced typewritten notes provided to the author by Nancy Deptula from her files.

16. Marshall Bouton, interviewed by the author, New York, October 10, 2007. Bouton went on to become president of the Chicago Council on Global Affairs.

17. *MLBJA*, p. 114.

18. Michael J. Smitka, telephone interview by the author, February 21, 2008.

19. Orville Schell, telephone interview by the author, March 19, 2008.

20. Edwin O. Reischauer, interviewed by the author, Belmont, Mass., May 17, 1981.

21. John K. Fairbank, *Chinabound: A Fifty-Year Memoir* (New York: Harper and Row, 1982), p. 377.

22. John Curtis Perry, e-mail exchange with the author, April 30, 2008, and January 19, 2003.

23. Albert M. Craig, remarks at the Reischauer Memorial Service at Harvard, October 19, 1990, from Nancy Deptula's notes.

24. Albert M. Craig, interviewed by the author, Cambridge, Mass., November 28, 2007.

25. Letter to parents, December 1948, Edwin O. Reischauer Correspondence, Family Correspondence, 1945–1966, HUGFP 73.6, Harvard Archives. His description of the fifth man (tall, thin, and homely) is of course a humorous reference to himself. The team was sent by the Defense Department from September 1948 to January 1949 to study the condition of the humanities and social sciences in Japanese universities.

26. John Curtis Perry, interviewed by the author, Lincoln, Mass., June 23, 1994. The reference to Oomi came from their reading of Sir George Sansom's *A History of Japan to 1334* (Stanford, Calif.: Stanford University Press, 1958), p. 38.

27. Remarks for the Reischauer Memorial Service at Harvard, October 19, 1990, from Nancy Deptula's notes. Jansen was a professor of Japanese history at Princeton and author of the highly praised *The Making of Modern Japan* (Cambridge, Mass.: Harvard University Press, 2000).

28. Robert Scalapino, interviewed by the author, San Francisco, April 25, 1994.

29. Peter Grilli, interviewed by the author, Cambridge, Mass., January 9, 2008. Grilli would become president of the Japan America Society of Boston.

30. Remarks for the Reischauer Memorial Service at Harvard, October 19, 1990.

31. *MLBJA*, p. 83.

32. Craig, interviewed November 28, 2007.

33. James W. Morley, interviewed by the author, New York, February 10, 1999; and James W. Morley, letter to the author, January 14, 2003.

34. Kent Calder, e-mail exchange with the author, January 27, 2009. Calder holds the Reischauer Chair in East Asian Studies at the Johns Hopkins School of Advanced International Studies.

35. Reischauer Memorial Lecture, published in the *International House of Japan Bulletin* 17, no. 2 (Summer 1997), p. 1.

36. Fairbank, *Chinabound*, p. 145, italics added.

37. *MLBJA*, pp. 114, 81.

38. Howard Hibbett, interviewed by the author, Cambridge, Mass., January 8, 2008.

39. James C. Thomson Jr., interviewed by the author, Cambridge, Mass., June 22, 1994. The most influential Mish-kid was Henry Luce, founder of *Time* magazine.

40. Perry, interviewed June 23, 1994.

41. *MLBJA*, p. 115.

42. The Harvard-Yenching Institute was established in 1928 with the proceeds from the estate of Charles M. Hall, inventor of a process for easily refining aluminum and the founder of the Aluminum Company of America (Alcoa). The institute is a nonprofit foundation dedicated to the advancement of higher education in the humanities and social sciences with emphasis on culture in East and Southeast Asia (from the institute's Web site at http://www.harvard-yenching.org). The institute had fostered close ties with missionary schools in China, but when the United States and China broke relations in 1949, it provided fellowships to students from East Asia. Unfortunately, many of them did not return to their native countries. Under Reischauer's leadership, the institute supported research councils in Japan, Korea, Taiwan, and Hong Kong, and brought to Harvard visiting scholars who were already established in their fields.

43. *MLBJA*, p. 115.

44. Letter to Ann Reischauer Heineman, December 27, 1964, copies of Reischauer's letters to his family 1961–66 provided to the author by Nancy Deptula, unless otherwise noted.

45. *MLBJA*, p. 82.

46. Karl Marx (1818–83) was of course the chief theorist of modern socialism and communism. Max Weber (1864–1920) was a German sociologist, economist, and political scientist. Emile Durkheim (1858–1917) was a French sociologist.

47. Perry, interviewed April 30, 2008.

48. *MLBJA*, p. 74.

49. Edwin O. Reischauer to John S. Service, March 17, 1950, Edwin O. Reischauer Correspondence, 1933–67, Box 1, HUGFP 73.8, Harvard University Archives.

50. Robert N. Bellah, "McCarthyism at Harvard," *New York Review*, February 10, 2005. Bellah's criticism of McGeorge Bundy is recounted in greater detail in Kai Bird, *The Color of Truth: McGeorge Bundy and William Bundy: Brothers in Arms* (New York: Simon and Schuster, 1998), pp. 128–29.

51. Robert N. Bellah, e-mail exchange with the author, February 14, 2005.

52. *MLBJA*, p. 118.

53. Ibid, p. 119. His mature view was reflected in the 1981 edition of Edwin O. Reischauer, *Japan: The Story of a Nation* (New York: McGraw-Hill). More recent scholarship has tended to support Reischauer's positive evaluation of the Tokugawa Era. See, for instance. Ikegami Eiko's *Bonds of Civility* (Cambridge, U.K.: Cambridge University Press, 2005).

6. A FAMILY TRAGEDY AND A NEW START

1. From the title of part IV of Edwin O. Reischauer, *My Life Between Japan and America* (New York: Harper and Row, 1986), hereafter *MLBJA*.

2. This title would later be changed to "professor of Japanese history." From 1956 to 1960, he was also director of the Center for East Asian Studies at Harvard.

3. This organization later adopted its current name, the Association for Asian Studies.

4. Edwin O. Reischauer, *The United States and Japan* (Cambridge, Mass.: Harvard University Press, 1950). The book was subsequently revised and updated in 1957 and 1965, and became the "bible" for readers wishing to understand Japan's character and the American occupation.

5. *Mainichi Shimbun*, August 23, 1950.

6. From the English text of an article dated December 23, 1952, "Japan and America: Do We Understand Each Other?" submitted to *Mainichi Shimbun* and published on page one of the newspaper on January 5, 1953; a copy is included in Edwin O. Reischauer Correspondence, 1933–67, Box 1, HUGFP 73.8, Harvard Archives.

7. Edwin O. Reischauer to Takata Ichitaro, Foreign Editor, *Mainichi Shimbun*, June 1, 1951, Edwin O. Reischauer Correspondence, 1933–67, Box 1, HUGFP 73.8, Harvard Archives.

8. *New York Times*, August 26, 1956.

9. *MLBJA*, p. 148.

10. Robert D. Reischauer, high school composition, dated only 1959, Edwin O. Reischauer Correspondence, 1933–67, Box 1, HUGFP 73.8, Harvard Archives. Edwin Reischauer clearly loved this essay and quotes extensively from it in *MLBJA*, pp. 134–35.

11. Robert D. Reischauer, interviewed by the author, Washington, D.C., January 21, 2003.

12. Joan Reischauer Simon, interviewed by the author, New York, February 27, 2003.

13. *MLBJA*, pp. 136–37.

14. Robert D. Reischauer, interviewed January 21, 2003.

15. *MLBJA*, p. 137.

16. Ibid., pp. 137, 47.

17. Robert D. Reischauer, interviewed January 21, 2003.

18. Winburn T. Thomas to Edwin O. Reischauer, June 10, 1955, Edwin O. Reischauer Correspondence, 1933–67, Box 1, HUGFP 73.8, Harvard Archives.

19. Joan Reischauer Simon, interviewed February 27, 2003.

20. Edwin O. Reischauer to Takata Ichitaro, February 5, 1952, Edwin O. Reischauer Correspondence, 1933–67, Box 1, HUGFP 73.8, Harvard Archives.

21. *MLBJA*, p. 121.

22. Letter to his daughter Ann, December 16, 1961, copies of Reischauer's letters to his family 1961–66 provided by Nancy Deptula, executive director of the Edwin O. Reischauer Institute of Japanese Studies, Harvard University, unless otherwise noted.

23. Reischauer, *The United States and Japan* (1965 ed.), p. 233.

24. *MLBJA*, p. 123.

25. Letter to family, December 3, 1948, E. O. Reischauer Correspondence, Family Correspondence, 1945–66, HUGFP 73.6, Harvard Archives.

26. In a blurb praising Lawrence Taylor's book *A Trial of Generals: Homma, Yamashita, MacArthur* (South Bend, Ind.: Icarus Press, 1981), Reischauer wrote, "MacArthur instead displays some of the seamy side of his strange dual character. He shows how bombastic, petty and vengeful he could be."

27. Blurb by Reischauer in Taylor, *A Trial of Generals*.

28. Edwin O. Reischauer, review of *Failure in Japan* by Robert B. Textor, *New York Times*, June 3, 1951.

29. Unpublished manuscript version of *MLBJA*, p. 251, copy provided to the author by Nancy Deptula.

30. Edwin O. Reischauer, review of *Time of Fallen Blossoms* by Allan S. Clifton, *New York Times*, February 18, 1951. "It is a profoundly moving book," he wrote, "with its intimate glimpses into the hearts of simple people." In using the words "little people of Japan," he was referring not to physical stature, but to the ordinary citizens as opposed to government officials.

31. Unpublished manuscript version of *MLBJA*, p. 274.

32. *MLBJA*, pp. 127–28. Colegrove's accusation would be picked up by the right-wing columnist Holmes Alexander and would be discussed during Reischauer's confirmation hearing before the Senate Foreign Relations Committee on March 23, 1961 (see chapter 7).

33. From a memo by John Condliffe, "A Report Prepared by the Working Party of the Ford Foundation," February 1953, in which he cites a memo by Reischauer, "Some Thoughts on Our Problem in Asia with Specific Reference to Japan" (1952), Call Number 013372, Ford Foundation Archives, New York. Condliffe, a professor of economics at the University of California, Berkeley, included Reischauer's memo in his report to the Ford Foundation, "Bringing to Japan the Teachings and Practices Which Form the Intellectual Foundations of Western Democracy" (1953, unpublished).

34. Reischauer's memo in Condliffe, "Bringing to Japan the Teachings and Practices," pp. 2, 4.

35. Edwin O. Reischauer, *Wanted: An Asian Policy* (New York: Alfred A. Knopf, 1955). Subsequent references are indicated by page number in the text.

36. This may have been the first use of the word *quagmire* in connection with Vietnam. By the late 1960s, when more than five hundred thousand American troops were fighting in Vietnam, the term became a standard description of that enterprise.

37. *MLBJA*, p. 130.

38. *MLBJA*, p. 139.

39. Haru Matsukata, *Samurai and Silk: A Japanese and American Heritage* (Cambridge, Mass.: Harvard University Press, 1986), p. 1. I have drawn heavily on this book for the biographical information about Haru Matsukata in this chapter. The quotes come from pp. 4–15.

40. *MLBJA*, p. 141.

41. Ibid., pp. 141–42.

42. Letter to parents, December 24, 1955, and letter to Margaret, Helen, and Ken, January 10, 1956, Edwin O. Reischauer Correspondence, Family Correspondence, Box 1, HUGFP 73.6, Harvard Archives.

43. *MLBJA*, p. 141.

44. Ibid., p. 142.

45. Unpublished manuscript version of *MLBJA*, pp. 293–94.

46. Matsukata, *Samurai and Silk*, p. 15.

47. Robert D. Reischauer, interviewed January 21, 2003.

48. Selma Janow, interviewed by the author, Washington, D.C., March 24, 2003.

49. The personal information on Senator John D. Rockefeller IV comes from an interview of him by the author, Washington, D.C., June 6, 2008. Jay would use his deep understanding of politics in Japan to explain the real background of the anti–Security Treaty demonstrations of 1960 in seminal articles in *New York Times Magazine*, June 5, 1960, and *Life* magazine, June 20, 1960.

50. Unpublished manuscript version of *MLBJA*, p. 318.

7. A TIME TO "PUT UP OR SHUT UP!"

1. Susan Jacoby, *The Age of American Unreason* (New York: Random House, 2008), p. xii. It was in this period from 1961 to 1963 that Richard Hofstadter defined the problem in his seminal work *Anti Intellectualism in American Life* (New York: Knopf, 1963).

2. Kai Bird, *The Color of Truth: McGeorge Bundy and William Bundy: Brothers in Arms* (New York: Simon and Schuster, 1998), pp. 185 ff. See also Richard Neustadt, Presidential Power (New York: Wiley, 1960).

3. Ibid., p. 186.

4. In an odd quirk of history, Schlesinger, Galbraith, and Reischauer shared an October 15 birth date.

5. Edwin O. Reischauer, *My Life Between Japan and America* (New York: Harper and Row, 1986), p. 145, hereafter *MLBJA*. Today this condition would probably be called "atrial fibrillation."

6. Documents declassified in 2008 by the George Washington University's National Security Archive reveal that at a cabinet meeting in mid-August 1958, General Nathan F. Twining, chairman of the Joint Chiefs of Staff, proposed using ten- to fifteen-ton nuclear bombs on selected fields in the vicinity of Amoy (Xiamen) in the event that the Communist Chinese blockaded Taiwan. President Eisenhower ruled out this option, refusing to accept the contention that nuclear weapons were as conventional as high explosives. *Washington Post*, April 30, 2008.

7. Edwin O. Reischauer to John Foster Dulles, September 29, 1958, Edwin O. Reischauer Correspondence, 1956–60, Box 1, HUGFP 73.8, Harvard Archives.

8. John Foster Dulles to Edwin O. Reischauer, October 31, 1958, Edwin O. Reischauer Correspondence, 1956–60, Box 1, HUGFP 73.8, Harvard Archives.

9. Edwin O. Reischauer, letter to the editor, *New York Times*, March 30, 1959.

10. Edwin O. Reischauer to J. Graham Parsons, August 27, 1959, Edwin O. Reischauer Correspondence, 1956–60, Box 1, HUGFP73.8, Harvard Archives.

11. Marshall Green interview, January 15, 1997, Cold War Interview , Episode 15, National Security Archives, George Washington University, Washington, D.C.

12. J. Graham Parsons to Edwin O. Reischauer, November 23, 1959, Edwin O. Reischauer Correspondence, 1956–60, Box 1, HUGFP 73.8, Harvard Archives.

13. Edwin O. Reischauer to J. Graham Parson, December 2, 1959, Edwin O. Reischauer Correspondence, 1956–60, Box 1, HUGFP73.8, Harvard Archives.

14. Winthrop Knowlton, *My First Revolution* (White Plains, N.Y.: EastBridge Signature Books, 2001), p. 5.

15. James Reed, "In Memoriam, Perspectives," publication of the American Historical Association, February 2003.

16. Theodore Sorenson, *John F. Kennedy* (New York: Harper and Row, 1965), pp. 253–57.

17. Geoffrey Kabaservice, *The Guardians: Kingman Brewster, His Circle, and the Rise of the Liberal Establishment* (New York: Henry Holt, 2004), p. 160.

18. Arthur M. Schlesinger Jr., *A Thousand Days: John F. Kennedy in the White House* (New York: Random House, 1966), pp. 151–52.

19. Peter Lowe, *The Origins of the Korean War* (London: Longman, 1986), p. 14. Lowe also describes Rusk as a member of the "hawkish elements" in the U.S. State Department who favored sending United Nations forces north of the thirty-eighth parallel in the period between July and September, 1950 (p. 181).

20. James Thomson, interviewed by the author, Washington, D.C., October 24, 1965.

21. Tireless in his effort to find a fresh approach to China, Thomson also recommended to Bowles that either Robert Scalapino or A. Doak Barnett be appointed deputy assistant secretary of state for Far Eastern affairs. There is no record of Bowles's reaction. Memorandum to Chester Bowles from James C. Thomson, March 23, 1961, James C. Thomson Papers, Series 1, Department of State, 1960–66, Box 2, State and Embassy Staffing, 1960–61, General, 3/61, John F. Kennedy Memorial Library, Boston.

22. Edwin O. Reischauer, "The Broken Dialogue with Japan," *Foreign Affairs* (October 1960), quotes from pp. 11, 13, 25–26.

23. *MLBJA*, p. 154.

24. "Nippon to no Shiteki na Taiwa" (Our Private Dialogue with Japan), *Sekai*, January 1961.

25. James C. Thomson Jr., "How Could Vietnam Happen?" *Atlantic Monthly* 221, no. 4 (April 1968), p. 47.

26. James C. Thomson, interviewed by the author, Cambridge, Mass., June 22, 1994.

27. Unpublished manuscript version of *MLBJA*, p. 306, copy provided to the author by Nancy Deptula, executive director of the Edwin O. Reischauer Institute of Japan Studies,

Harvard University. The last sentence is omitted from the published version, p. 147, suggesting that Reischauer later had reservations about Bundy's role in promoting the war in Vietnam.

28. Quoted in Bird, *The Color of Truth*, p. 135.

29. Joseph Kraft, "The Two Worlds of McGeorge Bundy," *Harper's* (November 1965), p. 106, quoted in Kabaservice, *The Guardians*, p. 161.

30. Henry Stimson and McGeorge Bundy, *On Active Service in Peace and War* (New York: Harper, 1948).

31. The *McNeil-Lehrer News Hour*, August 6, 1985, transcript no. 2572, quoted in Bird, *The Color of Truth*, pp. 97–98.

32. Quoted in Kabaservice, *The Guardians*, p. 124.

33. Dean Rusk, *As I Saw It* (New York: W. W. Norton, 1990), pp. 85, 607, 533.

34. Bird, *The Color of Truth*, p. 188.

35. Bird quoting an interview of Riesman by David Halberstam, in ibid., p. 153.

36. Quoted in Larissa McFarquar, "East Side Story," *The New Yorker* (February 25, 2008), p. 63.

37. *MLBJA*, p. 165.

38. Ibid., p. 162.

39. Ibid.

40. Ibid., p. 163.

41. Ibid., pp. 163, 164.

42. Haru Matsukata, *Samurai and Silk: A Japanese and American Heritage* (Cambridge, Mass.: Harvard University Press, 1986), p. 16.

43. James Thomson, interviewed October 24, 1965.

44. *MLBJA*, p. 167.

45. *Time* magazine, February 24, 1961.

46. Edwin O. Reischauer, interviewed by Dennis O'Brien, April 25, 1969, Oral History Program, John F. Kennedy Memorial Library, Boston, transcript pp. 4–5.

47. Paraphrased from *Zenei*, April 1961.

48. Paraphrased from article by Sakanishi Shiho, *Chuo Koron*, May 15, 1961.

49. From the summary of press comments in the English-language *Japan Times*, March 16, 1961.

50. *Japan Times*, March 16, 1961.

51. See U.S. Congress, Senate, *Hearings Before the Committee on Foreign Relations*, 87th Cong., 1st sess., January 10 and 12, 1961. Rusk testified on January 12: "I see no prospect at the present time that normal relations could be established with the authorities in Peiping [*sic*] because they seem to feel that the abandonment of the government and people on Formosa would be a prerequisite to any such normal relations" (p. 7). Bowles's response was virtually identical (January 10, 1961), p. 8.

52. U.S. Congress, Senate, Committee on Foreign Relations, Ambassadorial Nominations, 87th Cong., 1st sess., March 23, 1961. Quotations from the committee nomination hearing come from pp. 5–7, 10, 12, 15, 17.

53. In the biographical statement Reischauer submitted to the record on that date, he took pains to note that Haru had received an American education. "When my wife acquired American citizenship through marriage to me and subsequent residence in this county, she was, in

a sense, rounding out legally a basic Americanism that she had received by upbringing and education. I might mention that her brother and three of her four sisters have also become American citizens."

54. *MLBJA*, p. 169.

55. The Institute of Pacific Relations was an international organization set up in 1925 to provide a forum for discussion of issues among the nations of the Pacific Rim. Members included "national councils" from the United States, the Soviet Union, China, Japan, and ten other countries. Founded in the spirit of Wilsonian internationalism, it was supported by major grants from John D. Rockefeller and the Rockefeller Foundation, the Carnegie Corporation, and other major corporations. It also attracted a number of Communist Party members and collaborators with Soviet intelligence agencies. Philip Jessup was a distinguished diplomat, scholar, and jurist, a longtime professor of international law at Columbia University, and a justice on the International Court of Justice (1961–70). Senator Joseph McCarthy accused him in 1950 of pro-Communist sympathies, but Jessup was later cleared of all charges by the State Department's Loyalty Board. McCarthy also accused China specialist Owen Lattimore in 1950 of being a "top Soviet agent." In 1952, after hearings in the McCarran Committee, Lattimore was indicted on seven counts of perjury. Within three years, all charges were dismissed.

56. Fulbright doesn't give any specific information about the Alexander article he quotes here, but the hearings are cited in note 52 of this chapter, U.S. Congress, Senate, Ambassadorial Nominations.

57. Unpublished manuscript version of *MLBJA*, p. 344.

58. Letter to family, December 24, 1961, copies of letters to family 1961–66 provided to the author by Nancy Deptula.

8. ONE SHINING MOMENT

1. Sheila K. Johnson, *American Attitudes Toward Japan, 1941–1975*, American Enterprise Institute–Hoover Policy Study no. 15 (Washington, D.C.: American Enterprise Institute, November 1975), pp. 83–84.

2. Quoted in *New York Times*, March 29, 1964.

3. Quoted in *Asahi Shimbun*, English-language weekend edition, December 17–18, 2005.

4. Kennedy named Philip H. Coombs to be the first assistant secretary of state to run the new bureau, with a mandate to put the embassies in closer touch with leading cultural and educational figures and organizations overseas. However, Coombs resigned in mid-1962, telling Secretary of State Dean Rusk that bureaucratic obstacles and a dearth of funds had hampered his mission. *New York Times*, March 7, 2006.

5. Quoted in the *Yomiuri* (English language), April 20, 1961.

6. Edwin O. Reischauer, *My Life Between Japan and America* (New York: Harper and Row, 1986), p. 179, hereafter *MLBJA*.

7. Ibid., p. 180.

8. U.S. Department of Defense, *Deployment of Military Personnel by Country* (Washington, D.C.: U.S. Government Printing Office, September 30, 1961). Another 38,658 U.S. troops were stationed in Okinawa, which was until 1972 under U.S. administration.

9. FEN, which changed its name to AFN (Armed Forces Network) in 1997 was still on the air in 2009!

10. Letter to family, March 15, 1964, copies of letters to family 1961–66 provided to the author by Nancy Deptula, executive director of the Edwin O. Reischauer Institute of Japanese Studies, Harvard University, unless otherwise cited.

11. Edwin O. Reischauer, interviewed by Dennis O'Brien, April 25, 1969, Oral History Program, John F. Kennedy Memorial Library, Boston, transcript p. 12.

12. Ibid., p. 23.

13. Unpublished manuscript version of *MLBJA*, pp. 408–9, copy provided to the author by Nancy Deptula.

14. Ibid., p. 521.

15. Okinawa, largest of the 140 Ryukyu Islands, is 67 miles long and 2 to 17 miles wide, covering 454 square miles. Then and now it is host to about half of the U.S. troops and bases in Japan.

16. U.S. Department of State, "Joint Communiqué of June 21, 1957, Issued by President Eisenhower and Prime Minister Kishi," *Department of State Bulletin* 37 (July 8, 1957), pp. 51–53.

17. Quoted in *Asahi Shimbun*, November 30, 1969.

18. Unpublished manuscript version of *MLBJA*, p. 426. This view was slightly oversimplified. Many older Okinawans had memories of the final days of battle in April 1945 when the Imperial Japanese Army was alleged to have forced Okinawans to commit massive suicides rather than to submit to American invaders. How Japan's Education Ministry should depict this incident in high school textbooks is still a matter intense controversy. See, for example, *Asahi Shimbun*, October 2, 2007.

19. Unpublished manuscript version of *MLBJA*, p. 425.

20. Reischauer interview, April 25, 1969, JFK Library Oral History Program, transcript p. 13.

21. *MLBJA*, p. 204.

22. Letters to family, February 4, 1962, and July 26, 1964.

23. The massive bombing raid on the huge oil-refining complex at Ploesti, Romania, was aimed at destroying an important source of German oil.

24. *MLBJA*, pp. 247, 246.

25. Edwin O. Reischauer, interviewed by the author, Belmont, Mass., May 17, 1981. President Kennedy had decreed in 1961 that the U.S. ambassador to every country would head up a country team that included key representatives of all the top agencies in that country, such as Treasury, Commerce, the military attaches, Central Intelligence Agency, and so on. Reischauer felt that the case of Japan was different.

26. *New York Times*, November 16, 2006.

27. Saito Setsuko, telephone interview by the author, April 23, 2008.

28. Reischauer, interviewed at Belmont, May 17, 1981.

29. *MLBJA*, p. 248.

30. Letter to family, January 20, 1963.

31. Letter to family, October 13, 1963.

32. Speech to the Research Institute of Japan, "The Meaning of the Japanese-American 'Partnership,'" October 5, 1961.

33. For a fuller account of this period, see George R. Packard, *Protest in Tokyo* (Princeton, N.J.: Princeton University Press, 1966).

34. Reischauer interview, April 25, 1969, JFK Library Oral History Program, transcript p. 19.

35. Roy Mlynarchik, chief of the Office of Translation Services, U.S. Embassy, Tokyo, interviewed by the author, Tokyo, April 12, 1994.

36. In 1973, in what the Foreign Service jokingly called the "Emancipation Proclamation," ambassadors were forbidden to require lower-level spouses to work at official functions.

37. Mlynarchik interview, April 12, 1994.

38. Albert Seligmann, telephone interview by the author, Washington, D.C., January 11, 2007.

39. Over the next five years, Reischauer made a point of bringing Japanese-language officers into key embassy positions: John Emmerson became his deputy chief of mission and Burton Fahs his cultural minister; David Osborne, Owen Zurhellen, John Stegmeier, Thomas Shoesmith, William L. Givens, Ulrich Strauss, and Toshio Tsukahira were among this talented group.

40. Letter to family, January 1, 1962.

41. Kenneth B. Pyle, *The Japanese Question: Power and Purpose in a New Era*, 2d ed. (Washington, D.C.: American Enterprise Institute, 1996), p. 34.

42. Unpublished manuscript version of *MLBJA*, p. 436.

43. *MLBJA*, pp. 212–13.

44. Quoted in *Asahi Shimbun*, July 26, 1966.

45. Memorandum dated July 16, 1965, declassified in September 30, 1996, by the National Security Archive, George Washington University, and reported in the *New York Times*, March 31, 1997.

46. Tim Weiner, *Legacy of Ashes: The History of the CIA* (New York: Doubleday, 2007), pp. 116–21.

47. Seligmann interview, January 11, 2007.

48. Reischauer, interviewed at Belmont, May 17, 1981.

49. From the moment of his and Haru's arrival in Tokyo, Reischauer wrote a weekly letter to his family—sometimes banging it out on a portable typewriter, with many abbreviations and misspellings, or sometimes dictating it on a Sony tape recorder for transcription by his secretary. Haru would often add a note of her own. His father preserved all of these letters in Belmont. Taken together, they provide a complete historical record of his time as ambassador, which is exactly what he, as an historian, wanted to preserve. The complete set, made available to me by his assistant, Nancy Deptula, in 1994, offers fascinating glimpses into his innermost thinking. In quoting from these letters, I have cleaned up typographical and punctuation errors for purposes of clarity.

50. Letter to family, March 1, 1964.

51. Letter to family, May 28, 1961.

52. Letter to family, June 11, 1961.

53. Reischauer interview, April 25, 1969, JFK Library Oral History Program, transcript p. 9.

54. Unpublished manuscript version of *MLBJA*, p. 368.

55. Edwin O. Reischauer to Derek Bok, December 11, 1978, Edwin O. Reischauer Correspondence, Box 4, HUGFP 73.10, Harvard University Archives.

56. Letter to family, March 9, 1963.

57. Letter to kids, September 24, 1961.

58. Edwin O. Reischauer, "Increased Contact with Japanese 'Intellectuals,'" June 26, 1961, (limited use only), p. 1, Ford Foundation International Training and Research (ITR), Box no. 035696, Japan ITR Program folder, Ford Foundation Archives, New York.

59. Ibid., pp. 2–3. 4–5.

60. Letter to father, August 6, 1962.

61. Letter to family, December 6, 1964. For a Marxist view of Reischauer's "offensive," see Kurahara Korehito, "Raishawa Shi no Tetsugaku to Amerika no 'Heiwa Senryaku'" (Mr. Reischauer's Philosophy and America's Strategy), *Bunka Hyoron* (January 1964): 1–26.

62. Letters to family, January 27, 1963, and October 20, 1962.

63. Letter to friends who had sent Christmas greetings, January 1964. With tongue in cheek, he labeled this report, "An Unbiased Report on the Reischauers."

64. Letter to family, September 22, 1963.

65. Unpublished manuscript version of *MLBJA*, p. 420. See Oda Makoto, *Nan Demo Mite Yaro* (Let's Look at Everything) (Tokyo: Kawade Shobo Shinsha, 1961).

66. Edwin O. Reischauer, "The Broken Dialogue with Japan," *Foreign Affairs* (October 1960), p. 20.

67. Aoki's account of this incident was published in *Nikkei Shimbun*, October 14, 2007, and later appeared in his book *Watashi no Rirekisho* (My Personal History) (Tokyo: Nippon Keizai Shimbun Sha, 2008).

68. Several ambassadors who followed Reischauer continued this practice; James W. Morley, Michael H. Armacost, Edward J. Lincoln, and Kent Calder served in similar capacities.

69. Reischauer, interviewed at Belmont, May 17, 1981.

70. *Asahi Shimbun* alone carried 297 articles in which Reischauer's name appeared in the headline between January 30, 1961, and August 19, 1966.

71. Letter to family, October 7, 1962.

72. *Shufu no Tomo*, April 1961.

73. *Fujin Koron*, July 1961.

74. Quoted in *Chicago Tribune Magazine*, May 15, 1966.

75. Letter to family, December 3, 1961.

76. Richard Halloran, telephone interview by the author, July 9, 2009.

77. Letter to kids, November 27, 1962. Reischauer had suggested using Peace Corps volunteers to teach English in Japan, but his idea was rebuffed in both Washington and Tokyo. Because President Kennedy had launched the Peace Corps as an American initiative to aid the Third World nations, the Japanese were naturally reluctant to be placed in this category. In his farewell press conference in Washington in 1966, Reischauer said that his failure to persuade the government of Japan to accept Peace Corps volunteers was his greatest failure as ambassador.

78. John K. Emmerson, *The Japanese Thread* (New York: Holt, Rinehart and Winston, 1978), p. 366. Hashimoto's letter was dated June 21, 1963.

79. Letter to family, September 10, 1962.

80. Letter to family, July 15, 1962, emphasis in original.

81. Letter to family, August 26, 1962.

82. Haru Reischauer to Ann Heineman, June 16, 1963, copy provided to the author by Nancy Deptula.

83. Haru Reischauer to Ann and Steve Heineman, June 24, 1961, copy provided to the author by Nancy Deptula.

84. Letter to family, July 2, 1961.

85. Robert D. Reischauer, interviewed by the author, Washington, D.C., January 21, 2003.

86. Letter to Miye Matsukata (Haru's sister), September 20, 1961, letter provided by Nancy Deptula.

87. Edwin O. Reischauer to Arthur Billings, January 18, 1962, copy provided to the author by Nancy Deptula.

88. Haru Reischauer to Ann and Steve Heineman, August 6, 1961; Haru Reischauer to Kitty Galbraith, August 6, 1961; copies of both provided by Nancy Deptula.

89. The group consisted of William L. Givens, John Horgan, Nathaniel Thayer, Eugene Windchy, and the author.

90. Among occasional Japanese participants were Kiuchi Akitane, who later became ambassador to France; Sassa Atsuyuki, who became a leading authority on security issues in the National Police Agency; and Wakaizumi Kei, a writer and intellectual who would later become a secret intermediary between Kissinger and Sato on the negotiations over Okinawa. Wakaizumi describes his role in *The Best Course Available: A Personal Account of the Secret U.S.–Japan Reversion Negotiations* (Honolulu: University of Hawaii Press, 2002).

91. I was the aide who drafted the letter.

92. The expression usually refers to a situation where a senior person offers a younger person some financial or other help but does not expect anything in return. It implies "you do not have to pay me back, but do your best in your endeavors" and is a particularly Japanese notion.

93. See Jacques Barzun and Henry F. Graff, *The Modern Researcher* (New York: Harcourt Brace and Jovanovich, 1977), pp. 271–72 n. 14

94. *MLBJA*, p. 229.

95. Letter to family, June 10, 1961.

96. *MLBJA*, p. 208.

97. Ibid., p. 234.

98. Ibid., p. 235.

99. Ibid.

100. Ibid., p. 238.

101. Ibid., p. 249.

102. Had Bobby Kennedy been elected president in 1968, I am certain he would have offered Reischauer a high post in his administration—possibly even secretary of state. Reischauer spent a day campaigning for Kennedy in California in the spring of 1968, a highly unusual step into politics for him.

103. William L. Givens, telephone interview by the author, July 9, 2009.

104. In a famous interpreting gaffe, Sato said in Japanese, "Zensho itashimasu," which was wrongly interpreted as "I will do it" rather than "I will do my best." Nixon, who had been elected in 1968 with a "southern strategy," felt he could repay his southern supporters by getting Japan to curb the flood of inexpensive Japanese textiles that was injuring southern textile manufacturers. When Sato was unable or unwilling to curb the flow, Nixon felt he had been betrayed, and the result was the "Nixon Shocks" of 1971, in which he applied a 10 percent tariff to Japanese imports, invoking the Trading with the Enemy Act of World War I; abruptly took the United States off the gold standard, thus raising the price of Japanese goods; and recognized Communist China with almost no warning to Japan.

105. Recently declassified U.S. documents dated November 12 and 13, 1969, confirm that there was a secret agreement between the two governments allowing U.S. nuclear weapons to be brought into Okinawa in emergency situations in exchange for Okinawa's reversion to Japan in 1972. *Japan Times*, October 8, 2007.

106. *Asahi Shimbun*, November 30, 1969, Edwin O. Reischauer Correspondence, Box 2, HUGFP 73.10, Harvard University Archives.

107. *MLBJA*, p. 250. It appears that Reischauer was not telling the full story (see note 109).

108. U.S. Department of State, *Security Treaty Between the United States of America and Japan* (and related documents), vol. 11 of *United States Treaties and Other International Agreements*, TIAS 4509 (Washington, U.S. Government Printing Office, 1961), pp. 1633–35.

109. *MLBJA*, p. 251. According to secret U.S. State Department documents declassified June 4, 1996, Reischauer actually handed Ohira the English and Japanese classified records of a discussion of January 6, 1960, in which the U.S. understanding of the term *mochikomi* was agreed to by both sides. U.S Department of State, Secret/Eyes Only Incoming Telegram from U.S. Ambassador Edwin Reischauer to Secretary of State, no. 2335, April 4, 1963, obtained by Yoshitaka Sasaki from the U.S. National Archives, College Park, Md.. For more on this issue, see Haruna Mikio, "Nichi-Bei Mitsuyaku: Kishi-Sato no Uragiri," *Bungei Shunju*, July 2008. See also Wampler, Robert A., ed., Electronic Briefing Book, Nuclear Noh Duamg: Tokyo, Washington and the case of the missing Nuclear Agreements, National Security Archive, October 13, 2009. Nevertheless, the Japanese government continued in October 2009 to insist that no such agreement existed. *Tokyo Shimbun*, June 1, 2009.

110. Letter to family, April 6, 1963.

111. *Asahi Shimbun*, August 1, 2005. This report, citing recently declassified documents from the National Security Archives at George Washington University in Washington, D.C., also said that Prime Minister Ikeda told Rusk in November 1961 that several members of his cabinet favored nuclear armaments for Japan.

112. Ibid. Another *Asahi* report published on December 22, 2008, citing documents recently declassified by the Foreign Ministry of Japan, said that Prime Minister Sato, in a meeting with Defense Secretary Robert McNamara, requested that in the event of an outbreak of war between Japan and China, the United States be prepared to deploy nuclear weapons for a retaliatory attack against China.

113. Declassified documents have revealed that secret minutes to the Security Treaty signed

on June 23, 1960, by Foreign Minister Fujiyama Aiichiro and Ambassador to Japan Douglas MacArthur II allowed the United States to use its bases in Japan without prior consultations with the Japanese government in the event of a contingency on the Korean Peninsula. See *Asahi Shimbun*, June 4, 2008. It is not clear whether Reischauer knew of the existence of these minutes during his term as ambassador.

114. Letters to family, May 28, September 11, and October 15, 1961.

115. Unpublished manuscript version of *MLBJA*, pp. 433–34.

116. Letter to family, April 22, 1962. The strenuous action he urged was presumably for the United States to sweeten Japan's offer to South Korea by a substantial grant.

117. Edwin O. Reischauer to Professor Jun-yop Kim, Asiatic Research Center, Korea University, September 4, 1973, Edwin O. Reischauer Correspondence, Box 3, HUGFP 73.10, Harvard University Archives. Kim Dae Jung would be released and would later become president of the Republic of Korea. He would adopt a "sunshine policy" in seeking reconciliation with the Democratic People's Republic of Korea (North Korea), a stance Reischauer would have applauded.

118. Letter to family, December 16, 1962.

9. A DARKENING SKY

1. Edwin O. Reischauer, interviewed on April 8, 1969, for the Oral History Project of the Lyndon B. Johnson Memorial Library, Austin, Texas.

2. U.S. Embassy Tokyo press release, March 24, 1964.

3. *Asahi Shimbun,* March 25, 1964. The page one headline in *Asahi's* evening edition was "Yuketsu de Konketsuji no yo" (From Receiving Blood, Feel Like a Mixed-Blood Child).

4. *New York Times*, March 24–25, 1964.

5. Edwin O. Reischauer, *My Life Between Japan and America* (New York: Harper and Row, 1986), p. 263, hereafter *MLBJA*.

6. Both cables quoted in *Los Angeles Times*, March 25–26, 1964.

7. I am indebted for this account of Shiotani's life to Okamura Ao's book *Jukyusai Teroru no Kisetsu* (Nineteen Years Old—the Season of Terror) (Tokyo: Gendai Shokan, August 20, 1989).

8. *Chicago Tribune*, March 25, 1964.

9. Seishin Hoken Fukushi Kenkyukai (Study Group for Mental Health and Welfare), *Seishin Hoken Fukushi Ho Shokai* (Explanation of the Mental Health and Welfare Law) (Tokyo: Chuo Hoki Shuppan, October 2002), and *Wagakuni no Seishin Hoken Fukushi* (Mental Health and Welfare in Japan) (Tokyo: Koken Shuppan, 2000).

10. Quoted in the *Washington Post*, March 28, 1964.

11. *New York Times*, March 26, 1964

12. Letter to family, March 27, 1964, copies of letters to his family 1961–66 provided to the author by Nancy Deptula, executive director of the Edwin O. Reischauer Institute of Japan Studies, Harvard University.

13. *MLBJA*, p. 264.

14. Quoted in *Washington Post*, April 16, 1964.

15. *MLBJA*, p. 275.

16. Letter to family, June 20, 1964.

17. Quoted in *New York Times*, July 20, 1964.

18. *MLBJA*, p. 275.

19. Letter to family, July 12, 1964.

20. Letter to family, July 19, 1964.

21. Kai Bird, *The Color of Truth: McGeorge Bundy and William Bundy: Brothers in Arms* (New York: Simon and Schuster, 1998), p. 255.

22. Ibid., p. 272.

23. Quoted in ibid., p. 221.

24. Forrestal, son of former secretary of war James Forrestal, was a highly intelligent lawyer from the New York firm of Shearman and Sterling, but he lacked any specialized knowledge of Asian affairs.

25. Kennedy partisans argue to this day that had President Kennedy lived, he would never have escalated U.S. military involvement in the Vietnam War. They point out that Kennedy had approved a plan to begin withdrawing U.S. forces in December 1963, with almost all the rest withdrawn by the end of 1965. But the plan was contingent on McNamara and General Maxwell Taylor's judgment that sufficient progress would have been made that Hanoi and the Vietcong could not win the war in the South. What Kennedy would have done if faced with the choice that Johnson faced in 1965 cannot be known. Letter from Francis M. Bator, former deputy national security advisor to President Lyndon B. Johnson, *New York Review*, January 17, 2008.

26. For this account of decision making on Vietnam, I am indebted to Kai Bird's masterful book *The Color of Truth*, chapters 12–14.

27. Letter to family, June 5, 1964.

28. Transcript of interview with Ambassador Marshall Green, interviewed by Charles Stuart Kennedy, Foreign Affairs Oral History Project, Box 1, Fold 48, 1956–71, Georgetown University, Washington, D.C.

29. Reischauer, interviewed April 8, 1969, LBJ Memorial Library Oral History Project.

30. Robert J. Hanyok's study of National Security Agency documents released November 30, 2005, concluded that "the overwhelming body of reports, if used, would have told the story that no attack had happened. So a conscious effort ensued to demonstrate that an attack had occurred." Quoted in *New York Times*, December 2, 2005.

31. Letter to family, January 31, 1965.

32. Letter to family, February 28, 1965.

33. Letter to family, March 28, 1965.

34. Letter to family, April 4, 1965.

35. Gordon M. Goldstein, *Lessons in Disaster: McGeorge Bundy and the Path to War in Vietnam* (New York: Henry Holt, 2008), p. 20, citing Robert S. McNamara, with Brian VanDeMark, *In Retrospect: The Tragedy and Lessons of Vietnam* (New York: Times Books, 1995).

36. In an extraordinary revelation by Thomas L. Hughes, director of the State Department's Bureau of Intelligence and Research, published in 2004, top Washington officials who harbored private doubts about whether the war could be won and whether the United States had any national interest at stake in Vietnam included Chester Bowles, Hubert Humphrey, Clark Clifford, Bill Moyers, Dean Acheson, Richard Helms, Richard Russell, and even Presi-

dent Johnson himself. "To a far greater extent than was imagined in the 1960's, prominent officials in Washington engaged in a combined patriotic, political and careerist suppression of their strong personal doubts about the war," wrote Hughes in "A Retrospective Preface Thirty-five Years Later," his introduction to *Intelligence and Vietnam: The Top Secret 1969 State Department Study*, National Security Archive Electronic Briefing Book no. 121 (Washington, D.C.: National Security Archive, 2004), p. 1.

37. James C. Thomson Jr., "How Could Vietnam Happen? An Autopsy," *Atlantic Monthly* 221, no. 4 (April 1968), p. 49.

38. Edwin O. Reischauer, interviewed by the author, Belmont, Mass., May 17, 1981.

39. Thomas Havens, *Fire Across the Sea: The Vietnam War and Japan, 1965–1975* (Princeton, N.J.: Princeton University Press, 1987), p. 76. Asked in 1969 whether there was adequate consultation or any consultation with the Japanese government prior to the various crucial decisions that were made by our government that year, Reischauer replied, "No, there was not." From the April 8, 1969, LBJ Memorial Library Oral History Project interview, transcript p. 6.

40. Havens, *Fire Across the Sea*, pp. 27, 88.

41. H. R. McMaster, *Dereliction of Duty* (New York: Harper Collins, 1997), p. 334.

42. Letter to family, March 26, 1966.

43. *MLBJA*, p. 281.

44. Letter to family, November 15, 1964.

45. Letter to family, June 6, 1965.

46. Letters to Ann, May, September, and November 1965.

47. Letter to family, November 6, 1965.

48. Handwritten letter to Ann, December 1965.

49. Ibid.

50. Letter to family, June 18, 1966. Zinn would go on to write *A People's History of the United States* (New York: HarperCollins, 1980), a best-selling grassroots history of dissent and resistance to power in America.

51. *MLBJA*, p. 290.

52. Samuel Jameson article in *Chicago Tribune*, July 31, 1966.

53. Edwin O. Reischauer to George Packard, November 4, 1965.

54. Omori Minoru, "Raishawa wa Futari Ita" (Reischauer Was Two Persons), *Bungei Shunju* (June 1966), pp. 192–200. Omori was even more critical in his subsequent book, *Ishi ni Kaku: Raishawa Jiken no Shinsou* (Writing on Stone: The True Account of the Reischauer Incident) (Tokyo: Ushio Shuppansha, 1971). The book sold well.

55. Letter to family, May 23, 1965.

56. *MLBJA*, pp. 292–93, quoting a letter to family.

57. *Akahata*, the Communist Party newspaper, reported on September 7, 2008, that recently declassified documents at the U.S. National Archives revealed that the Japanese government in 1964 requested that the nuclear-powered submarines entering Japanese ports should not discharge any liquid or solid radioactive waste, but that the United States refused, saying that "it is necessary to discharge a small amount of low-level radioactive (cooling) water during the nuclear reactor's primary warm-up."

58. Reischauer briefly mentions this incident in *MLBJA*, p. 299. The incident also gets

a brief mention in Takemae Eiji's *The Allied Occupation of Japan* (New York: Continuum, 2002), p. 526.

59. Letter to family, April 23, 1966. This statement is strong evidence that this incident took place in 1966, not 1961, as Reischauer would later assert. See note 60.

60. A *New York Times* article by Richard Halloran on May 23, 1981, recounts these events but quotes both Reischauer and Johnson as asserting that the events happened in 1961. Either their memories were faulty in 1981, or they intended to minimize the length of time in which the United States was in violation of the treaty. Daniel H. Ellsberg held a press conference on May 22, 1981, in which he released a ten-year-old memo dated simply July 1971 that asserted that the weapons were still at Iwakuni in 1967. I accept the account by William Givens, who had access to all the key players (see note 61 and the long quote of Givens in the text).

61. William L. Givens, telephone interview by and e-mail exchange with the author, January 7, 2008.

62. Memorandum for Mr. Bundy, January 6, 1966, classified secret and approved for release October 19, 1999, NLK-37-008-2-1-2, with redactions. The memo is dated January 6, 1965, but the contents make it clear that it had to have been written in January 1966.

63. Quoted in Bird, *The Color of Truth*, p. 346, based on an interview with James C. Thomson Jr., February 13, 1995.

64. Ibid.

65. Ibid., p. 373.

66. I was the diplomatic correspondent for *Newsweek* who received and reported this leak.

67. Letter to family, March 7, 1966.

68. Embassy of the United States, confidential letter from Edwin O. Reischauer to James C. Thomson Jr. Esquire, TKY-39, 10F2, Series A, March 23, 1966, declassified June 16, 1997, copy provided to the author by Nancy Deptula.

69. Letter to kids, July 9, 1966.

70. From the April 8, 1969, LBJ Memorial Library Oral History Project interview, transcript p. 13.

71. Ibid., p. 21.

72. Letter to Ann, April 1966, and letter to family, May 15, 1966.

73. Quoted in *New York Times Book Review*, November 30, 2008, p. 13.

74. Lippmann and Schlesinger quoted in Bird, *The Color of Truth*, pp. 347–48.

75. Goldstein, *Lessons in Disaster*. Goldstein, who served as a researcher for Bundy, noted, "It was clear from the beginning that Bundy was distinctly uninterested in the topic of Vietnamese nationalism and the origins of the communist insurgency" (p. 29). In other words, Bundy still didn't get it. See note 35 for McNamara's book.

76. Arthur Schlesinger Jr., "The Missionary Enterprise and Theories of Imperialism," in John K. Fairbank, ed., *The Missionary Enterprise in China and America* (Cambridge, Mass.: Harvard University Press, 1974), p. 373.

77. Unpublished manuscript version of *MLBJA*, p. 624, copy provided to the author by Nancy Deptula.

78. *MLBJA*, p. 301.

79. Statement of Senator Mike Mansfield at the Senate Foreign Relations Committee Sub-

committee on State Department Organization Affairs hearings, 89th Cong., 2d sess., July 22, 1966.

80. *MLBJA*, p. 288.

81. James C. Thomson Jr., *While China Faced West* (Cambridge, Mass.: Harvard University Press, 1969); James C. Thomson Jr., Peter W. Stanley, and John Curtis Perry, *Sentimental Imperialists* (New York: Harper and Row, 1981).

82. Unpublished manuscript version of *MLBJA*, p. 627.

83. *Japan Times*, July 27, 1966.

84. Richard Halloran article in *Boston Sunday Globe Magazine*, June 12, 1966.

85. As remembered by Robert Immerman, interviewed by the author, New York, March 31, 2004. In November 1961, Reischauer and Foreign Minister Kosaka Zentaro hatched a plan to send one hundred American Peace Corps volunteers to Japan to teach English and to bring one hundred Japanese counterparts to the United States to teach the Japanese language as well as Japanese arts and crafts. The Education Ministry and Nikkyoso (the Teachers' Union) swiftly opposed the idea, and it died shortly thereafter.

86. Letter to kids, August 13, 1966.

87. *Face the Nation*, CBS News, August 28, 1956.

88. Letter to Ann, June 25, 1966.

89. Letter to family, August 13, 1966.

10. A HARD LANDING

1. "A Conversation with Former Ambassador Reischauer," *Harvard Alumni Bulletin* (October 15, 1966), p. 19.

2. Ibid., pp. 18–24.

3. U.S. Congress, Senate, *Hearing Before the Committee on Foreign Relations*, 90th Cong., 1st sess., January 31, 1967.

4. *New York Times*, February 1, 1967.

5. *Washington Post*, April 6, 1967.

6. Edwin O. Reischauer, *Beyond Vietnam: The United States and Asia* (New York: Random House, 1967), pp. 5–6.

7. Ad Hoc Committee on Vietnam, Harvard University, press release, January 16, 1968. A total of 341 faculty members, 3,077 Harvard and Radcliffe undergraduates, and 772 other Harvard students, faculty, and staff signed this message..

8. U.S. House of Representatives, *Hearings Before the Subcommittee on Asian and Pacific Affairs of the Committee on Foreign Affairs*, 90th Cong., 2d sess., February 29, 1968, p. 16.

9. Quoted in Randall Bennett Woods, *Fulbright: A Biography* (New York: Cambridge University Press, 1995), p. 476.

10. I was the White House correspondent for the *Philadelphia Bulletin* and a member of the small press pool that flew with Johnson to Texas on Air Force One the following day, April 1, 1968. Johnson, in off-the-record remarks, talked for most of the way about his bitterness and anger toward Bobby Kennedy and the other JFK advisors who, he claimed, got him into the war in Vietnam and were now bailing out.

11. *New York Times*, March 28, 1968.

12. *New York Times*, May 12, 1968.

13. In M. R. Montgomery, "The Reischauer Shock: Reflections on a Career and Controversy," *Boston Globe Magazine*, September 27, 1981.

14. Quoted in Michael Schaller, *Altered States: The United States and Japan Since the Occupation* (New York: Oxford University Press, 1997), p. 236.

15. Edwin O. Reischauer to Graham Allison, August 28, 1972, Edwin O. Reischauer Correspondence, Box 2, HUGFP 73.10, Harvard University Archives.

16. *Washington Post*, June 5, 1981. The *New York Times* carries a full account of this affair in an article by Richard Halloran, May 19, 1981.

17. Edwin O. Reischauer, *Japan: The Story of a Nation* (New York: Knopf, 1981), pp. 357–58.

18. This controversy has not died down in Japan. In an article in *Bungei Shunju* of July 2008, "Secret Agreements Between Japan and the U.S.: Treacherous Acts by Kishi and Sato," by former Kyodo correspondent Haruna Mikio, Reischauer is accused of lying when he claimed that only a verbal agreement on this point existed. Haruna charges that Reischauer had to be fully aware of the existence of a secret written agreement. He based his report on a cable from Reischauer to Secretary of State Dean Rusk dated April 4, 1963, that was briefly declassified and then a month later reclassified in 1999. In this cable, Reischauer allegedly referred to a Record of Discussion, 2A and 2C, in English, dated January 6, 1960. Haruna argues that this record was a written secret agreement allowing U.S. nuclear-armed ships to transit Japanese ports. If such a document exists, Haruna asserts, it means that Reischauer lied when he claimed in his memoir it was only an oral agreement and that the Japanese government is even today lying when it claims such a document does not exist. Reischauer is in fact vague on this point; as noted in chapter 8, he asserts in his 1986 memoir that he was relying entirely on his memory and that he "had understood that in the negotiations leading up to the revised security treaty of 1960," there had been an oral agreement (unpublished manuscript version of Edwin O. Reischauer, *My Life Between Japan and America* [New York: Harper and Row, 1986], hereafter *MLBJA*, p. 250), but he does not say whether there was also a written document or not. Subsequent revelations in Japan indicate that there had indeed been a written document. In June 2009, several former vice ministers of the Department of Foreign Affairs revealed that a secret written agreement did exist. (*Tokyo Shimbun*, July 1, 2009). As of October 2009, the Japanese government continued to deny that any agreement existed.

19. U.S. Department of State, "Security Treaty Between the United States of America and Japan," and related documents, *United States Treaties and Other International Agreements* 11, TIAS 4509, pp. 1633–35.

20. *Washington Post*, June 2, 1981.

21. Quoted in *Yomiuri Shimbun*, May 19, 1981, my translation.

22. Montgomery, "The Reischauer Shock," p. 48.

23. *MLBJA*, p. 716.

24. Ezra Vogel, *Japan as Number One: Lessons for America* (Cambridge, Mass.: Harvard University Press, 1979).

25. Norman Isaacs to Edwin O. Reischauer, May 19, 1970, Edwin O. Reischauer Correspondence, Box 2, HUGFP 73.10, Harvard University Archives.

26. John K. Fairbank, Edwin O. Reischauer, and Albert Craig, *East Asia: Tradition and Transformation* (Boston: Houghton Mifflin, 1973).

27. Edwin O. Reischauer, *The Japanese Today: Change and Continuity* (Cambridge, Mass.: Belknap Press of Harvard University Press, 1988; originally published as *The Japanese* in 1977), updated in 1995 by Marius Jensen after Reischauer's death and republished in 2003.

28. *Bungei Shunju* bought the rights to publish the book in translation for thirty-five thousand dollars and published it in the fall of 1977.

29. Both quotes come from Frank Gibney, review of *The Japanese* by Edwin O. Reischauer, *New York Times Book Review*, June 12, 1977.

30. Albert M. Craig and Donald H. Shively, eds., *Personality in Japanese History* (Berkeley: University of California Press, 1970).

31. Edward Friedman and Mark Selden, eds., *America's Asia: Dissenting Essays on Asian American Relations* (New York: Pantheon Books, 1969). Quotations come from the editors' introduction to the volume, p. xi.

32. John Whitney Hall, "Changing Conceptions of the Modernization of Japan," in Marius Jansen, ed., *Changing Japanese Attitudes Toward Modernization* (Princeton, N.J.: Princeton University Press, 1965), p. 19.

33. Edwin O. Reischauer, "Toward a Definition of Modernization," a lecture given at Nihon University on September 26, 1964, and published in *Jiyu* in January 1965.

34. The term *liberal* has many meanings in American politics. Reischauer's views were close to those of Arthur Schlesinger (*The Vital Center*, 1949), George Orwell (*1984*, published in 1949), and Richard Crossman (*The God That Failed*, 1950), all books that made the case for liberal anticommunism. Unlike many of his contemporary liberal anti-Communists, however, Reischauer had never been a member of the Communist Party nor a "fellow traveler." He reached his conclusions from his study of history, as noted in chapter 3: dialectical materialism, class struggle, and historical determinism made no sense to him. Individuals mattered. Nor was he ever tempted to join in a movement or to write for a partisan publication. He was content to let his books speak for themselves.

35. *MLBJA*, p. 155.

36. John W. Dower, "E. H. Norman, Japan, and the Uses of History," in E. H. Norman, *Origins of the Modern Japanese State: Selected Writings of E. H. Norman*, edited by John W. Dower, pp. 3–101 (New York: Random House, 1975).

37. E. H. Norman, *Japan's Emergence as a Modern State: Political and Economic Problems of the Meiji Period* (New York: Institute of Pacific Relations, 1940); this book was recently reprinted in an edition edited by Lawrence T. Wood (Vancouver: University of British Columbia Press, 2000).

38. E. H. Norman, *Ando Shoeki and the Anatomy of Japanese Feudalism* (Tokyo: Asiatic Society of Japan, 1949).

39. For a discussion of Norman's guilt or innocence, see the excellent biography by Roger Bowen, *Innocence Is Not Enough: The Life and Death of Herbert Norman* (Armonk, N.Y.: M. E. Sharpe, 1988). Bowen argues persuasively that Norman was not a Communist agent.

40. Eto Jun, "Modernization and Japan [in Japanese], Dialogue with Edwin O. Reischauer," in Eto Jun Zen Taiwa, *The Collected Conversations of Eto Jun* (in Japanese), vol. 2 (Tokyo:

Ozawa Shoten, 1974), pp. 158–71. This was an account of a dialogue that took place in February 1965.

41. Ouchi Hyoe, "Nichi-Bei Kankei no Shorai" (The Future of U.S.–Japan Relations), in Ouchi Hyoe Chosaku-shu, *The Collected Works of Ouchi Hyoe* (in Japanese), vol. 7 (Tokyo: Iwanami Shoten, 1975), pp. 432–33.

42. See *Jiyu*, January 1965.

43. The quotes are from the 1944 essay "Feudal Background of Japanese Politics," in Norman, *Origins of the Modern Japanese State*, pp. 323, 358.

44. Reischauer, *Japan: The Story of a Nation*, 3rd ed., p. 136.

45. Norman, *Origins of the Japanese State*, p. 358. For a deeper look at this dispute, see John W. Hall, "E. H. Norman on Tokugawa Japan," and George Akita, "An Examination of E. H. Norman's Scholarship," *Journal of Japanese Studies* 3, no. 2 (Summer 1977): 365–419, and the rejoinder by Herbert Bix, "The Pitfalls of Scholastic Criticism: A Reply to Norman's Critics," *Journal of Japanese Studies* 4, no. 2 (Summer 1978): 391–411. For another thoughtful review, see Richard H. Minear, "Cross-Cultural Perception and World War II: American Japanists of the 1940's and Their Images of Japan," *International Studies Quarterly* 24, no. 4 (December 1980): 555–80.

46. John W. Dower's *Embracing Defeat: Japan in the Wake of World War Two* (New York: W. W. Norton and New Press, 1999) won a number of awards, including the Pulitzer Prize in 2000.

47. Herbert Bix, *Hirohito and the Making of Modern Japan* (New York: HarperCollins, 2000).

48. For another discussion of this topic, see Warren I. Cohen, *The Asian American Century* (Cambridge, Mass.: Harvard University Press, 2002). Recent studies of the Tokugawa Era have been critical of Norman's interpretation—for example, Ikegami Eiko's *The Taming of the Samurai* (Cambridge, Mass.: Harvard University Press, 1995).

49. Patrick Smith, *Japan: A Reinterpretation* (New York: Random House, 1997), p. 25. It is perhaps useful to recall the words of Reischauer's friend Ken Galbraith on academic battles: "All academic disciplines have their feuds—intense conflicts much cherished by the participants and regularly combining differences in scholarly method or conclusion with deep personal dislike. They are large in the minds of those involved and usually unknown to the world outside." John Kenneth Galbraith, *A Life in Our Times* (Boston: Houghton Mifflin, 1981), p. 55.

50. E. H. Norman, book review of *Japan: Past and Present*, by Edwin O. Reischauer, *Pacific Affairs* (September 1947), p. 358.

51. Edwin O. Reischauer, "Herb Norman: The Perspective of a Lifelong Friend," in Roger Bowen, ed., *E. H. Norman: His Life and Scholarship* (Toronto: University of Toronto Press, 1984), p. 12.

52. Roger Bowen to the author, January 3, 2003.

53. Reischauer, "Herb Norman," pp. 11–12.

54. Akita, "An Examination of E. H. Norman's Scholarship."

55. Edwin O. Reischauer to George Akita, June 21, 1976, Edwin O. Reischauer Correspondence, Box 3, HUGFP 73.10, Harvard University Archives.

56. Edwin O. Reischauer to Professor Maurice Miesner, University of Wisconsin, Decem-

ber 8, 1974, quoted in Edwin O. Reischauer to George Akita, July 14, 1976, Edwin O. Reischauer Correspondence, Box 3, HUGFP 73.10, Harvard University Archives.

57. Selma Janow, interviewed by the author, Washington, D.C., March 24, 2003.

58. After a merger in 1974, the Browne and Nichols School became known as the Buckingham Browne and Nichols School.

59. Nancy Deptula, interviewed by the author, Cambridge, Mass., June 22, 1994.

60. Edwin O. Reischauer, *Toward the Twenty-first Century: Education for a Changing World* (New York: Knopf, 1973), quotes from pp. 150, 5.

61. *MLBJA*, p. 340.

62. *Varices* is the plural of *varix*, which is defined as "a permanent abnormal dilation and lengthening of a vein, usually accompanied by some tortuosity" (*Random House Dictionary of the English Language*, 1971).

63. *MLBJA*, p. 351.

64. Edwin O. Reischauer, interviewed by the author, Belmont, Mass., July 20, 1983.

65. *MLBJA*, p. 352.

66. I had become dean of the Johns Hopkins School of Advanced International Studies in 1979.

67. Harvard had for several years been considering naming its own Japan Institute for Reischauer, but had failed to do so on account of faculty jealousy and competition for funds with its China program. It then realized to its dismay that it might lose out to Johns Hopkins in the competition for scarce funds and quickly placed Reischauer's name on its institute in the following year, 1985.

68. Haru Matsukata, *Samurai and Silk: A Japanese and American Heritage* (Cambridge, Mass.: Harvard University Press, 1986). Harvard's Belknap Press had earlier published Edwin O. Reischauer's *The Japanese* (1977).

69. Martin Tolchin and Susan J. Tolchin, *Selling Our Security* (New York: Knopf, 1992).

70. Paul Kennedy, *The Rise and Fall of the Great Powers* (New York: Random House, 1987). Luce made his prediction in *Life* magazine, February 17, 1941.

71. Theodore H. White, "The Danger from Japan," *New York Times Sunday Magazine*, July 28, 1985.

72. Chalmers Johnson, "Their Behavior, Our Policy," *The National Interest*, no. 17 (Fall 1989), p. 25. Johnson later recanted: "In retrospect I probably did overstate the nature of the Japanese challenge," he told the *New York Times* (July 3, 2005).

73. Clyde Prestowitz, *Trading Places: How We Are Giving Our Future to Japan and How to Reclaim It* (Ann Arbor: University of Michigan Press, 1988).

74. A conservative southern textile maker seeking protection against Japanese imports, Milliken joined labor unions in providing the seed money for Prestowitz's think tank, according to Paul Krugman in "Who's Buying Whom? The Milliken Man March on Washington," *Slate*, posted September 26, 1997, 7.

75. Morita Akio and Ishihara Shintaro, *No to Ieru Nippon*, translated into English and published as *The Japan That Can Say No: Why Japan Will Be First Among Equals* (New York: Simon and Schuster, 1990).

76. *New York Times*, February 13, 1984.

77. See, for example, Tom Clancy, *Debt of Honor* (New York: G. P. Putnam, 1994).

78. Michael Crichton, *Rising Sun* (New York: Knopf, 1992), afterword.

79. Comment made in June 1991, quoted in the *Washington Post*, June 16, 1991.

80. James Fallows, "Containing Japan," *Atlantic Monthly* (May 1989), pp. 53–54. See also Kurt Singer, *Mirror, Sword, and Jewel: A Study of Japanese Characters* (London: Croom Helm, 1973).

81. James Fallows, "The Japan Handlers," *Atlantic Monthly* (August 1989), 14–23.

82. Ibid., p. 20.

83. I did challenge Fallows's allegations in "The Japan-Bashers Are Poisoning Foreign Policy," *Washington Post*, October 8, 1989.

84. Karel von Wolferen, *The Enigma of Japanese Power: People and Politics in a Stateless Nation* (New York: Knopf, 1989). See also his article, "No Brakes, No Compass," *The National Interest*, no. 25 (Fall 1991): 26–35.

85. Pat Choate, *Agents of Influence: How Japan Manipulates America's Political and Economic System* (New York: Knopf, 1990).

86. George Friedman and Meredith Lebard, *The Coming War with Japan* (New York: St. Martin's Press, 1991); James Fallows' review of the book appeared in the *New York Review of Books* on May 30, 1991.

87. John Creighton Campbell, "Japan Bashing: A New McCarthyism?" *Japan Foundation Newsletter* 18, no. 4 (March 1991): 1–5.

88. Alan Murray, interviewed by the author, Washington, D.C., March 20, 1994.

89. Edwin O. Reischauer to Barry Bingham, June 15, 1970, Edwin O. Reischauer Correspondence, Box 2, HUGFP 73.10, Harvard University Archives.

90. Edwin O. Reischauer to Yoshi Tsurumi, April 15, 1990, copy of letter sent to the author by Yoshi Tsurumi, March 8, 1991.

91. Quoted in *Boston Globe*, January 26, 1986.

92. My account is based on listening to and reading a complete transcript of the dialogue. All quotes are excerpted from a fourteen-page, single-spaced transcript.

11. NEARING THE RIVER'S MOUTH

1. Lafcadio Hearn, *Japan: An Attempt at Interpretation* (New York: MacMillan, 1904), pp. 9–10.

2. Some of these characters come to life in Christopher Benfey's *The Great Wave: Gilded Age Misfits, Japanese Eccentrics, and the Opening of Old Japan* (New York: Random House, 2003).

3. George Sansom, *Japan: A Short Cultural History* (Stanford, Calif.: Stanford University Press, 1931).

4. On Needham, see Simon Winchester, *The Man Who Loved China* (New York: Harper Collins, 2008).

5. Jim L. Anker of Eureka, California, to Edwin Reischauer, May 1, 1972, and Edwin O. Reischauer to Jim L. Anker, May 9, 1972, Edwin O. Reischauer Correspondence, Box 2, HUGFP 73.10, Harvard University Archives.

6. Edwin O. Reischauer, *My Life Between Japan and America* (New York: Harper and Row, 1986), p. 120, hereafter *MLBJA*.

7. Quoted in James Thomson, "E. O. Reischauer, Missionary," *New York Times Book Review*, June 12, 1977, p. 39.

8. Reischauer became interested in environmental issues late in his life and joined the board of Energy Conversion Devices Inc., a firm in Michigan that was developing clean energy systems.

9. William Watts, *How Americans Look at Japan: What the Data Say*, preliminary report for the Commission on U.S.–Japan Relations for the 21st Century (Washington, D.C.: U.S. Government Printing Office, November 17, 1989).

10. E-mail from Reischauer's physician Dr. Paul J. Pockros, Scripps Clinic, La Jolla, California, to the author, May 12, 2004.

11. Unpublished manuscript version of *MLBJA*, p. 731, copy provided to the author by Nancy Deptula, executive director of the Edwin O. Reischauer Institute of Japanese Studies, Harvard University.

12. A. K. Reischauer, *Studies in Japanese Buddhism* (New York: AMS Press, 1917), p. 264.

13. Edwin O. Reischauer and John K. Fairbank, *East Asia: The Great Tradition* (Boston: Houghton Mifflin, 1958), p. 143.

14. Ann Reischauer, interviewed by the author, San Diego, Calif., June 7, 2004.

15. "Raishawa Hakushi: Nihon Omoinagara Songenshi. Haru Fujin Kataru: Taiheiyo Nozomu Byoin De," *Shinano Mainichi*, September 3, 1990.

16. "Kicho na Rikaisha Ushinau," *Yomiuri*, September 2, 1990; "Sengo no NichiBei Yuko ni Jinryoku," *Mainichi Shimbun*, September 2, 1990.

17. *Asahi Shimbun*, September 3, 1990.

18. Text of speeches given at the memorial service for Reischauer, October 19, 1990, quotes from pp. 23, 30, 34, copy provided to the author by Nancy Deptula.

19. Memorial Minute adopted by the Faculty of Arts and Sciences, Harvard University, October 15, 1991, proposed by John Fairbank, Howard Hibbett, Robert Hightower, and Albert Craig, chairman. Published in the *Harvard Gazette*, November 22, 1991.

20. Edwin O. Reischauer, "Toward a Definition of Modernization," originally a lecture given in English on September 26, 1964, and published in *Jiyu*, January 1965.

21. Richard J. Samuels, *Securing Japan: Tokyo's Grand Strategy and the Future of East Asia* (Ithaca, N.Y.: Cornell University Press, 2007), p. 195.

22. In Japan's most recent general (Lower House) election on August 29, 2009, 69.3 percent of eligible voters cast their votes. In the U.S. presidential election of 2008, voter turnout was 61.5 percent, the highest since 1968.

23. *Washington Post*, January 16, 2007.

24. *MLBJA*, p. 355.

25. Chicago Council on Global Affairs, "Public Opinion Study 2008," available at http://www.thechicagocouncil.org. This view represented a dramatic shift from 1990 and 1994, when 71 percent of Americans thought Japan practiced unfair trade.

26. This cork reference was made famous by Major General Henry C. Stackpole of the U.S. Marine Corps in an interview with the *Washington Post* in March 1990.

27. John F. Smith Jr., remarks made at the annual dinner of the Japan Chamber of Commerce and Industry, New York, November 16, 1995, published in the *Washington-Japan Journal* 4, no. 3 (Fall 1995), quotes from pp. 17–18.

28. From Reischauer's last interview at Harvard, *Harvard Gazette*, January 12, 1990.

29. Ibid.

30. Edwin O. Reischauer, *Wanted: An Asian Policy* (New York: Alfred A. Knopf, 1955), p. 43.

31. From a speech Reischauer gave to the LTV Washington Seminar sponsored by LTV Corp. (a major defense contractor) and published in its house organ *American Foreign Policy in the '80s* (1980).

32. The term *soft power* was made popular by Joseph S. Nye Jr. in his book *Bound to Lead: The Changing Nature of American Power* (New York: Basic Books, 1990).

33. See, for example, the article by Waseda University professor Yamamoto Taketoshi in *Bungei Shunju*, November 2003, in which he claims that Reischauer was a cold, indifferent, calculating researcher-diplomat who looked down on the Japanese public.

34. Andrew Gordon, *A Modern History of Japan from Tokugawa Times to the Present* (New York: Oxford University Press, 2003).

35. Among the best are Iriye Akira of Harvard (history, the United States in East Asia); John Curtis Perry of the Fletcher School of Law and Diplomacy, Tufts University (maritime history, diplomacy); Richard Samuels of MIT (security); Gerald Curtis of Columbia (politics and foreign policy); Kenneth Pyle of the University of Washington (history); and Michael Schaller of the University of Arizona (U.S.–Japan relations).

36. According to the Japan Foundation's Survey of Overseas Organizations Involved in Japanese Language Education, 58,181 primary and secondary school students were studying Japanese in 2006 at 553 schools in the United States, with 807 teachers. At U.S. institutions of higher education, 66,605 students were studying Japanese in 2006, according to the Modern Language Association. Japanese was the sixth most commonly taught language, after Spanish, French, German, American Sign Language, and Italian. The number of students studying Chinese was increasing rapidly, whereas the number of those studying Japanese had declined since 2002.

37. Edwin O. Reischauer, *The Japanese Today: Change and Continuity* (Cambridge, Mass.: Belknap Press of Harvard University Press, 1988; originally published as *The Japanese* in 1977), p. 8. This edition was updated after his death by Marius Jansen and published as *The Japanese Today: Change and Continuity* (Cambridge, Mass.: Belknap Press of Harvard University Press, 1995; new printing, 2003). Quotations in the text come from the 1988 edition, pp. 8, 387, 390, and 408.

38. Edwin O. Reischauer, interviewed by Kawachi Takashi, *Mainichi Shimbun*, February 20, 1989. This statement was almost certainly a reaction to the book he had just read by Morita Akio and Ishihara Shintaro, *No to Ieru Nippon*, translated into English and published as *The Japan That Can Say No: Why Japan Will Be First Among Equals* (New York: Simon and Schuster, 1990).

39. *Washington Post*, September 24, 1986.

40. E. O. Reischauer, "Not Westernization but Modernization," in Harry Wray and Hilary Conroy, eds., *Japan Examined: Perspectives on Modern Japanese History* (Honolulu: University of Hawaii Press, 1983), p. 374, italics added.

41. Excerpted from a tape-recorded interview with Kawachi Takashi, reporter for *Mainichi Shimbun*, La Jolla, California, February 20, 1989, recording made available to the author by

Kawachi. At this writing, Ishihara is the popular governor of Tokyo. See note 38 for a full citation of his and Morita's book.

42. Ibid.

43. Ozawa Ichiro coined the term *futsu no kuni* (normal nation) in his book *Nippon Kaizo Keikaku* (Tokyo: Kodansha, 1993) and its English edition *Blueprint for a New Japan* (Tokyo: Kodansha, 1994).

44. *Mainichi Shimbun*, September 3, 1990.

EPILOGUE

1. Susan J. Pharr, e-mail exchange with the author, December 3, 2008.

Index